EDWARD SCHILLEBEECKX AND CONTEMPORARY THEOLOGY

EDWARD SCHILLEBEECKX AND CONTEMPORARY THEOLOGY

Edited by
Lieven Boeve
Frederiek Depoortere
Stephan van Erp

t&t clark

Published by T&T Clark International
A Continuum Imprint
The Tower Building, 11 York Road, London SE1 7NX
80 Maiden Lane, Suite 704, New York, NY 10038

www.continuumbooks.com

British Library Cataloguing-in-Publication Data
A catalogue record for this book is available from the British Library

ISBN 13: 978-0-567-18160-2 (Hardback)

Typeset by Fakenham Photosetting Ltd, Fakenham, Norfolk
Printed and bound in Great Britain by the MPG Books Group

Dedicated to the memory of Edward Schillebeeckx, OP (1914–2009)

.

CONTENTS

CONTENTS

CONTENTS

In Memoriam Edward Schillebeeckx, OP (1914–2009)

Prof. dr. Lieven Boeve, Dean of the Faculty of Theology, Katholieke Universiteit Leuven, Belgium

Prof. dr. Ben Vedder, Dean of the Faculty of Theology, Radboud University Nijmegen, The Netherlands

The Dominican theologian Edward Schillebeeckx died on 23 December 2009 in Nijmegen, the Netherlands. Schillebeeckx has played a major role in twentieth century and contemporary theology and worked on the fracture separating a bygone era from a new one. He is recognized by many people as a pioneer in theology who connected faith, Church and theology with modern humanity in a secular society. Schillebeeckx was open to other religions because, as he put it so strikingly, 'God has such an abundance of truth that he cannot be fully interpreted by just one religion'. 'On the other hand, our knowledge of God cannot be grasped in the best of all religions combined. God is forever new and larger than all religions put together.'

Edward Schillebeeckx was born in Antwerp, on 12 November 1914. He received his secondary education at the Jesuit College of Turnhout in Belgium. In 1934, he entered into the order of the Dominicans and he was ordained as a priest in 1941. After his graduation in Theology, in 1943, he was appointed as a lecturer of Dogmatic Theology at the Dominican Studium of Leuven and at the Higher Institute for Religious Studies in Leuven. The central idea of his lectures was that God is not an abstraction but a living God who engages with humanity and the world. This implies that theologians will have to constantly re-evaluate God's presence in the here and now. Tradition is not unchanging; it constantly relates to the spirit of the times.

From 1945 onwards, Schillebeeckx pursued his academic career in Paris. He attended lectures given by the Dominican theologians Yves Congar and Marie-Dominique Chenu, and he was introduced to the works of writer and philosopher Albert Camus. Around the same time, a clerical labour movement arose in France. Its aim was to reduce the distance between the Church and daily life by having priests work and live alongside labourers. Although this movement was eventually banned by the leaders of the Church, its influence was clearly tangible in the later council documents that sought to reformulate the relation between Church and world.

Late in 1957, Schillebeeckx was appointed Professor of Dogmatics and History of Theology at the Catholic University of Nijmegen, the current Radboud University. He lectured at this university until his retirement in 1983. Shortly after his appointment, Pope John XXIII announced the Second Vatican Council (1962–65). The Dutch bishops asked Schillebeeckx to accompany them as their advisor during the Council. In 1960 he wrote a pastoral letter on the bishops behalf to the faithful informing them about the Council. This letter gained international fame because of the way in which Schillebeeckx described the relationship between the faithful and the Church hierarchy: he believed that the bishops' and the pope's task is to express the life of the faithful, rather than the other way around.

At the time of the Council, Schillebeeckx delivered various lectures in Rome which established his international reputation. Thanks to his close cooperation with the Dutch episcopate and his appearances on television, he became the foremost theological spokesperson on Dutch Roman-Catholicism. His name and fame also reflected favourably upon the theological faculty at Nijmegen, which gained a reputation for innovative, open and high-standard theological pursuits.

Schillebeeckx aimed to promote theology among a wider audience. In 1961 he took the initiative to found the *Tijdschrift voor theologie* which exists to this day and which aims to connect current affairs with theological reflection. In 1965, Schillebeeckx and a number of other theologians, including Yves Congar, Hans Küng, Johann Baptist Metz and Karl Rahner, started the international journal *Concilium*. The purpose of this journal was to continue the debate on the central issues of the Second Vatican Council.

In 1974, he published the first volume of his renowned trilogy on Christology, *Jezus, het verhaal van een levende* (translated in English in 1979 as *Jesus: An Experiment in Christology*), and in 1977 *Gerechtigheid en liefde, genade en bevrijding* (translated in English in 1980 as *Christ: The Christian Experience in the Modern World* [in the UK] and *Christ: The Experience of Jesus as Lord* [in the US]). In these books, Schillebeeckx clearly shows that a scholarly examination of the texts of the New Testament of the Bible, in particular of those concerning the life of Jesus of Nazareth, is not at odds with the tradition of the Church, but rather brings it up to date. Moreover, Schillebeeckx presented Christian faith as a source of inspiration for people who want to stand up for the poor and the oppressed and who want to change the world for the good. These books broke new ground for twentieth-century theology and are still widely read and studied.

Schillebeeckx continued to be involved in the internal affairs of the Church after the Second Vatican Council. In addition to his earlier works on the sacraments of the Church (*De sacramentele heilseconomie*, 1953), his later publications deal with the priesthood and the role of the faithful in the Church (*Kerkelijk ambt*, 1980 and *Pleidooi voor mensen in de kerk*, 1985, translated as *Ministry* and *The Church with a Human Face: A New and Expanded Theology of Ministry*). Due to the innovative character of his work, Church authorities asked Schillebeeckx to justify himself on three separate occasions. However, he was not condemned. During this same time, Schillebeeckx received many honorary doctorates, including an honorary doctorate from the Catholic University of Leuven in 1974. Shortly before his retirement in 1983, he received the prestigious European Erasmus prize.

Schillebeeckx remained active after his retirement. In 1989, he published the final part of his Christological trilogy, *Mensen als verhaal van God* (translated as *Church: The Human Story of God*). His proposition that no salvation can be found outside this world (*extra mundum nulla salus*) conflicted at that time with the official Church point of view, which stated that there is no salvation outside the Church. As late as 2000, Schillebeeckx surprised many people with an article in the *Tijdschrift voor theologie* in which he discussed recent developments in anthropology and ritual studies.

Schillebeeckx's approach is largely responsible for completing the turn towards hermeneutics in Catholic theology. Indeed, it is almost impossible now to conceptualize the experience of faith without taking into account the interaction of experience and interpretation in which tradition and the faith community are continuously involved. Being Christian has to do with the specific ways of experiencing and interpreting concrete reality. God reveals Godself as justice and love in the concrete history of human beings, in the everyday activities of living and loving together. While this was the case in the past, it also is true for Christians today and will continue to be true for Christians in the future. Theology, therefore, can only be credible and relevant when it engages itself with the present-day (faith) experience of ordinary men and women and when it brings this experience into relationship with the experience of divine salvation with which Jesus' first disciples were familiar.

Two crucial experiences are of vital importance for Schillebeeckx: first, the 'Abba' experience of Jesus himself, which expresses the extraordinarily intimate bond between Jesus and the Father, and secondly, the resurrection experience of the first disciples after the Crucifixion: 'He is alive, and He will return.' The disciples' Easter experience is one of conversion, an experience of salvation that restores their relationship with Jesus and brings them together once again to form the kernel of the Christian faith community. It is this experience of divine salvation in Jesus Christ which is expressed in multiple ways throughout the New Testament. This same foundational experience serves as the driving force behind the Christian experiential tradition: taking a different form each time language, history and context changes.

For Schillebeeckx, believers are once again faced with the task of reflecting on God as salvation for the world today by the emergence of modernity and secularization. To this end, men and women must explore human experience in an effort to determine where the basic Christian experience is to be found and unlocked. According to Schillebeeckx, the 'contrast experience' grants modern Christians, living in a secularized culture, access to this basic Christian experience. At the same time, this secular (pre-religious) experience of being taken aback by suffering and injustice unlocks the desire for a better future. A 'hope-filled Yes', a belief in the humanness of humanity, is revealed in our 'unconditional No' to suffering and oppression. For Schillebeeckx, today's Christian identity is granted significance when the contrasting secular experience is brought into relationship with the basic Christian experience of salvation. In our human struggle for justice and liberation, the God of love and grace is articulated and expressed. Our concrete engagement on behalf of those who are suffering, our struggle in support of the '*humanum*', is the privileged location in which God's engagement with humanity can be experienced.

Grounded in his conviction that faith involves contextual interpretations of fundamental experiences of salvation, Schillebeeckx was particularly concerned about the obstinate maintenance of traditional formulations, practices and structures. In his opinion, they impede the unlocking of the basic Christian experience. This position frequently led him to be sharply critical both of the Church and of the tradition. For example, he accused the Church and its hierarchical procedures of alienating the faithful and threatening the very existence of the Eucharist and of the faith community itself by clinging to an obsolete understanding of ministry that restricted priesthood to celibate men.

The influence which Schillebeeckx exercised over two generations of believers and theologians is almost beyond comprehension. He taught theologians to enter into dialogue with new philosophical movements and with the human sciences, with the surrounding culture and society. He demonstrated the impossibility of a theological perspective on Jesus Christ without the input of historical-critical research into the Jesus of history. He insisted that salvation should not be understood as exclusively individual and spiritual, but that it also has practical, political and ecological dimensions. Perhaps the most important lesson we learned, however, from Schillebeeckx is the fact that being Christian has to do with concrete human existence – that 'dogma' is nothing without life itself. Only when faith, Church, tradition and world are able to mediate divine salvation in an ongoing and tangible way will they ultimately find grace in the eyes of God. God, after all, is always 'new'.

Letter from Edward Schillebeeckx to the Participants in the Symposium 'Theology for the 21st Century: The Enduring Relevance of Edward Schillebeeckx for Contemporary Theology' (Leuven – 3–6 December 2008)

It is my pleasure to be invited by the Dean of the Theological Faculty of Nijmegen to send a letter of welcome to this symposium of theological research. I thank you all for your willingness to take my thought as the starting point for doing theology for the 21st century – but only as a starting point.

The Dean asked for a brief message – just a few words. Therefore, I have chosen one theme; namely, *extra mundum nulla salus*. Some Christians and even some theologians misinterpret this expression because they think – wrongly – that it refers only to humanism and not to salvation by God. This is because they put the accent on *mundum* instead of *salus*. *Salus* always comes from God, but it is experienced in the world. God is always the foundation – the source of salvation – and that is the core point of the Christian religion. This is the key point I want to make in this letter to the symposium.

The expression *extra mundum nulla salus* has to do with the reality that the creative, saving presence of God is mediated in and through human beings. The Old Testament and the New Testament – the Bible therefore – is very clear about the incomprehensibility of God. Many Christians give the emphasis to the God who cannot be known – the silent God. Yet the official Church is not speaking about the silent God, but always speaking about dogmas. The truth is that the silent God is always going out ahead of us in the world. We cannot say this in the sense of human history with past, present, and future, because God is eternal. But, for us, God is new each moment.

People are always in search of a meaningful existence in their own lives. The question of salvation has to do with people's ordinary lives – work, family, politics – this is where they meet the Living God who is always near to each person. Yet, this salvation is always mediated by others in the world.

The expression *extra mundum nulla salus* also has consequences for our understanding of the Trinity (although I have not time to develop this here). Let me just say, in the Christian Tradition, and above all in the Great Catholica – there are two modes of Christian thinking. One is to speak of Father, Son, and Holy Spirit in that order. But there is also another tradition of speaking first of God, then of the Holy Spirit, and then of the human Jesus of Nazareth, called the Christ, the Son of God.

In the resurrection, Jesus becomes the enduring presence of God to human beings. The resurrected One is always present for us in the neighbour, the one nearby. In the resurrection Jesus is taken into God – he belongs to God and he belongs to human beings – the One of whom St. Paul said, 'He is the image of the invisible God, the first born of every creature' (Col. 1.15).

The invisible God can be encountered everywhere in creation. Faith in God is our hope, but the existence of God is not rationally provable. Faith is always a risk, but a risk that is not incredible. As St. Augustine and St. Thomas Aquinas claimed, the invisible, incomprehensible God both transcends the human and is nonetheless immanent in the human.

As Lord and Shepherd, God is the origin, the ever-present ground, and the power of all good – a good that human beings themselves must do freely in order to make a better world. Yet, every human action for justice, peace, and the integrity of creation is at the same time the gift of the silent God.

Thank you, and have an inspiring symposium.

Edward Schillebeeckx, OP
1 December 2008

Courtesy of Mirjam
Ates-Snijdewind;
used by permission.

PREFACE

Frederiek Depoortere

The present volume offers the results of the international expert symposium *Theology for the 21ˢᵗ Century: The Enduring Relevance of Edward Schillebeeckx for Contemporary Theology*, which was organized in Leuven from 3–6 December 2008. This expert meeting was the culmination point of a joint research project of the Research Group 'Theology in a Postmodern Context', Faculty of Theology, Katholieke Universiteit Leuven (Belgium) and the Faculty of Theology, Radboud University Nijmegen (The Netherlands). This project, which ran between 2005 and 2008, investigated the contribution of the Low Countries to the debate on theology and method in the 21ˢᵗ century. For the three initiators of the project – Lieven Boeve (Katholieke Universiteit Leuven), Erik Borgman (at that time still at the Radboud University Nijmegen, now at Tilburg University) and Stephan van Erp (Radboud University Nijmegen) – it was evident to focus on the methodological reflections of the Flemish-Dutch theologian Edward Schillebeeckx (1914–2009). Both in Leuven and in Nijmegen, theology has to a large extent been shaped by the work of Schillebeeckx and, moreover, both Boeve and Borgman have been the proponents of a continuation of Schillebeeckx's legacy for the present day and age – although both of them are aware that it is not sufficient to simply repeat what Schillebeeckx has said and that his theology should be developed further as the context has shifted from a rather 'late modern' to a rather 'postmodern' one.

The aim of the aforementioned expert symposium was therefore not merely to commemorate the legacy of Schillebeeckx, but to take his work as a starting point to repeat what he had done for his time, namely engaging with the context to develop a contemporary understanding of faith, an understanding of the faith which is plausible and accessible for today's women and men. It is from this broader perspective, then, that reference has been made to Schillebeeckx's theology. It was the conviction of the organizers of the symposium that precisely by engaging in an attempt at 'faith seeking understanding' for our own time we would follow Schillebeeckx's lead. Thus, the symposium's main objective was to enquire what theology in the current and coming age should look like. The focal questions during the discussions, therefore, were: What are contemporary theology's challenges?

What are its fruitful approaches? Who are its promising contributors? With these focal questions in mind, the participants engaged with eight topics during the symposium: (1) the question of God in modernity, (2) the social role of theology, (3) theology of/and the dialogue between the religions, (4) Christology and suffering, (5) experience, tradition and hermeneutics, (6) community, Eucharist and ministry, (7) philosophy and theology, and (8) history of salvation and eschatology. Each topic was the focus of one session for which each time two papers had been commissioned. Moreover, each one of these sessions, except for the session on philosophy and theology, was entitled with the help of a famous phrase from the work of Schillebeeckx: 'God Is New Each Moment', 'Everything Is Politics But Politics Is Not Everything', 'God Is Bigger Than All Religions Put Together', '*Deus humanissimus*', 'It Began with An Experience', 'The Church with a Human Face' and '*Extra mundum nulla salus*'. Next to the eight sessions which formed the heart of the symposium, there was also an opening lecture and a concluding plenary discussion on the basis of the observations of two observers. As the reader will be able to note as he or she reads through the pages that follow, the material as it appears in print here has been slightly restructured in order to reflect the content of the final versions of the papers. In the end, it turned out that it would make more sense to divide the papers, apart from the opening lecture (Boeve), under the following headings: (1) the question of God in modernity (Godzieba and Depoortere), (2) the social role of theology (Miller and Manemann), (3) the dialogue between the religions (Cruz and Souletie), (4) suffering and experiences of negative contrast (McManus, Hilkert and Tillar), (5) Church and tradition in an age of globalization and liquidization (Sander, Davies and Dumas), (6) philosophy and theology (van Erp and Bourgine) and (7) the past and future of Edward Schillebeeckx's theological project (Borgman, Schreiter and Dolphin). This restructuring had the unfortunate consequence that the phrases 'The Church with a Human Face' and '*Extra mundum nulla salus*' are now no longer in use as headings of a part. Yet, they are not absent from the book either: 'The Church with a Human Face' reappears as the title of a chapter in Part V and '*Extra mundum nulla salus*' is given prominence by Schillebeeckx himself in the letter of welcome he wrote to the symposium, a letter which was read out loud during the opening session and has also been printed at the beginning of this volume.

As the symposium which gave rise to the present book did not intend to be a meeting devoted to the exegesis of Schillebeeckx's work, the organizers have opted to bring together a stimulating mix of Schillebeeckx scholars (Borgman, Dolphin, Hilkert, McManus, Schreiter and Tillar), scholars whose current research may not be focused on Schillebeeckx, but who are familiar with his work via earlier research (Boeve, Cruz, Depoortere, Dumas, Godzieba, Miller, van Erp), and scholars who substantially engaged with Schillebeeckx for the first time at the occasion of the symposium, but who could precisely for the reason of being outsiders to Schillebeeckx scholarship look at his work with fresh eyes (Bourgine, Davies, Manemann, Sander, Souletie). Given the different levels of familiarity and involvement with Schillebeeckx scholarship of the authors who have contributed to the present volume, it may not come as a surprise that the essays gathered in this book differ in the extent to which they engage with the work of Schillbeeckx. A number of the essays proceed by means of a close reading of Schillebeeckx's work in order to formulate answers to the questions of Schillebeeckx's enduring relevance and of the direction to be taken by theology in the twenty-first century, while other essays rather testify to this enduring relevance by adopting one or a number of Schillebeeckx's intuitions as a starting point. We are convinced, however, that each paper has in its own way fulfilled the aim of taking Schillebeeckx as a starting point to reflect on the directions theology should take in the twenty-first century. We intend to demonstrate this further on in this Preface.

The symposium at the origin of the present book has also been explicitly conceived as an exercise in crossing boundaries between theological traditions. All too often theologians from different language areas remain in isolation from each other and do not have opportunities to interact. This symposium, however, brought together theologians from Flanders (Boeve and Depoortere) and the Netherlands (Borgman and van Erp), from the UK (Davies) and the US (Cruz, Dolphin, Godzieba, Hilkert, McManus, Miller, Schreiter and Tillar), from France (Souletie), Quebec (Dumas) and the Francophone part of Belgium (Bourgine), as well as from Austria (Sander) and Germany (Manemann). By gathering theologians from the Dutch-speaking, the English-speaking, the French-speaking and the German-speaking world, a unique opportunity was created for theological conversation across linguistic borders and national settings. As the contributors to the present volume are at home in different language areas and therefore also in different styles of academic work, the essays collected in the present volume also testify to these different academic styles. This leads us to a note on some aspects of the editorial work. When submitted, a number of the papers referred to the Dutch original of Schillebeeckx's works or to translations of it in French and German. To enhance the consistency of the book all references to translations in French or German have been replaced by references to the English equivalent. Where reference was made to the Dutch original of one of Schillebeeckx's works, that reference has been kept, but the reference to the English version has been added. The same has been done for other works which were cited in a non-English translation: when an official English translation was available, the references to that non-English translation have been replaced by references to the official English translation and when the original version of a non-English work was cited, a reference to the English translation has been added if such translation was, to our knowledge, available. (There is one important exception to this rule, namely Johann Baptist Metz's *Glaube in Geschichte und Gesellschaft*, the older translation of which is, according to Manemann, not accurate and the revised translation was not yet known to him at the time of finishing the manuscript.) Furthermore, all translations made by contributors themselves have been replaced by the official translation if such a translation was available. This entails that a quote is only an author's own translation when the note following it does not mention an English work. Or, to put it differently: if an English translation is mentioned in a note, the translation is taken from that work. This general rule explains why notes do not mention when a quote is an author's own translation.

As the papers collected in the present volume are very diverse with regard to length, theme, scope, methodology, sources they use and the degree in which they engage with the work of Schillebeeckx, it is worthwhile to reflect, at the beginning of the book, on how the several contributions fit together. To this aim, we want to indicate how each paper has in its own way fulfilled the aim of the aforementioned expert symposium in taking Schillebeeckx as a starting point to reflect on the directions theology should take in the twenty-first century.

The book opens with a chapter by **Lieven Boeve** (Katholieke Universiteit Leuven) in which he introduces the issue of Schillebeeckx's enduring significance and relevance. He does this by taking the reception of Schillebeeckx in the Low Countries as his point of departure. As he notes, the work of Schillebeeckx has been developed in two rather divergent directions by Erik Borgman and himself. Boeve develops the hypothesis that this is due to a duality which is present in the theology of Schillebeeckx himself, namely the duality between a 'theo-ontological' or 'creation-theological' Schillebeeckx on the one hand and 'an increasingly hermeneutical' Schillebeeckx on the other. Boeve shows how creation faith – entailing that it is possible to speak of God 'from below', so to speak, tracing God in world and history – has determined Schillebeeckx's thought from his first publications in the mid–1940s. Yet, from the mid–1960s onwards, Boeve states, Schillebeeckx has, at least in his methodological reflections, become increasingly aware of the problematic nature of that transition from world/history to God, entailing that one is only able to discern God in the world and in history because of the tradition. What characterizes our context is that it no longer seems possible to hold creation faith and hermeneutics in unison in the way Schillebeeckx could still do and this, in turn, Boeve adds, explains the difference between Borgman and himself: the former radicalizes the creation-theological Schillebeeckx (favouring the move from world to tradition and only arriving at the tradition in so far as the world allows or needs it) while he himself seeks to radicalize the hermeneutical Schillebeeckx; which is, according to Boeve, the direction theology in the twenty-first century should take. This does not entail, Boeve emphasizes, that creation faith is now ruled out, but it does entail recognizing it as a particular perspective on the world, a perspective which is informed by a particular tradition.

The following two chapters deal with the question of God in modernity. First, **Anthony J. Godzieba** (Villanova University) takes issue with a rather bold statement of the later Schillebeeckx in which he rejects any argument for the existence of God. Diagnosing the contemporary situation, with the help of Eyal Chowers and Charles Taylor, in terms of 'entrapment' in immanence, Godzieba argues that theology is still in need of a transcendental argument or natural theology. Schillebeeckx's blunt rejection of any such argument is, Godzieba defends, a mistake because precisely such an argument is what we need to break free from the entrapment in immanence which is characterizing our current situation. In his paper, **Frederiek Depoortere** (Katholieke Universiteit Leuven) subscribes to Godzieba's conclusion that we indeed need an argument for the existence of God, but he takes another road to the same outcome. Depoortere starts from the view of the early Schillebeeckx on the character of religion and faith, showing that in this view *true* religion and *true* faith are not possible without God's existence. He subsequently argues that the way in which some theologians try to resolve the conflict between science and religion results in a plea for a faith in a non-existent God, a faith which thus collapses into atheism. If such a collapse is to be avoided, we are therefore in need of a natural basis for faith and this need for a natural basis of faith is precisely what the early Schillebeeckx has defended. Thus, remarkably, Depoortere argues on the basis of the early Schillebeeckx for the position which Godzieba is defending against the later Schillebeeckx. This of course suggests that, at least concerning the need for an argument for the existence of God, there has been an important shift in the thought of Schillebeeckx and that therefore, at least with regard to this issue, the earlier Schillebeeckx is more promising than the later Schillebeeckx.

The next two chapters deal with the social and political role of theology. In his contribution, **Vincent J. Miller** (University of Dayton) investigates how Schillebeeckx's political theology can be continued in the contemporary United States. Miller begins by replying to Frederick Bauerschmidt's criticism of Schillebeeckx's view on the relationship of faith and politics and continues by investigating the situation in which Schillebeeckx developed that view; a situation characterized by the phenomenon of 'columnization'. However, the contemporary US context is very different from that situation. It is characterized by, on the one hand, secularization, detraditionalization and religious deregulation, and, on the other hand, the emergence of new cultural intermediaries and a growing impact of special agenda organizations. Miller concludes by pointing out the challenges posed by this new context to Schillebeeckx's political theology, but emphasizes that the latter remains insightful and relevant in the changing context of Western societies. **Jürgen Manemann** (Forschungsinstitut für Philosophie Hanover) offers in his paper a comprehensive overview of the current state of the so-called 'new political theology' in Germany, a theology which was instigated by Johann Baptist Metz. As Manemann notes, Metz's political theology is not merely concerned with the relation between Church and State or between faith and politics in the limited sense of statecraft, but entails the all-embracing project of 'a theology with its face towards the world'. It is appropriate to have such a discussion of contemporary German political theology included in this volume on Schillebeeckx and contemporary theology. First, Schillebeeckx was, together with Metz, one of the most prominent representatives of the turn to the world which was experienced by the Catholic Church and Catholic theology in the 1960s. Secondly, Schillebeeckx has developed his political theology in continuous dialogue with Metz. It is therefore worthwhile to investigate, as Manemann does in his paper, the enduring significance of political theology for politics.

The two chapters that follow discuss the issue of the dialogue between the religions, an issue in which Schillebeeckx was increasingly interested. **Gemma Tulud Cruz** (DePaul University) brings in the perspective of both Asian theologians and feminist theologians, in this way arguing that the dialogue between the religions has hitherto been characterized by a Western and androcentric bias. In her paper, Cruz points to three particular perspectives which promise to be fruitful to remedy this one-sidedness of the interreligious dialogue, namely: the 'triple dialogue' as espoused by the Asian bishops and Asian theologians, Elizabeth Johnson's idea of religious plurality as a gift from God and her emphasis on the role of the Spirit and, finally, Jeanine Hill Fletcher's view of hybrid identities. Cruz also points out how these perspectives resonate in the work of Schillebeeckx. She mentions that Schillebeeckx has adopted a position on the issue of inter-religious dialogue that is not unlike the position of some Asian theologians and she also notes similarities between Schillebeeckx and Johnson. In this way, Cruz's paper testifies to the way how intuitions of Schillebeeckx have been furthered in today's work on interreligious dialogue by both Asian and feminist theologians. **Jean-Louis Souletie** (Institut Catholique de Paris) searches for Christological tools for the dialogue between the religions. Starting from Schillebeeckx's insight that no religion, not even Christianity, is absolute and endorsing his view that orthodoxy is accomplished through orthopraxy, Souletie raises the question of how the Gospel can be embodied in the praxis of dialogue between the religions. To this aim, he discusses the debate in the French-speaking theological world on Jacques Dupuis' proposal to distinguish more clearly between the *Logos* qua incarnated and the *Logos* as such. Souletie continues by subscribing to Joseph Doré's plea for a so-called 'paschal fulfilment theology', which entails that Jesus' life, death and resurrection should be understood as the prefiguration of an as yet incomplete eschatological fulfilment, and he concludes by developing the view that the dynamic of salvation in Jesus Christ is love.

The fourth part of the book collects three papers which were initially presented in three different sessions, but which are rightly brought together here as all three focus on the issue of suffering and so-called 'experiences of negative contrast', experiences of resistance against the violation of the *humanum*. Such experiences are of utmost importance in the work of Schillebeeckx as they not only form the basis of his anthropology and his ethics, but also play an important role in his political theology and are even foundational for his method of correlation (as can be seen in for instance *The Understanding of Faith*). In her paper, **Kathleen McManus** (University of Portland) discusses Schillebeeckx's theology of suffering together with ecofeminism (in particular Ivone Gebara and Mary Grey) and feminist mystical theology (Beverly Lanzetta). She develops the similarities between Schillebeeckx's epistemology of concrete experience and ecofeminist epistemology and applies Schillebeeckx's idea of experience of negative contrast to the suffering of women today; both the global suffering of poverty and the spiritual suffering in the Church. Aim of this is to discern 'the feminine Body of Christ hidden in the tradition' in order to enflesh it in the present. **Mary Catherine Hilkert** (University of Notre Dame) examines the enduring relevance of Schillebeeckx's theology for contemporary anthropology and ethics. Hilkert is aware of the fact that Schillebeeckx may have been too optimistic in considering experiences of negative contrast as the universal and spontaneous reaction of human beings when they experience violations of the *humanum* (she refers to Metz, Copeland and Lonergan in this regard). Yet, she still considers Schillebeeckx's concept of the *humanum* as a fruitful basis for the development of a global ethic. In her paper, Hilkert further discusses the anthropological constants as well as the issue of the relationship between the Christian story and the human story. The third paper in which Schillebeeckx's idea of the experiences of negative contrast plays a key role is written by **Elizabeth Kennedy Tillar**. Tillar explores Schillebeeckx's mysticism. She links the experiences of negative contrast as developed by Schillebeeckx with Jan Van Ruysbroeck's 'dark light' and points out that it is often traumatic experiences which enable someone to gain deeper insight into the human condition and which stimulate ethical action. In this way, Tillar develops Schillebeeckx's fundamental insight that experiences of suffering bring with themselves a special type of knowledge, a type of knowledge in which the theoretical and the practical are conjoined and, which therefore, possess a special authority.

The three papers gathered in the next part tackle the issue of how the Church should react to the contemporary context characterized by pluralization and globalization. **Hans-Joachim Sander** (University of Salzburg) sketches, with the help of Zygmunt Bauman, how the contemporary context is characterized by an increasing 'liquidization', entailing that foundations become eroded and that fixed distinctions (so-called 'binary codes') become blurred. Sander describes how the Church is also confronted with this liquidization, as it increasingly becomes clear that history is not offering any ultimate guarantee for Christian faith, but only a plurality of narratives on Jesus. Sander describes two possible reactions to the contemporary liquidization. On the one hand, there is the utopian/apocalyptic way, which entails turning to scenarios about the future in order to deal with the hurly-burly of the present (as exemplified by fundamentalists but, according to Sander, also by political theologians such as Metz). This reaction is rejected by Sander, however, as dangerous and inherently violent. He in contrast pleads to focus on the present and the 'heterotopias' which appear here and now. He argues for this on the basis of *Gaudium et spes* and also defends that Schillebeeckx has increasingly become aware of both the liquidity characterizing the present age and the need to react to that liquidity in a flexible way. That is why, according to Sander, Schillebeeckx should be designated as 'a theologian with the size of a century'. **Oliver Davies** (King's College London) raises the question of how Christians, given the twin phenomena of globalization and pluralization, and the relativism that seems to follow from them, can still be 'non-relativistically present' in today's world. In order for the Christian tradition to avoid becoming merely one tradition among many we should, according to Davies, distinguish more clearly between 'history' and 'tradition' and we should, moreover, reconceive Christ's presence in history and the world by rehabilitating the core of the doctrine of the Ascension, namely the conviction that Christ remains actively present in time and space. The turn to history as defended by Davies is characterized by him as 'strongly non-cognitivist' and in this way, Davies claims, it aligns with Schillebeeckx, who has both stressed praxis as a way to grasp the world and the knowledge gained in experiences of negative contrast. The most important lesson Davies takes from Schillebeeckx is however that faith and action in the world are not opposites, but that the former grounds the latter. **Marc Dumas** (Université de Sherbrooke) offers an analysis of how Church and theology in his native Quebec seem to have reached 'rock bottom'. He nevertheless remains optimistic about the possibilities for renewal. Dumas subscribes to Schillebeeckx's 'plea in favour of humans in the Church'. In his paper, he distinguishes between three 'reflexes of the theological act', which are in his view exemplified by Schillebeeckx and which should be repeated today by contemporary theologians. These reflexes are: interrogating the tradition, participating in contemporary life and using those epistemological and methodological tools which are comprehensible for people living today. Every age, Dumas defends, is called to appropriate the dynamic of faith anew: theology cannot but be 'native' and more than ever before the Church is called to reinvent herself. Dumas concludes his paper with a proposal to rebuild the Church from the bottom-up. He envisages this renewed Church as a lot less hierarchical and centralized, but as consisting of 'ecclesial cells in all sorts of associations'.

The next two papers deal with the importance of philosophical reflection for theology. **Stephan van Erp** (Radboud University Nijmegen) begins his paper by rejecting Milbank's separation of philosophy and theology, arguing instead that contemporary theology needs philosophy, especially when it comes to understanding 'implicit faith', the belief of non-believers, and that we therefore need to develop further philosophical theology. In his paper, van Erp deals with the philosophical background of the early Schillebeeckx, offering a reconstruction of the theory of implicit intuition as developed by Dominicus De Petter, Schillebeeckx's philosophy teacher. Van Erp also discusses the issue of Schillebeeckx's dissociation from his former teacher, a dissociation which seems to be inspired by a rejection of metaphysics in favour of history. Van Erp contends, however, that Schillebeeckx was too radical in his dissociation from his former teacher. According to van Erp, De Petter's metaphysics is much more open towards history than Schillebeeckx acknowledged and the former's philosophy and the latter's theology are therefore not irreconcilable, but can both be helpful tools in the development of a contemporary theology of 'implicit faith'. **Benoît Bourgine** (Université catholique de Louvain) follows Schillebeeckx's lead in taking philosophy seriously and presents us with an overview of the challenges at stake in the interaction between philosophy and theology. He summarizes these challenges under two headings, 'conversation with modern rationality' and 'the postmodern quest for identity'. Modernity, Bourgine notes, is characterized by three projects: the project of science, the project of democracy and the project of individual autonomy in matters of ultimate concern. Consequently, modernity has distinguished between three types of truth: 'truth that is worthy of our *knowledge*', 'truth that we can propose to our individual and collective *action*' and 'truth in which we might rightfully *believe*'. As a result, theology is called to learn the language of modern science and democracy, and it has to come to terms with the plurality of religions and cultures. In this respect, Bourgine defends the need to develop an eschatological concept of truth. When it comes to the relation of theology and the postmodern quest for identity, Bourgine suggests that it is in particular a number of recent philosophical readings of Saint Paul which are promising, as they are opening the prospect of identity consisting in non-identity.

The final part of the book collects three papers that reflect on the past and future of Schillebeeckx's theological project. **Erik Borgman** (Tilburg University) begins by situating Schillebeeckx in the landscape of twentieth-century theology, discussing him against the background of the *nouvelle théologie* and the struggle of the correct interpretation of Vatican II. At stake in this struggle is the issue of how far the council, and the document *Gaudium et spes* in particular, constitutes a rupture with the past. An important lesson to be learnt from Schillebeeckx, Borgman defends, is that we can allow for genuine newness and development in the history of the

Church without subscribing to what Ratzinger rejects as 'a hermeneutic of discontinuity and rupture'. Schillebeeckx's point, Borgman argues, is that Vatican II not so much constitutes a rupture as the emergence of a different way of thinking about the continuity of the Christian tradition. Borgman calls to mind that Schillebeeckx designated God as being 'new each moment' and that we are therefore called to continuously 'retrieve the place where we are established as "holy ground" (Exod. 3.5)'. **Robert J. Schreiter** (Catholic Theological Union, Chicago) was the first of the two scholars invited to participate in the symposium as an observer. In his reflections offered at the beginning of the closing session and printed in this volume, Schreiter takes three steps. First, he proposes the phrase '*extra mundum nulla salus*' as offering a frame for the discussion of Schillebeeckx and contemporary theology that had taken place during the symposium. Secondly, he continues by pointing to five areas that had turned out to be important in the discussions among the participants in the symposium, sharing some thoughts on how Schillebeeckx's theology can contribute to theological work in these areas. These five areas are: (1) method, (2) God, (3) the human, (4) the social and (5) suffering. Thirdly, in conclusion, Schreiter also mentions two topics that were left unaddressed during the symposium and as a result also in this book: aesthetics and neo-augustinianism. The second observer was **Kathleen Dolphin** (Saint Mary's College, Notre Dame). Adopting the method of Schillebeeckx as developed by Don Browning, Dolphin examines how the participants in the symposium have dealt with the eight topics under discussion (*see supra*) with the assistance of Schillebeeckx as a resource, using 'incarnationality', 'relationality' and 'transformationality' as the criteria guiding her reflection.

This introduction to the material collected in the present volume shows that the challenges facing theology in the twenty-first century are numerous and diverse, but it also suggests that the work of Edward Schillebeeckx indeed offers fruitful approaches, insights and intuitions which can be taken up by contemporary theology when it deals with these challenges – something to which the eighteen essays collected here indeed testify.

At the end of this Preface, we would like to express our gratitude to all the contributors to this volume for the fine and pleasant collaboration. Secondly, we should also mention a number of people who have helped us in preparing the manuscript of this book: Patrick Cooper, who has assisted us in the editing of the text, has proofread most of the contributions and has compiled the bibliography of the 'Other Works Cited'; Phillip Davies and Colby Dickinson, who have done supplementary proofreading; Ming Yeung Cheung for looking up references; and Joeri Schrijvers for taking care of translations from the French. Last, but not least, we want to extend a special word of thanks to Ted Mark Schoof for his advise on the bibliography with works on Schillebeeckx and to Mirjam Ates-Snijdewind for making available the picture of Schillebeeckx which is printed in this book (and to Erik Borgman for contacting her).

And, finally: while working on the manuscript of this book, we learnt the news that Edward Schillebeeckx had passed away at a quarter past five in the afternoon of Wednesday 23 December 2010 at the age of 95. We thought it appropriate to dedicate this volume, in which eighteen theologians from different countries reflect on the enduring relevance of his theology and its contribution to twenty-first-century theology, to his memory. We are also happy that Lieven Boeve, in his capacity as Dean of the Faculty of Theology of the Katholieke Universiteit Leuven, and Ben Vedder, Dean of the Faculty of Theology of the Radboud University Nijmegen were prepared to write an 'In memoriam' for Schillebeeckx to be published here. We hope the present book may contribute to the continuation of the spirit that has moved the work of this great theologian.

26 January 2010.

LIST OF CONTRIBUTORS

Lieven Boeve is Professor of Fundamental Theology in the Faculty of Theology at the Katholieke Universiteit Leuven (Belgium), where he is the co-ordinator of the Research Group 'Theology in a Postmodern Context'. He was the International President of the European Society of Catholic Theology (2005–2009) and is currently serving as Dean of his faculty. His main publications in English include *Interrupting Tradition: An Essay on Christian Faith in a Postmodern Context* (Leuven: Peeters/Grand Rapids, MI: Eerdmans, 2003) and *God Interrupts History: Theology in Times of Upheaval* (London/New York, NY: Continuum, 2007).

Erik Borgman is Full Professor of Systematic Theology in the Faculty of the Humanities at Tilburg University (The Netherlands). He is editor in chief of *Tijdschrift voor theologie* that Schillebeeckx founded in 1961 and a vice-president of *Concilium: International Journal for Theology*, co-founded by Schillebeeckx in 1965. He is author of *Edward Schillebeeckx: A Theologian in His History. Volume 1: A Catholic Theology of Culture 1914–1965* (London/New York, NY: Continuum, 2003), the (first part of) the first full biography of Edward Schillebeeckx and a widely read and acclaimed book. He wrote, in the tradition of Schillebeeckx's theological approach, on liberation theology: *Sporen van de bevrijdende God: Universitaire theologie in aansluiting op Latijnsamerikaanse bevrijdingstheologie, zwarte theologie en feministische theologie* (Traces of the Liberating God: Academic Theology Following Latin American Liberation Theology, Black Theology and Feminist Theology) (Kampen: Kok, 1990). His current research is about the intricate relations between contemporary culture and the Christian tradition; cf. his *Metamorfosen: Over religie en moderne cultuur* (Metamorphoses: On Religion and Modern Culture) (Kampen: Klement, 2006); *... want de plaats waarop je staat is heilige grond: God als onderzoeksprogramma* (For the Place Where You Stand is Holy: God as a Research Program) (Amsterdam: Boom, 2008); *Overlopen naar de barbaren: Het publieke belang van religie en christendom* (Going Over to the Barbarians: The Public Importance of Religion and Christianity) (Kampen: Klement, 2009).

Benoît Bourgine is Professor of Dogmatic Theology in the Faculty of Theology at the Université catholique de Louvain (UCL) in Louvain-la-Neuve (Belgium). His research deals with the meaning and significance of the work of Karl Barth and also with the dialogue of theological rationality and other rationalities (as found in science, politics and philosophy). He is the author of *L'herméneutique théologique de Karl Barth: Exégèse et dogmatique dans le quatrième volume de la* Kirchliche Dogmatik (Leuven: Peeters, 2003) and co-editor of *Religions, sciences, politiques: Regards croisés sur A.N. Whitehead (Louvain-la-Neuve, 31 mai–2 juin 2006)* (Franfurt: Ontos Verlag, 2007).

Gemma Tulud Cruz holds a PhD in Theology from Radboud University Nijmegen in the Netherlands. She is currently Visiting Assistant Professor in the Catholic Studies Department at DePaul University in Chicago (Illinois, USA) and an affiliate of the Center for World Catholicism and Intercultural Theology, also at DePaul. She has published about thirty book and journal articles and has served as consultant and speaker in various conferences in Asia, Europe, North America, and Australia. She is author of *Pilgrims in the Wilderness: An Intercultural Theology of Migration* (Leiden: Brill, 2010).

Oliver Davies is Professor of Christian Doctrine at King's College London (UK) and currently President of the Society for the Study of Theology. He worked on the German medieval theologian Meister Eckhart before publishing *A Theology of Compassion: Metaphysics of Difference and the Renewal of Tradition* (London: SCM Press, 2001/Grand Rapids, MI: Eerdmans, 2003) and *The Creativity of God: World, Eucharist, Reason* (Cambridge: Cambridge University Press, 2004). In *Transformation Theology: Church in the World* (London/New York, NY: T&T Clark, 2007) he presented with colleagues at King's a new direction in theology which places sensibility, space and time and ecclesial commissioning at the centre of Christian revelation. He is currently working with colleagues inside and outside King's on the development of this new theology, focusing on current areas of practical and ethical engagement, as well as doctrinal and philosophical debate.

Frederiek Depoortere is a Postdoctoral Fellow of the Research Foundation – Flanders (FWO) in the Faculty of Theology of the Katholieke Universiteit Leuven (Belgium), where he is a member of the Research Group 'Theology in a Postmodern Context'. He is the author of *The Death of God: An Investigation into the History of the Western Concept of God* (London/New York, NY: T&T Clark, 2008), *Christ in Postmodern Philosophy: Gianni Vattimo, René Girard, Slavoj Žižek* (London/New York, NY: T&T Clark, 2008) and *Badiou and Theology* (London/New York, NY: T&T Clark, 2009).

LIST OF CONTRIBUTORS

Kathleen Dolphin, PVBM is Director of the Center for Spirituality and Lecturer in the Religious Studies Department at Saint Mary's College in Notre Dame (Indiana, USA). She obtained her PhD at the University of Chicago with a dissertation on the integration of theology and spirituality in the sermons of Edward Schillebeeckx. Her research interests focus on Schillebeeckx's theology/spirituality as a resource for faith communities, especially as that applies to current ecclesial issues in the US.

Marc Dumas is Professor in the Faculty of Theology, Ethics and Philosophy at the Université de Sherbrooke (Canada). His current research deals with the translations of and commentaries on Paul Tillich and with the topic of experience in theology. He also has a specific interest in both the identity of theology and its current transformations, in the collaboration between theologians and people/communities in search for meaning, and in the multiple forms of the contemporary religious experience. He published as editor the following books: *Paul Tillich, prédicateur et théologien pratique: Actes du XVIe Colloque International Paul Tillich Montpellier 2005* (Berlin: LIT, 2007), *Théologie et culture: Hommages à Jean Richard* (Québec: PUL, 2004) (together with François Nault et Lucien Pelletier), and *Pluralisme religieux et quêtes spirituelles: Incidences théologiques* (Montréal: Fides, 2004) (together with François Nault). He has also written a number of articles on experience and correlation in the theology of Edward Schillebeeckx.

Stephan van Erp is a Senior Researcher and Lecturer in Systematic Theology and Theory of Religion and Culture in the Faculties of Theology and Religious Studies at the Radboud University Nijmegen (The Netherlands). He is managing editor of *Tijdschrift voor theologie* that Schillebeeckx founded in 1961 and editor in chief of *ET Studies*, the journal of the European Society for Catholic Theology (ESCT). His main publications include *The Art of God: Hans Urs von Balthasar's Theological Aesthetics and the Foundations of Faith* (Leuven: Peeters, 2004) and *Vrijheid in verdeeldheid: De geschiedenis van religieuze tolerantie* (Freedom in Diversity: The History of Religious Tolerance) (Nijmegen: Valkhof Pers, 2008).

Anthony J. Godzieba is Associate Professor of Theology and Religious Studies at Villanova University (USA) and the editor of *Horizons*, the journal of the College Theology Society. He specializes in fundamental theology, theology of God, Christology, theological anthropology, and philosophical theology. He is the author of *Bernhard Welte's Fundamental Theological Approach to Christology* (New York, NY: Peter Lang, 1994) and the co-editor, together with Anne M. Clifford, of *Christology: Memory, Inquiry, Practice* (New York, NY: Orbis, 2003). He is currently completing

xxxi

a book on the theology of God for Crossroad/Herder, and is researching the intersection of art, music, theology, spirituality, and embodiment in early modern Catholicism.

Mary Catherine Hilkert, OP is Professor of Theology in the Department of Theology at the University of Notre Dame (Indiana, USA) and a past president of the Catholic Theological Society of America (CTSA). She specializes in contemporary systematic theology with particular interest in theological anthropology, fundamental theology, and feminist theologies. She is the author of *Naming Grace: Preaching and the Sacramental Imagination* (New York, NY: Continuum, 1997) and *Speaking with Authority: Catherine of Siena and the Voices of Women Today* (Mahwah, NJ: Paulist Press, 2008). She co-edited, together with Robert J. Schreiter, both *The Praxis of Christian Experience: An Introduction to the Theology of Edward Schillebeeckx* (San Francisco, CA: Harper & Row, 1989) and *The Praxis of the Reign of God: An Introduction to the Theology of Edward Schillebeeckx* (New York, NY: Fordham University Press, 2002). Her next book, *Words of Spirit and Life: Theology, Spirituality, and Preaching*, will be based on the Lyman Beecher Lectures which she will deliver at Yale University in October 2010. She is also working on a volume on theological anthropology titled *Grace Enfleshed: A Sacramental Anthropology*.

Jürgen Manemann is Director of the Forschungsinstitut für Philosophie Hanover (Germany). He is the author of, among others, *Carl Schmitt und die Politische Theologie: Politischer Anti-Monotheismus* (Münster: Aschendorff, 2002), *Rettende Erinnerung an die Zukunft: Essay über die christliche Verschärfung* (Mainz: Grünewald, 2005) and *Über Freunde und Feinde: Brüderlichkeit Gottes* (Topos-Taschenbuch; Kevelear: Topos, 2008). He is editor of and co-founder of the *Jahrbuch Politische Theologie*.

Kathleen McManus, OP is Associate Professor of Systematic Theology at the University of Portland (Oregon, USA.) Her research focuses on Christology, suffering, and intercultural feminist and ecofeminist theology. She is the author of *Unbroken Communion: The Place and Meaning of Suffering in the Theology of Edward Schillebeeckx* (Lanham, MD: Rowman & Littlefield, 2003). Her publications include articles related to Schillebeeckx and suffering in *Theological Studies*, *The Way* and *Doctrine & Life*.

Vincent J. Miller is the first Gudorf Chair in Catholic Theology and Culture in the Department of Religious Studies at the University of Dayton (Ohio, USA). He is author of *Consuming Religion: Christian Faith and Practice in a Consumer Culture* (New York, NY: Continuum, 2003) and is currently working on a book about how globalization is affecting religious belief and communities.

Hans-Joachim Sander is Full Professor of Dogmatics in the Faculty of Catholic Theology at the University of Salzburg (Austria). He is the author of *Macht in der Ohnmacht: Eine Theologie der Menschenrechte* (Freiburg: Herder, 1999), *Nicht verleugnen: Die befremdende Ohnmacht Jesu* (Würzburg: Echter, 2001), *Nicht ausweichen: Die prekäre Lage der Kirche* (Würzburg: Echter, 2002), *Nicht verschweigen: Die zerbrechliche Präsenz Gottes* (Würzburg: Echter, 2003) and *Einführung in die Gotteslehre* (Darmstadt: Wissenschaftliche Buchgesellschaft, 2006). He published a commentary on the Pastoral Constitution *Gaudium et spes* of Vatican II in *Herders Theologischer Kommentar zum Zweiten Vatikanischen Konzil*, (ed. P. Hünermann and B.J. Hilberath; vol, 4; Freiburg: Herder, 2005), pp. 581–886.

Robert J. Schreiter holds the Vatican Council II Professorship of Theology at the Catholic Theological Union in Chicago (Illinois, USA) and is one of the most prominent theologians in North America. In 1974 he wrote his PhD thesis 'Eschatology as a Grammar of Transformation' under supervision of Edward Schillebeeckx. In the period 2000–2006 Schreiter held the 'Theology and Culture'-chair which was established by the Edward Schillebeeckx Foundation at the Faculty of Theology in Nijmegen. His many books include *Constructing Local Theologies* (Maryknoll, NY: Orbis, 1985) and *The New Catholicity: Theology between the Global and the Local* (Maryknoll, NY: Orbis, 1997). He is editor of *The Schillebeeckx Reader* (New York, NY: Crossroad, 1984) and co-editor, together with Mary Catherine Hilkert, of both *The Praxis of Christian Experience: An Introduction to the Theology of Edward Schillebeeckx* (San Francisco, CA: Harper & Row, 1989) and *The Praxis of the Reign of God: An Introduction to the Theology of Edward Schillebeeckx* (New York, NY: Fordham University Press, 2002).

Jean-Louis Souletie is Professor of Fundamental and Systematic Theology in the Theologicum, the Faculty of Theology and Religious Studies of the Institut Catholique de Paris (France). His research topics are 'Theology, culture and society', 'Transmission of faith in postmodernity', and 'Truth and method in systematic theology'. He is the author of *La croix de Dieu: Eschatologie et histoire dans la perspective christologique de Jürgen Moltmann* (Paris: Cerf, 1997), *La crise une chance pour la foi* (Paris: L'Atelier, 2002), *Les grands chantiers de la christologie* (Paris: Desclée, 2005), *Catholicisme* (Paris: Armand Colin, 2006), and 'Social Sciences and Theology after L.-M. Chauvet', *Sacraments: Revelation of the Humanity of God: Engaging the Fundamental Theology of Louis-Marie Chauvet* (ed. Philippe Bordeyne and Bruce T. Morrill; Collegeville, MN: Liturgical Press, 2008).

Elizabeth Kennedy Tillar has obtained her PhD from Fordham University in 2000 with a dissertation entitled 'Suffering for Others in the Theology of Edward Schillebeeckx'. Her work on Schillebeeckx has been published in three subsequent volumes of *The Heythrop Journal*: 'The Influence of Social Critical Theory on Edward Schillebeeckx's Theology of Suffering for Others', *The Heythrop Journal* 42/2 (2001), pp. 148–72, 'Eschatological Images of Prophet and Priest in Edward Schillebeeckx's Theology of Suffering for Others', *The Heythrop Journal* 43/1 (2002), pp. 34–59, and 'Critical Remembrance and Eschatological Hope in Edward Schillebeeckx's Theology of Suffering for Others', *The Heythrop Journal* 44/1 (2003), pp. 15–42.

INTRODUCTION

The Enduring Significance and Relevance of Edward Schillebeeckx? Introducing the State of the Question in Medias Res

Lieven Boeve

Introduction: *Enduring Relevance and Significance?*

Determining the enduring significance of the theology of Edward Schillebeeckx is no simple task. The question itself seems to suggest that the continuing significance of his theology is no longer evident: could it have become – at least in principle – completely outmoded? Perhaps. I would argue that there are three reasons for this state of affairs.

(1) The *first* reason is to be located among contemporary theologians themselves. Over the years, a certain distance has established itself between the theological endeavour and work of Schillebeeckx, which took shape for the most part, in terms of structure, content and method, between 1965 and 1990. This is due primarily to the fact that the context itself has not remained static, but has evolved rather from a so-called late-modern to a postmodern culture and society, of which today's theologians are a part. Nevertheless, other theologians from times gone by, have remained relevant for later generations, albeit in a mediated fashion, via a hermeneutical inter-action with their work, which takes the said historical distance seriously. So why not Schillebeeckx?

(2) The *second* reason would appear at first sight to be more complex and perhaps problematic. It seems that the late-modern manner of theologizing has lost some of its credit and that the plausibility of a theological project of engaging in critical dialogue with modernity has somehow lapsed. Indeed, from the perspective of the institutional church, it is apparent that the theological tendency that had expressed serious reservations with respect to such a dialogue with modernity has subsequently gained considerable

ground in the last decennia and is now making the decisions. Indeed, what has come to be known as the 'Communio group' appears to have survived the change of context in better shape than its rivals. It goes without saying that this has to do with the prominence of one of the leading theologians of the group – Joseph Ratzinger – and with the popularity of the work of H.U. von Balthasar. Furthermore, the group in question was reinforced by certain so-called post-liberal and postmodern theological tendencies, such as the Yale School and Radical Orthodoxy, each of which based themselves in their own way on the power and rationality of the Christian narrative itself, before turning to the relationship of Christian faith within its context. This second reason for doubting the enduring relevance of Schillebeeckx's work clearly belongs to a different order than the first. The least that can be said, however, is that every reflection on the relevance of Schillebeeckx for today's theology will be obliged to declare its position with regard to this evolution.

(3) A *third* reason for questioning the relevance of Schillebeeckx's theology for today has to do with Schillebeeckx himself. It has to be said that Schillebeeckx's theologizing was already an exercise in what Metz was to call '*Korrektivtheologie*'.[1] While Metz' own political theology criticized and revised the transcendental theology of Karl Rahner, Schillebeeckx's theology appears to have undergone its own evolution from being a neo-Thomistic – albeit one already under revision – to a late-modern, hermeneutically oriented theology. We are thus left with a question: is Schillebeeckx's theology, itself being '*Korrektivtheologie*', not subjected to the same process of correction? Especially when we account for the insight – for which we are indebted to Schillebeeckx – that all theology is in relationship to the context or situation in which it desires to understand the faith. In short, if all theology is '*Korrektivtheologie*', then Schillebeeckx's theology also requires reconsideration.

Our goal in the present contribution is to confront the question of Schillebeeckx's continuing relevance primarily from the perspective of this third question, trusting that an answer thereto will provide some indications for a response to the first and second reasons for doubting his relevance. To this end we will focus our attention on the contemporary reception of Schillebeeckx in the Low Countries.

1. *Point of Departure: The Reception of Schillebeeckx in the Low Countries Reveals a Duality in His Theology*

As the basis for a discussion of the enduring relevance of Schillebeeckx's thought for present-day theology I know turn my attention to the debate surrounding the varied reception of Schillebeeckx in the Low Countries,

---

[1] Cf. Johann Baptist Metz, *Glaube in Geschichte und Gesellschaft: Studien zu einer praktischen Fundamentaltheologie* (Mainz: Grünewald, 1977) p. 12.

especially by Erik Borgman and myself. It should be clear from the outset that I do not intend to limit the reception of Schillebeeckx's thought in Flanders and the Netherlands to this debate. Nevertheless, I have been wondering – on more than one occasion – how two theologians, formed and challenged by the same master, and in spite of the common ground between them, could ultimately arrive at such distinct theological positions; so much so that the tension between both positions would appear to be irresolvable. The search for an answer to this question has made me aware of the fact that evident variation in the reception of Schillebeeckx is most likely to have its roots in a twofold 'givenness' in his theology as such, a duality that typifies it and ultimately constitutes its vigour. At the same time, however, it also introduces a degree of tension, unevenness and even ambiguity. It is this duality that I hope to demonstrate in the present contribution and develop as a key to reading Schillebeeckx's work, not only in support of our understanding of his position, but also as the starting point for a discussion with respect to his enduring relevance. I therefore begin by briefly outlining the contours of the discussion.

a. *Erik Borgman: Reading the Present-Day Religious Situation – God as a Research Programme*

After the completion of his doctoral dissertation,[2] Erik Borgman (b. 1957), former research fellow at the Radboud University in Nijmegen and currently professor at the University of Tilburg, published four monographs, one of which was the unsurpassed first volume of his Schillebeeckx biography (1999, also translated in English).[3] In the three books that followed, which were often heavily edited collections of previously published articles, Borgman positioned himself within the present-day theological landscape.[4] In line with Schillebeeckx, Borgman describes his theology as 'cultural',[5] a

---

[2] Erik Borgman, *Sporen van een bevrijdende God: Universitaire theologie in aanslui-ting op Latijnsamerikaanse bevrijdingstheologie, zwarte theologie en feministische theologie* (Kerk en theologie in context, 7; Kampen: Kok, 1990).

[3] Erik Borgman, *Edward Schillebeeckx: Een theoloog in zijn geschiedenis. Deel 1: Een katholieke cultuurtheologie (1914–1965)* (Baarn: Nelissen, 1999); English trans-lation: *Edward Schillebeeckx: A Theologian in His History. Volume 1: A Catholic Theology of Culture (1914–1965)* (trans. John Bowden; London/New York, NY: Continuum, 2004).

[4] Erik Borgman, *Alexamenos aanbidt zijn God: Theologische essays voor sceptische lezers* (Zoetermeer: De Horstink, 1994); *Metamorfosen: Over religie en moderne cultuur* (Kampen: Klement, 2006); and more recently, on the reception of his appointment in Tilburg: *... want de plaats waarop je staat is heilige grond: God als onderzoeksprogramma* (Amsterdam: Boom, 2008).

[5] Cf. Erik Borgman, 'Van cultuurtheologie naar theologie als onderdeel van de cultuur: De toekomst van het theologisch project van Edward Schillebeeckx', *Tijdschrift voor theologie* 34 (1994), pp. 335–60. On the question of continuity with Schillebeeckx: *Metamorfosen*, p. 19 and pp. 50–51.

description he further specifies as 'religious intellectual', 'not only thinking *about* religion' in and on the basis of our culture 'but also engaging anew in *religious* thinking'.[6] Borgman's goal is the unearthing of a religious core present in human existence and in society, a core to which religious traditions refer, while allowing themselves to be relativized in doing so. He is not so interested in the *content* of religious claims but rather in the *basis upon which* such claims are made. He thus hopes to find traces of what it is that fundamentally binds human beings together (before concrete religions and religious convictions separate them). According to Borgman, theologians today can only achieve this 'not by presenting the Christian traditions and arguing in support of their enduring importance, but by reading the present situation ... as a religious situation'.[7] Indeed, the metamorphosis our culture has undergone also leads us to understand God in a new way.[8] Those who desire to find God, or traces of a relationship with the sacred, should reflect first and foremost on the way '"religion after religion" is taking shape in our culture',[9] how religion today is not secularized and absorbed into the world, but emerges rather from a secularized culture. This emergence is not only a consequence of our growing awareness that human beings are not their own master – or of the alienation accompanying such an awareness – but also of a metamorphosis of the religious as such, a transformation of the way in which God makes Godself known today. The metamorphosis in question is so radical that it confronts theology with the boundaries of its classical ways of thinking and speaking and calls for new ways to bear witness to God:

> There are traces of God in creation and redemption ... *Something* is recognized in the good, the meaningful and the compassionate, in the horror elicited by evil, meaninglessness and indifference, and in our longing for a situation in which the reality of which we are a part speaks of goodness, meaningfulness and compassion in all its dimensions and with complete clarity.[10]

Borgman continues: it is this *something* that is 'confessed with religious faith when the Christian traditions refer to God as "creator"'.[11] It is also this same something that resonates in every religious tradition as that which bears the tradition and at the same time transcends it. It is for this reason that Borgman speaks in his most recent book of theology as 'service to

---

[6] Borgman, *Metamorfosen*, p. 11.

[7] Borgman, *Metamorfosen*, p. 23.

[8] Cf. Erik Borgman, 'Gods gedaanteverandering: De metamorfosen van de religie en hun theologische betekenis', *Tijdschrift voor theologie* 44 (2004), pp. 45–66.

[9] Borgman, *Metamorfosen*, p. 32.

[10] Borgman, *Metamorfosen*, p. 92.

[11] Borgman, *Metamorfosen*, p. 92.

the world, which is of God' and describes God as a 'research programme':
reading the world from 'the salvific perspective in which this world is given
its due and bears witness to God as its origin, support and goal'.[12]

In a number of places, Borgman explicitly aligns himself with Edward
Schillebeeckx's cultural-theological project. He introduces two elements in
this regard, which he considers important. First, Schillebeeckx's theological
approach is based on the intuition that 'the Catholic tradition [albeit
in changed circumstances] can become surprisingly significant, precisely
in confrontation with the contemporary situation and contemporary
culture.'[13] Secondly, the fact that for Schillebeeckx 'all of human culture
and human knowledge ... is a *locus theologicus*' contributes to the
enduring relevance of his work.[14] God 'can be known only from contact
with concrete everyday life', and from 'the desire for and the experiences
of salvation that are alive within it'.[15] Borgman particularly appreciates
the notion of contrast experience and radical resistance to suffering and
oppression in this regard.

In 1994, Borgman argued that Schillebeeckx had ultimately not
succeeded in his plan. 'In spite of its extensive interest in human history,'
he wrote, 'Schillebeeckx's theology does not penetrate to [the concrete]
level of human existence. As such, he is unable to make Christian tradition,
with its concrete narratives and theories, relevant at this level for contemporary readers' – something Borgman considered to be the fault of western
theology as a whole during that time.[16] Borgman argues that this has
to do with Schillebeeckx's apparently unquestioned presupposition of
church and tradition, which serves as a screen between concrete human
existence and God's salvation. Schillebeeckx too easily and too frequently
takes for granted that 'faith comes first, that the church and its tradition
are a reality that he can analyse, exposing the openness thereof to the
situation of contemporary men and women'.[17] Borgman goes on to argue
that Schillebeeckx is bent on establishing the continuity of the church and
its tradition: they represent both the presupposition and the goal of his
theology. It is here that his cultural theology encounters its limitations
today. Borgman concludes the first part of his Schillebeeckx biography in
programmatic terms:

> Theologians need to abandon the fiction that the truth of the tradition
> and the authority of the church form a firm foundation on which they

---

[12] Borgman, *... want de plaats*, pp. 22–23.
[13] Borgman, *Edward Schillebeeckx: A Theologian*, p. 371; see also p. 380.
[14] Borgman, 'Van cultuurtheologie naar theologie als onderdeel van de cultuur',
pp. 350–51.
[15] Borgman, *Edward Schillebeeckx: A Theologian*, p. 369.
[16] Borgman, 'Van cultuurtheologie naar theologie als onderdeel van de cultuur', p. 358.
[17] Borgman, 'Van cultuurtheologie naar theologie als onderdeel van de cultuur', p. 359.

can build further, up to and including the last remnants and traces. Theology has no other foundation than the God of salvation, whose mystery it may and must constantly decipher and clarify. If it takes that completely seriously, it will inevitably change fundamentally, time and again.[18]

b. *Lieven Boeve: Christian Identity in a Postmodern Context of Detraditionalization and Pluralization*

The two monographs I have published on theology and contemporary culture, have been conceived of, and to a significant degree, in dialogue with Schillebeeckx's work. In *Interrupting Tradition*, I focused my attention on the problems surrounding the persistence of the Christian tradition in the present-day European context.[19] How does one live as a Christian in a context that has, for the most part, lost touch with Christianity, without abandoning dialogue with the said context? Rooted in a critical-constructive conversation with a postmodern critical awareness and its insistence on otherness and difference, I then endeavoured to understand the Christian narrative as an open narrative, able to detect unexpected opportunities to expose God's presence in the interruption of its own tradition by otherness or the other. The cultural interruption of the Christian tradition – which is no longer self-evident on account of the processes of detraditionalization – thus becomes the point of departure for a discussion of the ongoing theological interruption of the Christian tradition. In the last analysis, it is God who breaks open narratives that have closed themselves, including the Christian narrative when it locks itself up within itself.

The methodological consequences of the insight that God interrupts history are then further unfolded in my similarly titled monograph *God Interrupts History*.[20] In continuous dialogue and discussion with theologians such as Edward Schillebeeckx and Johan Baptist Metz, but not excluding Joseph Ratzinger and John Milbank, I set out in search of a theological method that endeavours to learn from the difficulties confronting modern correlation theology today while likewise maintaining one of its basic intuitions, namely that dialogue with the context is theologically necessary and indeed inevitable. Indeed, the crisis of modern theology should not lead to the end of dialogue with the context, but rather to a revision of the nature of this dialogue, on account of the altered relationship with the

---

[18] Borgman, *Edward Schillebeeckx: A Theologian*, p. 381.

[19] Lieven Boeve, *Interrupting Tradition: An Essay on Christian Faith in a Postmodern Context* (Louvain Theological and Pastoral Monographs, 30; Leuven: Peeters/Grand Rapids, MI: Eerdmans, 2003).

[20] Lieven Boeve, *God Interrupts History: Theology in a Time of Upheaval* (New York, NY: Continuum, 2007).

context.[21] In contrast to a secularization paradigm, detraditionalization and pluralization sharpen our awareness that to be Christian implies an identity construction rooted in particular narratives and practices, with its own specific truth claims in a context of dynamic plurality and often-conflicting truth claims. A postmodern critical consciousness, moreover, warns us not to be too quick to include or exclude the truth of the other, but rather to reflect on our own truth claims in relationship to the truth claims of others. It is at this point that the concept of interruption may play a pivotal role.

In the midst of dialogue with the present-day context, 'interruption' can be made productive not only as a contextual category but also, and in line with Metz, as a theological category. As a matter of fact, this category serves to reflexively elucidate the way in which God reveals Godself in history and the way in which Christians bear witness to this reality in narratives and practices. God's interruption then constitutes the theological foundation for a continuous and radical hermeneutic of both context and tradition. Just as (and because) every concrete encounter with the other/Other is a potential *locus* for God to reveal Godself today, it is only in concrete narratives and practices that the interrupting God can be testified to in today's context. Ultimately, it is the event of Jesus Christ narrated in this tradition that constitutes both the foundation and the hermeneutical key thereto. Just as (and because) the Christian narrative is interrupted, the same narrative succeeds in bearing witness to the interruption without domesticating it. Furthermore, just as (and because) the Christian narrative is interrupted by God, Christians are called to interrupt themselves and others when their own narratives and those of others close themselves off. In this sense, 'interruption' is not only a formal, methodological notion, but also a substantial theological category, narratively signified by the same tradition it interrupts. In the last analysis, it is because interruption is such a thick theological category that it legitimates and motivates its formal and methodological use.

It may be evident that the influence of Edward Schillebeeckx is not alien to such a profoundly hermeneutical-theological approach to tradition. Schillebeeckx's theological application of Gadamer's model of the 'fusion of horizons', and his own dynamic interplay between experience and interpretation, are radicalized therein – in part under the influence of postmodern thought. Tradition becomes a living tradition when Christians experience their being-Christian in their concrete, contextually situated existence. The fact that the relationship between tradition and context is intrinsic, then, and that the context is co-constitutive for tradition, also remains normative for present-day theology.

---

[21] For this and the following paragraph, see also the conclusion of my *God Interrupts History*.

This latter dimension, nevertheless, required a reassessment of the late-modern correlation theology – based on a dialogue between Christian tradition and secular culture – practiced by Schillebeeckx. Instead of a secularization-based analysis, present-day postmodern culture is better explained in terms of detraditionalization and pluralization, as a post-Christian as well as post-secular culture – a point I was able to discuss with Schillebeeckx in person in 2001:

> The Christian faith is in my perspective ... no longer a mere partner of an in essence secular culture. On the contrary, it is to be found in the midst of an internally pluralized domain, where it is obliged to determine its own position in relation to others. While this task is both social and cultural, it is also (inter)subjective; and to the extent that our own identity has also become pluralized, even intra-subjective.[22]

The modern presupposition of continuity between the human and the Christian is thus placed under pressure by postmodernity. Dialogue with the context today forces theology to redefine the – living – Christian tradition in a context of plurality (including religious plurality) and difference.

c. Hypothesis: A Duality in Schillebeeckx's Project Itself

As noted above, I think that the different ways in which Erik Borgman and myself receive Schillebeeckx can probably be traced to a duality in the theology of Schillebeeckx itself. I will endeavour to describe this duality in more detail by way of a hypothesis.

We can speak, on the one hand, of the 'theo-ontological Schillebeeckx', who sets considerable store by the presence of God in creation and history – without regard to our knowledge and interpretation of the said presence.[23] This creation-theological intuition constitutes the ontological support for the proposition that history and salvation history are one and the same. In its origin, this intuition stems from his Thomistic background and can be qualified premodern. In reaction to the dynamism of secularization, however, Schillebeeckx has turned it into a generally-human religious anthropology, starting from experiences of contingency and a longing for wholeness. It is this Schillebeeckx, then, who – rooted in contrast experience – critically yet constructively associates Christian faith praxis and community with modern emancipation and liberation movements. Modernity and Christianity, therefore, are not fundamental strangers,

---

[22] Lieven Boeve, 'Schatbewaarder en spoorzoeker: het één niet zonder het ander', *Jezus, een eigentijds verhaal* (ed. Maurice Bouwens, Jacobine Geel and Frans Maas; Zoetermeer: Meinema, 2001), pp. 87–91 (89).

[23] Cf. Edward Schillebeeckx, 'Theologie als bevrijdingskunde', *Tijdschrift voor theologie* 24 (1984), pp. 388–402 (401).

because they are both characterized by the same desire for wholeness and liberation. It is this Schillebeeckx, I would argue, who reverberates in Erik Borgman's project, even today.

At the same time, however, there is also the increasingly 'hermeneutical Schillebeeckx', who employs the hermeneutical approach with increasing intensity when he speaks of church and tradition, in the conviction that only a contextual re-translation of Christianity – rooted in the interplay of experience and interpretation – can uphold Christianity's present-day plausibility. This Schillebeeckx would appear to be intent on evolving – by analogy with the experience of Paul Ricœur – in the direction of a 'no longer essentialist' hermeneutics (without simultaneously abandoning – in the words of Ricœur – its ontological 'vehemence' and truth claim). It is this evolution that allows Schillebeeckx – in spite of its difficulty and being subject to critique – to uphold the Christian tradition and church community as the hermeneutical horizon and community of interpretation. It is this Schillebeeckx who invites us, as Christians and theologians,[24] by way of follow up to his 'theological understanding of faith' (anno 1983) and his 'human story of God' (anno 1989),[25] to establish a 'theological understanding of faith for 2010', in relation to today's (no longer late-modern) context.

2. Creation Faith and the Hermeneutics of Tradition

In this section, then, I will elaborate on both theological presumptions and try – albeit in brief – to sketch their development. First I will explore the creation-theological intuition, starting off with a presentation of Schillebeeckx's thinking on the natural and the supernatural in 1945.

---

[24] Comp. Edward Schillebeeckx, 'Het nieuwe Godsbeeld, secularisatie en politiek', *Tijdschrift voor theologie* 8 (1968), pp. 44–66 (50); English translation in: Edward Schillebeeckx, *God the Future of Man* (trans. N.D. Smith; Theological Soundings, 5/1; London/Sydney: Sheed and Ward, 1969) pp. 167–207 (179):

> I will simply take my own situation in the reality of Christian faith as the point of departure and, on the basis of this, as a believer, clear up the problem of the cultural transformation in which believers are, of course, also involved. I will examine the possibilities of an experience of God that is really integrated into the new culture and of a new concept of God that really has its roots in this culture.

[25] 1983: cf. the publication of Schillebeeckx's valedictory lecture in Nijmegen: Edward Schillebeeckx, *Theologisch geloofsverstaan anno 1983* (Baarn: Nelissen, 1983); 1989: cf. *Mensen als verhaal van God* (Baarn: Nelissen, 1989); English translation: *Church: The Human Story of God* (trans. John Bowden; New York, NY: Crossroad, 1990/London: SCM, 1990).

Consequently I will then endeavour to situate his hermeneutical approach, and its less and less essentialist character.

a. *Creation Faith*

The 'ontological', or perhaps better 'theo-ontological Schillebeeckx', is closely bound up with the creation-theological anchoring of his theology. In *The Praxis of the Reign of God*, Philip Kennedy notes in this regard that 'The idea of creation is the oxygen and lifeblood of Edward Schillebeeckx's theology.'[26] While he never wrote a book on the topic (only an abundance of course material), the theme serves as a basic intuition behind his entire theological oeuvre, from his sacramentology to his Christology. It is because God created the world that God can also be observed in the contingency and finality of world and history. Kennedy – and Borgman in his biography – refer in this regard to the Thomistic foundations of this basic intuition: 'God can be spoken of, because creation exhibits the effects, so to speak, of divine activity. Put differently, by what is perceived in a created world, believers can speak of the cause of all things.'[27] The opposite is likewise true: human beings cannot have direct knowledge of God; such knowledge is always mediated by creation.[28] Schillebeeckx's creation faith, moreover, not only underpins his theological epistemology, it should also be understood in soteriological terms:[29] the God made manifest in salvation history is the God who created the world – and once again the reverse is true: it is because God created the world that God is salvifically present in world and history. Salvation history begins with creation. It is in line with this creation theology that Schillebeeckx takes the modern world seriously, including the processes of secularization.

This position is already evident in three early articles published in the Flemish Dominican journal *Kultuurleven* (1945) on the *Christian situation*, in which Schillebeeckx – still writing under his religious name Henricus – attempts to make room for the world, for 'the natural' in relation to 'the supernatural': 'The facts invite us to recognize that the mutilation and misunderstanding of nature also has a ruinous effect on the supernatural ... If the natural order is crippled, how can the opulence of the supernatural blossom?'[30] Schillebeeckx refuses to continue to see any opposition between

---

[26] Philip Kennedy, 'God and Creation', *The Praxis of the Reign of God: An Introduction to the Theology of Edward Schillebeeckx* (ed. Mary Catherine Hilkert and Robert J. Schreiter; New York, NY: Fordham University Press, 2nd edn, 2002), pp. 37–58 (37).

[27] Kennedy, 'God and Creation', p. 40.

[28] See also Borgman, *Edward Schillebeeckx: A Theologian*, pp. 374–75. Borgman makes detailed reference in this regard to the influence of the Flemish Dominican and Thomistic philosopher D. De Petter on Schillebeeckx.

[29] See, for example, Borgman, *Edward Schillebeeckx: A Theologian*, pp. 252–69.

[30] Henricus Schillebeeckx, 'Christelijke situatie', *Kultuurleven* 12 (1945), pp. 82–95, 229–42, 585–611 (88).

humanity and its enthusiasm for life, on the one hand, and the life of grace that demands the sacrifice of the truly human, on the other. The flourishing of human potential in culture, 'the pursuit of self-development and cultural growth is simultaneously [within the natural order] the pursuit of God. Furthermore, in this same yearning for self-refinement, our yearning for God is most profound, most important and all-determining.'[31] The fundamental and radical self-renunciation, which the sanctification of humanity implies, might relativize this 'self-development and cultural growth' but it does not destroy it: the supernatural life of grace gives our natural yearnings perspective and brings them to completion: 'Everything human is simply the *material* that has to be divinized and supernaturalized.'[32] The natural order thus maintains its own autonomy, dealing with its own business in its own way. Inner-worldly problems require inner-worldly solutions. While grace recognizes this independence, it simultaneously integrates it and raises it above itself.[33] It is for this reason that Catholics should not be cultural pessimists, in spite of their awareness of the relativity of the natural in the light of the supernatural.[34] In this sense, 'earthly mysticism' is allowed to interact with 'supernatural religious mysticism'.[35] There can be no opposition, therefore, between the truly human and the life of grace.[36] The distinct perspectives of God as Creator and God as Saviour are thus combined. It is for this very reason that Catholic laity should be expected to take responsibility in culture and society. It goes without saying that the desired 'bond between the natural and the supernatural ... in this world [remains] an incomplete symphony, an evolving harmony that can be destroyed at any moment'.[37] From the eschatological perspective, an inner tension exists between religion and culture, which – according to Schillebeeckx – also calls cultural Christianity into question when the latter clings to earthly positions of power.

Some years later, Schillebeeckx's endeavour to create space within the existing classical theological framework for world and history, and humanity's stake therein – including the natural relationship with the divine – undergoes a transformation when he speaks of the world as a

---

[31] Schillebeeckx, 'Christelijke situatie', p. 231.

[32] Schillebeeckx, 'Christelijke situatie', p. 239.

[33] Schillebeeckx's definition of original sin is also significant in this regard: it does not paralyse our natural life energy, rather it removes its goal: the human person thus becomes so inner-worldly and autonomous that he/she 'ultimately loses his/her natural ethical-religious creaturely awareness' (Schillebeeckx, 'Christelijke situatie', p. 237).

[34] Schillebeeckx, 'Christelijke situatie', p. 603.

[35] Schillebeeckx, 'Christelijke situatie', p. 604.

[36] 'Humanism is thus the other side and surplus of the supernatural exclusivism' (Schillebeeckx, 'Christelijke situatie', p. 607).

[37] Schillebeeckx, 'Christelijke situatie', p. 608.

11

secular reality in relation to which the Christian faith must position itself. The vertical pattern of nature and super-nature turns over to constitute a horizontal mutuality between the Christian faith and the modern context. The autonomy of the world becomes even greater, although it continues to be conceptualized from a perspective of essential continuity: the Christian faith continues to be relevant and meaningful today, precisely because there are experiences in the context that can be unlocked from within the Christian tradition as experiences of salvation. Contrast experience is given a crucial role to play at this juncture in the correlation or interrelation between faith and context.

Schillebeeckx identifies secularization as the rationalization of the world in which we live. According to Schillebeeckx in 1967, this process not only leads to an increasing loss of function with respect to the church and religion in general, but also brought a new secular world into existence side-by-side with the church.[38] As a cultural phenomenon, however, secularization should not be identified unequivocally with the atheistic interpretation thereof, which envisages the end of faith and religion. Schillebeeckx's ultimate goal is to render a legitimate place to secularization as a cultural phenomenon from within a Christian framework of interpretation. This is only possible when 'our secular experience of existence itself contains elements which inwardly *refer* to an absolute mystery. ... if our human reality *itself* contains a real reference to God, which is therefore part of our experience.'[39] It is in line with such experiences, therefore, that the reinterpretation of the Christian faith ought to take place. In this sense, the secular world as a hermeneutical situation does not offer a critique of religion itself, but rather of the old ways of expressing religion, while religion, for its part, offers a critique of purely atheistic interpretations of the present-day secularized experience of existence. Schillebeeckx calls at this juncture for a revaluation and rediscovery of natural theology. The fact that people ultimately believe – even prior to their association thereof with religion – that, in spite of everything, the good has more right to exist than the bad, and that life in the last analysis has meaning, leads to a religious question, 'because this trust cannot be justified when it is viewed only within the perspective of man himself taken as a whole'.[40] It is at this anthropological, pre-religious level that people make a choice for or against God:

[38] Cf. Edward Schillebeeckx, 'Zwijgen en spreken over God in een geseculariseerde wereld', *Tijdschrift voor theologie* 7 (1967), pp. 337–59; English translation in: Schillebeeckx, *God the Future of Man*, pp. 51–90. See also: Schillebeeckx, 'Het nieuwe Godsbeeld, secularisatie en politiek'; English translation: *God the Future of Man*, pp. 167–207.

[39] Schillebeeckx, 'Zwijgen en spreken', p. 347; English translation: *God the Future of Man*, p. 71.

[40] Schillebeeckx, 'Zwijgen en spreken', p. 350; English translation: *God the Future of Man*, p. 74.

The so-called proof of the existence of God which is based on the experience of contingency is therefore only the reflective justification, made afterwards, of the conviction that this unconditional trust in the gift of a meaningful human future is not an illusion, not a projection of frustrated wishful thinking, but that it has an objective basis in experienced reality – the reality in which the God who is to come manifests himself, and in a very intimate manner, as the one who is absent, but approaching nevertheless.[41]

The unlocking of this experience dimension with respect to God serves as the ontological basis for making God's offer of salvation in Jesus Christ comprehensible for men and women today. At the same time, it motivates Christian engagement in support of a better society on theological grounds, bearing in mind that this engagement is the very place in which God's promise of salvation can and must be made manifest. Moreover, as Schillebeeckx indicated in 1968: the verification principle of the Christian faith and its eschatological hope consists precisely in discerning whether Christians 'show in practice in their lives that their hope is *capable* of changing the world now and of making our history a real history of salvation which brings well-being to all men'.[42]

Schillebeeckx further elaborates this new insight in the same 1968 article through the notion of contrast experience and the cognitive and ethical-practical theological consequences thereof.[43] This notion continues to be determinative for the remainder of Schillebeeckx's theological career and serves as a point of anchor/connection between Christian faith and its context.[44] In his *Theological Testament* (1994), he states: 'I refer here

---

[41] Schillebeeckx, 'Zwijgen en spreken', p. 350; English translation: *God the Future of Man*, p. 75.

[42] Schillebeeckx, 'Het nieuwe Godsbeeld, secularisatie en politiek', p. 53; English translation: *God the Future of Man*, p. 182.

[43] For this paragraph, and for a broader reflection on Schillebeeckx's concept of experience, see my *God Interrupts History*, chapter 5; and my 'Experience according to Edward Schillebeeckx: The Driving Force of Faith and Theology', *Divinising Experience: Essays in the History of Religious Experience from Origen to Ricoeur* (ed. Lieven Boeve and Laurence Paul Hemming; Studies in Philosophical Theology, 23; Leuven: Peeters, 2004), pp. 199–225.

[44] Cf. e.g. Edward Schillebeeckx, *Tussentijds verhaal over twee Jezusboeken* (Bloemendaal: Nelissen, 1978) p. 65; English translation: *Interim Report on the Books* Jesus *&* Christ (trans. John Bowden; London: SCM, 1980/New York, NY: Crossroad, 1980) p. 55. Here Schillebeeckx uses the category of 'contrast experience' in order to point – positively – to our ineradicable expectation, persisting in the modern secular context, of a sustainable future for humanity. On the other hand, this experience witnesses – negatively – to the equally persistent distress unsettling all of us because suffering and senseless injustice continue to threaten this future for an overwhelming majority of people.

13

to a basic experience common to all human beings, which is thus also pre-religious and therefore accessible to all human beings.'[45] The veto against all forms of suffering and injustice carries within itself a fundamental 'faith in the humanity of humanity' together with a sense of hope for a future without suffering, oppression and injustice. 'Without this hope, the indignation present as existential experience becomes inexistent, impossible in itself, meaningless and without human content. Without at least a latent positive hankering for human dignity, this human indignation is absurd.'[46] For Schillebeeckx, it is precisely this link between the modern human experience of searching for liberation and the Christian message of salvation that presents the best argument in support of the plausibility and relevance of Christian faith today, both within and with respect to secular society. Even though these experiences have to do with life's most profound meaning, however, they do not necessarily call for a religious interpretation. Nevertheless, Schillebeeckx affirms – in *Church* – that in order to understand their fundamental character, 'which so deeply affects human existence', one 'is helped ... by the word of God'. He continues: 'I say, "[one] is helped"; [and] not "give[n] a better understanding of" this experience than the agnostic explanation':

> So I am talking about universally shared experiences which are fundamental to any human existence, which by the introduction of belief in God's saving presence manifest a distinctive comprehensibility which can be understood by others (even if they do not accept them), which is not present in other interpretations in which belief in God is not expressed.[47]

Schillebeeckx's creation faith thus expresses itself in the course of time in the establishment of the desire for God in pre-religious, human experience. As we have said, this causes the vertical nature-super-nature pattern to evolve into a horizontal juxtaposition of faith and secular world. Reading secular experience of existence in search of God then constitutes his natural theology,[48] to which he attaches God's salvation-historical presence. At the same time, it constitutes the precondition for sustaining credibility and the plausibility of Christianity for Christians as well as non-Christians.

---

[45] Edward Schillebeeckx, *Theologisch testament: Notarieel nog niet verleden* (Baarn: Nelissen, 1994) p. 128.

[46] Schillebeeckx, *Theologisch testament*, p. 130.

[47] Schillebeeckx, *Church*, p. 84.

[48] See in this regard also: Edward Schillebeeckx, 'Een nieuwe aarde: Een scheppingsgeloof dat niets wil verklaren', *Evolutie en scheppingsgeloof* (ed. Sjoerd L. Bonting; Baarn: Nelissen, 1978), pp. 167–76.

b. *The Hermeneutics of Tradition*

It goes without saying that Schillebeeckx's vision of the hermeneutics of tradition is not detached from what we have said thus far. The fact that God reveals Godself in the concrete mediation of history in fact transforms this tradition primarily into a testimony to the presence of God in history. The extent to which God is present today also implies that the tradition is not closed but rather open and continuing. Tradition becomes a living tradition when it succeeds in allowing people to live and practice God's presence in history in a concrete way. The epistemological and soteriological cohesion of Schillebeeckx's creation-theological intuition therefore must ultimately lead to a hermeneutics of tradition.[49]

Schillebeeckx systematically addresses the problem of hermeneutics in the articles he will later include in *The Understanding of Faith: Interpretation and Criticism*. Not only does he there recognize the Christian hermeneutical circle between understanding and pre-understanding, but in relating the critical theory of Jürgen Habermas, among others, to hermeneutics, he also explicitly initiates the ideology-critical dimension of hermeneutics and makes it praxis-oriented. He furthermore argues for a critical correlation between theology and critical social theory. The hermeneutics of tradition can no longer be understood as a theoretical re-actualization of the tradition, but must substantiate itself in orthopraxis. Theology as the understanding of faith thus becomes the critically reflexive 'self-consciousness of Christian praxis'.[50]

Having illustrated and commented upon his hermeneutical-theological approach in his two Jesus volumes, his *Interim Report* offers an initial synthesis of the hermeneutical insights he had developed thus far. In concrete terms, this hermeneutics takes the form of a *critical correlation between tradition and the modern situation*, which in fact can be rightly referred to as a 'correlation between experiences'. While concrete contrast experiences help us to perceive within the Christian tradition the liberating claim of the God of salvation in a different light, the same tradition – as the interpretation history of experiences of salvation – provides perspectives that allow for this modern context of experience to be structured from a Christian point of view. The result is a contemporary Christian faith in which the current 'situation is an intrinsic element of the significance of the Christian message for us'. Schillebeeckx continues:

---

[49] For earlier, highly cautious attempts at tradition critique and the hermeneutics of tradition, see Schillebeeckx, 'Christelijke situatie', pp. 608–09.

[50] Cf. Edward Schillebeeckx, *Geloofsverstaan: Interpretatie en kritiek* (Theologische Peilingen, 5; Bloemendaal: Nelissen, 1972) p. 205; English translation: *The Understanding of Faith: Interpretation and Criticism* (trans. N.D. Smith; London: Sheed and Ward, 1974/New York, NY: Seabury, 1974) p. 143.

It is therefore striking that the times in which men [sic] refer to their own experiences, individual and collective, with renewed emphasis, are always times of crisis in which they experience a gap between tradition and experience instead of continuity between, e.g. the Christian tradition of experience and their contemporary experience. Of course even old experiences have power to make men question and transform; ... But even new experiences have their own productive and critical force; otherwise, a reference to 'interpretative elements' of old experiences would do no more than solidify and hold back our ongoing history.[51]

During his valedictory speech in 1983, Schillebeeckx preferred to speak of this hermeneutical approach as 'interrelation'.[52] He thereby emphasized the dynamic-dialectical relationship between both poles, a dynamic that is already at work when Christians endeavour to understand their faith in the contemporary context. Because the Christian message is always passed on in particular cultures, it can never be presented in its trans-cultural core: 'Thus, there is a durable faith substance [een blijvende geloofssubstantie], which is time and again actualized and acclimatized in a particular culture, while we can never catch sight of that faith substance in an unhistorical or supra-cultural way.'[53] At the same time, this implies that the said cultural mediation also represents the precondition for the continuation of the Christian message; it has 'a positive mediating function, precisely because the trans-culturality of the Gospel can only be found *in* the particularity of certain cultural structures of understanding'.[54] These historical mediations therefore cannot simply be relativized in a unilateral manner, since they constitute our historically conditioned access to the Gospel. It is at this juncture that Schillebeeckx applies his theological approach to the model of 'fusion of horizons' and claims the 'fundamental identity of meaning'

[51] Schillebeeckx, *Interim Report*, p. 55.
[52] Cf. Schillebeeckx, *Theologisch geloofsverstaan anno 1983*, p. 9 (compare with: *Church*, p. 36). Schillebeeckx argues at this juncture that the terminology of correlation is misleading, because authentic theologizing happens in two phases (not three) which together constitute one dynamic whole.
[53] Schillebeeckx, *Theologisch geloofsverstaan anno* 1983, p. 10. Compare with: *Church*, p. 36: 'So there is the constantly young, abiding "offer of revelation", but on each occasion this is acclimatized in a particular culture, while that offer can never be found in an unhistorical and supra-cultural form.'
[54] Schillebeeckx, *Theologisch geloofsverstaan anno* 1983, p. 11. Compare with: *Church*, p. 39:

The mediation of revelation varies, depending on place, society and period, but it nevertheless comes within the interpretation of faith which is presented on each occasion. Thus any possible understanding of faith takes place on the basis of and through the medium of the human understanding of reality – distinctive to a particular culture in which the gospel is proclaimed and heard.

of the subsequent corresponding relationships between the historically situated form of tradition, on the one hand, and the socio-historical context of the day, on the other. This is why 'dogmas or confessions of faith are on the one hand irreversible', while at the same time they can 'become really irrelevant for later generations' because of their cultural-historical forms. However, 'even irrelevant dogmas continue to be theologically important. ... The Christian identity *in* cultural breaks or shifts is what is at stake.'[55]

In his inclusion of this text in the fifth chapter of the first part of *Church*, Schillebeeckx further radicalizes his hermeneutical insights and speaks, for example, of an 'offer of revelation' instead of a 'faith substance', further emphasizing the non-objectifiable significance thereof. Likewise, the dynamic and indissoluble bond between experience and interpretation, the constitutive bond between experience and experiential tradition, reinforce his insight into the hermeneutical circle from which we are unable to extricate ourselves. At the same time, Schillebeeckx also underlines the critical-productive dynamic that is activated within this circle when experiences are given meaning on the basis of an experiential tradition, and simultaneously, as experiences of revelation, place the same tradition under pressure. Allusion to the fact that experiences of suffering and narratives of suffering enjoy cognitive priority in this dynamic because they bear witness *ex negativo* to the *humanum* desired by all, brings his hermeneutical observations into contact once again with the modern translation of his creation-theological intuition.

3. Theology after Schillebeeckx

Both the creation-theological foundation and hermeneutical-theological approach are deeply woven into Schillebeeckx's theology, providing it with its specifically late-modern profile.

As early as 1994, Borgman argued that this synthesis was subject to pressure and appeared to have lost its plausibility for many of our contemporaries: 'Experience of teaching students and interested "ordinary believers" makes it clear that young people find it difficult to access Schillebeeckx's work and that the latter appeals for the most part to people

---

[55]Schillebeeckx, *Theologisch geloofsverstaan anno* 1983, p. 16. Compare with *Church*, pp. 43–44:

> ... dogma's, are on the one hand irrevocable and irreversible: ... But on the other hand, in their cultural and historical forms they can become irrelevant and meaningless ... But even dogmas which have become irrelevant with the passing of time remain theological, i.e. important ... there is Christian identity *in* cultural breaks and shifts, ...

older than 55.'[56] The context would appear to have changed to such an extent that people have difficulty with Schillebeeckx's project, and that the next generations deal with it and draw from it in a different way. In my presentation of the twofold reception of Schillebeeckx, I have already noted that Borgman has particular difficulty with Schillebeeckx's maintenance of tradition and church, which would prevent him from pointing to concrete faith in concrete life. His theology thus gets bogged down, Borgman claims, in a 'search for the core of what it is to be Christian via an analysis of the Christian past'.[57] Schillebeeckx thus misses the opportunity to discover traces of God in new and different ways in the world today. It will come as no surprise that I do not fully share this analysis, but prefer to point to the late-modern rootedness of Schillebeeckx's theology to emphasize why its persuasiveness no longer functions today. In a context that can no longer be described as evidently Christian, in which it is difficult to accept that the experience of contingency and solidarity can function almost automatically as a sort of natural theology, any overhasty association between such experiences and Christian belief in God runs the risk of eroding the latter and transforming it into a sort of narrative reduplication of what people already know.[58] From a contemporary perspective, the problem with the reception of his theology, in my opinion, is not so much that Schillebeeckx engages in too much tradition hermeneutics, but rather not enough. It is on this particular point, however, that Schillebeeckx can also lead the way to an ever more hermeneutical hermeneutics: the Christian faith is rooted in a narrative and a common history of interpretation 'in which [– as he writes in 2001 –] the temporal and the particular are understood from a temporal and particular context'.[59] As Schillebeeckx continues: 'In the highly concrete aggregate of fragmentary, personal and collective events

[56] Borgman, 'Van cultuurtheologie naar theologie als onderdeel van de cultuur', p. 359 n. 86.
[57] Borgman, 'Van cultuurtheologie naar theologie als onderdeel van de cultuur', p. 358.
[58] In this sense we can turn Schillebeeckx's proposition from 1967 on its head: when he spoke of secularization, he wrote that the Christian faith is reduced to a 'useless' superstructure when a breach is established between the modern secular context and that said faith. The truth claims of the faith thus become a question of fideism and can no longer be taken seriously (Schillebeeckx, 'Zwijgen en spreken', p. 349; English translation: God The Future of Man, pp. 71–73). The opposite is the case, however, in the present day: too much continuity between faith and context transforms Christian faith into a 'useless superstructure'. At the same time, however, I would add, also discontinuity does not have the last word in the matter, although the precise mediation of the Christian salvific message still requires our reflection in a post-Christian, post-secular and pluralized context.
[59] Edward Schillebeeckx, 'Het gezag van de traditie in de theologie', Jezus, een eigentijds verhaal (ed. Maurice Bouwens, Jacobine Geel and Frans Maas; Zoetermeer: Meinema, 2001), pp. 76–87 (87) – with reference to Theo de Boer.

[and narratives], likewise and precisely within our present-day situation, it becomes possible to detect the profile of a liberating God.'[60]

Borgman's and my differing diagnosis leads to differing theological projects, in which the work of Schillebeeckx is differently received, and with consequences, as we have seen, for both of our evaluations of the enduring relevance of Edward Schillebeeckx for present-day theology. Allowing for a potential lack of nuance, I would describe this difference in theological approach as follows:

(a) Because the world is ultimately of God, Borgman searches for traces of God in the world, and it is only to the extent that tradition and community are of service in this regard that they continue to count. Indeed, the relationship is in fact the reverse: only insofar as we can demonstrate where God is manifest today, can we introduce the said tradition into the discussion. Where the transmitted tradition and community have an alienating effect, theology is faced with the task of reading reality in a new – post-secular and post-traditional – religious way. The present-day transformation of the religious to which we have referred serves then as the outcome of such a re-reading.

(b) My own point of departure is theology's task of reflecting on the experience of being Christian in a transformed context. It starts from the experience that being Christian – with legitimate variety – is a specific position in the domain of religious and other fundamental life options, which brings with it a specific hermeneutical approach to reality. Informed by the so-called 'linguistic turn', it is fundamental in this regard that our access to reality is linguistic and thus interwoven in interpretations. Insofar as this access is situated today in a dynamic, irreducible and often conflicting plurality of narratives and discourses, each narrative is likewise challenged to determine its own position in relation to difference and otherness. Naturally, whatever post-liberals may pretend, this need not imply that we are locked within our own language and experience, rather that we must bear witness to the interruption of our language and narratives in precisely linguistic terms. It is for this reason that tradition and community are crucial. That is, tradition must be understood as a process of continual recontextualizing, a living tradition; and community therefore as a concrete hermeneutical community in which theology locates itself on the basis of its own task. If we are to detect traces of God in reality, to see where God interrupts history *and* the Christian narrative, both the narrative in question and the interpreting community are important – at the same time putting pressure on both narrative and community to recontextualize when interruption takes place.

I myself would thus be inclined to link Erik Borgman's theological project to Schillebeeckx's creation-theological intuition, driven by the 20th

---

[60] Schillebeeckx, 'Het gezag van de traditie in de theologie', p. 87.

century endeavour to rethink the relationship between the natural and the supernatural in a world that has become increasingly alienated from both church and tradition. The theological truth claim that the world is of God would then appear to be heading towards a hermeneutic that is less and less connected to the linguistic foundations from which it ultimately emerged, precisely because of the aforementioned alienation. The generally-human religious anthropology that is claimed, as far as I am concerned, on merely theological grounds, then receives the primacy. In my own theological approach, I would explicitly locate this truth claim – i.e. the world is of God – within the particular linguistic horizon of interpretation in which it took shape. It is precisely because the Christian narrative of God's saving presence in the world makes us read the world in this way that Christians make such a claim and live from such a claim. The contemporary situation of plurality and difference in which they now find themselves then results in putting pressure on this particularity. The crucial question then is: how do we uphold and express this narratively embedded truth claim, without allowing it to become totalitarian – without allowing the Christian narrative to evolve into a hegemonic master narrative – and creating victims on account of its proclamation to the world of the same truth claim?

Schillebeeckx writes somewhere that 'profane history is salvation history, independent of our knowledge thereof'.[61] For sure, this may be correct, but if there were not the narratives concerning the God who makes salvation history with us, this would probably have gone unnoticed, and most certainly would have made little difference in the praxis of our lives. For God does not reveal Godself in experience as such, but in interpreted experience. Context, history and narrative are co-constitutive for revelatory experiences.

4. *Theology Today*

In the conclusion to his *The Praxis of the Reign of God*, Robert Schreiter proposes the following four elements as characteristic of the enduring relevance of Schillebeeckx's theology. First, there is his inductive approach, which focuses on experiences and interpretation, and ascribes to the insight that God can only reveal Godself through the concrete mediation of world and history. Schreiter refers in the second instance to the narrative character of experience, both for the first disciples of Jesus as for ourselves, and the dangerous memory that lies hidden in narratives of human suffering. Thirdly, and related to the latter, he alludes to the cognitive importance of the contrast experience, including the asymmetrical structure thereof, which leads in a postmodern context to the critique of master narratives.

[61] Schillebeeckx, 'Theologie als bevrijdingskunde', p. 401.

Schreiter concludes by reminding us of the primacy of Schillebeeckx's soteriology, not only in his Christology, but in his theology as a whole, including his teachings on creation. Schreiter adds that the fact that many of these insights are now widely accepted in contemporary theology is due in the first instance to the work of Schillebeeckx: 'While certain elements in his theology may come to be superseded by more recent reflection and research, these foundational elements remain.'[62]

From my own perspective I would add the following to Schreiter's list. I would argue that an elaboration of Schillebeeckx's hermeneutical-theological line – certainly when in dialogue with the later thought of Ricœur – leads to the insight that his natural theology is a forceful *theological* reading of reality. This is not only true with respect to Schillebeeckx's earlier work, but also his later works and his creation-theological reading of secularity, including the contrast experience. The latter is no longer presumed to result in a broadly human religious anthropology, one which can serve as the basis for the plausibility and relevance of the Christian narrative, to be understood potentially by all. The question remains, however, whether the insight into the theological character of this claim ultimately disqualifies it. For Christians, who experience and substantiate the Christian narrative in their everyday lives, such disqualification does not make the claim any less true. It becomes clear, nevertheless, that the cultural plausibility of such a claim can no longer be rooted in continuity. This need not, of course, imply that dialogue with the context should be abandoned – as some anti-modern and postmodern theologians are often too pleased to insist. It is in this regard that thinkers who point – as Schreiter indicates – to radical asymmetry in the contrast experience, to the experience of difference and conflict, raise the question of justice. Such thinkers are often too quick to forget that the question of justice is also mediated through language and the asymmetry of which they speak is not discussed out of context. They all too frequently lapse with ease, like John Caputo, into patterns of 'religion without religion', 'pure religion' and 'messianity without messianism', which are then taken to be more original and claimed to underlie concrete religions.[63] It is precisely Schillebeeckx's (likewise creation-)theological insight that concrete experiences, narratives, history and context – and thus language – make a difference, that informs the position Christians adopt in their lives today, and can lead to the establishment of a contemporary

[62] Robert J. Schreiter, 'Edward Schillebeeckx: His Continuing Significance', *The Praxis of the Reign of God: An Introduction to the Theology of Edward Schillebeeckx* (ed. Mary Catherine Hilkert and Robert J. Schreiter; New York, NY: Fordham University Press, 2nd edn, 2002), pp. 185–94.

[63] See, e.g., the analysis in my 'Theological Truth, Particularity and Incarnation: Engaging Religious Plurality and Radical Hermeneutics', *Orthodoxy: Process and Product* (ed. Mathijs Lamberigts, Lieven Boeve and Terrence Merrigan; BETL, 227; Leuven: Peeters, 2009), pp. 323–48.

Christian open narrative that is capable of seeing where the God of creation and salvation history is revealed today. Furthermore, it also determines the conditions under which Christians can introduce this claim into dialogue with others – not as something that others should already know and share in advance, but as something that is already part of the game for Christians, something to which they wish to bear witness in dialogue and praxis, in the hope that God's engagement in history and context can become more apparent.

PART I
'GOD IS NEW EACH MOMENT': THE QUESTION OF GOD IN MODERNITY

GOD, THE LUXURY OF OUR LIVES: SCHILLEBEECKX AND THE ARGUMENT

Anthony J. Godzieba

At a time when everyone seems to be writing a book about God, Edward Schillebeeckx has always resisted the temptation. God, of course, has always been on his mind. His more recent thoughts might be gleaned from a careful reading of the combination of Christology and ecclesiology presented, for example, in *Mensen als verhaal van God* (*Church: The Human Story of God*). Here he discusses God's relation to the world and to humanity through Jesus, in whom 'God's purposes with men and women and in them God's "own character" have become revelation'. Indeed, Jesus is 'the supreme density of divine revelation in a whole history of experiences of revelation'.[1] But at the same time, as Schillebeeckx argues elsewhere, Jesus is the one whose contingency 'reveals God but also conceals him'.[2] Do these claims play any role in postmodern (and even post-postmodern) debates over God and the possibility of transcendence?

There is one claim in particular from Schillebeeckx's later writings that I wish to examine here. In the late 1980s, he published a small book that, at least in its English translation, has received little notice: his 1986 Abraham Kuyper-lectures at the Vrije Universiteit Amsterdam entitled *Als politiek niet alles is... Jezus in onze westerse cultuur*.[3] The book summarizes

---

[1] Edward Schillebeeckx, *Church: The Human Story of God* (trans. John Bowden; New York, NY: Crossroad, 1990) p. 26.

[2] Edward Schillebeeckx, *On Christian Faith: The Spiritual, Ethical, and Political Dimensions* (trans. John Bowden; New York, NY: Crossroad, 1987) p. 2.

[3] Edward Schillebeeckx, *Als politiek niet alles is... Jezus in onze westerse cultuur: Abraham Kuyper-lezingen 1986* (Baarn: Ten Have, 1986). In Britain, the translation was entitled *Jesus in our Western Culture: Mysticism, Ethics and Politics* (trans. J. Bowden; London: SCM, 1987); in the U.S., *On Christian Faith*. All translated citations are taken from the U.S. edition.

25

christological, ecclesiological, and soteriological themes that are typical of his later work. In addition, it calls for the end of 'the liberal pluralism of many modern theologies',[4] arguing instead for a crucial ethical link between mysticism and politics.[5]

What I wish to focus on is the following remarkably blunt statement:

> No one prays to some 'condition of possibility' or another. ... God is not there as an 'explanation' but as a gift. The idea which people are so fond of these days, that God is 'the condition of the possibility' of human subjectivity, has taken not only the heart but also the 'logos' out of all belief in God and theology. By contrast the post-modern 'we do not need God' is precisely the supreme luxury of any human life. It is precisely that which a person 'needs'. Thus for believers God is the supreme luxury of their life – our luxury, not so much our cause or our final goal, but sheer, superfluous luxury (Zo is voor gelovigen God de luxe van hun leven, onze weelde, niet zozeer onze oorzaak of ons einddoel, wel puur overtollige weelde).[6]

Schillebeeckx's emphasis on God as 'gift' should have inserted him directly into recent discussions of religious experience and transcendence. But his work has played no role there. The rest of his bold and unusually harsh rejection of a 'transcendental' starting point, indeed of any argument for the existence of God, clashes with traditional Christian attempts to craft a 'natural theology' that might serve as a preparation for a 'theological theology' (e.g., as in Walter Kasper's work), as well as current arguments for the reality of transcendence and the human need for it (e.g. Charles Taylor's A Secular Age). Schillebeeckx's statement, then, demands attention. I will analyze it, then give an indication of the current context in which we read this claim, and then indicate whether Schillebeeckx's claim remains vital and critically productive, or is a 1980s period-piece and a theological dead-end.

1. The Question of God

Schillebeeckx's polemic comes in the midst of his argument against any approach to God that does not recognize God's fundamental hiddenness, 'the specific and distinctive religious relationship of Jesus to this hidden

---

[4] Schillebeeckx, On Christian Faith, p. 84.
[5] Schillebeeckx, On Christian Faith, pp. 65–84.
[6] Schillebeeckx, On Christian Faith, pp. 5–6; Als politiek niet alles is, p. 13.

God',[7] and the necessary historical and cultural situatedness of salvation.[8] God's hiddenness is a non-negotiable challenge to human experience: 'We cannot derive the active saving presence of God from our awareness or our experience of this presence which challenges us to make sense on our side'.[9] And so the catalyst for Schillebeeckx's wholesale dismissal of transcendental argument and the human need for God is his firm opposition to human 'force' or power, which in turn would lead to the illusion that we possess God and control salvation: if we force God to fit human categories such as 'importance, efficiency or utility'[10] and thereby 'possess' God according to human understanding, this would deny God's freedom to give God's self.

Jesus himself represents a paradox that defeats any claim to possess his meaning. Jesus has an 'indescribably special relationship with God' and yet 'as a historical phenomenon he is a contingent event' – a contingency that produces the insight that 'God has not revealed himself exclusively and exhaustively in Jesus Christ and therefore that when it comes to talking about God, any man or woman has a right to his or her say'.[11] While talk about God is always bound up with talk about human experience and the world, God transcends the human categories of necessity and utility. 'God is not to be reduced to a function of humanity, of society or of the world. For all this God is a useless, superfluous hypothesis. For us, God as a remedy for the human condition has completely disappeared.'[12] The possibility of cogent arguments for the existence of God – whether cosmological, metaphysical, ethical, or political – has also disappeared. This context is not debilitating, Schillebeeckx argues, but freeing: 'In this Western social climate of secularization and religious indifference,' he says, 'the question of God becomes the freest and most gratuitous question that one can ask, and the way to God also becomes the freest career to choose.'[13] This human freedom, in turn, allows God's gracious and saving freedom to become visible, a freedom in which God chooses to need us. 'God himself determines in all freedom who he is and also who he wants to be for us',[14] the absolute saving presence of human beings within their history, a saving presence that began with creation.[15]

[7] Schillebeeckx, On Christian Faith, p. 3.
[8] Regarding God's fundamental hiddenness, Schillebeeckx, On Christian Faith, p. 3 cites Isa. 45.15 ('Truly, you are a God who hides himself') and Jesus' words on the cross. Cf. also Edward Schillebeeckx, For the Sake of the Gospel (trans. John Bowden; New York, NY: Crossroad, 1990) pp. 85–87.
[9] Schillebeeckx, On Christian Faith, p. 7.
[10] Schillebeeckx, On Christian Faith, p. 4.
[11] Schillebeeckx, On Christian Faith, pp. 3–4.
[12] Schillebeeckx, On Christian Faith, p. 4.
[13] Schillebeeckx, On Christian Faith, p. 5.
[14] Schillebeeckx, On Christian Faith, p. 5.
[15] Schillebeeckx, On Christian Faith, p. 7.

These claims are supported by Schillebeeckx's familiar steadfast refusal to consider the history of salvation apart from 'secular history', which, due to creation, already has a sacramental structure before believers recognize it. A 'secular event' already bearing a human meaning which 'is already relevant in human terms without reference to God must necessarily form the basis for the interpreting eyes of faith to recognize history as the sacrament of God's presence. The signs which the believer can interpret as salvific are primarily acts of liberation, those which open human beings to others, and 'human love which has a preference for the poor'.[16] This in turn is supported by Schillebeeckx's famous hermeneutical link between experience and interpretation.

Now, I want to emphasize that this was and remains a vital theological *exhortation*, especially when Schillebeeckx urges us to 'look for points of expectation in human experience, echoes, traces or even held-back sounds which betray or suggest God's existence, his free presence within a hair's breadth of us'.[17] But as a convincing theological *argument* it is muddled; whatever power it has had in the late 1980s has today completely dissipated. The confusion stems first of all from Schillebeeckx failing to provide adequate criteria for recognizing revelation in history. He does indeed provide some criteria (liberation, open human relationships, the contrast experience of suffering). And in turn, he grounds such criteria in the praxis of Jesus, introducing it as a more fundamental criterion for judging these ordinary experiences as ultimately life-affirming. But we are given no justification as to why or how we are to recognize and to name them as fundamentally 'religious' or 'revelatory', as having a transcendental referent. What indeed allows us to point to events of liberation as moments of grace? What allows us to acknowledge human acts of love as God's 'presence within a hair's breadth of us'? It is one thing to seek to preserve the coherence of historical events and claim they act as a mediation for recognizing 'the countenance of God'.[18] But precisely how does theology plausibly derive the latter from the former? It is inadequate to claim simply that 'religious language with its own spirituality gets its material from our human experience of contingency as a possible (but never compulsive) "deciphering" of deeper dimensions which can nevertheless be experienced'.[19] This thin claim is, to put it simply, a type of modern liberal theology with low expectations.

---

[16] Schillebeeckx, *On Christian Faith*, pp. 11–12.
[17] Schillebeeckx, *On Christian Faith*, p. 5.
[18] Schillebeeckx, *On Christian Faith*, p. 13.
[19] Schillebeeckx, *On Christian Faith*, p. 12.

2. *Diagnosing the Contemporary*

Transcendental arguments about the conditions for the possibility of human experience are less about the use of rational 'force' and more properly explorations of *limits*. And when used in Catholic theology, especially in reaction to the 'turn to the subject' that is rooted not only in modern philosophy but also in Renaissance humanism's 'revival of the classical ideal subsumed under the biblical ideal of Man as the image of God',[20] it is an exploration of human limit-experiences and the possibility of divine revelation precisely as mediated by those limit-experiences, as well as an attempt to begin with a publically available and discussable argument about ultimacy. David Tracy's argument for the necessity of the transcendental perspective, part of his larger argument for a revised method of critical correlation, is as valid today as it was when he first made it in 1989:

> That some form of transcendental reflection is needed by theology seems as clear now as it was 20 years ago, and that for the same reason: if one understands the logic of the claim Jews, Christians, and Muslims make when they affirm their belief in a radically monotheistic God, transcendental reflection is that mode of rational inquiry appropriate to considering that claim.[21]

He argues further that 'the strictly transcendental question of the nature of ultimate reality' is a question that theological reflection cannot avoid asking 'if theologians are faithful to the logic of the subject matter they presume to study'.[22]

This kind of theological reflection is especially necessary in the current context, in light of recent vital discussions about the limits – indeed, the closure – of human experience and the relation of religion to the secularization that dominates the West. I cite here only two examples. First, Eyal Chowers, in his book *The Modern Self in the Labyrinth*, argues that since the end of the eighteenth century there has been a rift between the self and the social institutions that the self creates. Rather than promoting

---

[20] Brendan Bradshaw, 'Transalpine Humanism', *The Cambridge History of Political Thought 1450–1700* (ed. James Henderson Burns and Mark Goldie; repr., Cambridge: Cambridge University Press, 2004), pp. 95–131 (105). See also the classic work on this theme: Charles Trinkaus, *In Our Image and Likeness: Humanity and Divinity in Italian Humanist Thought* (Chicago, IL: University of Chicago Press, 1970). Cf. Anthony J. Godzieba, '"Refuge of Sinners, Pray for Us": Augustine, Aquinas, and the Salvation of Modernity', *Augustine and Postmodern Thought: A New Alliance against Modernity?* (ed. Lieven Boeve, Mathijs Lamberigts and Maarten Wisse; BETL, 219; Leuven: Peeters, 2009), pp. 147–65.

[21] David Tracy, 'The Uneasy Alliance Reconceived: Catholic Theological Method, Modernity and Postmodernity', *Theological Studies* 50 (1989), pp. 548–70 (559).

[22] Tracy, 'The Uneasy Alliance Reconceived', p. 568.

humanization, these institutions instead are seen by many to promote a sense of 'entrapment' that 'sap moderns of their distinct identities'. A more optimistic nineteenth century believed it could alleviate this condition, but by the late nineteenth and throughout the twentieth century it was considered to be an inescapable threat (especially in the thought of Weber, Freud, and Foucault, all of whom are Chowers' main examples). The limits to human ability, then, become symbols of the loss of human identity:

> This rift leads the self to experience itself as under threat of subjection – not to any specific person or transcendental entity – but to collective institutions, the self's 'great double'. Moreover ... entrapment involves a sense that the source of dehumanization is human inventiveness itself. ... [Entrapment] is the notion that human action is not answerable to nor harnessed by any natural or divine scheme that haunts the modern imagination: entrapment occurs in a world experienced as self-fabricated. ... [23]

Chowers's solution is to reimagine the self, but the scope of that reimagining is constricted and even lifeless in the face of an amorphous and all-too-powerful social world: 'The main option left for the self in resisting this predicament is one of coping, of an individualistic-agnostic response that does not aspire to devise an encompassing vision of emancipation.'[24]

This discussion of human life collapsed inwards behind its limits is intensified by Charles Taylor's recent analysis of secularization and its effects. For Taylor, the hallmark of Western culture after modernity is the bounded and disenchanted 'buffered' self that results from the 'exclusive humanism' of the modern secular order. Unlike the pre-modern 'porous self' that was open to transcendent influences and forces (the chief of which were acts of God), the buffered self is 'disengaged' from any possible transcendence that lies 'beyond the boundary', and rather 'giv[es] its own autonomous order to its life'.[25] This modern moral order infiltrates what Taylor terms the 'social imaginary', that is, 'the ways in which [people] imagine their social

---

[23] Eyal Chowers, *The Modern Self in the Labyrinth: Politics and the Entrapment Imagination* (Cambridge, MA: Harvard University Press, 2004) pp. 2–3. He notes that:

> Weber, Freud, and Foucault reject the belief that human beings are the authors of history, able to stand above current events, rationally deliberating about their aims and needs and steering the future in desirable directions. In the entrapment vista, history is a train careening out of control, and we can neither willfully divert it to a new track nor simply pull the emergency brake and step off. Instead of piloting history, the best we can do is to cope with its dehumanizing effects, mostly through individual projects (p. 181).

[24] Chowers, *The Modern Self*, p. 8.
[25] Charles Taylor, *A Secular Age* (Cambridge, MA: Belknap Press/Harvard University Press, 2007) pp. 38–41.

existence, how they fit together with others, how things go in between them and their fellows, the expectations which are normally met, and the deeper normative notions and images which underlie these expectations'.[26] The social imaginary that we inherit is thus rooted in the Enlightenment's legacy, a 'powerful humanism' that presupposes and affirms, among other things, 'an eclipse/denial of transcendence which tends to make this humanism an exclusive one'.[27] The narrow, immanent frame of reference of this disenchanted autonomy, however, does not produce the sense of human 'fullness' which is at the heart of what we desire. This overall yearning, while not unambiguous, is that which a flattened-out secularization ultimately will fail to satisfy. And so we must look beyond framing life as pure immanence to the possibility of spiritual ascent 'beyond the boundaries'.[28]

Each of these diagnoses wrestles with the limits of human subjectivity and with it, the realization that occurs at those limits. In Chowers' account, the limits crush us; change will come only if the 'self' is radically re-imagined. In Taylor's account, the re-imagining takes the form of a counter-narrative to the dominant narrative of exclusive humanism and the 'immanent frame' within which it is practiced, a counter-narrative that appears primarily Catholic and sacramental.[29] He thus emphasizes specifically the issue of transcendence as essential to human meaning and fullness, and does not shy away from arguing for what Schillebeeckx expressly forbids, namely, the fundamental human *need* for God's presence.

It is that *sacramental imagination* which is the key element – the way of envisioning reality through the eyes of faith that recognizes the presence of transcendence within immanence, the infinite mediated by the finite, the mediation of grace by created being. The force of this theological claim, in turn, depends on recognizing the fundamental possibility of immanence intentionally opening out into transcendence. However, especially today when the productive power of the imagination is constrained and even sapped by a tight network of images constructed by consumer and media cultures, it is theology's crucial task to emphasize the fundamental human yearning for God's presence and to make a publically-accessible argument for the dynamic intentionality of embodied subjectivity and especially of the imagination. This is precisely what any transcendental argument does, by revealing the double-sidedness of the limits of subjectivity: such

[26] Traylor, *A Secular Age*, p. 171. In another definition of the 'social imaginary', Taylor says that 'it consists of the generally shared background understandings of society, which make it possible for it to function as it does' (p. 323).

[27] Taylor, *A Secular Age*, p. 371.

[28] Taylor, *A Secular Age*, pp. 770–72. See also Taylor's argument (pp. 768–71) that the 'modes of fullness' recognized by exclusive humanisms indeed respond to transcendent reality but 'misrecognize it'.

[29] See Taylor's acknowledgment of this in his chapter on 'Conversions' (pp. 728–72, esp. at p. 765).

arguments describe our inescapable finitude while revealing a hint of what exceeds the limit, a hint that makes finitude both conceivable and frustrating. This glance beyond experience's limits toward its intentional goal is what Fergus Kerr has called our 'immortal longings': 'We do not have to choose between the leap in the dark of radical transcendence and hiding in the pure immanence of the familiar world.'[30] A transcendental argument, then, renders the mediated immediacy of the supernatural plausible, without reducing transcendence to immanence. It articulates, in Maurice Blondel's famous phrase, how the supernatural is '*indispensable* and at the same time ... *inaccessible* for man'.[31] God's gracious presence can still be portrayed as 'gift', as Schillebeeckx argues. But without this kind of 'method of immanence', theology will fail to make plausible to those dominated by the 'immanent frame' how the reality of God intersects with human experience. Transcendence, then, would remain extrinsic to human experience – how, then, could salvation be a salvation which fulfills my personal identity and my historically-situated life with others? Despite Schillebeeckx's intentions and assertions, in jettisoning the need for any transcendental argumentation he ends up espousing an extrinsicist position where secular history and the history of salvation proceed on parallel tracks or parallel planes, with ultimately no philosophical-anthropological way to discern their connection.[32]

3. *The Need for a Natural Theology*

As a counter-narrative to exclusive humanism in 'the immanent frame', what is needed is a natural theology that demonstrates the *a priori* transcending character of human subjectivity and the possibility of the natural knowledge of God – that is, a contemporary version of what the Neo-Scholastic manuals called the *demonstratio religiosa*. As inadequate as the term 'natural theology' is, I want to insist on it here (rather than use an alternative like 'philosophical theology') in order to emphasize its embodied, historically- and culturally-situated character. This, of course, is not 'natural theology' in the textbook sense of 'rational knowledge of God without special revelation'. It is rather the deeply Catholic sense of a theology that seeks to demonstrate what Walter Kasper calls 'the natural

---

[30] Fergus Kerr, *Immortal Longings: Versions of Transcending Humanity* (Notre Dame, IN: University of Notre Dame Press, 1997) p. 184.

[31] Cf. Blondel's *Letter on Apologetics* (1896). See: Maurice Blondel, *The Letter on Apologetics and History and Dogma* (ed. and trans. Alexander Dru and Illtyd Trethowan; Grand Rapids, MI: Eerdmans, 1994) p. 161.

[32] Note that the argument in *On Christian Faith* differs from the argument for faith as an 'anthropological constant' that Schillebeeckx makes in *Christ: The Experience of Jesus as Lord* (trans. John Bowden; New York, NY: Crossroad, 1981) pp. 740–41.

"access-point" of faith' and 'the internal reasonableness of a faith which has its substantiation in and from itself' by demonstrating the possibility of the natural knowledge of God.[33] In other words, the believer claims that human experience by its very nature participates in a dynamic intentional movement toward transcendent mystery that can be even more fully articulated through faith in God's further self-revelation in and through created being – a claim that is at the heart of the Catholic sacramental imagination.

Natural theology attempts to disclose the fundamental *religious* character of the structure of human experience, a 'clearing' within experience, its intentional openness to infinite mystery that forms its transcendental horizon. It is true that the *precise* character of this mystery is revealed only by the mystery itself. But the natural knowledge of God, while ultimately inadequate, opens a vista onto the revelation of the true nature of divine mystery, without daring to claim to actually reach it; here we join both Moses on the heights of Mount Nebo (Deut. 34.1–4) and Thomas Aquinas' view of the simultaneous power and impoverishment of the natural knowledge of God (*Summa theologiae* Ia, q. 2, a. 2). An authentic natural theology demonstrates that one of the fundamental conditions of human experience is its faith-intentionality, its orientation in the direction of transcendence. It also gives us a glimpse – but only a glimpse – of the character of the transcendence for which we long. In this clearing within experience, at the threshold of the natural access-point of faith, we encounter not only the transcendent horizon of our life and actions, the all-encompassing infinite mystery which we do not hesitate to call 'God'.[34] We also discover a hint (*Vorgriff*) of the non-negotiable benevolence of that mystery which gives itself to us on its own initiative, a glimpse of the character of absolute freedom which reveals itself to us in a relationship that can best be described as personal and ultimately fulfilling.[35] The key elements here are the 'givenness' of this experience and the personal relationship that this revelatory 'giving' engenders. At the limits of our experience, divine transcendence can best be described in personal, relational terms: as a gracious giver who encounters us in a personal fashion, freely granting us the space that makes our lives and actions possible. In turn, we give ourselves over to the infinite mystery, trusting that the mystery will be revealed as the personal and loving fulfillment that we believe it to be. Human intentionality outwards towards

---

[33] Walter Kasper, *An Introduction to Christian Faith* (trans. V. Green; New York, NY/Ramsey, NJ: Paulist, 1980) p. 20 ('access-point'); *The God of Jesus Christ* (trans. M.J. O'Connell; repr., New York, NY: Crossroad, 2005) p. 71 ('internal reasonableness').

[34] Cf. Karl Rahner, *Foundations of Christian Faith: An Introduction to the Idea of Christianity* (trans. W.V. Dych; New York, NY: Crossroad, 1978) pp. 57–75.

[35] Kasper, *The God of Jesus Christ*, pp. 114–15, 154–57.

ultimacy, as an act of faith in meaning, meets the divine thrust inwards as revelation.

The task of establishing the sheer possibility of transcendence and of human intentionality stretching toward it in search of 'fullness' within a contemporary context or 'entrapment', or where the social imaginary discounts religion and transcendence, is the first necessary step toward demonstrating the plausibility of the religious imagination and of the possibility of the revelation of the God who saves. These aspects are discoverable through a phenomenology of the religious imagination, the kind of rational reflection that Schillebeeckx takes great pains to dismiss.[36] It is clear why he does so: his insistence on the substantiality of secular history as the arena for salvation history counteracts any attempt to turn salvation into pure abstraction, and his emphasis on the post-modern 'we do not need God' as 'the supreme luxury of any human life'[37] is done in order to make a mystical move, turning the issue of 'need' on its head and applying it to God.

> It is a matter of our making clear to men and women something of God's completely gracious and saving, gratuitous nearness which never leaves us in the lurch, not even when we leave him in the lurch. *Dieu a besoin des hommes*, God needs men and women, not in order to be God but in order to be a God of men and women. God himself determines in all freedom who he is and also who he wants to be for us.[38]

As noted above, there is no denying the exhortatory force and meditative value of such a claim. But in making this move in the context of his blunt rejection of any 'transcendental' starting point, Schillebeeckx is dangerously close to going down the same anti-humanist road that Jean-Luc Marion, Jacques Derrida, John Caputo, and others have travelled, where in order to establish the literally overwhelming character of transcendence, human agency must be severely diminished, even negated.[39] In light of the philosophical analysis of Chowers, Taylor, and others, but also in light of the fragile political and economic situations present around the globe, such an anti-humanist stance is revealed to be a late twentieth-century period-piece, as well as perhaps an abdication of responsibility for the planet.

---

[36] For an example of such a phenomenology of the religious imagination, see Anthony J. Godzieba, 'Knowing Differently: Incarnation, Imagination, and the Body', *Louvain Studies* 32 (2007), pp. 361–82.

[37] Schillebeeckx, *On Christian Faith*, p. 6.

[38] Schillebeeckx, *On Christian Faith*, p. 6.

[39] For a criticism of such anti-humanism in Marion's work, see Anthony J. Godzieba, 'As Much Contingency, As Much Incarnation', *Religious Experience and Contemporary Theological Epistemology* (ed. Lieven Boeve, Yves De Maeseneer and Stijn Van den Bossche; BETL, 188; Leuven: Peeters, 2005), pp. 83–90.

But if our post-Christian, post-9/11 aestheticized and secularized Western situation is anything like the way Chowers, Taylor, and others have described it, what is needed is precisely what Schillebeeckx dismisses, namely an *argument*. Specifically, what is needed is a constructive and optimistic anthropological argument with a theological intentionality, one that is about limits and limit-experiences, as well as about the open-ended intentional character of human embodied experience – in short, an argument for the possibility of transcendence and for the existence of God. Recently, many others have seen the need for exploring and analyzing the possibilities at the limits of human experience; this is clear from the quickly-developing interests in theological aesthetics and scriptural reasoning that mark current theological reflection. How else might the theologian break the grip of the entrapment imagination, or disclose the breaks in 'the immanent frame', without arguing for our need for transcendence, for the very possibility of salvation, and for the love of God? Once the human imagination begins again to view these as indeed *real possibilities*, once the power of the religious imagination can be shown to be life-affirming rather than life-denying, then theology can retrieve Schillebeeckx's mystical insight and point with assurance to God who is the luxury of our lives, and to Jesus whose liberating praxis incarnates that luxury as sheer, life-giving love.

TAKING ATHEISM SERIOUSLY: A CHALLENGE FOR THEOLOGY IN THE 21ST CENTURY

Frederiek Depoortere

During his 1958 inaugural address as professor at the University of Nijmegen, Edward Schillebeeckx designated atheism as 'the most important phenomenon of our time'.[1] A few years ago, however, such a statement would have seemed completely outmoded as 'post-secularism' and 'the return of religion' were the talk of the town. Furthermore, in 2004, British theologian Alister McGrath described the 'fall of disbelief in the modern world' and announced, not without sniggering triumphalism, 'the twilight of atheism'.[2] Today, atheism is hot again and it has returned to the centre of public debate. The most visible sign of this return are the best-selling books of authors such as Richard Dawkins, Daniel Dennett, Sam Harris and Christopher Hitchens.[3] With this in mind, the aim of the present article is to indicate why atheism, that is: the denial of God's existence, remains an important challenge for theology in the 21st century. The argument will proceed in three steps. I will begin by examining Schillebeeckx's view

---

[1] Edward Schillebeeckx, *Op zoek naar de levende God* (Redes uitgesproken aan de Katholieke Universiteit Nijmegen; Utrecht: Dekker en van de Vegt, 1959). Included in: Edward Schillebeeckx, *God en mens* (Theologische peilingen, 2; Bilthoven: Nelissen, 1965), pp. 20–35. English translation: Edward Schillebeeckx, 'The Search for the Living God', *God and Man* (trans. Edward Fitzgerald and Peter Tomlinson; Theological Soundings, 2; London/Sydney: Sheed and Ward, 1969), pp. 18–40 (here p. 34). Where I refer, in what follows, to the Dutch text, I refer to the version from the *Theologische peilingen*.

[2] Alister E. McGrath, *The Twilight of Atheism: The Rise and Fall of Disbelief in the Modern World* (Garden City, NY: Doubleday, 2004).

[3] See, for instance: Richard Dawkins, *The God Delusion* (London: Bantam Press, 2006); Daniel C. Dennett, *Breaking the Spell: Religion as a Natural Phenomenon* (New York, NY: Penguin, 2005); Sam Harris, *The End of Faith: Religion, Terror, and the Future of Reason* (New York, NY: Norton, 2005); Christopher Hitchens, *God Is Not Great: The Case Against Religion* (London: Atlantic Books, 2007).

on the characteristics of religion and faith. As it will become clear, in Schillebeeckx's view, *true* religion and *true* faith imply God's existence: they cannot exist without God. Though this may sound self-evident, it is not. In the second section, I will show that the particular ways in which some theologians try to resolve the conflict between science and religion results in a plea for faith in a non-existent God, a faith which thus collapses into atheism. If we want to avoid this coincidence of faith and atheism, we are therefore in need of a natural basis for faith. And as it shall be pointed out in the third section, this need is precisely what Schillebeeckx has defended during his inaugural address in 1958. I shall conclude the third section by saying a few words on the enduring relevance of Schillebeeckx, which was the topic of the symposium during which an earlier version of this paper was originally presented.

1. *Edward Schillebeeckx on Religion and Faith*

To examine Schillebeeckx's view on the characteristics of religion and faith, I will make use of his contribution on the lemma 'Theology' in the third volume of the *Theologisch woordenboek* (Theological dictionary), which was published in 1958.[4] In the first section of the first paragraph of this article, Schillebeeckx defines religion as 'a personal communion between God and human beings' and he continues by stressing God's initiative in bringing about this personal communion, which cannot come about by human effort, but only by divine grace and revelation. At the same time, Schillebeeckx also stresses the importance of *faith*: it is thanks to faith that the first contact in the encounter between human being and God is established and this act of encounter is what amounts to salvation.[5] This suggests that faith is what is giving us access to the salvific encounter with the living God.

Continuing then from the first section of the first paragraph of the 1958 article on theology, we find two further elements that are part of Schillebeeckx's answer to the question of what is faith. (1) First, Schillebeeckx mentions the link between faith and revelation. In the official English translation of the article, as it is printed in *Revelation and Theology*, this remark reads as follows: 'Faith is conditioned by this

---

[4] Edward Schillebeeckx, 'Theologie', *Theologisch woordenboek* (vol. 3; Roermond/ Maaseik: Romen, 1958), col. 4485–542. Included as 'Wat is theologie?' in Edward Schillebeeckx, *Openbaring en theologie* (Theologische peilingen, 1; Bilthoven: Nelissen, 1964), pp. 71–121. English translation: Edward Schillebeeckx, 'What Is Theology?', *Revelation and Theology* (trans. N.D. Smith; Theological Soundings, 1/1; London/Melbourne: Sheed and Ward, 1967), pp. 95–183. Where I refer, in what follows, to the Dutch text, I refer to the version from *de Theologische peilingen*.

[5] Schillebeeckx, 'What Is Theology?', p. 103; Dutch original: 'Wat is theologie?', p. 75.

revelation [i.e. the revelation in Christ continued in the Church], in which we are addressed by God.' If we take a look at the Dutch original, however, we find that a number of the elements present there have not been rendered in the English translation. Next to the fact that Schillebeeckx is speaking about *theological* faith (Dutch: *theologaal geloof*) and it being *intrinsically* conditioned (Dutch: *innerlijk bepaald*), it is particularly noteworthy here that Schillebeeckx claims that faith is conditioned by the *content* of revelation (Dutch: *openbarings*inhoud). (2) This stress on the content of revelation helps explain what follows, namely that 'faith is therefore a way of knowing'. Schillebeeckx immediately adds to this that 'This knowing has a distinctive character in that it is a knowledge which comes about by our being addressed, by our being confidentially informed, through God's mercy'. Schillebeeckx further points to two ways in which we are addressed by God. On the one hand, there is the *locutio interior*: 'God speaks to us inwardly, through the inward grace of faith'; on the other hand, there is also the aspect of *fides ex auditu*: 'we are addressed from outside by the God of revelation'.[6]

In the beginning of the second section of the first paragraph of the article currently under discussion, Schillebeeckx offers us further clues about his understanding of faith. He distinguishes between the subjective side of faith, i.e. the act of faith, and the objective side of faith, i.e. its content. (1) He then continues by defining the act of faith in terms of consent to a mystery. This implies in his view that rest and unrest are simultaneously present in the one act of faith. In faith, 'firm consent' and 'intellectual speculation' go hand-in-hand. In this respect, he refers to a formula Aquinas adopted from Augustine: *credere est cum assentione cogitare*, 'to believe is to reflect with consent'.[7] (2) The fact that Schillebeeckx considers the act of faith as entailing consent to a mystery does not imply that the content of faith can be completely obscure. On the contrary, Schillebeeckx even stresses that the act of faith is only possible when the mystery to which assent is given is 'to some extent ... clear to the human mind' and when the content of faith appears as answering to 'a problem of human life' (Dutch: *een menselijke levensproblematiek*).[8]

From our study of the first two sections of the first paragraph of Schillebeeckx's article on theology, it becomes clear that in his view, faith is intimately connected with (a particular type of) knowledge. This is confirmed in the third section, which deals with the scientific character of theology and in which Schillebeeckx bases this scientific character of

---

[6] Schillebeeckx, 'What Is Theology?', p. 104; Dutch original: 'Wat is theologie?', p. 76.

[7] Schillebeeckx, 'What Is Theology?', pp. 105–06; Dutch original: 'Wat is theologie?', pp. 76–77.

[8] Schillebeeckx, 'What Is Theology?', pp. 107–09; Dutch original: 'Wat is theologie?', pp. 78–79.

theology on 'the supernatural cognitive aspect of the act of faith' in which 'contact [Dutch: *kennend contact*, knowing contact] is made with the reality of revelation [Dutch: *de openbaringswerkelijkheid*]'.[9] This of course raises the question of what kind of knowledge is at stake here. To delve further into this, we can now turn to the sub-section on 'the basis of the possibility of a speculative theology' in the second section of the third paragraph of the 1958 article on theology. In it, Schillebeeckx distinguishes between 'natural knowledge of God' and 'supernatural knowledge of faith'.

(1) Let us first take a look at what Schillebeeckx writes about natural knowledge of God. This type of knowledge consists in the application of creaturely concepts to God. This does not result, however, in an 'idea of God or of any of his attributes that is both positive and can be properly predicated of him'. Given the unbridgeable difference between the Creator and creation, our (creaturely) concepts are not able to reach God as God is in Godself. This does not mean, however, that 'our natural knowledge of God is merely a blind shot in the dark, aimed at a completely unknown reality'. In Schillebeeckx's view, the creaturely concepts we use to talk about God possess 'an inner dynamism': each of these concepts 'refers, beyond its content, to the divine, which must be in the direction indicated by this concept; but the content of my concept can tell me nothing at all about the specifically divine reality that I do grasp by knowing'. This entails that, even when our concepts are not able to grasp God conceptually as God is in Godself, they nevertheless refer objectively to God. Or, to put it differently: by the help of creaturely concepts it is possible for human beings to 'grasp something of the reality of God'. Yet, this does not prevent our natural knowledge of God from being only negative: what we know of 'what is specifically God's' (Dutch: *het eigene van God*) is, in the end, only that we don't know it. Precisely because our natural knowledge of God is dependent on (creaturely) concepts, it can never grasp the reality of God in itself (who, as Creator, transcends creation). In this regard, Schillebeeckx speaks about a 'conscious unknowing' or 'conscious ignorance' (Dutch: *bewuste onwetendheid*). Yet, his claim is precisely that this not-knowing is nevertheless 'a true *knowledge*'. This is the case because negative knowledge 'is implicit [Dutch: *geborgen*] in a positive knowledge, the conscious content of which also objectively applies to God, the one who is totally different, even though we can neither know nor express *the way in which* this applies to God'. (2) Subsequently turning now to what Schillebeeckx writes on the supernatural knowledge of faith, we see that Schillebeeckx begins his discussion of supernatural knowledge by talking about '*concepts of faith*' (Dutch: *geloofsbegrippen*). This suggests that the divide between conceptual and non-conceptual knowledge is actually running across both natural and supernatural knowledge so that both types of knowledge

---

[9] Schillebeeckx, 'What Is Theology?', p. 109; Dutch original: 'Wat is theologie?', p. 79.

make use of concepts and in both types of knowledge there is a move beyond the conceptual. Indeed, in the supernatural knowledge of faith the mystery remains intact as such supernatural knowledge is also analogical. In the supernatural knowledge of faith, the 'noetic value' (Dutch: *noëtische kenwaarde*) of concepts also consists in 'a projective act of the mind in which we reach out for God, without actually grasping him conceptually, in the firm conviction that God really is in the direction towards which we are reaching', a conviction which is justified because these concepts are opened to the transcendent by revelation. This brings us to the difference between natural and supernatural knowledge of God. In our natural knowledge of God, we use concepts, the so-called *transcendentalia* or transcendentals, which possess 'a *natural* openness for the transcendent' while the concepts of faith (like 'Father' and 'Son') open onto the transcendent by God through 'positive revelation', which guarantees that the concepts of faith refer *objectively* to God.[10]

To conclude our discussion of Schillebeeckx's view on faith as presented in the 1958 dictionary article on theology, we will summarize his view with the help of a number of propositions: (1) faith is the appropriate response to God's initiative of grace; (2) it is through faith that the first contact between God and human being is established; (3) faith is intrinsically conditioned by the content of revelation; (4) the act of faith consists in consent to a mystery and therefore both firm consent (rest) and intellectual speculation (unrest) as simultaneously present in it; (5) the act of faith is only possible when the mystery to which assent is given is to some extent clear to the human mind; (6) faith has a cognitive aspect, it is a way of knowing, in it a *knowing* contact is made with the reality of revelation, though this does not mean that we have conceptual knowledge of God's specificity – our concepts are not able to grasp God, but they nevertheless refer to God *objectively*; ultimately, our knowledge of God is a conscious unknowing.

Moreover, it should have become clear by what has been said until now that religion and faith (as Schillebeeckx understands them) are dependent upon God and become impossible in the case that God would not exist. For, if God would not exist, humankind cannot enter into a personal relation with him and there is nobody to give us the virtue of faith in grace. So, if there is no God, the conditional possibility of human faith would be impossible and there is no such thing as faith. This may seem self-evident, but it is not. Faith without belief that God exists has been seriously defended. This has been done, for instance, by philosophers who plead for a non-realistic perception of religion. These voices express a commonly established *doxa*, namely that in religion it ultimately does not matter what one believes,

---

[10] Schillebeeckx, 'What Is Theology?', pp. 132–36; Dutch original: 'Wat is theologie?', pp. 92–94.

as long as one has faith. These antirealists state that the specific beliefs of religion can no longer be subscribed to. However, they don't think of this as a bad thing: religious statements are not cognitive in nature anyway. They do not concern a state of affairs in reality and, as a result, they simply don't have any truth value. Religious statements express, on the other hand, a certain attitude towards life. According to the antirealists, it is possible to continue this attitude without believing that God exists. This faith without belief that God exists is not limited to the study rooms of armchair philosophers. In 2007, a Dutch preacher echoed this sentiment in a published book with the title: *Geloven in een God die niet bestaat: Manifest van een atheïstische dominee* (Having faith in a God who does not exist: Manifesto of an atheistic minister).[11] Even sound theological arguments may tend in this direction. We will see that in particular the way some theologians attempt to resolve the conflict between science and religion runs the risk of ending up with defending faith in a non-existent God. An example of this tendency can be found in the work of Taede Smedes, a Dutch specialist in the field of science and religion, to whom we now turn.

2. Having Faith in a Non-Existent God: The Example of Taede Smedes

Smedes's solution of the conflict between science and religion is straightforward: in principle, there is simply no such conflict, whereas, given the fact that so many people think otherwise is the result of a mistaken understanding of what it means to believe. In general, the verb 'to believe' is understood as meaning to 'think, suppose, be of the well-founded conviction, agree with an authority, trust in something on the basis of probability'.[12] In line with this colloquial understanding, the verb 'to believe' is in a religious context also often considered to refer to the acceptance of convictions, like the one that God exists, which are unproven and/or cannot be proven. According to this common view, we believe something because we don't know for sure: if we would, it would no longer be necessary to believe it, we would simply know it. This view situates believing somewhere in the middle between unknowing and knowing: we believe when there is not enough evidence to be sure about something, for instance, about God's existence, but when there are nevertheless sufficient reasons that point in that direction. In this way, it becomes of course a matter of utmost importance to find a sufficient number of such good reasons to believe. Or, as Smedes

[11] Klaas Hendrikse, *Geloven in een God die niet bestaat: Manifest van een atheïstische dominee* (Amsterdam: Nieuw Amsterdam Uitgevers, 2007).
[12] Cf. Wolfgang Beinert, 'Faith', *Handbook of Catholic Theology* (ed. Wolfgang Beinert and Francis Schüssler Fiorenza; New York, NY: Crossroad, 1995), pp. 249–53 (249).

puts it, one has to find the traces of God's activity in the universe and in the history of humankind in order to be justified to believe that God exists. This search for the traces of God's activity in the universe and in history is, in Smedes's view, highly problematical because it entails that there are events in time and space that escape from the chain of cause and effect as natural science can find out. As a result, it becomes quite pointless to attempt a scientific explanation of a phenomenon. A scientific explanation entails that a phenomenon is described in terms of general laws of nature, but if at each moment God can intervene, it becomes impossible to do so: one can never be sure whether the laws of nature applied or whether God has intervened to temporally suspend these laws. Or, to put it differently: science is only possible precisely on the basis of the assumption that nature is a closed whole in which no supernatural interventions occur. There is no room in science for supernatural agents.[13]

Yet, trying to make room for supernatural causes within natural science is precisely what not only the adherents of the intelligent-design movement, but also a lot of scholars engaged in the so-called dialogue between science and religion are attempting to do (with the help of, for instance, chaos theory or quantum mechanics). In Smedes' view, these attempts not only result in bad science, but are also theologically unsound. Indeed, Smedes offers a number of strong theological arguments for his rejection of any attempt to make room for God in our scientific theories. He points to the fact that Christian theologians have always stressed God's transcendence: 'God is *more* than the world, goes *beyond it*, but God is also *radically different* than the world.' Indeed, there is an unbridgeable difference between the Creator and all that has been created. God and world are totally separated: 'All that is the world, is not God. The reality of God and our world are therefore actually radically incomparable: there is no common standard with the help of which God and world can be compared with each other.'[14] Thus, God is not a part of the universe which is studied by natural science, but is completely apart from it. Due to the impact of science on culture, however, believers have forgotten this fundamental distinction between God and world. As a result, God has become an entity *in* the world, next to other objects such as houses, cars, trees, cows and apple-pies (to repeat the examples used by Smedes).[15] This confusion calls into being the problem of the relation between science and religion: since God's existence and activity are placed at the same level of the existence and activity *within* created reality, the belief that God exists seems only justified if, in one way or another, God's traces can be scientifically recorded.

[13] Taede A. Smedes, *God en de menselijke maat: Gods handelen en het natuurweten-schappelijk wereldbeeld* (Zoetermeer: Meinema, 2006) pp. 211–12.
[14] Smedes, *God en de menselijke maat*, pp. 218–19.
[15] Smedes, *God en de menselijke maat*, p. 214.

But is it correct to understand the verb 'to believe' in its religious sense as referring to the acceptance of unproven/improvable convictions like the one that God exists? According to Smedes, this is not the case. But what does 'to believe' mean then, if not the acceptance of convictions which are unproven/ cannot be proven? To answer this question, Smedes falls back on a number of sources. His first source is the Flemish philosopher Walter Van Herck who writes in a book on religion and metaphor that 'The believer and the unbeliever see and hear the same. Yet, the believer sees and hears something more. Or maybe we should say: he sees and hears in a different way.'[16] This suggests that believing implies a 'seeing-as' or perspectival seeing, an idea that has been developed by the philosopher Ludwig Wittgenstein. To illustrate this 'seeing-as', Smedes offers a paraphrase of a parable originally put forward by the British philosopher John Wisdom. This parable, known as the 'Parable of the Invisible Gardener', tells the story of two men who return to their garden after a long period of absence. They find that, despite the amount of weeds, some of their old plants are still doing very well. From this the one concludes that a gardener must have taken care of the garden during their absence. The other does not agree: there are too many weeds for that being the case. They interrogate the neighbours, but none of them has seen a gardener. The first person is not convinced: maybe the gardener comes during night? So, they decide to begin an investigation. But after they have both considered all the clues, the first person still thinks that there is a gardener, while the other one still does not agree. Wisdom concludes his parable as follows:

> At this stage, in this context, the gardener hypothesis has ceased to be experimental, the difference between one who accepts and one who rejects it is now not a matter of the one expecting something the other does not expect, [but] a difference in how they feel towards the garden, in spite of the fact that neither expects anything of it which the other does not expect.[17]

From this, Smedes draws the conclusion that facts are not decisive in the final decision of both men. For, while they see the same garden, the one concludes from what he sees that there must be a gardener while the other draws the opposite conclusion that there cannot be one. This shows that religious belief is not the outcome of an argumentation on the basis of facts, but that it has to do with 'a particular attitude vis-à-vis reality, a way of relating to the world, which is determined by how this world is

---

[16] Walter Van Herck, *Religie en metafoor: Over het relativisme van het figuurlijke* (Tertium Datur; Leuven: Peeters, 1999) p. 110. Quoted in Smedes, *God en de menselijke maat*, p. 222.

[17] John Wisdom, 'Gods', *Proceedings of the Aristotelian Society: New Series*, 45 (1944–45), pp. 185–206 (192).

experienced [Dutch: *beleefd*]'.[18] The difference between the believer and the unbeliever is like the difference between two people who are watching the same painting: one can see a fantastic piece of art, while the other just sees paint on a canvas. It is the same with two people listening to a piece of music: if one is unmusical, he may only hear a succession of sounds, while the other, if he is musical, hears the melody. As a last example, Smedes refers to jokes: one person gets a joke immediately while the other simply does not see it.[19]

But if religious language is essentially metaphorical, figurative or symbolical, as Smedes is claiming, the question of course pops up of what then do we *really* mean when we use it. But for Smedes this is the wrong question: there is no way to look behind the metaphors we use to refer to God to see what they *really* mean. These metaphors are all we have. This also entails that the question of how we know all this is simply a mistaken one, as well, because it presupposes that there is some way in which we would be able to describe God objectively. All we can talk about is 'God *pro nobis* [i.e. 'for us']', while 'God *in se* [i.e. 'as such']' or '*sine nobis* [i.e. 'without us']' remains for ever beyond our grasp. Whether there is a correspondence between religious language and the reality of God and how we can assess that correspondence is simply not to the point.[20] It only seems a small step however from the statement that all religious language is metaphorical to the conclusion that God is *only* a metaphor. But if God is *only* a metaphor, the question then becomes what is then the difference between a believer and an atheist. To explain this further, I will fall back on the paraphrase of Wisdom's parable found in the famous paper on *Theology and Falsification* of Antony Flew, at that time still a leading atheist. This paraphrase concludes as follows:

> Yet still the Believer is not convinced. 'But there is a gardener, invisible, intangible, insensible to electric shocks, a gardener who has no scent and makes no sound, a gardener who comes secretly to look after the garden which he loves.' At last the Sceptic despairs, 'But what remains of your original assertion? Just how does what you call an invisible, intangible, eternally elusive gardener differ from an imaginary gardener or even from no gardener at all?'[21]

---

[18] Smedes, *God en de menselijke maat*, p. 224.

[19] Smedes, *God en de menselijke maat*, pp. 222–25.

[20] Smedes, *God en de menselijke maat*, pp. 73–76, 77–79.

[21] Antony Flew, R.M. Hare and Basil Mitchell, 'Theology and Falsification', *New Essays in Philosophical Theology* (ed. Antony Flew and Alasdair MacIntyre; 7th impression, London: SCM, 1969), pp. 96–130 (96). Reprinted as: Antony Flew, R.M. Hare and Basil Mitchell, 'Theology and Falsification: A Symposium', *The Philosophy of Religion* (ed. Basil Mitchell; Oxford Readings in Philosophy; Oxford: Oxford University Press, 1971), pp. 13–22 (13).

Indeed, how does an 'an invisible, intangible, eternally elusive gardener differ from an imaginary gardener or even from no gardener at all?' It is remarkable that this question is not answered, and not even mentioned, by Smedes. This is meaningful because the concluding question of the unbeliever is also the major question one can raise against Smedes: Is the only difference between a believer and an atheist that the former says that God is not traceable while the latter simply says that God does not exist? And is this a *real* difference or only a matter of semantics, of phrasing things slightly differently? In this regard it is worthwhile mentioning the Dutch philosopher Herman Philipse, who writes in his atheistic manifesto that somebody who is even interpreting God's existence symbolically can no longer be said to believe in God's existence.[22] Or, to refer once more to Flew who, in the aforementioned paper on *Theology and Falsification*, points to the fact that the statement 'God exists' can become 'so eroded by qualification that it [is] no longer an assertion at all', but has died the death of a thousand qualifications.[23] So, to put it with a bold statement: the way Smedes resolves the conflict between science and religion leaves him with a faith in a non-existent God, a faith which can no longer be distinguished from an atheistic position. This suggests that, if we want to avoid this collapse of faith into atheism, the issue of God's existence cannot be avoided. As we shall see in the next section, this is precisely what Schillebeeckx has defended in his inaugural address when he became a professor at the University of Nijmegen in 1958.

3. *Schillebeeckx on the Necessity of a* Praeambula Fidei

During his inaugural address, Schillebeeckx stated that the absence of God should be considered as something positive. For, only an *absent* God can truly be God, given the difference between God and experienced reality. The divine way of being *present* entails that we can experience God only as *absent*. This further entails that God is not an object *in* the world and can,[24] as a result, never become an object of exact-scientific inquiry because the exact sciences can only deal with objects *in* the world. This means that God is, by definition, 'a reality which evades the exact sciences'.[25] So, when Smedes defends God's absolute transcendence, Schillebeeckx would agree.

---

[22] Herman Philipse, *Atheïstisch manifest: Drie wijsgerige opstellen over godsdienst en moraal en De onredelijkheid van de relgie: Vier wijsgerige opstellen over godsdienst en wetenschap* (Amsterdam: Bert Bakker, 2004) p. 29.

[23] Flew, Hare, Mitchell, 'Theology and Falsification', p. 98/15.

[24] Schillebeeckx, 'The Search for the Living God', pp. 22–23; Dutch original: 'Op zoek naar de levende God', pp. 22–23.

[25] Schillebeeckx, 'The Search for the Living God', p. 19; Dutch original: 'Op zoek naar de levende God', p. 21.

Yet, he differs from Smedes in how radically this distinction between God and world should be understood. Smedes writes that 'all that is the world, is not God'. Thus, everything which can be experienced, be it in the universe or in history, is not God. Schillebeeckx tends to agree when he writes that God is 'totally different from all experienced reality' and concludes that 'whenever we try to grasp and take hold of God as an object we find ourselves still in this finite world and never in the presence of God'.[26]

Nevertheless, Schillebeeckx seems to shrink from the radicality of his own conclusion when, in his inaugural address, he also says the following:

> It still remains to be seen whether, when we have once fully circumscribed man's horizon within earthly limits, there can still be room for a religious attitude towards God. *Unless it can already be seen from this natural, human standpoint that man, although existing in a relationship with the world, is in his real core*, which is called freedom, *nevertheless not of this world and cannot therefore be described simply as an earthly being*, then the supranatural religious orientation of man towards a God revealing himself becomes a priori utterly untenable. In other words, unless there is one, all-embracing dimension of human existence (that can nevertheless not yet be called *grace*) in which the full transcendent being, or the divine reality, is visible at the very source of human experience, then the ground is cut from under the feet of religion in life. And if we nevertheless continue to regard religion as the profoundest truth of our human existence, then by the nature of things religion will find itself in stultifying competition with human life in and of this world. *Modern atheist thought recognizes this perhaps more clearly than some Christians do.*[27]

This brings Schillebeeckx to a plea for independent philosophical reflection by believers. More than ever before, we need reflection on the so-called *praeambula fidei*, the elucidation of 'the natural basis of faith'. Schillebeeckx also emphasizes the importance of the *praeambula fidei* in the dictionary article from which we have read in Section 1 above. There he writes that religion, being a personal communion between God and human beings, 'presupposes a natural basis', namely 'the existence of two persons, God and man, who meet each other, with all the natural implications of what is implied in the human state of being a person'. Our conclusion, put forward at the end of Section 1, that Schillebeeckx's understanding of religion and faith implies God's existence, is thus

---

[26] Schillebeeckx, 'The Search for the Living God', p. 23; Dutch original: 'Op zoek naar de levende God', p. 23.

[27] Schillebeeckx, 'The Search for the Living God', pp. 32–33 (italics changed); Dutch original: 'Op zoek naar de levende God', pp. 29–30.

confirmed by Schillebeeckx himself. In the dictionary article, Schillebeeckx continues by adding what he also says in his inaugural address, that revelation is only meaningful when there is a point which is not yet grace but at which we nevertheless come into contact with God. In both texts he also stresses the importance of the fact that the Church has always held on to the view that God's existence is a *natural* truth and can be known by unaided reason. Moreover, Schillebeeckx states that, in a critical age like his, and ours, the *praeambula fidei* has to be developed in a critical-scientific manner. It is not something which is to be passed over lightly. It is not enough to produce some proof for the existence of God in half a shake. This should be done with all possible seriousness because the natural cognizability of God's existence has 'a necessity which has its foundation in faith itself' (Dutch: *innerlijke geloofsnoodzakelijkheid*). For, without its natural basis, faith is hindered and becomes impossible, untenable. Therefore, clarifying 'the natural theistic dimension in our Christian faith', the fact that the question of God arises from our being-in-the-world, is a matter of safeguarding faith.[28]

It is important, however, to understand this necessity of the *praeambula fidei* correctly. As Schillebeeckx points out, this does not mean that faith is grounded or justified on the basis of natural knowledge. Faith is only guaranteed by itself. It is not the outcome of an investigation which results in the conclusion that God has really revealed himself, but has a super-natural origin. The basis of faith is God himself, who invites the human being to enter into a personal communion. Ultimately, faith is grounded in God's grace and not upon natural knowledge. This suggests that we should keep in mind that the origin of faith and its justification are two separate issues. If we do this, it becomes clear that what Schillebeeckx is probably asking for when he requires a point which is not yet grace at which we come into contact with God is a matter of *justifying a faith which is already there*, not of convincing unbelievers. Beginning to believe is not a matter of being convinced by good arguments, these can only support a faith once it has already come into being. Yet, without natural basis faith is nevertheless hindered, impossible and untenable. In so far as faith is the outcome of God's salvific initiative, it may be infallible and absolutely certain, but in so far as it is a human act, it is always in need of justification. This human need for justification explains why, in Schillebeeckx's view, the natural cognizability of God's existence has 'a necessity which has its foundation in faith itself' and why the critical-scientific elaboration of the *praeambula fidei* is a matter of the utmost importance, in particular in an age which is characterized by secularization and atheism.

[28] Schillebeeckx, 'What Is Theology?', pp. 170–73; Dutch original: 'Wat is theologie?', pp. 113–15. See also: Schillebeeckx, 'The Search for the Living God', pp. 35–37; Dutch original: 'Op zoek naar de levende God', pp. 31–33.

Let us, finally, raise the question of whether there is any 'enduring relevance of Edward Schillebeeckx for contemporary theology' (as the sub-title of the symposium during which this article was presented suggests). If there is, it is at least the following: that we should take the challenge of atheism seriously. For, it is atheism which reminds Christian believers and Christian theologians of the fact that religion, understood in terms of a personal communion with the living God, and faith, as that which gives us access to that salvific encounter with God, cannot survive without a natural basis. Elucidating this natural basis of faith is and remains therefore an important task for theology, also in the 21st century.

PART II
'EVERYTHING IS POLITICS BUT POLITICS IS NOT EVERYTHING': THE SOCIAL ROLE OF THEOLOGY

WHEN EVERYTHING BECOMES POLITICAL: READING SCHILLEBEECKX ON FAITH AND POLITICS IN THE CONTEMPORARY UNITED STATES

Vincent J. Miller

1. *Introduction*

Edward Schillebeeckx wrote extensively on the relationship between religion and politics. His theology displays the concerns of the age in which they were written: i.e., the proper relationship between religious belief and political participation in a secular, pluralistic political sphere and the challenges posed by liberation theologies to traditional soteriologies. Schillebeeckx offered a sacramental account of Christian involvement in politics seeking to avoid the extremes of sectarian withdrawal, theocracy, and a totalitarian situation where 'politics becomes everything'.[1]

This essay attempts to use Schillebeeckx's perspective to engage the quite different context of the contemporary United States. Here, politics threatens to become everything in quite a different way. There is little threat of a totalitarian state absorbing civil society and religion. Sectarian withdrawal is not likely, as the protestant traditions most inclined toward such a stance have been deeply engaged in the political process for decades. Rather,

---

[1] Edward Schillebeeckx, *On Christian Faith: The Spiritual, Ethical, and Political Dimensions* (trans. John Bowden; New York, NY: Crossroad, 1987) p. 81.

we face a situation that Schillebeeckx did not foresee. The distinction between religion and politics has not been obscured by state action, but by the political activity of Christians and their churches. 'Everything has become political' because churches have entered into the political field and begun to function according to its rules. Rifts occur not along denominational lines, but between members of denominations along the fault lines of the American culture wars. These divides are not merely ideological. They are formed and sustained by particular social and communication infrastructures, interest groups, and certain sorts of opinion leaders. These create a new 'cultural ecology' in which contrasting identities and political polarization become the norm.

This context poses a particular challenge to Schillebeeckx's account of the relationship between religion and politics. It becomes more difficult to imagine a place of formation in the logics and telos of the Christian tradition that can serve as an inspiration for participation in secular projects of liberation in the political sphere. Both sides of this equation have become fractured. Religious traditions are shattered into myriad microtraditions. On the political side, state action ceases to be a unified field on which secular projects of liberation are carried out. Rather it is a place of deep conflict, where culture wars fundamentally divide the polity and destroy the possibility of practically oriented debate regarding shared goals of human emancipation. Thus we face a situation in which both religious formation and political agency are deeply fractured.

This essay begins by considering a critique of the conceptual framework of Schillebeeckx's political theology. It will then turn to Schillebeeckx's writings to answer that critique and uncover a different, more contextual set of assumptions within his theology that have become problematic. It will then turn to the contemporary political and religious context of the United States to sketch a new form of collective religious identity and action and consider its implications for formulating a contemporary theological engagement with public life.

2. Conceiving Schillebeeckx

Frederick Bauerschmidt's critique of Schillebeeckx's political theology provides a helpful starting point for our investigation. Bauerschmidt argues that Schillebeeckx's categories of 'mystical' and 'political' conform too closely to the modern privatization of faith and the reduction of politics to statecraft.[2] No matter how much Schillebeeckx 'seeks to overcome a sharp distinction between the two by relating them dialectically', 'they still

---

[2] Frederick C. Bauerschmidt, 'The Politics of Disenchantment', *New Blackfriars* 82 (2001), pp. 313–34 (313).

remain basic poles in his interpretation and thus continue to reproduce the very antinomies between sacred religion and disenchanted politics that he wishes to overcome'.[3] By constructing mysticism in distinction to politics, Schillebeeckx must strip Christianity of its distinctive politics: 'Despite his own warnings about a formalized eschatological proviso, Schillebeeckx consistently speaks of love of God as providing only an "orientation" or "direction" or "inspiration" to political activity.' For Bauerschmidt, Schillebeeckx's theology 'is predicated on the interiorization and depoliticization of Christianity; as with Weber, religion must become "mysticism" so that politics might become autonomous and rational'. Religion, in the form of the 'experience of God', can 'ensoul' politics, but it cannot 'embody' it.[4]

The other side of the dichotomy is equally problematic for Bauerschmidt. He finds in Schillebeeckx's laudable concern that theology not be reduced to politics an assumption that politics 'take the form of coercive use of power by nation states'.[5] Schillebeeckx's dichotomy between the mystical and political assumes the political is an autonomous and neutral construction. The Church is forced to conform to the form of politics allowed in the modern state, which Bauerschmidt describes as a Hobbesian monopoly on power and a Weberian administrative bureaucratic rationality. Lost as a result, the Church's ability to model a distinct politics that can challenge the modern political order.

Bauerschmidt's critique poses well the threat of the political domestication of religion into mystical interiority. It does not, however, sufficiently engage Schillebeeckx's theologies of revelation and salvation, and for that reason, it overstates the privatization of mysticism and the captivity of the Church in statecraft. Despite the difficulty of escaping this dichotomy (which Schillebeeckx describes as a 'gulf') between public and private, Schillebeeckx insists on a fundamental connection between faith and politics.[6]

Schillebeeckx does not posit the political as simply a matter enacting prior belief (private or not). Rather, for him, the liberative struggles of human history are the 'medium and material' of revelation itself. God continues to act in history and has not ceased to be the 'biblical God'.[7] Revelation has a 'sacramental structure' built upon this divine action within 'secular' history. Historically 'meaningful' events of liberation and

[3] Bauerschmidt, 'Politics of Disenchantment', p. 325.
[4] Bauerschmidt, 'Politics of Disenchantment', p. 327.
[5] Bauerschmidt, 'Politics of Disenchantment', p. 328.
[6] Derek J. Simon, 'Salvation and Liberation in the Practical-Critical Soteriology of Schillebeeckx', *Theological Studies* 63 (2002), pp. 494–520. 'Gulf' from Edward Schillebeeckx, *Christ: The Experience of Jesus as Lord* (trans. John Bowden; New York, NY: Crossroad, 1981) p. 906.
[7] Edward Schillebeeckx, *Church: The Human Story of God* (trans. John Bowden; New York, NY: Crossroad, 1990) p. 37.

the reaction against suffering in contrast experiences form its material. This shared history; a 'general salvation history' becomes revelation proper in 'interpretative experience ... in relation to what God is actively bringing about in this world'.[8] Religious communities are the 'sacraments' of this salvation, the 'places where salvation from God is thematized or put into words, confessed explicitly, proclaimed prophetically and celebrated liturgically'.[9] Religious belief is 'a gracious answer to that which precedes all talk of believers: God's creative action within history in and through men and women for human salvation'.[10]

Likewise, Schillebeeckx's understanding of mysticism is not one of private interiority detached from the world. He draws from Dominican spirituality, which sees mysticism as an intensification of the ordinary. Mystical experiences transcend 'the political and personal ethical commitments of Christians', by implicating the whole, rather than excluding the everyday.[11] Martha, not Mary is the true fulfillment of the *via eminentiae*. Her 'concern for God makes her solicitous for human beings'.[12] The mystical is not interiority or privacy. It is an intensification of all dimensions of life in relationship to God. For that reason, it pushes against human categories and concepts, including the reduction of politics to statecraft and bureaucratic rationality.

If he is not wedded to a Weberian privatization of faith, why does Schillebeeckx emphasize that the relationship of religion and politics is one of inspiration and motivation? This arises from his theology of creation and transcendence. God is the creator and sustainer of finite human freedom. 'Creation faith sets us free for our own task in the world.' The Christian God is not a *conservator* of a preordained order. Creation faith prevents humans from passing 'over to God what is our task in this world'. 'Overcoming suffering and evil, wherever we may encounter them ... is our task and our burden ... not a matter for God, except that this task is performed in his absolute presence.'[13] God's salvific actions in human history are always veiled as much as revealed.[14]

This notion of finite freedom is Schillebeeckx's point of articulation between theology, pluralism and liberalism. 'Christian revelation gives no precise instructions for the economic, social and political ordering of human society.' Yet the message of the Gospel is relevant to these questions.

---

[8] Schillebeeckx, *Church*, p. 12.

[9] Schillebeeckx, *On Christian Faith*, p. 32; Schillebeeckx, *Church*, pp. 12–13.

[10] Schillebeeckx, *Church*, p. 14; Schillebeeckx, *On Christian Faith*, p. 34.

[11] Schillebeeckx, *Church*, pp. 69–70.

[12] Schillebeeckx, *Church*, p. 77.

[13] Cf. the text 'I Believe in God, Creator of Heaven and Earth', included in: Edward Schillebeeckx, *God Among Us: The Gospel Proclaimed* (trans. John Bowden; New York, NY: Crossroad, 1983) pp. 94–96.

[14] Schillebeeckx, *On Christian Faith*, p. 33.

Caritas impels toward a just social order, demands the abolition of 'social and political alienations'. '[H]uman solidarity and social responsibility' must be fostered 'all over the world'. Politics in the strictest sense of directly overseeing and enacting a social and political order is outside the authority of the Church. It is however, a matter for Christians to engage in along with other citizens. It is in this sense the Gospel provides 'motives' and 'inspiration' for their political decisions. The Church does have a proper role in politics in the more general sense of the broad historical project of forming human society into a '*polis* ... in which it is good for everyone to live'. On this level, the Church's interventions are not direct involvements in power struggles, but 'in the way of spiritual power, critical and ethical'.[15] Although this engagement is not 'separate from its proclamation of faith' the Church must contribute to 'social discussion' not with dogmatic confession, but by arguing on a 'rational basis' in a manner 'accessible to non-believers'.[16]

Nevertheless, Schillebeeckx explicitly rejects Kuitert's confidence in the autonomy of political reason and his council of Church neutrality save in times of political emergency. Even within a state system that is deeply democratic, Schillebeeckx hesitates. His questions are based not on ideological suspicions of the violent roots of modern liberalism and the nation state. Rather, they are undertaken in the name of a more thorough going democracy whose boundaries include not just citizens of first world nations, but the entire world, where economic and military policies distort the distributions of resources and shatter human flourishing. Here, political reason and even the most scrupulously exercised state democracy functions ideologically by ignoring the broader human 'ecumene of human suffering'. This poses a fundamental challenge to the 'liberal pluralism of modern theologies'.[17]

Schillebeeckx's political theology is also deeply influenced by his soteriology. Humans are not capable of complete salvation under their own power. While divine salvation takes place within the world, it is never reducible to any political party or program.[18] Human projects are forever hindered by chance, contingency in a history marred by sin, and by their

[15] Schillebeeckx, *On Christian Faith*, p. 78.

[16] Schillebeeckx, *On Christian Faith*, pp. 81–82.

[17] Schillebeeckx, *On Christian Faith*, pp. 81–84.

[18] Cf. Erik Borgman, 'Theology as the Art of Liberation: Edward Schillebeeckx's Response to the Third World Theologians', *Exchange* 32/2 (2003), pp. 98–108 (103):

> At the same time, however, he was certain that no political program or political order could ever embody the Christian values completely. In his discussion with Jacques Maritain's idea of a New Christendom, he developed the strong conviction that every human humanism would necessarily be incomplete and stay an unfinished symphony.

own ignorance and sinfulness.[19] The question of divine salvation arises from the 'impossibility of a total, universal and final liberation through emancipation'.[20] This limit points to salvation not because of an eschatological proviso, but in terms of an 'eschatological superabundance' that points to inner 'positive' connection between the Kingdom of God and human emancipatory struggles.[21]

Schillebeeckx's resistance to a directly political role for Christian faith is also driven by his understanding of the Paschal Mystery:[22]

> As the intrinsic consequence of the radicalism of its message and reconciling practice, the crucifixion of Jesus shows that any attempt at liberating redemption which is concerned with humanity is valid *in and of itself* and not subsequently as a result of any success which may follow.[23]

Christian salvation transcends politics as it aims forever beyond what is humanly achievable. In so doing, it also fundamentally challenges any model of politics as violent domination or bureaucratic control.

Schillebeeckx's Christological project is a fundamental challenge to Bauerschmidt's critique that his politics lacks a distinctively Christian form. Christianity does not lack a model of action, it is found in the life praxis of Jesus of Nazareth. Schillebeeckx's turn to the historical/theological study that became the Christological trilogy after his engagement with Critical theory led him to a concern that pure critical negativity could provide no guidance for politics.[24] The New Testament contains the early Church's response to Jesus in their life praxis. In this we can gain an image of Jesus' own praxis.[25] The 'profound connection between the life praxis, death, and Resurrection of Jesus remains pivotal in Schillebeeckx's understanding of the productive difference between sociopolitical liberation and definitive eschatological salvation.'[26]

---

[19] Schillebeeckx, *God Among Us*, p. 101.

[20] Schillebeeckx, *Christ*, p. 768.

[21] Edward Schillebeeckx, 'Terugblik vanuit de tijd na Vaticanum II: De gebroken ideologieën van de moderniteit', *Tussen openheid en isolement: Het voorbeeld van de katholieke theologie in de negentiende eeuw* (ed. Erik Borgman and Anton van Harskamp; Kampen: Kok, 1992), pp. 153–72 (170–71). Cited in Simon, 'Salvation and Liberation in the Practical-Critical Soteriology of Schillebeeckx', p. 517.

[22] Simon, 'Salvation and Liberation in the Practical-Critical Soteriology of Schillebeeckx', p. 503.

[23] Schillebeeckx, *Christ*, p. 837.

[24] William Portier, 'Interpretation and Method', *The Praxis of Christian Experience: An Introduction to the Theology of Edward Schillebeeckx* (ed. Robert J. Schreiter and Mary Catherine Hilkert; New York, NY: Harper and Row, 1989), pp. 18–34 (31).

[25] Schillebeeckx, *On Christian Faith*, p. 35.

[26] Simon, 'Salvation and Liberation in the Practical-Critical Soteriology of Schillebeeckx', p. 519.

When considered in its whole, Schillebeeckx's conception of the relationship of Christian faith and politics does not seem adequately described by Bauerschmidt's critique. Christian faith is not private. It begins and remains in history in a manner that does not accept the modern distinction of spheres any more than it accepted sacral boundaries in ages past. Mysticism is not understood as an experience of private interiority, but as a disruptive deepening of the human encounter with the divine in the midst of any human activity, including politics. Far from accepting the rules and confines of statecraft, Schillebeeckx situates all politics within the context of human finitude against the encompassing horizon of God's presence and history's destiny in the Kingdom of God.

3. A Different Dichotomy arising from Schillebeeckx's Context

Nevertheless, Bauerschmidt's critique still haunts Schillebeeckx's theology. The default account within Schillebeeckx's political theology seems to be the one Bauerschmidt describes: a religious community conceived voluntaristically within a secular, pluralistic context where political action is carried out not primarily by the community itself but in a shared secular space of state and civil society. Schillebeeckx clearly rejects the Weberian dichotomy on ideological grounds. Perhaps it is present in a weaker form as a pair of sociological assumptions about the nature of church and society.

Schillebeeckx's theology of revelation presumes the ongoing existence of a community of memory with socialization substantial enough to ground an ongoing interpretation of God's saving activity in history. Likewise, Schillebeeckx's implicit description of the space of shared struggle for emancipative politics bears a close resemblance to the modern nation state. Here members of the Church come, guided by the interpretive frameworks of the Christian tradition to work side by side with other citizens in a pluralistic context. The context is framed by their overarching understanding and experience of God acting in history through and beyond politics. Their engagement in political action and their political communication use consensus means and language. Both of these assume a unity and stability that may no longer be present.

These assumptions are likely as much a matter of Schillebeeckx's historical context as any intellectual commitments. These assumptions are particularly resonant within the Low Countries socio-religious structure of *verzuiling* or 'columnization'. In this system multiple social groups (the Reformed churches, the Roman Catholic Church and the Socialist party) maintained their distinct identities in the midst of a pluralistic culture with the help of separate educational, social and media institutions. Each group participated in the public realm through its own separate column.

The maintenance of such a massive institutional establishment required an enormous number of lay professionals who became accustomed to reflecting on their work from an explicitly confessional perspective. Furthermore, columnization entailed a massive communications network. There were scores of confessional organizations all of which required clerical spiritual advisors. At one point, up to one quarter of the Dutch clergy was involved full time in such work.[27] This system of communications also involved the extensive system of media that provided both the construction of a shared imagined community (e.g., coverage of church events, community news, etc.) and a distinctive Catholic perspective on broader professional issues, issues of the day, and on politics.

While Schillebeeckx grew up in Belgium, a similar structure had been in place there. More importantly, this was the prehistory of the Dutch Church in which he laboured during his professional career. It was particularly relevant as he wrote in the 1960s, while assisting the Dutch Church through its major transformations and engaging in theological debates on secularization and political theology. It was this post-columnized context to which his theological reflections on the church and politics were addressed. And thus, these historically contingent facts form the basis of his assumptions. In the 1960s and 1970s Dutch Catholicism could still presume a strong identity and robust formation in the faith as a legacy of columnization. Likewise, he could sketch the realm of politics and civil society as relatively coherent and shared, even as the various liberation movements emerged in the 1960s and 1970s. For all their radical challenges and often-radical tactics, these still addressed a shared civil society.

This softer dichotomy is less ideological, but it may be every bit as problematic as the concerns raised by Bauerschmidt. If Schillebeeckx's theology implicitly assumes such a context, what happens, when, as in the current North American situation, it no longer holds? Religious communities have ceased to exercise sufficient religious formation of their members to guide such a sacramental engagement. The social/political field has also become fundamentally transformed by the rise of various new communication technologies, infrastructures, and organizational technologies. These fragment the public sphere both as a place of discourse and a realm of shared action.

---

[27] John A. Coleman, *The Evolution of Dutch Catholicism, 1958 – 1974* (Berkeley, CA: University of California Press, 1978) pp. 86–97.

4. *The Contemporary U.S. Context*

The contemporary ecclesial context in the United States is markedly different from the one implicit in Schillebeeckx's theology in both fronts. Religious communities currently lack the ability to socialize their members into a deep understanding of their religious traditions and the social political field is deeply divided and fragmented. We will consider both dimensions of the contemporary U.S. context. First, we will explore the decline of religious formation in terms of secularization, detraditionalization, and religious deregulation. Second, we will consider changes in the social and political field such as the deepening of choice and its impact upon the constitution of religious and political communities, and the rise of the new cultural intermediaries and special agenda organizations.

a. *Secularization, Detraditionalization, and Religious Deregulation*

The United States enjoyed a period of stable, strong religious identities similar to columnization in the post-war period.[28] In Europe, however, traditional religious institutions and authorities have since experienced a profound decline in influence. It is now commonplace to note that the secularization thesis that had once so dominated sociology (and theology) in the 1960s has simply not come to pass outside of Western Europe.[29] The decline once described in terms of an all-encompassing secularization appears, rather, to have been a more specific decline in the social and cultural power of religious institutions and leaders. The symbols, practices, and myths that they once stewarded continue to inform people's lives, but authorities and institutions exercise less control over how these are used. Drawing metaphors from economics, some speak of the 'deregulation' of religion or the decline of religious 'monopolies'.[30]

Religious deregulation brings with it detraditionalization: the loss of collective authority over religious belief and practice. The modern individual is empowered to pick and choose among elements of tradition,

---

[28] Robert Wuthnow, *After Heaven: Spirituality in America since the 1950s* (Berkeley, CA: University of California Press, 2006).

[29] Peter L. Berger, *The Desecularization of the World: Resurgent Religion and World Politics* (Grand Rapids, MI: Eerdmans, 1999) pp. 2 and 10. For a more detailed account of various forms of secularization and various configurations of religion and public life in Europe see: Grace Davie, *Religion in Modern Europe: A Memory Mutates* (Oxford: Oxford University Press, 2000). See also Lieven Boeve, *God Interrupts History: Theology in a Time of Upheaval* (New York, NY: Continuum, 2007) pp. 13–21.

[30] David Lyon, *Jesus in Disneyland: Religion in Postmodern Times* (Cambridge: Polity Press, 2000) p. 34; *The Steeple's Shadow: On the Myths and Realities of Secularization* (Grand Rapids, MI: Eerdmanns, 1987).

and to employ them in constructing their own religious synthesis.[31] Detraditionalization is, in this account, the other side of the coin of individualization.[32] But it is not simply a matter of the discrete freedom for individuals to lift cultural resources from the various traditions at their disposal. This new relationship to tradition has cumulative consequences for culture and religion. One generation's freedom from the strictures of previous tradition becomes the foundation upon which the next begins. This happens in a host of ways: the decline of primary religious socialization within the family, the disappearance of religious practices in everyday life, and the decline of religious authorities' status. In Danielle Hervieu-Léger's words, we are experiencing 'the collapse of the framework of collective memory which provided every individual with the possibility of a link between what comes before and his or her own actual experience'.[33] Schillebeeckx spoke of precisely this predicament in a homily to the critical community IJmond:

> [The] situation has ... fundamentally changed, in the sense that the younger ones among you ... do not even know the content of these traditions which their parents opposed ... [T]hey not only do not know what was oppressive in many traditions, but perhaps also they do not know the precise content of this great tradition, the basic story of Israel and Jesus.[34]

These changes challenge Schillebeecxk's vision of the Church as a community rooted in a shared tradition that can sustain a shared interpretation of history and act within it. Hervieu-Léger discusses how the shattering of the 'chain of memory' in modern societies leads to the collapse of this shared interpretation. 'The complexity of the world shown in the vast incoherent mass of available information is decreasingly amenable to being ordered in the more less impromptu way that collective memory was able to achieve by finding explanatory links.' The individualized religious context sustains no shared 'interpretative process'. Our individualized memories are 'anomic ... made up of isolated recollection and scraps of information which are increasingly incoherent'.[35]

---

[31] Paul Heelas, 'Introduction: Detraditionalization and Its Rivals', *Detraditionalization: Critical Reflections On Authority And Identity* (ed. Paul Heelas, Scott Lash and Paul Morris; Malden, MA/Oxford: Blackwell, 1995), pp. 1–30 (3–7).

[32] Boeve, *God Interrupts History*, p. 22.

[33] Danielle Hervieu-Léger, *Religion as a Chain of Memory* (trans. Simon Lee; New Brunswick, NJ: Rutgers University Press, 2000) pp. 130–31.

[34] Cf. the text 'I Still Have Much to Say to You', included in: Edward Schillebeeckx, *For the Sake of the Gospel* (trans. John Bowden; New York, NY: Crossroad, 1990) pp. 170–71.

[35] Hervieu-Léger, *Religion as a Chain of Memory*, pp. 128–29.

b. *Deregulation and the New Cultural Intermediaries*

Hervieu-Léger views the breaking of the chain of memory from the perspective of European secularization. This outcome of detraditionalization is not apparent in the U.S. context. On the contrary, it has become increasingly present in public life. In order to understand the specific threat these dynamisms pose in the U.S. we will need to consider new forms of religious authority and collective identity at work in that context. Traditional religious authority is being reworked to conform to the default forms of authority in contemporary culture: the new cultural intermediary and the special agenda organization.

Pierre Bourdieu identified new cultural intermediaries as serving the needs of a new bourgeois class employed in new professions such as cultural production, therapeutic and professional services that do not fit into traditional class hierarchies.[36] They provide guidance for life choices in the post-traditional culture where the heads of each nuclear family are expected to make their own choices concerning sexuality, child rearing, etc. The assimilation of religious leaders to this cultural location influences their reception, as they exchange traditional communication infrastructures for the mass exposure granted by the secular media. In the process they lose the complex articulations of authority and doctrine into local communities. Believers encounter their religious authorities not in ecclesial contexts, but in popular culture. As a result they apply the habits of interpretation and use from popular culture to religious authorities, commodifying religion in the process.[37]

The new cultural intermediaries are often associated with therapeutic spirituality and narcissism. Although the association is apt, a historical perspective gives greater insight into the nature of the challenge this social position poses. Religious new cultural intermediaries are helpfully understood as transitional figures. The therapeutic transformation of religion corresponds in the U.S. with the post-war increase in prosperity, education, and suburbanization. Pre-war urban modes of religious belonging were highly ascriptional. Church membership was a matter of ethnicity and geographic community. In the suburbs, association became elective, voluntary, and more reflexive. Ecclesial cultural intermediaries (e.g., Bishop Fulton J. Sheen, Thomas Merton) served the transitional needs of these populations. Mark Massa critiques Merton from this perspective. Merton's transcendental and interior spirituality 'offered a model of post-immigrant,

---

[36] Pierre Bourdieu, *Distinction: A Social Critique of the Judgement of Taste* (trans. Richard Nice; Cambridge, MA: Harvard University Press, 1984) pp. 359–69; Mike Featherstone, *Consumer Culture and Postmodernism* (London: Sage, 1991) pp. 43–44.

[37] Vincent J. Miller, *Consuming Religion* (New York, NY: Continuum, 2004) pp. 94–106.

post-working-class spirituality to newly arrived middle class Catholics looking for role models in the strange suburbs'.[38]

As transitional figures however, they don't fully describe the contexts to which they bridge. They presume the stabilities in process of being left behind. Individual freedom and agency were emphasized in the break from more collective forms of religion. After a few generations, however, the cultural inertia of the previous moment fades and new principles of organization appear. Thus the new cultural intermediaries fit well into the story of religious deregulation and detraditionalization.

c. New Cultural Intermediaries and Special Agenda Organizations

The new cultural intermediary analysis suggests that religion will become increasingly influenced by lifestyle and experience gurus catering to an individualistic religious market. While that is certainly the case, such an analysis, does not account for the massive presence of collective religious identities in the United States and the new forms of religious leaders associated with them. These new collective identities are sustained by 'special purpose' or 'special agenda' organizations.

Robert Wuthnow has analyzed 'special purpose groups' that exist independently of traditional denominations. They are comprised of members with specific identities or concerned with particular issues.[39] Special purpose groups are more adaptable than churches, which are wedded to fixed liturgical rituals and structures. Sects are similarly focused, but require more all-encompassing commitment. Special purpose groups allow for high levels of commitment to a focused cause, while not disturbing other commitments and associations. These groups do not compete with denominations. They work around and within them. Churches continue to gather people in traditional worship settings, but the engaged practice of faith within these communities takes place within focused special purpose groups focused on spirituality, justice or even shared hobbies.[40]

Wuthnow argued that such groups contribute much to the vitality of American denominations. He worried, however, that their homogeneity 'heightened potential for religious communities to become fractured along the lines of larger cleavages in society'.[41] They sort out allegiances within denominations and congregations and thus lessen the ability of religious communities to sustain the complex unities their traditions demand. New

---

[38] Mark Massa, *Catholics and American Culture: Fulton Sheen, Dorothy Day and the Notre Dame Football Team* (New York, NY: Crossroad, 1999) p. 56.

[39] Robert Wuthnow, *The Restructuring of American Religion* (Princeton, NJ: Princeton University Press, 1990) pp. 101–05.

[40] Wuthnow, *Restructuring of American Religion*, p. 130.

[41] Wuthnow, *Restructuring of American Religion*, p. 130.

forms of prayer (e.g., charismatic, eastern meditative practices) split off from the shared liturgical tradition, while social action groups fraction into justice and peace and pro-life concerns. James Davison Hunter studied this divisiveness in his study of American '*Culture Wars*'. Such 'special agenda organizations' include, 'a wide variety of religiously based public affairs organizations, political lobbies, and associations' which are 'concerned with promoting particular social or political agenda in the public domain'.[42] This work to attract and organize a committed membership resembles Arjun Appadurai's description of how globalization creates an ecology which favors elements of culture that have the most power to mark difference.[43] Leaders of such groups are drawn to elements of religious traditions and practices that elicit strong emotions or set a community apart from others. Attachment to tradition may remain strong, but it is not practiced in a comprehensive manner. Such selective appropriations of tradition are abetted by commodification, deregulation, and detraditionalization. Believer's lack sufficient knowledge and respected authorities to resist such manipulative representations.

These organizations reach over traditional religious communications infrastructures such as seminaries, universities, and denominational print media. They can assemble broad transdenominational religious, cultural, and political movements. Not only can such organizations reach into existing religious communities to address their members, they possesses the cultural power to challenge their traditional authorities and to reframe their theological discourses. Special agenda organizations, with their sophisticated communications capabilities and their deftness operating in the current politicized cultural ecology have more power than traditional Church authorities to define the major concerns of religious traditions and their most pressing engagements with public life. Such groups have been central to the rise of the religious right in the United States, which has in the past four decades remade the face of American religion in the public sphere, in the popular imagination, and within denominations.

d. *The U.S. Episcopate and the Special Purpose Organization: The 2008 Presidential Election*

The consequences of this new, politicized cultural ecology were particularly evident during the 2008 U.S. elections. The United States Conference of Catholic Bishops issued its quadrennial statement on faith and public life, *Forming Consciences for Faithful Citizenship*. This document addressed

---

[42] James Davison Hunter, *Culture Wars: The Struggle to Define America* (New York, NY: Basic Books, 1991) p. 90.

[43] Arjun Appadurai, *Modernity at Large: Cultural Dimensions of Globalization* (Minneapolis, MN: University of Minnesota Press, 1996) pp. 33–41.

the entire range of Catholic concern in an American context where both of the major parties hold positions at odds with Catholic social teaching. The document was distributed through a wide range of media. Abridged versions were widely distributed as bulletin inserts. It also had its own dedicated website (FaithfulCitizenship.org), which offered webcasts by issue experts, and even an online novena.

Despite these impressive communications innovations, the meaning of the document was decided within broader media and political space where special agenda groups struggled to support or marginalize the document in the context of a partisan political campaign.

The range of bishops' roles in the process is telling. Many promoted *Faithful Citizenship* and its breadth of Catholic political concern in their diocesan papers. Such actions had little impact. The bishops who were most effective in the debate, were those that augmented their episcopal role and resources with the new cultural intermediaries: focusing on single issues and working through secular media and the networks of special agenda organizations. Archbishop Charles Chaput of Denver stands out as the most effective in this regard. He published a book on political responsibility that offered a prudential argument that Catholics could not in good conscience vote for a candidate that supports abortion rights. The book appeared around the time of the political conventions in late summer. Media picked up his argument within the widespread frame that equated Catholic participation in public life with the issue of abortion.[44] A LexisNexis search returns 94 hits for *Faithful Citizenship* from June through the election, Archbishop Chaput received 97, 3 times that of Cardinal Francis George, the president of the USCCB at the time.

The contrast between the USCCB strategy regarding *Faithful Citizenship* and the bishops who pursued the strategies of special agenda organizations is illuminative. It shows that the new communicative structures overwrite the old. The USCCB's expansion into new media space did not rewrite its rules. The broad range of issues and the diverse concerns of the Catholic Church cannot be easily communicated in this ecology.

5. *Conclusion*

We can summarize three interrelated challenges posed by this cultural ecology. First, through detraditionalization and the transformation of religious authority into the role of new cultural intermediaries, religious communities experience a profound decline in the formation of believers in their living traditions. Second, religious community and authority is

---

[44] Charles J. Chaput, O.F.M. CAP, *Render Unto Caesar: Catholic Witness and American Public Life* (New York, NY: Doubleday, 2008).

subsequently reformed in the model of special agenda organization. In the process, religious communities cease to gather heterogeneous communities that bridge cultural and political divides. Rather, they are increasingly riven along those fractures themselves. This media and cultural ecology preferences of contrastive identities and rewards focus on a narrow range of issues. Unformed believers are susceptible to the partisan manipulation of religions for political ends. Finally, the political sphere itself becomes increasingly fragmented as the complex overlaps of heterogeneous communities are replaced with smaller scale, contrastive collective identities.

Each of these poses a profound challenge to Schillebeeckx's political theology. Detraditionalization deprives the Church of the strong formation that is needed in order for Christians to bring the interpretive lens and positive insights of the Gospel to their participation in shared public life. The rise of contrastive, politicized identities severely circumscribes the scope of the Church's engagement in public life in a manner different from that which Bauerschmidt fears. Politics is not reduced to statecraft but to narrow partisanship, mutual recrimination, and the truncating of elements of the tradition that do not clearly distinguish one group from another. In this sense politics does threaten to become 'everything' in a manner different from the context in which Schillebeeckx developed his theology. Finally, the fragmentation of the political sphere makes shared political projects more difficult to imagine. For all its manifest problems, the technocratic liberalism of the 1960s provided a shared political project in which diverse groups could participate. In our more fractious moment, debate has degenerated into vituperation.

Schillebeeckx's, political theology remains insightful and relevant. But these changes require new supplemental tasks to fulfill his project. First, in order to avoid defaulting to the special agenda model requires that we take seriously the task of forming the faithful in the complexity of the tradition in a post-traditional milieu. Theology must adjust its communicative practices to suit this new field, which provides little opportunity for the expression and reception of complex arguments and comprehensive orthodoxy. This does not mean however, that complexity must be abandoned. What is needed is not a reduction of theological discourse to partisan sound bites, but targeted engagement to push common discourse toward a more theologically adequate and doctrinally more complex state. This may very well require that ecclesial discourse be deployed tactically in sound bite scale units, but in service to a comprehensive theological vision. Such interventions take place in a discursive terrain marked by the cultural rifts, simplistic assumptions, political interests, and discursive frames of the contemporary mediascapes. A more comprehensive theological discourse will, of necessity, be communicated piecemeal and indirectly; oftentimes in response to inadequate or distorting questions and narrative frames. Second, this new context calls for a renewed focus on the task of Catholic unity, both for the Church and as a witness to a broader fractious society. The stable differences of the twentieth century are long gone. In a fractious ecology, holding traditions and communities together becomes a task that must now be accomplished intentionally.[45]

Schillebeeckx's political theology remains germane in the changing context of Western societies. His fundamental insight into the sacramental role of the Church in witnessing to God's salvific presence in human history remains sound, if more difficult to achieve in our more fractious contemporary context.

---

[45] See Vincent J. Miller, 'Where Is The Church? Globalization And Catholicity', *Theological Studies* 69 (2008), pp. 412–32.

NEW ORIENTATIONS OF THE POLITICAL: ON THE CONTEMPORARY CHALLENGE OF POLITICAL THEOLOGY

Jürgen Manemann

1. *Theology in the 21ˢᵗ Century*

a. *The Importance of Experience*

Raising the question of theology in the 21ˢᵗ century we have to ask ourselves as theologians in a new way, how events in the world effect the ways in which we think about God. This question contains a presupposition, which I would like to emphasize. It is guided by the insight that we do not so much need theories – which often collaborate in the process of alienation. What seems to be necessary are, to the contrary, not so-called facts, but experiences. Thus it makes very much sense in this context to refer to Edward Schillebeeckx, who connected theology in a radical way with experiences or more precisely with counter-experiences. If it is true that we need more experiences than theories, one has to recognize that this insight has to be understood in a dialectical way. That means: this statement is not made against theory. Rather, we need experience as the source of theory.

b. *Nihilism in the 21ˢᵗ Century*

Speaking from a Western European perspective about late modern societies, we are confronted with what I call nihilistic tendencies. Let me briefly explain what I mean by this. If human beings invent cultural forms of life in order to persuade each other that one's own life and the life of the other is worth living, then today we recognize that something has gone wrong with our cultural foundations. In particular, new forms of violence indicate that our symbolic order has been shattered. Therefore, along the lines of Friedrich Nietzsche, I differentiate between three forms of nihilism: active, passive and a re-active nihilism. (1) *Active nihilism* is defined here as the inability to speak emphatically 'No' to the non-being of the other, even if this leads to one's own non-being. This active nihilism is the nihilism of suicide attackers and persons running amok. The violence of the extreme-right among young people is also an expression of it. (2) *Passive nihilism* is characterized as the inability to speak emphatically 'No' to one's own non-being. The consequences of this inability are of course obvious: depression, suicidal attempts, etc. (3) And by *reactive nihilism* I refer to answers given by politicians. Here I differentiate between (a) a *decisionist nihilism*, which is well expressed in the Hobbesian axiom '*Auctoritas non veritas facit legem*' (authority, not truth makes the law), (b) a *paternalistic nihilism*, expressed in the view that human beings are unable to live a life in solidarity, a life according to the teachings of Jesus Christ. This position could be summarized in the phrase: 'Church, yes – Kingdom of God, no!'. And lastly, (c) a *technical-pragmatic nihilism* which focuses on economic problems and is grounded by an optimistic mentality. This technical-pragmatic nihilism is very widespread. Here we are confronted with two problems. First, more and more people are unable to live their lives even when they have a job; secondly, we don't need optimism: 'Optimism is a lack of information' (H. Mueller). This form of reactive nihilism is therefore, consciously or unconsciously, a way of repressing reality. What people need in today's situation is not optimism, but hope. Yet, there is no hope without anxiety. One cannot hope for someone without also being worried about someone. Hope includes an awareness that action could fail. But hope also guarantees not forgetting the major questions, the question of humankind and the world. Thus, I am going to ask in this socio-cultural situation for new political orientations on the basis of a theology that turns its face towards the world.

2. *The Political in the New Political Theology*

a. *Theology of the World*

In order to define the relationship between theology and politics in the present we should refer to theological paradigms that explicitly bring focus to this question. Referring to theology as conceived by Johann Baptist Metz we recognize that the starting point for his theological-political thinking has never been the question of defining the relationship between religion and politics. The new political theology is nothing other than the attempt to pursue a theology 'with its face towards the world' (J.B. Metz).[1] This turn towards the world stems from a deep rootedness within theological history. None other than Thomas Aquinas himself has formulated the insight that an error about the world results in false thinking about God. And so Johann Baptist Metz was able to begin developing a *theology of the world* with reference to Thomas Aquinas, Karl Rahner, Harvey Cox and others, a project which can be viewed within his overall commitment in contributing to the becoming world of the world (*Weltwerdung*). This theology has been designed so as a participation in the project of making life more human and maintaining it.[2] This, according to Aristotle, is a political project, because politics aims at the common good. In this sense, the activity of God is also political. This is the only way to prevent *Gottesrede* (God-talk) from becoming *Gottesgerede* (gossip-talk). Theology is therefore forced to become political. The view taken of political life thus indicates whether we really believe in God or just in our believing of God; for if we say God, then this word must change our life.[3]

Theo-logy, if it is intended to be God-talk, may not lose sight of the world, of the whole. Both theology and politics are concerned with the whole. This is why Friedrich Nietzsche was able to define politics as the 'organ of general thinking'.[4] Anyone who wishes to recognize theology and politics in this sense as the means of conceiving the whole, is therefore obliged not to forget the whole. At this point a distinction has to be made between the whole and the total. The new political theology does not conceive the political, as in the case of the 'crown-jurist of the "Third Reich" (W. Gurian)', Carl Schmitt, as 'the total'.[5] To see the whole as total

---

[1] Cf. Bernd Wacker and Jürgen Manemann, '"Politische Theologie": Eine Skizze zur Geschichte und aktuellen Diskussion des Begriffs', *Politische Theologie – gegengelesen* (ed. Jürgen Manemann and Bernd Wacker; Jahrbuch Politische Theologie, 5; Münster: LIT, 2008), pp. 28–65. See also: Johann Baptist Metz, *Zur Theologie der Welt* (repr., Mainz: Grünewald, 1984). English translation: *Theology of the World* (London: Burns and Oates/New York, NY: Herder and Herder, 1969).

[2] Cf. Metz, *Zur Theologie der Welt*; *Theology of the World*.

[3] Cf. also Johann Baptist Metz, *Glaube in Geschichte und Gesellschaft: Studien zu einer praktischen Fundamentaltheologie* (repr., Mainz: Grünewald, 1984) pp. 47–49.

[4] Cf. Nietzsche's letter to Carl von Gersdorf, in: Friedrich Nietzsche, *Werke in drei Bänden* (ed. Karl Schlechta; vol. 3; repr., Munich: Hanser, 1966) p. 992. See also: Tiemo Rainer Peters, *Johann Baptist Metz: Theologie des vermissten Gottes* (Mainz: Grünewald, 1998) p. 10.

[5] Carl Schmitt, *Politische Theologie: Vier Kapitel zur Lehre von der Souveränität* (repr., Berlin: Duncker & Humblot, 1993) p. 7. English translation: *Political Theology: Four Chapters on the Concept of Sovereignty* (ed. and intr. George Shwab; foreword by Tracy B. Strong; Studies in Contemporary German Thought; Cambridge, MA: MIT Press, 1985).

is an error. What is necessary is to have an understanding of the whole that is not total, because it protects the particular in its non-identity instead of drawing it into identity. Seen in this way, the category of the whole guarantees the identity of the non-identical. This difference should certainly not be taken to mean that relationships are not possible. As will be shown later, this difference consists in non-indifference, in the impossibility of indifference.

The new political theology, committed to 'talk about God in this time' (J.B. Metz), takes this insight seriously: the theologian will only realize what theology is ultimately about when he or she takes the socio-historical context into account. Metz's view that the concept of 'political theology' is actually a pleonasm, becomes comprehensible from this perspective.

b. *Against Privatization: The Programme of the New Political Theology*

For the new political theology, the predicate 'political' therefore means more than merely reflecting on the political-ideological and the political-practical consequences of religion and theology. However, the word 'political' is also to be understood in an attributive manner and as such represents a reaction to the critique of religion. Both the critique of religion and new political theology are linked by demonstrating the socio-political implications of theology and religion.[6] The new political theology does not ask 'How can religion be politicized again?' but 'What can be done to prevent politics from becoming religious again?'[7] As self-reflexive talk about God, it understands that theological questions have lost their historical, social and cultural innocence. The constitutional question of theology, according to Metz, can now be formulated: 'Who talks – when and where – for whom and with what intention – about God?'

The project of the new political theology is not a retreat behind 'the separation of state and society that was effected by the political Enlightenment'.[8] Such an anti-totalitarian separation is always taken as a given. At the same time, it must be remembered that because of this differentiation a political change took place, through which the political order became manifest as an order of freedom, so that the predicate 'political' now refers to the history of freedom.[9] A 'basic framework of secularization' is to be understood by this, through which a modern community

---

[6] Cf. Johann Baptist Metz, '"Politische Theologie" in der Diskussion', *Diskussion zur politischen Theologie* (ed. Helmut Peukert; Mainz: Grünewald, 1969), pp. 267–301 (268).

[7] Jürgen Moltmann, *Politische Theologie – Politische Ethik* (Fundamentaltheologische Studien, 9; München: Kaiser, 1984) p. 72.

[8] Metz, '"Politische Theologie" in der Diskussion', p. 269.

[9] Cf. Metz, '"Politische Theologie" in der Diskussion', p. 270.

is committed to the detachment and emancipation of secular spheres from religious institutions.[10] But this does not necessarily mean that religions are completely restricted to the private sphere. The new political theology opposes such radical demands for privatization and secularization by maintaining that the Enlightenment and the modern world do not necessarily lead to the strict division of religion and politics. The arena in which religion and politics enter into a relationship is not that of the state, nor that of the political in the narrow sense of the word, but that of civil society.[11]

The new political theology aims to save the human being in his or her uniqueness by talking about God. It is precisely for this reason that it works on a programme against the privatization of theology. It has always seen this as its primary theological task and still does so. It fights for the sake of the concrete human being against any attempt to replace the political self by the individual,[12] because any such substitution robs the person of his or her co-existence with others, taking him or her out of social space.

c. *The Temporal Aspect of the Political*

The concept of the political has normative implications within the new political theology. It therefore sees the goal of politics not as the state or the maintenance or consolidation of state order in its own right, but as peace.[13] And here the new political theology conceives peace as *shalom*, as an eschatological category. Peace is not a non-political concept but a concept that transcends purely political thinking, to which reference can only be made by an eschatological connotation. Therefore, a Messianic politics is demanded in this sense from a theological-political perspective.

However, the new political theology and its basic understanding of politics have a basic orientation that is neither simply contemporary nor eschatological but above all based in anamnesis. The new political theology takes its talk of future, freedom and hope from stories and memories of a

---

[10] Cf. Martin Heckel, 'Das Säkularisierungsproblem in der Entwicklung des deutschen Staatsrechts', *Christentum und modernes Recht: Beiträge zum Problem der Säkularisierung* (ed. Gerhard Dilcher and Ilse Staff; Frankfurt a.M.: Suhrkamp, 1984), pp. 35–95 (53).

[11] Cf. in addition: José Casanova, *Public Religions in the Modern World* (Chicago, IL: University of Chicago Press, 1994); Karl Gabriel, 'Religion und Kirche im Spiegel- und Diskursmodell von Öffentlichkeit', *Glaube und Öffentlichkeit* (ed. Ingo Baldermann *et al.*; Jahrbuch für Biblische Theologie, 11; Neukirchen-Vluyn: Neukirchen, 1996), pp. 31–51.

[12] Cf. Thomas Polednitschek, *Diagnose Politikmüdigkeit: Die Psychologie des nicht-vermissten Gottes* (Berlin: Wichern, 2003) p. 14.

[13] Cf. Dolf Sternberger, *Die Politik und der Friede* (Frankfurt a.M.: Suhrkamp, 1986) p. 76.

hope that is broken and unfulfilled. For this theology, the factor of what is to come is, so to speak, empirically mediated in what it calls dangerous memories.[14] It is precisely in such an anamnesis that the new political theology has Messianic implications.

d. *Politics in Second Place*

Both the messianic and the anamnestic mark the difference from the old catechontic political theology.[15] Where the old political theology of Carl Schmitt rested on the primacy of the political, the axiom of the new political theology is not 'Politics first!' but 'Politics second!' Politics is in second place.[16] It is therefore valuable to work out the nature of the instruction that precedes this order, breaks through it and transcends it: the responsibility for the other.

The starting point for the relationship of one person to another person is one neither of order nor enmity, but the 'nonpossibility of indifference'[17]: the asymmetrical responsibility for the other.[18] Politics and the political are to be reflected upon from the perspective of this pre-political experience of non-indifference, not *vice versa*. This relationship with the other thus fundamentally appeals to religion,[19] which does not bring the other into line.[20] Religion is the interruption of the act of violence and of negation; it is the refusal to reduce the other to such basic levels like that of the environment or context.[21] This affective plane of pre-political asymmetrical responsibility finally results in the principle of equality. It refers to the individual which cannot be replaced by another in its being addressed by the call of the other. The main signs of this responsibility are unpredict-

---

[14] Cf. Johann Baptist Metz, 'Under the Spell of Cultural Amnesia? An Example from Europe and Its Consequences', *Missing God? Cultural Amnesia and Political Theology* (ed. John K. Downey, Jürgen Manemann and Steven T. Ostovich; Münster: LIT, 2006), pp. 5–10.

[15] Cf. Jürgen Manemann, *Carl Schmitt und die Politische Theologie: Politischer Anti-Monotheismus* (Münster: Aschendorf, 2002) pp. 262–302.

[16] Cf. Jacques Derrida, *Adieu to Emmanuel Levinas* (trans. Pascale-Anne Brault and Michael Naas; Meridian: Crossing Aesthetics; Palo Alto, CA: Standford University Press, 1999) pp. 70–72, 105–129.

[17] Alain Finkielkraut, *The Wisdom of Love* (trans. Kevin O'Neil and David Suchoff; intr. David Suchoff; Texts and Contexts, 20; Lincoln, NE: University of Nebraska Press, 1997) p. 96.

[18] Cf. Jürgen Manemann, *Über Freunde und Feinde: Brüderlichkeit Gottes* (Kevelaer: Topos, 2008).

[19] Emmanuel Levinas, 'The Trace of the Other', *Deconstruction in Context* (ed. Mark C. Taylor; Chicago, IL: University of Chicago Press, 1986), pp. 345–59 (113).

[20] Levinas, 'The Trace of the Other', pp. 113 and 114.

[21] Levinas, 'The Trace of the Other', p. 115.

ability, foreignness and heteronomy. It is founded in *compassion*,[22] the *conditio sine qua non* of a moral sensibility.

This radical responsibility is admittedly interrupted when another other appears: a third person is a disturbance. Then the question becomes one of justice.[23] With justice, the basic pre-political place is left behind and the space of the political is entered. From the concrete other emerges the generalized other.

e. *Politics and the Political*

The political rests on the fact that people are different. It emerges only 'in the in-between, therefore it is completely *outside of* the human person. There is therefore no actual political substance.' The political emerges in the in-between and is relational.[24] It is the social question – the question of justice – that constitutes the space of the political.

The political is to be distinguished from the idea of politics as a field of special interest. In contrast to politics, i.e. all the discourses, institutions and practices that aim to create an order and to organize social existence, the political is a state of intensity, a state of interaction between people and groups of people which causes associations and dissociations.[25] Thus the place of the political could be related to fields that haven't previously been seen as fields of the political.

Such a conception of the political takes a critical stance towards the strict liberal division between the public and the private, for only permeable relations could ever be in the position to expose the forms of power and the hegemony of the private. But this should not lead to a mixing of the private and the public. The political is grounded in the need to lend a voice to suffering which is the condition of all justice.

f. *Consensus and Dissent*

The political is primarily orientated not towards consensus but towards dissent. It creates boundaries that are chiefly based on conflict. Impervious boundaries represent however a perversion of the political, because they

---

[22] Cf. Johann Baptist Metz, *Memoria passionis: Ein provozierendes Gedächtnis in pluralistischer Gesellschaft* (Freiburg/Basel/Vienna: Herder, 2006) pp. 166–78.

[23] Cf. Emmanuel Levinas, *Otherwise than Being: Or, Beyond Essence* (trans. Alphonso Lingis; Martinus Nijhoff Philosophy Texts, 3; The Hague: Nijhoff, 1981) p. 150.

[24] Hannah Arendt, *Was ist Politik? Fragmente aus dem Nachlaß* (ed. Ursula Ludz; intr. Kurt Sontheimer; München/Zürich: Piper, 1993) pp. 9–12.

[25] According to Böckenförde in reference to Carl Schmitt in: Ernst-Wolfgang Böckenförde, 'Was heißt heute eigentlich "politisch"?', *Demokratiefähigkeit* (ed. Jürgen Manemann; Jahrbuch Politische Theologie, 1; Münster: LIT, 1995), pp. 2–5 (4).

abolish the basic quality of difference. Consensus in a democratic society is primarily related to those institutions that constitute democracy and to certain ethical and political values;[26] whereas dissent, by contrast, is concerned with the question of the meaning of values and the methods of their implementation.[27] In democratic society, conflict is distinguished by the fact that it is limited. Democracy means the transformation of antagonism into agonism, of enmity into opposition. The agonistic basis of democracy is therefore categorized with the political, in that the necessary energies of transformation are set loose. A model of society primarily concerned with consensus risks allowing this source of energy to dry up.[28]

3. The Significance of the New Political Theology for Politics

a. The Democratic Challenge

The definition of the relationship between the political and politics that has been developed here resists every attempt to cement a unity. The people are not presented as a unity, as 'one', since the people as 'empiricized' is constructed from the 'many'. It is 'the people of flesh and blood with its individuals'.[29] This is the reason why the vital nerve of democracy does not lie in consensus but in dissent. Dissent guarantees the freedom of all citizens, i.e. the freedoms of the dissident with respect to the sovereign and of the majority with respect to itself. This democracy is a future democracy in the sense that it contains the promise of taking seriously a realistic view of people as 'the ensemble of conflicting individuals' (P. Flores d'Arcais). The democratic challenge consists in this, even if it is threatened constantly with defeat in democratic societies, whenever majorities drown out the voices of minorities. And while current democracies are primarily worried about majorities, the new political theology is concerned with voiceless minorities.

Both democracy and monotheism are less about becoming a people than about becoming a subject. If democracy can be defined as the 'institutionalized form of dealing with uncertainty in the public',[30] then biblical monotheism cannot be used to master this uncertainty. Exactly the opposite is true! It radicalizes uncertainty. Uncertainty allows for new scopes of

---

[26] Cf. Chantal Mouffe, 'Für eine antagonistische Öffentlichkeit', *Demokratie als unvollendeter Prozess: Documenta11_Plattform1* (ed. Okwui Enwezor *et al.*; Ostfildern: Hatje Cantz, 2002), pp. 101–12 (104).

[27] Cf. Mouffe, 'Für eine antagonistische Öffentlichkeit', p. 104.

[28] Cf. also Chantal Mouffe, *On the Political* (Thinking in Action; Abingdon/New York, NY: Routledge, 2005).

[29] P. Flores d'Arcais, 'Ist Amerika noch eine Demokratie?', *Die Zeit*, 20 January 2005.

[30] Helmut Dubiel, *Ungewißheit und Politik* (Frankfurt a.M.: Suhrkamp, 1994) p. 9.

action to arise. Biblical monotheism is in its very nature a call against deadlocks, a call into a productive exile.[31] Abraham is called by God to leave his home and he is told never to return to his origins. Uncertainty is the site of formation of the subject. In democracy, civil society is the place for becoming a subject. It is the site where moral forces are mobilized. Civil society is the genuine motor of democracy: the source of resistance, innovation and change. In other words, it is the place of sub-politics. Sub-politics grounded in the political can be distinguished from politics in that it changes the rules, whereas politics is led by the rules.[32]

Dissent is the driving force of democracy. The persistence of dissent can lead to the rise of something like an 'expanded way of thinking' (I. Kant) and as such, accumulates moral capital.[33] But it is not only this moral capital that binds; there are other phenomenal areas that allow similarities between different people to be recognized and to be felt. At this point, the point of view of the new political theology should be mentioned, the *analogia passionis* (P. Rottländer) that is the result of a dual vulnerability: every person is capable of suffering and is in turn affected by the suffering of the other. To this extent the experience of suffering can be categorized as common, even if in each case it is different.[34] The concept of *analogia passionis* that is considered here does not consist in 'remaining with the perception and the memory of personal suffering' but in moving out to the perception and the memory of the other's suffering. The coming together of internal and external perspectives, of witness and empathy, then opens possibilities that tend towards a universal understanding.'[35] For such memory is both well grounded in experience and the ground of experience.

Returning now to the previously mentioned nihilistic tendencies, this ability for *analogia passionis* seems to be lost. Why?

Reflecting on this question from a social-phenomenological point of view developed by the psychoanalyst Ronald D. Laing, we recognize that in the sharing of our experiences we are confronted with a paradox. On the one hand we have to notice, that what we experience is to us of highest evidence. While on the other hand 'we can see other people's behaviour, but not their experience.'[36] That is: 'Our experiences are invisible to one

---

[31] Jürgen Manemann, *Rettende Erinnerung an die Zukunft: Essay über die christliche Verschärfung* (Mainz: Grünewald, 2005).

[32] Cf. Ulrich Beck, *Die Erfindung des Politischen: Zu einer Theorie reflexiver Modernisierung* (Frankfurt a.M.: Suhrkamp, 1993) p. 207.

[33] Cf. Dubiel, *Ungewißheit und Politik*, p. 116.

[34] Cf. Peter Rottländer, 'Alterität versus anamnetische Ethik?', *Demokratiefähigkeit* (ed. Jürgen Manemann; Jahrbuch Politische Theologie, 1; Münster: LIT, 1995), pp. 238–49 (248).

[35] Rottländer, 'Alterität versus anamnetische Ethik?', p. 248.

[36] Ronald D. Laing, *The Politics of Experience* and *The Bird of Paradise* (repr., Harmondsworth: Penguin, 1977), p. 15.

another.' Experience is the invisibility of the one for the other and at the same time it is connected with highest evidence. Yes, experience is the only evidence that we have.

But how do we really know something about the experience of the other? What is experience about? Your experience is not evident to me, as it is not and never can be an experience of mine. The only thing we are able to do is to experience ourselves as experiencing. All of which entails that we don't not know each other so well when we attempt at hearing the other from the basis of what we think we have experienced. The way we make experience is expressed to others in the way we behave. Our behaviour is a function of our experience. If our experience is destroyed, our behaviour is destructive. In turn, from such destroyed experience, one not only loses one's self but participates in such loss by crossing out one's self. And if we face the challenges of nihilistic tendencies from these social-phenomenological insights we may start to get a hint about new potentials, as Laing correctly states: 'What we think (theory) is less than what we know (evidence by experience): what we know is less than what we love: what we love is so much less than what there is. And to that precise extent we are so much less than what we are.'[37] Experience deserves its name only if it transports us beyond what we think constitutes our nature, if it makes us aware that we are so much less than what we think we are. As such, experience is connected with the idea of infinity.

Religions – to the extent that they are receptive to suffering experiences – can be a source of experience or, more precisely, of counter-experience and therefore a source of the sort of politics that can change rules. If the God of the Bible is concerned with the suffering of the stranger, and if it is simultaneously clear on the grounds of belief in the God of the Bible that there is no suffering in the world that does not concern us (P. Rottländer), then the result of this sensibility is a potential for change, which compels not only religions but also democratic societies to go beyond themselves. This is a dissolving of boundaries that makes it difficult for democratic societies to remain indifferent to the claims of the stranger in their midst. This claim for justice is demanded even in the face of the enemy. By this it is meant that the other can always be discovered in the enemy, 'for whom there is a co-responsibility even in the excess of collective enmity, which cannot be renounced'.[38] From this point of view, a politics of enmity that is based on a dualistic rhetoric calls not for an intensification of the political but for its liquidation. The realm of the political is abandoned whenever somebody's right to exist is annihilated.[39]

---

[37] Laing, *The Politics of Experience*, p. 26.
[38] Burkhard Liebsch, *Gastlichkeit und Freiheit: Polemische Konturen europäischer Kultur* (Weilerswist: Velbruck, 2005) p. 167.
[39] Liebsch, *Gastlichkeit und Freiheit*, p. 167.

Advocates of a dualistic politics of friend and foe are walking the path into the anti-political for this very reason.[40]

b. *Doing Justice to the Concrete Other*

Democratic societies would do well to note the potential for change that is contained in biblical traditions, for the political debate must constantly reflect on the boundaries of justice.[41] Biblical monotheism constantly demands this kind of self-reflection, in that the biblical traditions remind us that morality does not originate in equality but in the service that is given to the poor, the orphan and the widow. An imperative is therefore generated of recognizing the suffering of the other, and through this imperative the theory and practice of justice as equality in liberal society is constantly questioned in respect to real human beings in their infinite dignity. In turn there is a demand to take into account the individual's unique perspective. A liberal democracy that understands justice as equality must be founded upon a responsibility oriented towards the other, for this is what drives justice. The problem, therefore, of liberal democracy bridging together justice and equality is that its very medium of doing so is unjust.[42] Thus, from the perspective of biblical monotheism, the theory and practice of justice as equality in liberal democracy is put under challenge in the light of the question of the non-identical. The audibility of the cries of individuals in reaction to any established practice of equality is what drives self-reflection.[43] The egalitarian attitude of the members of democratically constituted states is completed by doing justice to the concrete other. 'Here, doing justice to the individual means reacting with the other against that which causes the other to suffer and to lament.'[44] The idea of morality that is expressed here is to be found in proximity. Contrary to that, the longing for order as part of polemical politics is an ideology which seeks to justify the hatred of human beings. This hatred of other human beings is nothing other than a rejection of responsibility and not an expression that rejects multiplicity.[45]

The word 'democracy' is actually not to be found in biblical traditions, but Israel's understanding of the right of the other in his or her 'otherness'

---

[40] Cf. also Manemann, *Über Freunde und Feinde*.

[41] Cf. Christoph Menke, 'Grenzen der Gleichheit: Neutralität und Politik im Politischen Liberalismus', *Deutsche Zeitschrift für Philosophie* 50/6 (2002), pp. 897–906.

[42] Cf. Axel Honneth, 'Das Andere der Gerechtigkeit', *Freiheit oder Gerechtigkeit: Perspektiven Politischer Philosophie* (ed. Peter Fischer; Leipzig: Reclam, 1995), pp. 194–240.

[43] Cf. Christoph Menke, *Spiegelungen der Gleichheit* (Berlin: Akademie Verlag, 2000) p. 35.

[44] Menke, *Spiegelungen der Gleichheit*, p. 38.

[45] Finkielkraut, *The Wisdom of Love*, p. 177.

(E. Levinas), has constantly taken into account the very thing that is demanded by democracy: namely a profound sensibility that protects the right of the individual.

The churches can contribute to combating social fragmentation by giving encouragement so that the suffering experienced by the individual in society is not reduced to individual suffering but is correlated with the whole of society. This will affect society in two ways: first, the one who suffers can assume that nobody else wants to experience such pain and suffering, and would reject it; secondly, the resultant change affects the whole in that it gives a new orientation to the whole. Only then can talk of 'genuine politics' (S. Žižek) begin. Opposed to this is the current dominance of what Žižek calls 'post-politics': a politics that mobilizes the entire apparatus of experts, social workers etc. in order to reduce the collective demands of a minority group to minority relevance.[46] Yet, is it possible for a new orientation of the whole to find a foundation in liberal-secular societies?

c. The Political and the Symbolic

The basis of the political is neither the economy nor the common good, whether understood substantially or as guaranteed by tradition. Every definitive closure is incompatible with the political.[47] And this is how democratic societies, rooted in the political, establish themselves: through an institutionalized questioning.[48] Society, which is based on dissent that cannot be solved by consensus and transformed into a unity, depends on the symbol. The political, as the space in-between, does not destroy society; it shapes society, through giving meaning to social relations and through staging them.[49] Giving meaning is based on structuring distinctions of generative principles (just – unjust etc.), such as justice and human rights, for example, which prolong the conflict. The way that society takes shape cannot however be reduced to the social, but rather contains a whole complex of phenomena, including religious ones.[50] Society, without this religious dimension, is in danger of losing a difference that does not lie

---

[46] Cf. Slavoj Žižek, *The Ticklish Subject: The Absent Centre of Political Ontology* (Wo es war; London/New York, NY: Verso, pb edn, 2000). See also: Polednitschek, *Diagnose Politikmüdigkeit*.

[47] Cf. Oliver Marchart, 'Demonstrationen des Unvollendbaren: Politische Theorie und radikaldemokratischer Aktivismus', *Demokratie als unvollendeter Prozess: Documenta11_Platform1* (ed. Okwui Enwezor *et al.*; Ostfildern: Hatje Cantz, 2002), pp. 291–306.

[48] Cf. Dubiel, *Ungewißheit und Politik*, pp. 9 and 47.

[49] Cf. Claude Lefort, *Fortdauer des Theologisch-Politischen* (Vienna: Passagen, 1999) p. 39.

[50] Cf. Lefort, *Fortdauer des Theologisch-Politischen*, p. 44.

within the power of disposal of human beings.[51] Both the political and the religious spheres are connected with the symbolic and open up access to the world.[52] The 'secret of democracy' (C. Lefort) is the symbolic way in which society forms itself, in which a unity is produced that is open and that guarantees diversity.[53] This openness is made possible through the distance between the symbolic and the real, between the political and politics.

The political remains, however, only *one* form of symbolization (shaping, giving meaning, representation).[54] Religion offers another. Religion, unlike the political, does not give a form to society. Religion is the link with the whole; it breaks through borders in the way that it, as a giving of world, constitutes the world as world by remembering another world. This other world is not to be regarded in a dualistic manner. It does not involve any devaluation of this world but actually challenges this world to become world.

This rupture of the world by the polarization between a world that is willed by God and a world as human order, thus shows that the sacred pole in modern society can no longer be filled substantially – for instance through a king appointed by the grace of God or through a Hobbesian sovereign – and hence, must remain empty. This emptiness of the actual place of power allows for the members of civil society both participation and self-determination, and becomes the condition for the possibility of a non-totalitarian society, in that it resists identical symbolizations.[55]

While the political can be understood as the symbolic formation of a society,[56] religion contains a symbolization that radically ruptures boundaries – and therefore it locates the way the political forms the society by locating it into a space opened for the whole: 'That human society can only open onto itself by being held in an opening it did not create, is exactly what every religion *says*, each in its own way, just like philosophy, but religion said it first, albeit in terms that philosophy cannot make its own.'[57]

The political and religion as dimensions of the other are entangled in a way which cannot be unravelled. Politics and the political need religion, because without religion, both would be limited to the preservation of the given order, living in the illusion of a pure immanence.[58] What is needed is a permanence of the theological-political in modern democracy, which is indicated through the empty place of power, in order to withstand a resto-

---

[51] Cf. Lefort, *Fortdauer des Theologisch-Politischen*, p. 45.
[52] Cf. Lefort, *Fortdauer des Theologisch-Politischen*, p. 44.
[53] Cf. Lefort, *Fortdauer des Theologisch-Politischen*, p. 49.
[54] Cf. also. Manemann, *Über Freunde und Feinde*.
[55] Lefort, *Fortdauer des Theologisch-Politischen*, p. 50.
[56] Lefort, *Fortdauer des Theologisch-Politischen*, p. 49.
[57] Lefort, *Fortdauer des Theologisch-Politischen*, p. 45.
[58] Lefort, *Fortdauer des Theologisch-Politischen*, p. 47.

ration of the political-theological in the form of a political religion. The new political theology votes therefore for a de-corporation of power, which is essential for modern societies.

d. *Doing Politics Facing the Memory of the Other's Suffering*

What is necessary is a new way to link politics and morality. This does not mean falling back 'into the political canonization of a certain system of morality'; nor is the intent 'a "totalitarian" clash of political and ethical practice'. The demand is rather for 'the mobilization of spiritual and moral forces through a radical *democratization* on the basis of society, a resto-ration of freedom and of efficient responsibility from below'.[59] In this way, the 'subversion of political imagination and of political action into the pure business of planning' can be resisted.[60] 'Political imagination will not be ultimately sucked up by technological [and economic, J.M.] pressures, so long as it retains that moral-religious imagination and force for resistance that grows out of memory of accumulated suffering in history.'[61] The new political theology therefore pleads for a political consciousness *ex memoria passionis*.[62] Only then will we be able to talk about 'real politics' (S. Žižek), one which works for a change in parameters characterized as 'possible' and 'real', while actually representing the art of the impossible, i.e. a messianic politics.

On the basis of these clarifications, the task of a new political theology could be seen as involving the repolitization of the private sphere and the renormativization of the public sphere, in confronting personal morality with public problems and the public with questions of private morality.[63]

e. *The Task of Christians*

In order to be able to fulfil this task, theology would have to be reworked once again as a helping tool which gives a voice to the voiceless. Theology will not be able to reach the 'sources of the self' (C. Taylor) by using systemic philosophies, but by addressing everyday suffering, which is often hidden or dismissed as banal. Its political task would initially consist in helping people to articulate their thoughts and feelings, in such a way that would oppose manipulating opinions by merely surveying them or by working to make suffering visible when the sufferer believes that he or she is without importance for others or when he or she is not conscious

---

[59] Metz, *Glaube in Geschichte und Gesellschaft*, p. 90.
[60] Metz, *Glaube in Geschichte und Gesellschaft*, p. 91.
[61] Metz, *Glaube in Geschichte und Gesellschaft*, pp. 91 and 92.
[62] Metz, *Glaube in Geschichte und Gesellschaft*, p. 92.
[63] Cf. Casanova, *Public Religions in the Modern World*, pp. 5 and 6.

of their own suffering or simply forgets to share it.[64] This task could help to break through 'democratic melancholy' (P. Bruckner). It would not only be a step towards the democratization of democracy but also towards the *democratization of theology*.

f. *An Incomplete Democracy*

If the question – from the perspective of Christian theology – is that of defining the relationship between religion and politics, then this question should not be understood in the usual sense of the relationship between religion and state order. Democracy actually forms not a state, but a form of life, a way of being that is the result of bitter experiences. It is not an abstract sovereignty of the people that is foregrounded in democratic society but the recognition of the other in his or her otherness. This recognition is what links the two projects of Christianity and democracy.

Democracy possesses an eschatological dimension. It is the good that would vanish with its realization. But to talk of an incomplete democracy is not to refer to a future reality, or to a utopia, but to a 'democracy that is coming' (J. Derrida); it is to categorize a future present.[65] Talking of an incomplete democracy should be taken not to mean that there is an uncompleted democracy that possesses empirical deficits but – and this is much more significant – that there is a promise that democracy is in principle incapable of keeping. And therefore the strength of democracy does not lie in its drive to realize a particular good, but in this very promise.[66]

---

[64] Cf. in addition: Pierre Bourdieu *et al.*, *The Weight of the World: Social Suffering in Contemporary Society* (trans. Priscilla Parkhurst Ferguson; Cambridge: Polity Press, 1999) p. 795.

[65] Cf. Marchart, 'Demonstrationen des Unvollendbaren'.

[66] Cf. Marchart, 'Demonstrationen des Unvollendbaren'.

PART III
'GOD IS BIGGER THAN ALL RELIGIONS PUT TOGETHER': THE DIALOGUE BETWEEN THE RELIGIONS

GOD BEFORE US, GOD AMONG US: INTERRELIGIOUS DIALOGUE FROM AN INTERCULTURAL FEMINIST PERSPECTIVE

Gemma Tulud Cruz

1. *Introduction: Migration, Violence, and the Religions*

Religions have been a part of the human story ever since human beings have walked this earth. While there have been conflicts in the past with religious underpinnings, religions and their relationship with each other were relatively not of the utmost concern. Arguably, this is no longer the case in the contemporary world. Within Christianity, for example, this preoccupation with interreligious relations can be seen in the emergence of theologies on interreligious dialogue which, I believe, is largely due to three factors.

The first is migration. In earlier times, religions possessed clearer and more discernible geographical locations such that one could more or less speak of Europe or the United States as being Christian. But migration, particularly in the past few decades, has muddled this claim. In the case of the United States, the very title of Diana Eck's book *A New Religious America: How a 'Christian Country' Has Become the World's Most Religiously Diverse Nation*[1] points to this blurring of geographical religious boundaries and the increase in consciousness towards other religions.

This brings me to the second factor, that is, the changing attitude of peoples towards other religions. The Catholic Church, despite what can be argued as its historical belligerence towards other religions, is

[1] See Diana Eck, *A New Religious America: How a 'Christian Country' Has Become the World's Most Religiously Diverse Nation* (San Francisco, CA: Harper One, 2002).

85

emblematic of this change. Pope Paul VI, for instance, pointed out as early as 1964 in *Ecclesiam Suam* that 'dialogue is demanded nowadays ... by the dynamic course of action which is changing the face of modern society ... by the pluralism of society and by the maturity man has reached in this day and age' (*Ecclesiam Suam*, no. 79). The same document, which is usually regarded as the *magna carta* of dialogue, also lays down four levels of dialogue, including dialogue with other religions. In 1968 the Vatican Secretariat for Unbelievers even insisted that 'all Christians should do their best to promote dialogue ... as a duty of fraternal charity suited to our progressive and adult age'.[2] Other Church documents, particularly *Dialogue and Mission* (1984) and *Dialogue and Proclamation* (1991), as well as the considerable dialogical attitude of the late Pope John Paul II towards other religions, further testify to the progress in the thinking and practice of the Catholic Church toward other religions.

The third factor is the effect of the problematic co-opting of the religions, particularly through terrorism. From Bali to Bangkok, New York to London, Madrid to Glasgow, never before has religion been imbricated with violence and in such devastating proportions in just a few seconds as in the present time. To be sure, global terroristic attacks by persons who associate themselves and their acts with a particular religion have made people not just more aware and critical of other religions but also partly more willing to recognize the need for interreligious dialogue. Edward Schillebeeckx[3] explicitly tackles this factor with a view to interreligious dialogue in an essay titled 'The Religious and the Human Ecumene'[4] where he points out how religious wars or violence of religions in the past and present are a threat to living together in

---

[2] As quoted in Leonard Swidler, *After the Absolute: The Dialogical Future of Religious Reflection* (Minneapolis, MN: Fortress, 1990) p. 26.

[3] While he has not published a book or written substantially on the issue Schillebeeckx does have some writings or sections in his books that tackle or touch on the issue. Aside from the Schillebeeckx texts that will be cited in the succeeding pages see also Chapter 9 and 10 of Edward Schillebeeckx, *World and Church* (trans. N.D. Smith; Theological Soundings, 3; London/Sydney: Sheed and Ward, 1971) which offer glimpses of Schillebeeckx's thoughts on dialogue and cooperation between Christians and non-Christians.

[4] Edward Schillebeeckx, 'The Religious and the Human Ecumene', *The Future of Liberation Theology: Essays in Honor of Gustavo Gutiérrez* (ed. Marc H. Ellis and Otto Maduro; Maryknoll, NY: Orbis, 1989), pp. 177–88. Reprinted in: Edward Schillebeeckx, *The Language of Faith: Essays on Jesus, Theology and the Church* (intr. Robert J. Schreiter; Concilium Series; Maryknoll, NY: Orbis/London: SCM, 1995), pp. 249–64. Where I refer, in what follows, to this essay, I refer to the version from *The Language of Faith*.

community[5] and that the coexistence of religions is a key to the building of human community.[6]

2. *Trajectories of Christian Theologies on Interreligious Dialogue*

So how far have the religions gone when it comes to articulating and envisioning interreligious engagement? As far as Christianity is concerned it has the so-called Christian theologies of religions or theologies which measure the extent to which Christianity regards other religions as true or salvific. An often used paradigm to discuss this is that of Alan Race's exclusivism, inclusivism, and pluralism model.[7] Exclusivism is best represented by the axiom *extra ecclesiam nulla salus* (outside the Church, no salvation). This was propounded by the third century bishop Cyprian of Carthage for heretics and schismatics but the sentiment has since been appropriated to serve as condemnation of peoples of other religions. Inclusivism is a liberal progression of this first position. Karl Rahner's theory of the 'anonymous Christian' best captures this stance. Peoples of other religions can attain salvation but it is Christ who is secretly saving them, even as they know nothing about it. These people are saved not so much in and through their own religions but despite their belonging to them. Pluralism, meanwhile, basically asserts that no religion, including Christianity, can claim to be the norm or guide by which others are measured.

Exclusivist proponents primarily regard other religions as false, while seeking to conquer or replace them for, in their view, error has no right of existence. Paul Knitter labels this as the 'replacement model', which operates out of a conviction that there is only one true religion, that is, Christianity.[8] Its emphasis on 'no salvation outside the church' makes it ecclesiocentric in focus. The second position, inclusivism, which regards other religions as partially true, seeks to fulfill or perfect them. Knitter labels this the 'fulfillment model', where the one true religion is responsible for fulfilling the many other partially true religions. One could use

---

[5] Schillebeeckx believes that, as could be seen in religious wars, any theoretical or practical misuse of religion leads to the cruelest inhumanities. Hence as far as he is concerned coming clean over the violent history of the encounters between religions is a critical component of interreligious coexistence. Edward Schillebeeckx, 'Documentation: Religion and Violence', *Religion as a Source of Violence* (ed. Wim Beuken and Karl-Josef Kuschel; Concilium, 1997/4; Maryknoll, NY: Orbis/London: SCM, 1997), pp. 129–42 (130).

[6] Schillebeeckx, 'The Religious and the Human Ecumene', p. 249.

[7] See Alan Race, *Christians and Religious Pluralism: Patterns in the Christian Theology of Religions* (London: SCM, 1983).

[8] See Paul Knitter, *Introducing Theologies of Religions* (Maryknoll, NY: Orbis, 2002).

the dictum 'outside Christ, no salvation'[9] thus characterizing this position as Christocentric. The third position, pluralism, which acknowledges that other religions are genuine and true in their own right, seeks thus to develop relationships of mutuality and collaboration. Knitter uses two models to describe variations of this last position. The first is what he calls the 'mutuality model', where the many different and true religions are called into dialogue with one another. In his earlier writings he calls this the Theocentric model where salvation is no longer attributed to the Church or to Christ but to *ho Theos*.[10] Knitter later on sought to clarify and revise this so as to be inclusive of non-theistic traditions and posited in its turn the soteriocentric model, whereby *soteria* is understood broadly and encapsulates all struggles on behalf of human and ecological justice.[11] For Knitter, this shifts the basis for Christianity's relations with peoples of other religions from the Church to Christ, to God, to God's Kingdom.

Schillebeeckx himself considers religions as 'schools of wisdom and freedom'[12] with so-called 'family resemblances' (Wittgenstein) among them which can serve as bases for comparison.[13] He cautions, however, against a form of modern 'indifferentism' which presents religions as having the same value.[14] As far as Schillebeeckx is concerned, the statement that 'all religions are equal' is 'understandable to postmodern sensibilities' but he finds this 'fundamentally wrong',[15] for even their (religious) visions about humanity are rather divergent. For example, a religion that condones sending the eldest son to death is certainly not of the same value as a religion that expressly forbids it. For Schillebeeckx, 'the question of truth with regard to one's own religion in no way need be discriminatory in itself vis-à-vis other religions. No single religion exhausts the question of truth. Therefore *in religiosis* we must put behind us both absolutism and relativism.'[16]

---

[9] Hendrik Vroom, *No Other Gods: Christian Belief in Dialogue with Buddhism, Hinduism, and Islam* (Grand Rapids, MI/Cambridge: Eerdmans, 1996) p. 142.

[10] Paul Knitter, *No Other Name: A Critical Survey of Christian Attitudes toward the World Religions* (Quezon City: Claretian, 1985) pp. 145–67.

[11] Paul Knitter, 'The Place of the Church and Missionary Activity in Theocentric and Soteriocentric Approaches to Dialogue', *Mission & Dialogue: Theory and Practice* (ed. Leonardo N. Mercado and James J. Knight; Manila: Divine Word Publications, 1989), pp. 186–221 (195–200).

[12] Edward Schillebeeckx, 'Prologue: Human God-Talk and God's Silence', *The Praxis of the Reign of God: An Introduction to the Theology of Edward Schillebeeckx* (ed. Mary Catherine Hilkert and Robert J. Schreiter; New York, NY: Fordham University Press, 2nd edn, 2002), pp. ix–xviii (xiv).

[13] Schillebeeckx, 'The Religious and the Human Ecumene', p. 250.

[14] Schillebeeckx, 'The Religious and the Human Ecumene', p. 254. He mentions as an example here Paul Knitter's arguments in his aforementioned book *No Other Name?*.

[15] Schillebeeckx, 'The Religious and the Human Ecumene', p. 254.

[16] Schillebeeckx, 'The Religious and the Human Ecumene', p. 254.

3. When Culture Becomes a Factor: The Challenge of Asian Perspectives on Interreligious Relations

In Christian circles most theological discussions on interreligious dialogue have been provoked by the particular context of Asia where there have been substantial theological reflections on interreligious relations, some of which has posed a challenge to mainstream Christian theologies on religions, including those at the institutional level. For some Asian Christian theologians, the whole enterprise of the theology of religions is problematic. They ask: Why do we need to measure other religions against our own religious ideals and theological systems? Why do we need to categorize them in terms of their salvific efficacy? Why do we need to evaluate if peoples of other religions are saved or headed to eternal damnation? Felix Wilfred, for example, points to the predominantly Western epistemology grounded on the principle of non-contradiction as shaping the exclusivist-inclusivist-pluralist paradigm.[17] This epistemology hinges upon history where particular events or persons and their uniqueness matters. Whereas for many Asians, what matters is that the various religions are thriving, giving life, and are at peace with one another. After all, they have been partaking in the inexhaustible search for the divine for centuries.

Moreover, the Asian psyche is open to diversity and ambiguity. It is not at home with rigid exclusivism; nor is it at home with evaluating others on the basis of one's own religious and theological ideal. Malaysian-American theologian Amos Yong says as much when he points out that religious traditions are comprehensive ways, whole systems and not subject to comparison, especially on the basis of whether they are salvific or not. He asserts: 'In this case, Christian theologies of exclusivism, inclusivism, and pluralism all miss the mark because they do not engage other religious traditions on their own terms.'[18] Many Asian theologians (including Western theologians of Asian descent) do not typically use the uniqueness of Christ or the special position of the Church as norms by which other religions are gauged.[19] They do not normally abide by a hierarchical structure of religions which categorizes and quantifies things in gradated terms of 'goodness' or 'truth'. Unfortunately, these are attempts by Christians of trying to make sense of the presence of other religions within their own economy of salvation but without listening to what these other traditions have to offer.

---

[17] Felix Wilfred, 'Towards a Better Understanding of Asian Theology', *Vidyajyoti Journal of Theological Reflection* 62/12 (1998), pp. 890–915.

[18] Amos Yong, *Hospitality and The Other: Pentecost, Christian Practices, and the Neighbor* (Maryknoll, NY: Orbis, 2008) p. 52.

[19] Edmund Chia, 'Dialogue with Religions of Asia: Challenges from Within (1) (Part II)', http://www.sedos.org/english/within_chia.html (accessed on November 24, 2008).

Ordinarily, Asian Christians have no problem embracing a sort of epistemological humility by refraining from judging the religious other. If anything, the religious other's presence encourages them to witness to their own faith with greater zeal. In the words of Indian theologian Michael Amaladoss: 'People then learn to relativize their own belief systems without in any way relativizing the Absolute to which they are committed and which they witness to and proclaim.'[20] Problems begin when told that their Christian tradition makes claims to Christianity's uniqueness or the absoluteness of their savior or religion. As Stanley Samartha puts it, 'what is a stumbling block to neighbours of other faiths, is the Christian claim that *only* in Jesus Christ has God been revealed *once-for-all* to redeem all humanity'.[21] Noted Sri Lankan theologian Aloysius Pieris' position is that if the uniqueness language has to be used, then 'Jesus' uniqueness is found in his preferential option for the poor'. Pieris maintains the old formula 'no salvation outside the church' is now replaced by 'no salvation outside God's covenant with the poor'.[22] 'The medium *par excellence* for encountering God,' Pieris clarifies, 'are the excluded ones among whom God appeared in human flesh, thus putting God's Seal on God's eternal covenant with the poor.'[23]

Schillebeeckx's stance on interreligious relations or Christianity's relationship with other religions aligns in some ways with that of the Asian theologians under present consideration.[24] First he emphasizes not just the 'equality between all dialogue partners'[25] but also the 'relation to the other', particularly the poor, as bases for interreligious dialogue. In principle religions are subject to the critique of human dignity according to

---

[20] Michael Amaladoss, 'The Church and Pluralism in the Asia of the 1990s', *FABC Papers No. 57e* (Hong Kong: FABC, 1990) p. 12.
[21] Stanley Samartha, *One Christ, Many Religions: Toward a Revised Christology* (Maryknoll, NY: Orbis, 1991) p. 118.
[22] Aloysius Pieris, *God's Reign for God's Poor: A Return to the Jesus Formula* (Kelaniya: Tulana Research Centre, 1999) p. 60.
[23] Pieris, *God's Reign for God's Poor*, p. 57.
[24] Edmund Chia, 'Towards a Theology of Dialogue: Schillebeeckx's Method as Bridge between Vatican's Dominus Iesus and Asia's FABC Theology' (unpublished doctoral dissertation, University of Nijmegen, 2003) provides a good example of points of convergence between Schillebeeckx's and Asian theological approaches to Christianity and the religions. Schillebeeckx's critique of Aloysius Pieris' more mystical approach to the religions in Edward Schillebeeckx, *Church: The Human Story of God* (trans. John Bowden; New York, NY: Crossroad, 1990) p. 179 could serve as an example, in the meantime, of a point of divergence. In a footnote in a much later work, however, Schillebeeckx mentions Pieris as one of those who inspire him in concretely locating the universal openness and universal invitation of the gospel message in contemporary times in the context of aching structural poverty. See Schillebeeckx, 'The Religious and the Human Ecumene', pp. 260–61 and 264.
[25] Schillebeeckx, 'Documentation: Religion and Violence', p. 135.

Schillebeeckx. Like Pieris, Schilebeeckx believes that the preferential place of encounter with God is found in the countenance of the suffering person, the place of 'Jesus crucified'[26] and that God's name 'may not therefore be used to justify our existing economic system which exploits men and women structurally. Christians need to use the name of God only where it belongs: in solidarity with the victims of our economic situation ...'[27] For Schillebeeckx the proper self-definition of the Church, particularly in terms of its universality,[28] lies in the measure with which it chooses the side of the poor and those deprived of their rights, for this is not only a given from the very inception of Christianity (Jesus as the defender of the poor) but a contextual charge to be achieved historically.[29]

4. 'No Girls Allowed'? Women and Interreligious Dialogue[30]

In his book *Sunset in the East?* Felix Wilfred laments how interreligious dialogue 'has, by and large, remained a pursuit of an elite group and has confined itself to structured forms'.[31] I would like to add to this lament the fact that women and their concerns have significantly been absent in

[26] Schillebeeckx, 'The Uniqueness of Christ and the Interreligious Dialogue', A lecture delivered on April 22, 1997 at the Catholic Academy in Munich, Bavaria, unpublished manuscript, p. 24.

[27] Schillebeeckx, *Church*, p. 185. Moreover, Schillebeeckx maintains that the affirmation or repudiation of the other in his or her situation of otherness and as an alien is decisive for the salvation of the Jew, the Christian, the humanist or whomever. Schillebeeckx, 'Documentation: Religion and Violence', p. 140.

[28] For Schillebeeckx the poor have universal right and Christianity is only universal if Christians are concerned to reach all of humanity in its being lacerated into 'poor' and 'non-poor'. Suffering humanity is *the* chosen people of God in the eyes of Schillebeeckx (italics in text). See Schillebeeckx, 'The Religious and the Human Ecumene', p. 263.

[29] For Schillebeeckx, indeed, 'outside the world, there is no salvation' (*extra mundum nulla salus*) for before one can speak historically of religions, there was the reality of God's saving activity in profane history. Today this saving activity of God and, consequently, God's revelation takes place in the context of the 'negative contrast experiences' and the praxis that emerges from these experiences, notably the preferential option for the poor. See Schillebeeckx, 'The Religious and the Human Ecumene', pp. 253–54 and *Church*, pp. 5–7.

[30] Schillebeeckx does not explicitly touch on the gender issue, particularly in relation to interreligious dialogue, but some of his writings offer a glimpse of a gender-inclusive perspective. In his discussion on the claim on the uniqueness of Christ, for example, he raises the question whether this claim discriminates against other religions or whether it bears a message that is liberating for *all men and women* (emphasis mine). See Schillebeeckx, 'Documentation: Religion and Violence', p. 137.

[31] Felix Wilfred, *Sunset in the East?* (Madras: SIGA, 1991) p. 221.

'official' interreligious engagements. Maura O'Neill in *Mending a Torn World: Women and Interreligious Dialogue* contends that this is one serious deficiency in contemporary interreligious dialogue[32] since some of the critical problems within and across world religions have to do with women, e.g. gender discrimination.[33] Anne Davison also argues that women and gender issues need to take an important place in interreligious engagements because 'the issues of women, their social and religious roles, the perception of women's sexuality and bodily functions, the question of women's human rights are in themselves divisive issues'.[34] When one indeed factors in the reality that women and girls are, more often than men, at the receiving end of religious violence, the palpable absence of women at the table of dialogue or the lack of attention to gender issues in official inter-religious dialogue is a serious concern.

Christian feminist theologians working on interreligious dialogue argue that one can discern parallels between the Church's treatment of women and the Church's treatment of religions other than Christianity.[35] Marjorie Hewitt Suchocki sheds light on these parallels in 'In Search of Justice: Religious Pluralism from a Feminist Perspective'. Suchocki maintains that absolutizing one religion, such that it becomes normative for all others, is a dynamic with clear parallels to sexism, whereby one gender is established as the norm for human existence. Suchocki points out:

---

[32] O'Neill specifically points to her experience in the 1999 meeting of the Parliament of World Religions where some members even met to discuss the noticeable dearth of women's voices. In the succeeding meeting in 2004 the group formally reported the absence of the full range of women's voices that would have balanced the parliament's dialogue. See Maura O'Neill, *Mending a Torn World: Women and Interreligious Dialogue* (New York, NY: Orbis, 2007) pp. 5–6.

[33] Moreover, O'Neill advances the participation of women from different schools of thought, which she thinks, are at work among religious feminists. These include the conservatives or traditionalists, the centrists, and the progressives. By religious feminism O'Neill is referring specifically to those women who continue to have faith in their religious tradition and would exclude those who have already given up on it in favour of a secular approach to the problem of sexism. See O'Neill, *Mending a Torn World*, pp. 14–16.

[34] Anne Davison, 'Learning to Live in a Europe of Many Religions: A Curriculum for Interfaith Learning for Women', World Council of Churches (2000), http://www.wcc-coe.org/wcc/what/interreligious/cd35–18html (accessed on September 3, 2005), as quoted in O'Neill, *Mending a Torn World*, p. 6.

[35] Rosemary Radford Ruether, for example, has attempted to link the discussion on feminism with questions of Jewish-Christian dialogue around the theme of universalism and particularism. See Rosemary Radford Ruether, 'Feminism and Jewish-Christian Dialogue: Particularism and Universalism in the Search for Religious Truth', *The Myth of Christian Uniqueness: Toward a Pluralistic Theology of Religions* (ed. John Hick and Paul Knitter; Maryknoll, NY: Orbis, 1987), pp. 137–48.

Just as the norm of masculinity is applied to women regardless of women's protestations that their own experience of humanity is sufficient to generate their own norms, even so Christian norms are projected uncritically upon non-Christian religions. Such inclusivist stances toward other religions violate their integrity.[36]

But what makes women's participation in interreligious dialogue important aside from the abovementioned reasons? What can women concretely bring to the table for dialogue? Diane D' Souza[37] claims that one strength that women could bring is their tendency to operate from a worldview where personal relationships are central. D' Souza maintains that women, in meeting and conversing, form relationships on a more personal level than could be found in so-called 'objective' dialogue.[38] D' Souza writes that women *take time* to be with other women and to know one another as persons in a holistic way, not merely as bearers of a particular faith or ideology.

5. The Incomprehensible Mystery, Ever Greater, Ever Nearer: A Conclusion

Evidently, Christian theologies of religions have come a long way. However, there are still areas that need (re)consideration. First, any mention or talk about God will inevitably be from a religious lens and most likely, a particular religious lens. This could continue to pose problems in achieving clearer and more effective dialogue. For instance, what about religions like Buddhism which does not use the term 'God' as the Christian tradition has understood it? Moreover, the word 'God' is overwhelmingly tied with Christianity. In fact the word 'God' has often been understood by ordinary Christians to refer to the *Christian* God and has been used by Christians themselves to engage in exclusionary practices. Eck illustrates this following point:

When Muslims in Edmond, the suburb of Oklahoma City where the University Central of Oklahoma is located, planned to build a mosque

---

[36] Marjorie Hewitt Suchocki, 'In Search of Justice: Religious Pluralism from a Feminist Perspective', *The Myth of Christian Uniqueness: Toward a Pluralistic Theology of Religions* (ed. John Hick and Paul Knitter; Maryknoll, NY: Orbis, 1987), pp. 149–61 (153).

[37] See Diane D' Souza, 'Inter-faith Dialogue: New Insights from Women's Perspectives', *Ecclesia of Women in Asia: Gathering the Voices of the Silenced* (ed. Evelyn Monteiro and Antoinette Gutzler; Delhi: ISPCK, 2005), pp. 441–45 for more details on the project.

[38] D' Souza, 'Inter-faith Dialogue', p. 442.

in 1992, a move was made to deny a building permit because, as a Pluralism Project researcher reported, 'One of the minister's wives [sic] attended the first public hearing and vehemently opposed it. She said, "The constitution says One nation under God, and that's a Christian God. These people have no right to be here."'[39]

Indeed, we might still have to ask the questions 'Which God?' and 'Whose God?' which Jacques Dupuis asks in *Christianity and the Religions: From Confrontation to Dialogue.*[40] Then there is the problem of gender. The religions have to recognize the seriousness of gender issues that continue to plague them as well as acknowledge the critical role women (can) play in actual interreligious engagements. Last but not the least is the thorny question of whether religious pluralism exists *de facto*, meaning just a fact of the world today that is meant to be overcome, or *de jure* meaning it is a good intended by God in principle.

Clearly there remains a host of problems. As a concluding remark let me offer two possible ways in which some of these problems can be addressed. One way is Elizabeth Johnson's suggestion to think of God as 'the generous God of the religions' whereby the presence of other religions challenges us to realize that the divine design for the salvation of the world is multi-faceted. In Johnson's words:

Assuming that the real presence of grace and truth can only have divine origin, the religions can be seen as God's handiwork. In them we catch a first glimpse of the overflowing generosity of the living God who has left no people abandoned but has bestowed divine love on every culture. This is the grace of our age: encountering multiple

---

[39] Eck, *A New Religious America*, p. 309.
[40] These questions include: (1) Is it legitimate to think, from the standpoint of a Christian theology, that the Ultimate Reality to which those other religious traditions refer is, in spite of their vastly different mental constructs, the same which the monotheistic religions affirm as the God of Abraham, Isaac, and Jacob?; (2) Is there an 'Ultimate Reality' common to all religious traditions, even if it is differently experienced and variously conceptualized by the various traditions? One Divine Mystery with many faces?; (3) And, if such is the case, can this 'Ultimate Reality' be interpreted in terms of Christian Trinitarian theism, no matter how imperfectly apprehended? Or is it to be viewed as equally distant from all categories, theistic or otherwise?; (4) In this broad variety of standpoints, can there be a reduction *ad unum* in favor of a Christian Trinitarian theism? Is it theologically justified and practicable?; (5) If we speak of a universal hidden presence of the God of Jesus Christ in the 'Ultimate Reality' appealed to by the other traditions, do we not unduly 'absolutize' a particular 'referent' as the only possible hermeneutical key to any religious experience whatsoever?; 6) And can any evidence be put forward to substantiate such a Christian interpretation? See Jacques Dupuis, *Christianity and the Religions: From Confrontation to Dialogue* (New York, NY: Orbis, 2001) pp. 117–18.

religious traditions widens the horizon wherein we catch sight of God's loving plenitude. Thus we are enabled to approach the mystery ever more deeply.[41]

In Johnson's eyes, interreligious dialogue indeed opens broad and deep vistas onto God's unspeakable generosity to the human race. She does refer to Jesus Christ as one in whom this design reaches its highest historical density with significance for all, but she also makes it a point to say that the eternal Word of God is neither constrained, exhausted, nor completely used up in this one particular history, nor is the Spirit of God thereby limited in her outpouring into the world.[42] She asserts that the religions' positive wisdom and grace, brought about by the Spirit of God, make religious pluralism a divine gift.

Schillebeeckx, for his part, says that:

The multiplicity of religions is not just a historical fact that must be transcended, but a matter of principle. There are authentic religious experiences in other religions which are never realized or thematized in Christianity and, I added, perhaps cannot be without robbing Jesus' identification with God of its distinctiveness.[43]

Schillebeeckx also offers an interesting and more direct take on the significance of the role of the Spirit. He contends that 'the actual historical violence of Christianity and its Christology has its deepest roots in our continual and constant forgetfulness of pneumatology' and that 'only pneumatology can prevent christology from being violent ... for in [the Spirit] the redemption of Jesus becomes a historical and universal offer without any discrimination or virtual violence'.[44] The Logos of the pneuma blows where it wills, so to speak.

Another way which could also address the question of gender, and maybe even differing positions, in approaching the challenge of religious plurality is what Jeanine Hill Fletcher points to in *Monopoly of Salvation?*

---

[41] Elizabeth A. Johnson, *Quest for the Living God: Mapping Frontiers in the Theology of God* (New York, NY: Continuum, 2008) p. 163.

[42] Johnson, *Quest for the Living God*, pp. 174–75.

[43] Schillebeeckx, *Church*, p. 179. Schillebeeckx offers a more comprehensive and nuanced take on the highly contentious matter of the Christian claim to the uniqueness and universality of Jesus. He posits that, by virtue of his historical particularity, the person of Jesus is a relative personal manifestation of God who is absolute. He argues that absolutizing the historical humanity of Jesus of Nazareth contradicts the Christian belief in creation: God as transcendent is in no respect whatsoever an element in an earthly system or a human social and political order, nor is God the 'ingredient' of a religion. See Schillebeeckx, 'The Uniqueness of Christ and the Interreligious Dialogue', p. 16 and Schillebeeckx, 'Documentation: Religion and Violence', p. 137 respectively.

[44] Schillebeeckx, 'Documentation: Religion and Violence', p. 142.

A Feminist Approach to Religious Pluralism, arguing that we should engage in a dialogue that takes into account people's hybrid identities. Hill Fletcher argues that human beings, in all their manifold dimensions of identity and particularity, are themselves the self-communication of God.[45] In a sense, she submits that it is both our own as well as the other's hybrid identities – comprising of religion, class, gender, etc. – that allow, challenge, and give us several ways or possibilities to engage the religious other without erasing his/her (religious) particularity in the process. Let us look, for example, at the Asian bishops' approach to dialogue. First, the Asian bishops regard dialogue itself as a way of being-church, particularly in Asia.[46] Secondly, as a form of dialogue that engages the Asian religions (interreligious dialogue) in conjunction with the dialogue with Asian cultures (inculturation), and Asian poverty (integral liberation), their concept of triple dialogue arguably addresses the two hallmarks of Asian identity, i.e. poverty and cultural diversity, both of which coexist with the religious plurality that has marked the continent for centuries. It is clear for the Asian bishops that engaging these other facets of the Asian context offers not just glimpses of the incomprehensible mystery but also provides ways of making possible not just a Church *in* Asia but also a Church (that is truly) *of* Asia. They know that for many Asian Christians to be religious is to be interreligious. As Indian Jesuit theologian Sebastian Painadath affirms:

> When believers of various religions work together to bring about integral human liberation ... they discover the creative and redemptive forces in each religion and articulate the liberative and unifying potential of each religion. ... Concern for the poor, therefore, is the

---

[45] Hill Fletcher posits that while we may not have the same religious affiliation with our neighbour we might share other features which could serve as points of connection for conversation. The conversation partners could either be of the same gender, race, ethnicity, political ideology, or simply share a passion for justice. Hill Fletcher says that in the process of finding and engaging these commonalities we might have the opportunity to glimpse the incomprehensible mystery as it is seen through the other's eyes. See Jeanine Hill Fletcher, *Monopoly on Salvation? A Feminist Approach to Religious Pluralism* (New York, NY: Continuum, 2005) p. 134. See also Jeanine Hill Fletcher, 'Religious Pluralism in an Era of Globalization: The Making of Modern Religious Identity', *Theological Studies* 69 (2008), pp. 394–411 for more on Hill Fletcher's thesis on hybridity as a heuristic lens for theologically making sense of religious plurality.

[46] See Thomas C. Fox, *Pentecost in Asia: A New Way of Being Church* (New York, NY: Orbis, 2002) for elaboration on the triple dialogue. The four volumes of the documents of the Federation of Asian Bishops' Conferences, *For All the Peoples of Asia* (Quezon City: Claretian Publications, 1997/1997/2002/2007) also give ample evidence of how the Asian bishops conceive of this triple dialogue.

meeting point of religions; compassion is the hallmark of a religious person.[47]

With probable exception regarding issues over gender, Schillebeeckx nonetheless gathers the principles that are most constitutive of the theological positions presented in this paper, which are encapsulated in the following statement:

> The ecumene of world religions cannot be called peace among religions if one tones down the religious accents of the particular, diverging religions in favour of an abstract and also eclectic universality which joins all religions together and in so doing in fact becomes unreal. Anyone who, for example, seeks to make Christianity a mystical religion from which at least all the liberating accents of Jesus' distinctive image of God have disappeared – and that implies the partisan choice for the poor and oppressed – damages the originality of Christianity.[48]

Clearly there is a consensus among Christian theologians, Schillebeeckx included, that interreligious dialogue is an imperative, especially in an increasingly diverse, unjust, and violent world. In doing so we not only get a glimpse of an image of God that is before us and among us but also a sense of the incomprehensible mystery as ever greater, ever nearer.

---

[47] See Sebastian Painadath, 'Federation of Asian Bishops' Conferences' Theology of Dialogue', *Dialogue? A Resource Manual for Catholics in Asia* (ed. Edmund Chia; Bangkok: Federation of Asian Bishops' Conferences, 2001), pp. 102–05 (102). In Paul Knitter, 'Toward a Liberation Theology of Religions', *The Myth of Christian Uniqueness: Toward a Pluralistic Theology of Religions* (ed. John Hick and Paul Knitter; New York, NY: Orbis, 1987), pp. 178–200 (186) Knitter also suggests the option for the poor as a possible point of convergence among the religions. He writes:

> Because of its hermeneutical priority and potency, [therefore], the preferential option for the oppressed serves as an effective condition for the possibility of dialogue. ... If the religions of the world, in other words, can recognize poverty and oppression as a common problem, if they can share a common commitment to remove such evils, they will have the basis for reaching across their incommensurabilities and differences in order to hear and understand each other and possibly be transformed in the process.

[48] Schillebeeckx, *Church*, p. 186.

WHICH CHRISTOLOGICAL
TOOLS FOR THE
INTERRELIGIOUS DIALOGUE?

Jean-Louis Souletie

1. *Introduction*

We want to remember first that when Edward Schillebeeckx addresses the
subject of dialogue between religions he does not envision the divine absolu-
tization of historical particularity. On the contrary, Christian revelation in
Jesus of Nazareth is rather the index that forbids us from absolutizing
historical particularity in Christianity. Men and women thus encounter
God outside of Jesus in history.[1] God may be absolute, however, no religion,
not even Christianity, is absolute. Yet, against all forms of Docetism,
Schillebeeckx follows Col. 2.9 and claims that the fullness of deity dwells
in the human contingency of Jesus. It is he, therefore, who saves humanity
and not his majestic titles, as Schillebeeckx explains in accordance with the
Sri Lankan theologian Aloysius Pieris.

According to Schillebeeckx, when Christians proclaim that Jesus is
the saviour this implies that they have started bearing the fruits of the
Kingdom he announced. The historical path of Jesus is the *via crucis*;
this is the unicity of Jesus. Its conclusive force is that Christians must be
'completing what is lacking in Christ's afflictions' (Col. 1.24). The universality of salvation is not merely an idea, but rather the concrete expression
of what has happened in Jesus Christ and Lord through Christian praxis in
the fragmented structures of history. Universality is only achieved through
the spread of what happened as liberating praxis in and thanks to Jesus.
Thus, for Schillebeeckx, orthodoxy is accomplished through orthopraxy.
Yet, this is precisely the argument that Christology must confront in interreligious dialogue. Are the words and actions of Jesus, which constitute

---

[1] Edward Schillebeeckx, *Church: The Human Story of God* (trans. John Bowden;
London: SCM, 1990) pp. 165–66.

the Gospel of salvation, embodied in today's practice of interreligious dialogue? Or, is this dialogue compelled towards an inclusivism that hurts the non-Christian interlocutor? How is it possible to affirm and explain that in and thanks to Jesus, salvation is accomplished in other religions (*Gaudium et Spes* 22 no. 25) without discriminating against these other religions? Jacques Dupuis has sought to answer this question by making use of Chalcedonian Christology. In this contribution, I investigate whether Dupuis' Christological thesis offers a way to continue, in the context of interreligious dialogue, Schillebeeckx's fundamental intuition that orthodoxy is necessarily accomplished through orthopraxy.

2. Dupuis' Christological Thesis

Dupuis' argument in favour of Trinitarian Christology as an interpretative key unveils the mystery of the unicity and universality of Jesus Christ and the universal salvation of humanity. However, his work seems to initiate a dilemma between the constitutive value of Jesus Christ for the salvation of humanity and the salvific impact of the paths of salvation which other religions offer to their followers. Dupuis thus outlines his remarks:

> The three elements which are to be combined with each other are: 1) the permanent actuality and universal effectiveness of the Jesus Christ-event, despite the historical particularity of that event; 2) the universal active presence of God's Word whose activity is not limited to the human existence which It has assumed in the mystery of the incarnation; 3) the activity of the Spirit which is equally universal throughout the world and which is not limited nor exhausted by its descent through the risen and glorified Christ.[2]

Dupuis uses the Prologue to the Gospel of John as the starting point for his reflection. The Prologue may be interpreted as an account of universal saving action, not only of the *Logos* before the Incarnation, but also of the *Logos* as such after the Incarnation and the Resurrection. To develop this point, Dupuis refers to exegetical studies of the Prologue, and in particular of Jn 1.9, 'The true light, which enlightens everyone, was coming into the world'. Indeed, Dupuis emphasizes this by referring to the work of Xavier Léon-Dufour[3]:

---

[2] Jacques Dupuis, 'Le Verbe de Dieu, Jésus Christ et les religions du monde', *Nouvelle revue théologique* 123/4 (2001), pp. 529–46 (529). See also: Jacques Dupuis, *Toward a Christian Theology of Religious Pluralism* (Maryknoll, NY: Orbis, 1997) pp. 195–98.

[3] Xavier Léon-Dufour, *Lecture de l'Evangile selon Saint Jean* (vol. 1; Paris: Seuil, 1988) pp. 62–144.

The *Logos* has been active since the beginning of creation (v. 2–5), as the principle of life and light, establishing a personal relationship between God and human beings: 'coming into the world', … [The *Logos*] is the source of light for all humans, and to those who have welcomed It, It has given the 'power to become children of God' (v. 9.12). … If it is true that the *Logos* is God who communicates himself, the communication did not begin with the incarnation, but rather with creation, and has been continued throughout the entire history of revelation … Even so, meanwhile [i.e., since the incarnation], revelation is also and in particular concentrated in he who will be called by his name: Jesus Christ (1,17).[4]

According to Dupuis, the universal action of the Word in the world continues to enlighten all men and women. Through this enlightenment, men and women are educated and liberated, transfigured and sanctified, but also judged. Dupuis affirms, moreover, the possibility of salvation for all human beings who have not known the Word Incarnate, either before or after the Incarnation, by citing the knowledge they have had of the non-Incarnate Word (the Word as such). He therefore supports Yves Raguin's position based on Jn 1.9:

Those who won't have known the Father through the incarnated Word will be able to know Him in his non-incarnated Word. In this way, all human beings can know the Word of God, without knowing It in its incarnation. … We read in the Prologue to the Gospel of John that the Word of God is the life of everything and that this life becomes the light of all men and women. Well then, every human being can have this experience, in him- or herself, of life having become light, and in this way every person can enter into the intimacy of the Father, through union with the Word. This is why the larger part of humankind can enter in relation with God, source of all life and all love, through the mediation of the Word, without having encountered Jesus and without having known him.[5]

---

[4] Dupuis, 'Le Verbe de Dieu, Jésus Christ et les religions du monde', p. 534. In a similar vein, Jacques Dupont writes the following in his *Essais sur la christologie de Saint Jean: Le Christ, Parole, Lumière et Vie, la Gloire du Christ* (Bruges: Editions de l'Abbaye de Saint-André, 1951) p. 48:

> By using this term (*Logos*), the apostle does not want to say who Christ is in himself, but indicates that Christ's action in the world has not begun with his earthly life: his action is at the basis of the world, at the origin of all other things. John identifies Christ with the Word of God *ad extra*, with the creative Word with which God addresses the world, not to tell us who the person of Jesus is, but to show us how far his action extends in the universe.

[5] Yves Raguin, *Un message de salut pour tous* (Vie chrétienne: Supplément, 406; Paris: Vie chrétienne, 1996) p. 31.

Dupuis uses this exegetical study to consider how the continual illumination and life-giving action of the Word can be manifest in a world of religious pluralism. The Word as such 'correlates' with the 'focus' of divine salvation in the Word Incarnate Jesus Christ and the permanent relevance of the historical event through his resurrection. Dupuis thus maintains that 'The incarnation marks ... "the unsurpassed – and unsurpassable – profundity of God's self-communication to human beings; the supreme mode of immanence of his being-with-them", in fact, the "key of interpretation" of the entire process of self-commitment of God with human beings throughout history.'[6]

3. *Chalcedonian Dogma as a Tool*

Dupuis firmly establishes his position on the Christological dogma of two natures, divine and human, united in Jesus Christ. The author maintains the complementarity of the two natures, according to the terms of the Council of Chalcedon, 'without division, without separation', and 'without confusion or change', which entails that, although they are 'hypostatically united', the two natures remain nevertheless 'distinct'. Dupuis warns against the dangers of monophysitism (absorbing the authentic human nature of Christ into the divine nature). At present, this tendency continues to threaten, but in reverse, when it is assumed that the human nature absorbs the divinity of Christ, thus reducing the divine nature to the human measure. In this case, while the human nature of Jesus is united to the Word of God, the divine attributes of the person of the Word are lost, or at least somewhat diminished to the scale of human nature (as suggested by so-called 'kenotic' theories).[7] Chalcedonian dogma, in contrast, states, 'that the divine nature, just like the human nature, remains distinct and intact in the union of the two natures; and that, consequently, it is not possible to speak of either a diminution of divinity that would reduce the divine nature to the human measure or an absorption of the human by the divine'.[8] Given this, the two

---

[6] Dupuis, 'Le Verbe de Dieu, Jésus Christ et les religions du monde', p. 536. See also: Dupuis, *Toward a Christian Theology of Religious Pluralism*, pp. 320–21 and Jacques Dupuis, *Who Do You Say I Am? Introduction to Christology* (Maryknoll, NY: Orbis, 1994) pp. 144–48.

[7] Cf. Dupuis, 'Le Verbe de Dieu, Jésus Christ et les religions du monde', p. 537.

[8] Dupuis, 'Le Verbe de Dieu, Jésus Christ et les religions du monde', p. 537. The proclamation of the Council of Chalcedon, that is: the unity in distinction between two natures, has been taken up by the Third Council of Constantinople in terms of 'wills' and 'operations' ('two natural wills and two natural operations without division, without change, without separation and without confusion'). See for this: Gervais Dumeige (ed. and trans.), *Textes doctrinaux du Magistère de l'Eglise sur la foi catholique* (Paris: Editions de l'Orante, 1975) pp. 203–04.

natures remain distinct from one another without being separated. This means that the human action of Jesus is actually the work of the Word, and the divine work of the Word remains, nevertheless, distinct from his human action.

4. *Criticism of Dupuis*

One of the critics of Dupuis' thesis, Henry Donneaud, disagrees with the former's interpretation of the Chalcedonian dogma, calling it a 'hijacking [of] Chalcedon'. By such critique, Donneaud seeks to demonstrate that Dupuis interprets the doctrine to suit his own purpose, and that a hurried reader might not notice this:

> The author [i.e. Dupuis] illicitly mixes the distinction between the two natures of the incarnated Word – and the concrete actions which ensue from them – with the distinction of two concrete salvific activities: the one of the Word as such and the one of Jesus Christ. When the Chalcedonian dogma scrupulously maintains the distinction between the divine and the human nature, between the will and the activity that is appropriate to each of them, it is not to provide with two ways of salvation or two distinct salvific operations, the one of the Word as such and the one of Jesus, but with one unique concrete salvific activity which is performed by the divine nature of the Word through the instrumental mediation of Jesus' humanity.[9]

In response to Donneaud, Dupuis states that in their struggle against Nestorius and monophysitism, the Chalcedonian Fathers did not consider the existence of two complementary paths of salvation, one through Christ and the other through the non-Incarnate Word. And in turn, Donneaud replies that:

> To safeguard the distinction between the divine and the human, and to avoid that the divinity of the Word found itself changed by the suffering of the flesh, Nestorius contested the personal unity of the incarnated Word. The author [i.e. Dupuis], to preserve the distinction between the human and the divine activity, does he not end up by setting aside the concrete and singular unity of the work of salvation brought about for the good of all human beings by God and his incarnated Son, once and for all?[10]

[9] Henry Donneaud, 'Chalcédoine contre l'unicité absolue du Médiateur Jésus-Christ? Autour d'un article récent', *Revue thomiste* 102/1 (2002), pp. 43–62 (46).
[10] Donneaud, 'Chalcédoine contre l'unicité absolue du Médiateur Jésus-Christ?', p. 49. For comments on this statement, see: Dupuis, 'Le Verbe de Dieu, Jésus Christ et les religions du monde', pp. 533, 536–37 and 544.

Dupuis refutes this opinion and reaffirms his own position:

> As new and unexpected as it may seem, [the "illuminating" and 'life-giving' power of the Word of God, of which the Prologue to the Gospel of John speaks] affirms nothing more than that the Word of God, while becoming human, nevertheless remains in any case God; or to put it differently, that God remains God in becoming human. And if the Word remains God, It likewise continues to act in the capacity of God, beyond its own human action.[11]

Dupuis upholds his thesis of complementary paths of salvation by often using verbs such as: 'to exhaust', 'to restrict', 'to limit' and 'to circumscribe', and this in order to express that the incarnation neither exhausts nor restricts the action of the divine *Logos*. This is to say that, theoretically, he does reserve for the *Logos* the possibility of action beyond the humanity of Jesus Christ and his mediation. To which Donneaud responds:

> To be sure, from a theoretical point of view, who would dare to contest the legitimacy of an axiom such as: God is God and remains God? No one should deny God the power to act where he wants, when he wants, how he wants, beyond each spatio-temporal limit, including the one set by the historical particularity of Jesus Christ. This is moreover the unanimous answer given by theologians, at least since Augustine, to the question: Could God have saved humankind in another way than through mediation of the redemptive incarnation of the son-Word? Already the dogma of the almightiness of the divine is enough in forcing one to answer this question affirmatively.[12]

Thus, the universal mediation of salvation is achieved by and in Jesus Christ, the 'human face of God', 'a man himself', 'born of a woman', and at the same time the beloved Son of the Father: 'For if the many died through the one man's trespass, much more surely have the grace of God and the free gift in the grace of the one man, Jesus Christ, abounded for the many' (Rom. 5.15). Concerning the universal saving mediation of Christ, Claude Geffré prefers another response. 'As for myself,' Geffré writes, 'I am talking about *derivative mediations*. It is not a matter of paths which would be in competition with Christ's mediation. The[other] religions are only salvific insofar as they participate, in a mysterious way, in the mediating activity of Christ in the midst of history.'[13]

---

[11] Dupuis, 'Le Verbe de Dieu, Jésus Christ et les religions du monde', pp. 538–39.

[12] Donneaud, 'Chalcédoine contre l'unicité absolue du Médiateur Jésus-Christ?', p. 51.

[13] Claude Geffré, *Croire et interpréter: Le tournant herméneutique de la théologie* (Paris: Cerf, 2001) pp. 128–29. See: Donneaud, 'Chalcédoine contre l'unicité absolue du Médiateur Jésus-Christ?', pp. 54–55.

5. Joseph Doré's Suggestion

Dupuis' criticism has led to a rethinking of Christology and its relation to other religions in a way that – given the present aims and limits of my focus – can only lead to a suggestion. Namely, it would be necessary to explain that the unicity of the mediating lordship of salvation in Jesus Christ has been inscribed in human history as the forerunner of the final eschatological victory. According to an author like Joseph Doré, Christology would in this way acquire more credibility and intelligibility regarding the 'corporeal, tangible and social' aspects of revelation as understood by Karl Rahner.[14] It means being able to account for revelation in Jesus Christ as 'God's communication to man in grace and at the same time its categorical self-interpretation in the corporeal, tangible and social dimension'.[15] To sum up the article Doré published in the journal *Chemins de dialogue*, let us underline the key to his thought by saying that, strictly speaking, in Jesus Christ, God himself has come into history and has *really* come; that he has revealed himself and has *really* revealed himself; that he has completely and definitively communicated himself; and that it is in this way, emphasizing 'in this way', that he has opened for human beings the possibility of salvation. Well then, it is necessary to see and to say that this is only realized where it is realized in this way; and where it is in fact realized, it is realized once and for all. Yet, according to Doré, while Christ is the sole mediator of salvation for humanity, this salvation is first of all born by the Holy Spirit. This steers his theology towards a Trinitarian reflection. The Spirit brings to fulfilment that which had already started to bloom through its power in the means that other religions offer to their followers. Doré develops the idea of paschal fulfilment to explain the type of renunciation, both on the part of religions, which would thus find fulfilment, and, *mutatis mutandis*, on the part of Christianity which would somehow fulfil them. How can this type of fulfilment theology, already present in Justin Martyr's and continued by Karl Rahner's work, avoid being accused of appropriation or a new type of ecclesiocentrism masked as inclusivism?

To avoid this pitfall, Doré suggests four criteria for developing paschal fulfilment theology. The first criterion is the singularity of Jesus that cannot bear separating the Word and Jesus Christ, according to the principle of Chalcedonian faith recalled in *Redemptoris Missio* no. 6. The second criterion stems from the universality of salvation that Christ brings. It is

---

[14] Our understanding of Rahner's concept of revelation is mainly based on the following: Karl Rahner and Herbert Vorgrimler, 'Revelation', *Theological Dictionary* (ed. Cornelius Ernst; trans. Richard Strachan; New York, NY: Herder and Herder, 3rd edn, 1968), pp. 409–13 and Karl Rahner, *Foundations of Christian Faith: An Introduction to the Idea of Christianity* (trans. W.V. Dych; New York, NY: Crossroad, 1978) pp. 138–75, and in particular pp. 153–75.

[15] Rahner, *Foundations of Christian Faith*, pp. 174–75.

only as this unique man, a first-century Jew, that Jesus is the saviour in an exclusive way because 'No one comes to the Father except through me' (Jn 14.6). Yet, he is the saviour for all. The third criterion concerns Jesus' identity; and the fourth bears upon the unicity of his lordship. From these criteria, it follows that, if Christ Jesus is present and active in other religions, it is through his Spirit in the unicity of his mediation and as an expression of what happened in him, with him, and through him. Christ can indeed impact other religions only insofar as he is bound to the man from Nazareth and his history. On this point, it is impossible to oppose a functional Christology to an ontological Christology. The role Jesus Christ has in other religions is inextricably linked to his identity as both true man and true God, as Christ bound to Jesus and Jesus bound to Christ. The unicity of the fate and role designate Jesus Christ as the unique Lord and Saviour of the world. He is not the saviour without the Spirit which he announced at the Ascension and which was later poured out at Pentecost. Nor is he the Saviour without the Church he has established and the men and women who have been invited to cooperate in the work of salvation that they freely accept from God. Moreover, the unique lordship of Christ is brought about in his self-disclosure, in abandonment and kenosis. The lordship of Christ is also the *nexus mysterium* for the theology of interreligious dialogue.

Christ therefore saves *in* non-Christian religions, but does he save *through* them? This issue is still being researched because Scripture and the magisterial and theological tradition do not provide any perfectly clear answers. As a theologian, Doré formulates two suggestions for further discussion and debate. (1) His first suggestion is to make use of the theory of anonymous Christians with caution, in such a manner that it does not become the theory of anonymous Christianity. This theory, however, should not infer that followers of other religions would have to become members of the visible Church, even anonymously. The distinction between the Church and the Kingdom, which is not a separation, makes followers of other religions participants in the Kingdom Christ establishes, as the Reign of his Father, without belonging to the visible Church. Subordinated to the unique mediation of Christ, the mediation of the Church conforms to that of Christ through the kenosis of the Word, which is as a service of mediation and not annexation or appropriation.

(2) The second suggestion deals with the Trinity and stems from the task of relating Christocentrism and theocentrism. It is through the Spirit that the unique mediation of Christ reaches other religions to put them into relation with God's salvation. Yet, the spirit is always the Spirit of Christ because its outpouring is bound to the coming of the Son into the world. Can the followers of other religions, as participants in salvation *in a way known to God* through the Spirit of Christ, recognize the fruits of the Spirit in their ways of being and living and in their doctrines and rules? What are the means of Christ's action and presence in and through the religions they

practice? Doré wonders whether this would not be conceding too much to other religions. Scripture and Vatican II tradition, however, as well as the 'seeds of the Word'-theology (the *Semina Verbi* of St. Justin Martyr), provide important support for the view that Christ is indeed present *in* and acts *through* the non-Christian religions. Yet, even if this were accepted as a matter of principle, it would still be necessary to verify in detail the exact manner in which these religions would function as fruits of Christ's Spirit and could have a Christic function. Thus on this point, Doré suggests an area to be explored, ideas to be checked, and the coherency of certain aspects to be evaluated. In brief, he suggests that discernment be used at the service of a theology of interreligious dialogue.

6. *A Proposal*

In this perspective, I would like to suggest pursuing the paschal dimension of fulfilment that Doré mentions. Jesus' fate and preaching initiate a crisis that intensifies throughout the Gospel and leads to the passion and death of Jesus. How can it be that this crisis continues to have an impact in our day when the affair ended so catastrophically in Jesus' death? Faith in the Resurrection has been born from Jesus' cruel fate until the present day. Yet, the community of disciples is not purely and simply faithful to its martyr-prophet, who died too soon, by cultivating his memory. The community does not simply proclaim the everlasting value of his message, but rather announces, as does Paul, that he is alive: if Christ has not risen, our faith is in vain (cf. 1 Cor. 15.14).

What is the Word, which is capable of bringing about faith in the Resurrection? Jesus' return to life is, as such, not enough to cause one to believe in his resurrection, as the parable of the evil rich man and the poor man Lazarus shows (Lk. 16.19–31). Since the brothers of the evil rich man do not believe in Moses and the prophets, even someone returning from the dead cannot convince them to change their lifestyle. The counter example is the story of the walk to Emmaus (Lk. 24.13–35). The words spoken on the way warm the disciples' hearts and open their eyes to see the Resurrection in the breaking of bread.

The cross causes us to wonder whether or not the love that Jesus lives and preaches is an illusion. The Resurrection enables us to face the crisis of love. Jesus sums up all of his preaching in the double commandment of the Old Testament, to love God and neighbour. The pious men who condemned him saw in his behaviour and preaching a blasphemy which was punishable by death. Furthermore, he was abandoned by God and his own people. Who will do him justice? For him, as for us, it is clearly true that our good works do not make us worthy of God's love. One can only hold to that view if one understands the cross in terms of rewards or '*do ut des*' exchanges. Indeed, he who has not sinned dies as a sinner and a criminal, one abandoned by God. His claim to act in the name of the Father is belied by his death (cf. the 'Let God deliver him now, if he wants to' which is uttered by the onlookers in Mt. 27.43).

However, there is something luminous and pacifying in the love that endures without worry in the Cross of the Crucified One as revealed in the Gospel of Easter. This is what the first witnesses of salvation, the good thief (Lk. 23.39–45) and the centurion (Mk. 15.39) perceive. We are invited to place ourselves where these two men are, or where the angel is, on Easter morning, to hear the resurrected Word. That morning, the angel proclaims an impossible reality to the women who came to the tomb during the night; a reality which frightens them into silence (Mk 16.1–8). The truth of the message only appears to us when we face the cross and accept what is done there without worrying about compensation or performance, but rather abandon ourselves to the event like the good thief. To enter into the paschal mystery of our salvation means to love, not from duty or self-righteousness or as a goal to be pursued, but, rather, in place of these, to enter into the gaze of God, who sees Jesus crucified as his Son, whom He has showered with all of his love ...

The Gospel of love is neither an overpowering, condescending message nor a superhuman feat of accomplishment (i.e. a performance). We are free of this, as the apostle Paul says. The call of the Gospel, 'Be perfect, therefore, as your heavenly Father is perfect' (Mt. 5.48), can now be heard, but not as an endless quest for one's self (this is sinful). Men and women are freed from feeling anxious about having to fulfil the law with the feeble means at their disposal for meeting their obligations to God (cf. Paul's letter to the Romans). God invites us to be in relation with Him, in a relation without measure, where all is grace, and where the commandment to love our neighbour is understood as being made possible through the love of God which is then the source of human existence.

All religions seem to me to be called to verify how they propose to accomplish their fundamental purpose in history. Orthodoxy is verified in orthopraxis, and vice versa. What are the resources of their doctrines and praxis that could help them fulfil that final goal? And is this not, more or less, some form of salvation (in the Christian sense)? Christianity makes love the dynamic of salvation in Jesus Christ. Love that is, not as a theme or as a mysticism of feeling, but as understood in the way Meister Eckhart does, who says that the soul must be in a 'free nothing' ('*libre néant*'). This means that for the soul it is more essential to lose God than it is to lose the creature – when the soul no longer seeks God, no longer makes of Him an object or theme, it dies the highest possible death, it dies of itself to be born to its true liberty.[16] Angelus Silesius similarly speaks of

---

[16] Meister Eckhart, *Traités et sermons* (trans. F.A. and J.M.; intr. M. de Gandillac; Philosophie de l'esprit; Paris: Aubier, 1942) pp. 248 and 250.

access to God as an impossible possibility for those who come to love and want nothing. Salvation, in Christianity, is thus understood as the dynamic of love which enables the meeting of those who do not understand one another. Their mutual strangeness is not insurmountable, but it cannot be diminished or reduced to what is already familiar. Living in contact with another religion exposes us to 'not knowing', while challenging us to decipher their grammar of living. Even if there is some familiarity (shared language and cultural experience) between us, this does not erase the distance that separates us and the misunderstandings that constantly emerge. But even when the distance cannot be completely overcome and when misunderstandings cannot be entirely ruled out, other religions do nevertheless deepen and change the Christian self-understanding. They provoke Christians to a deeper awareness of the nature of their own faith, discovering that their own faith challenges them to encounter the other. God is relation and self-communication. But in the relationship of God to humankind, the incarnation unfolds itself as kenosis. This suggests that, for Christians, the encounter with another religion can only be done in the movement of divine kenosis. According to the Pauline doctrine of justification, to love no longer becomes a goal or a performance. Losing God in Eckhart's sense means to no longer take God's place in speaking of God, to no longer take love's place in speaking of love. Such a path *is* the *via crucis*, for the human will resists such a loss of place. Yet despite even the best of intentions, this desire for such a place quickly transforms our desire to share the Gospel into a form of propaganda. Who will save these best of intentions from attitudes which inevitably discriminate against other religions? To this dilemma the Gospel responds: love, as lived by Jesus and as understood by Paul. Such a love as compelled Paul to revisit Judaism, a faith that first impelled him to persecute Christians, before going on to revise Christianity, as it was understood in Jerusalem, in order to open it up for its encounter with pagans.

PART IV
'DEUS HUMANISSIMUS':
SUFFERING AND EXPERIENCES
OF NEGATIVE CONTRAST

SUFFERING, RESISTANCE, AND HOPE: WOMEN'S EXPERIENCE OF NEGATIVE CONTRAST AND CHRISTOLOGY

Kathleen McManus, OP

The global suffering of women in poverty, and the spiritual suffering of women in the Church together pose critical challenges for Christology in the 21st century. Understood and articulated through the lens of an eco-feminist epistemology, these two broad forms of women's suffering will be examined dialectically against the informing backdrop of the theology of Edward Schillebeeckx. Schillebeeckx's insistence on Jesus' constitutive relation to the coming of God's rule will be considered in conversation with the multiple starting points of global ecofeminisms and a first world 'feminist mystical theology'. The category of negative contrast experience will be engaged in relation to what Beverly Lanzetta has called the *via feminina*[1] in an effort to seek out the feminine Body of Christ hidden in the tradition so that it may be enfleshed in the present.

1. Suffering, Experience, and Knowing

a. *A Common Phenomenological Method*

a. 1. *Edward Schillebeeckx: Epistemology of Concrete Experience*

Schillebeeckx's early philosophical and theological formation resulted in a blend of phenomenological method and incarnational, creation-centered Thomism that has consistently grounded his theological project in an

---

[1] Beverly J. Lanzetta, *Radical Wisdom: A Feminist Mystical Theology* (Minneapolis, MN: Fortress, 2005).

111

epistemology of concrete experience. His particular concern for Christian experience in the world has always been focused by the pervasive reality of suffering, giving rise to the primacy of praxis that marks his methodology. For Schillebeeckx, there is a divine mystery at the heart of human experience that never can adequately be grasped by conceptual language. The revelation of God in human experience is particularly focused and interpreted through the lenses of the Christian tradition, although Schillebeeckx has expressed increasing concern for those outside of or marginalized by the Church.[2] Indeed, as we contemplate the challenges for theology in the twenty-first century, those on the edges of the Church, especially women, pose a critical claim for our attention.

a. 2. *Schillebeeckx and Ecofeminist Epistemology*

In his writings on eschatology, Schillebeeckx increasingly interchanges the term 'Promise' for the 'Mystery' that is the reality of God presenting itself to us in experience.[3] In the face of human suffering, 'Promise' acknowledges the profound fissure between the reality of salvation accomplished in Christ and the experience of that salvation by vast populations mired in poverty and afflicted with violence and oppression. Ecofeminist theologians, above all, stand in that fissure in an effort to discern the hidden and silent Promise of salvation in the very depths of human suffering that we now know to be inextricably entwined with the suffering and travail of our earth. Among such ecofeminists, Ivone Gebara of Brazil has reflected on the importance for women of 'knowing our knowing' within the interrelational web of life that is creation. While the ecofeminist epistemology she outlines arises from the same phenomenological method engaged by Edward Schillebeeckx, she takes pains to contrast it with traditional patriarchal ways of knowing, illumining a relational matrix that is, nevertheless, implicit in Schillebeeckx's approach.

According to Ivone Gebara, ecofeminist epistemology is not a 'knowledge to be acquired like a new book'. Rather, 'it is a stance, an attitude, a search for wisdom, a conviction that unfolds in close association with the community of all living beings'.[4] In Latin America, Gebara emphasizes, epistemological issues are practical, related to work among the poor; work on epistemology is work toward changing hierarchical

---

[2] See Mary Catherine Hilkert, 'Experience and Revelation', *The Praxis of the Reign of God: An Introduction to the Theology of Edward Schillebeeckx* (ed. Robert J. Schreiter and Mary Catherine Hilkert; New York, NY: Fordham University Press, 2nd edn, 2002), pp. 59–77.

[3] Robert J. Schreiter, 'Edward Schillebeeckx: An Orientation to His Thought', *The Schillebeeckx Reader* (Edinburgh: T&T Clark, 1984), pp. 1–24 (16).

[4] Ivone Gebara, *Longing for Running Water: Ecofeminism and Liberation* (Minneapolis, MN: Fortress, 1999) p. 23.

power structures.[5] Furthermore, ethical judgements are implicit in epistemologies. Gebara continues: 'In every act of knowing there is a vision
and an understanding of the world and of human beings ... that can
be observed in the act itself, as well as in its consequences. To know is
to take a stand ...'[6] Gebara critiques Aristotelian and Thomistic epistemologies as hierarchical and patriarchal; similarly, Schillebeeckx leaves
behind the Thomist framework instilled in him by De Petter 'because
the rational categories of this form of Thomism became too constraining
for the phenomena to be studied'. What Schillebeeckx retains, however,
is an approach to experience that is intuitive in nature, recognizing that
the act of knowing is an act of faith, not an act of logic.[7] This prizing of
intuition is a hallmark of the phenomenological method as engaged by
ecofeminist theologians contemplating the immediacy of suffering in an
alienated world.

b. *Women's Experience of Negative Contrast*

b. 1. *The Global Suffering of Women in Poverty*

Schillebeeckx has called suffering the scarlet thread woven throughout the
fabric of human history. While specific focus on the suffering of women
is a rather recent phenomenon, the reality of women's unique share in
the suffering of the world is older than our most ancient texts. Moreover,
in our contemporary world, it is impossible to consider the reality of
suffering due to poverty, oppression, and injustice apart from the reality
of globalization. While globalization has both positive and negative
characteristics, its market-place ethos is the pervasive force shaping life
and culture around the world. Because globalization impacts us mind,
body, and soul, British ecofeminist theologian Mary C. Grey likens it to
a spirituality, albeit a negative spirituality of distorted desire.[8] In Grey's
analysis, this globalized distortion has its roots in centuries of patriarchal
epistemologies responsible for a gradual and decisive turn away from the
earth. This turning away from the earth is also a turning away from the
earth's most vulnerable people, especially women and the children who
depend upon them. The suffering and well-being of women and nature
are inextricably entwined; like nature itself, women's responsibilities for
sustaining life are all affected by globalization's dark side. Corporate
wealth and the increasing demands of consumer lifestyles in the First

---

[5] Gebara, *Longing for Running Water*, p. 21.
[6] Gebara, *Longing for Running Water*, p. 24.
[7] Schreiter, 'Edward Schillebeeckx: An Orientation to His Thought', p. 15.
[8] Mary C. Grey, *Sacred Longings: The Ecological Spirit and Global Culture*
(Minneapolis, MN: Fortress, 2004) pp. ix–xii.

World increase poverty and further the exploitation of the earth, women, and children in the Two-thirds World. [9]

When the earth is ravaged and poisoned, whether *via* the byproducts of war or corporate production, women's bodies and the bodies of their yet-to-be born children bear the most profound scars. In nations afflicted by famine, it is women who suffer the anguish of being unable to feed their children as they helplessly watch them die of hunger. In the deserts of Africa and India, it is women who struggle daily to procure water for their families while foregoing it themselves. Water is a sacrament of life and symbol of God. Where the thirst for water that fuels daily labour and sacrifice nevertheless goes unquenched, it is not too much to say that women and their families are being deprived of their divine life and dignity. [10]

While global technologies unite the world community through enhanced means of communication and travel, this new 'world without borders' also allows for the globalization of organized crime, drug trafficking, and the sex trafficking of women and children. What we are contemplating here is the brokenness and sin of the world in global perspective. Women share uniquely in this brokenness – all women – those in poverty in the Two-Thirds World, and those in the First World who would seem to benefit the most from globalization's positive aspects. Let us turn now to consider not only First World women's relatedness to and implicit responsibility for the suffering of their sisters in poverty, but also to the particular spiritual suffering of such women in relation to the Church.

b. 2 The Spiritual Suffering of Women in the Church

Mary Grey, Ivone Gebara, Beverly Lanzetta, and a host of others attribute the structures of globalization that dominate our world to those patterns of patriarchal epistemology that result in a pervasive dualism and reinforcement of hierarchies of power and privilege. [11] Males are certainly not the only beneficiaries of this system; many women both benefit from and perpetuate the patriarchal system in secular and religious realms, conditioned as they are by a patriarchal epistemology of which they are unconscious. [12] Nevertheless, it is undeniable that male-dominated institutions occupy the upper echelons of the power pyramid and have considerable stakes in maintaining their hold on power. This is equally the case in both secular and religious institutions. The spiritual oppression of women is profoundly

---

[9] Grey, *Sacred Longings*, pp. 11–16.

[10] Grey, *Sacred Longings*, pp. 26–46.

[11] See especially Elizabeth A. Johnson, *Women, Earth, Creator Spirit* (Mahwah, NJ: Paulist, 1993).

[12] See Ivone Gebara, *Out of the Depths: Women's Experience of Evil and Salvation* (Minneapolis, MN: Fortress, 2002) p. 98.

related to the same systems responsible for the global suffering of women and of all who experience life on the margins. In the analyses of ecofeminist theologians, these systems are held in place by a patriarchal epistemology that has not only been reinforced by, but is preeminently embodied in, the public hierarchy of the Church.

In her critique of patriarchal epistemology, Ivone Gebara delineates the oppressive impact of its distinctive dimensions. First, she notes that patriarchal epistemology is essentialist. Such an essentialism holds that there is an ideal, constitutive essence of human beings that is willed by God. This ideal essence is established in the human imagination as the model we seek to emulate. However, it often functions as a denial of what is really there, i.e., it functions as an imposed denial of the phenomena that we actually observe. And this denial is a profound cause of suffering to all whose life experience do not fit the essentialist paradigm.

Gebara further identifies this patriarchal way of knowing as a 'monotheistic epistemology' (i.e., there is one God, and He is male). Also problematic is the epistemology of eternal truths which approaches supernatural revelation as another plane marked by a privileged and immutable certitude.[13] Finally, while Gebara acknowledges that the developments of Vatican II and, especially, liberation theology have moved beyond classical and medieval epistemologies, they remain fundamentally anthropocentric and androcentric. Their failure to raise questions about the repercussions, through history, of traditional or historically conditioned images of God marks them still as patriarchal.[14] In the wake of her deconstruction, Gebara moves forward to construct an ecofeminist epistemology adequate to a contemporary Christian theology.

In offering an ecofeminist epistemology, Gebara does not jettison the centuries of patriarchal epistemology that she critiques. On the contrary, she observes, 'we are one body in process ...'[15] So, too, Schillebeeckx asserts: 'The discoveries about reality we have already made ... become the framework in which we interpret new experiences, while at the same time this already given framework of interpretation is exposed to criticism and corrected, changed or renewed by new experiences.'[16] Moreover, he states, 'the constantly unforeseen content of new experiences keeps forcing us to think again ... Our thinking remains empty if it does not constantly refer back to living experience.'[17] Gebara indicts such disconnected thought as more than neutrally empty; her experience as a Latin American woman

---

[13] Gebara, *Longing for Running Water*, pp. 32–34.

[14] Gebara, *Longing for Running Water*, p. 47.

[15] Gebara, *Longing for Running Water*, p. 48.

[16] Edward Schillebeeckx, *Christ: The Experience of Jesus as Lord* (trans. John Bowden; New York, NY: Crossroad, 1981) p. 31.

[17] Schillebeeckx, *Christ*, p. 32.

theologian compels her to name it as oppressive: 'To the degree to which we distance (traditional) truths from their origins and from ourselves, we act as if they had some hidden power over us.'[18] The oppressive power of theological truths distilled through the patriarchal framework critiqued above is a source of spiritual suffering to women whose experience painfully clashes and contrasts with those truths.

Clearly, many of the affirmations of ecofeminist epistemology are assumed by Schillebeeckx and other phenomenologically grounded thinkers. That in ecofeminism which is new, different, and inherently critical of previous phenomenologies emerges precisely from its faithfulness to phenomenological method in owning its foundations in gender and ecology. As a gender-based, ecological epistemology, ecofeminism recognizes gender and ecology as *mediations*. 'In other words,' Gebara asserts, 'the feminine dimension is constitutive of the human reality, just as the ecological dimension is, despite the fact that both emerged only recently into the light of historical consciousness.'[19] Thus, the 'knowing' that emerges from women's experience is not only not reflected in traditional truths as rendered in the Christian theological tradition, but is also often actively denied by them. Schillebeeckx acknowledges the innate distrust authoritarian institutions show towards new experiences. In an analysis that is presciently illuminating of the contemporary position of ecofeminist epistemology and theology vis-à-vis the Church, he states:

> [Authoritarian institutions] instinctively feel that in experiences an authority can present itself which is a criticism of the normativeness of ... any authority which would merely assert itself as contingent facticity and thus as power. That they must nevertheless acknowledge the critical and productive force – the authority – of experiences emerges from the fact that they often seek to manipulate new experiences. Above all, experiences which put in question our established thinking and acting open up new perspectives. But precisely out of fear of the reflection or the change which they require, they are often manipulated: their critical force is not allowed, but they are integrated, and in this way their sting is taken away.[20]

As women articulate their experience of Christian faith from within their feminine being, they often experience one of two things: either they are censored and rejected, or they are manipulated and integrated. They are set apart from the Church, or they are manipulated into at least an overt conformity. In either case, the critical and epistemic force of their knowing-born-of-suffering is lost to the Church. This then becomes yet another

[18] Gebara, *Longing for Running Water*, p. 49.
[19] Gebara, *Longing for Running Water*, p. 58.
[20] Schillebeeckx, *Christ*, p. 37.

dimension of suffering for women who still struggle to do theology on behalf of women and all who are marginalized, and who, at the same time, still care to do it within and on behalf of the Church. This unique suffering experience of women has particular implications for Christology. We will argue here that Jesus' constitutive relation to the coming of God's rule intrinsically means that every implication of Incarnation is essential to salvation. In this case, the feminine and ecological dimensions of Incarnation are essential to the fullness of revelation and the immanent and final experience of salvation. Women's unique insight into this reality emerges from their particular experience of negative contrast – the only mediation for a thinking woman's experience of the hierarchical Church. We turn now to Schillebeeckx's understanding of Jesus' own experience of negative contrast as source of wisdom and salvation for women.

c. *Jesus' Experience of Negative Contrast as 'Good News' for Women*

The theme of negative contrast experience pervades Schillebeeckx's theology, especially as a means of dealing with those aspects of reality that thwart progress toward the *humanum*. The fullness and flourishing of life signified by this term is overshadowed by the suffering reality of the *threatened humanum*. The ambiguity of human experience is such that the reality of salvation we long for can never be adequately expressed in conceptual language. Rather, out of the depths of contrast experiences of suffering and evil there emerges an instinctive 'no' to all that threatens human well-being, giving rise to transformative action. What Schillebeeckx calls 'the critical and productive epistemic power of suffering' has its roots in the negative contrast experience of Jesus himself; moreover, it has vital implications for the flourishing of women who suffer oppression, whether the global oppression of poverty or the spiritual oppression of a patriarchal church.

Schillebeeckx maintains that nothing less than Jesus' 'special, original religious apprehension of God' can account for 'the unqualified assurance of salvation that characterized his message'.[21] The relational ground of Jesus' being-in-God sustained him through the contrast experience of the rejection of his person and message that culminated in his crucifixion. Moreover, even from the vantage point of the twenty-first century, it is not anachronistic to note that the structures of secular and religious power that colluded in his rejection, torture, and death were both political and patriarchal. Not only Jesus' teaching, but his practices of healing on the Sabbath, eating with sinners and outcasts, and his egalitarian relationships with women, posed a threat to those defined by male religious authority and/or political power. If Jesus' parables functioned to open up a new world that placed the structures

---

[21] Edward Schillebeeckx, *Jesus: An Experiment in Christology* (trans. Hubert Hoskins; New York, NY: Seabury, 1979) p. 267.

of the current one under judgement, so too did his person and manner of relating. Thus, Schillebeeckx's identification of Jesus as 'parable of God and paradigm of humanity' signifies good news for women today whose suffering is exacerbated, if not caused, by patriarchal structures.

In the rift or fissure between Jesus' own trusting intimacy and identification with God and the suffering shored up by unjust structures, there emerged his own instinctive 'no' expressed in a mysticism of resistance to everything contrary to God's reign. The revolutionary quality of this resistance was neither militant nor political, though it certainly had political repercussions. It was a resistance interpreted by the prevailing authorities as disruptive and disobedient; however, this 'no' was rooted in Jesus' more fundamental 'yes' to the coming reign of God which he knew as the positive ground of his own being. This mysticism of resistance was, in fact, enfleshed in Jesus' inclusive relationships of justice and love. It may be argued that, in our own day, Jesus' identification of the Reign of God in and through such relationships is experientially embodied in women's ways of being in the world over against patriarchal structures.

2. Hope in the Depths of Suffering: The 'Via Feminina', Contemplative Feminism, and Subversion in the Body of Christ

The positive ground of life and being that gives rise to a mysticism of resistance in communities of women suffering oppression in diverse contexts is what North American theologian Beverly Lanzetta seeks to identify and uncover through the spiritual path she names the *via feminina*.[22] Like ecofeminist theologians in other cultural contexts, Lanzetta understands gender as a mediation of experience and knowledge. Her work explores 'how gender differentiates the spiritual process in significant ways, playing a role in both the structure and content of mystical consciousness, as well as serving as an interpretive lens through which women negotiate the sacred'.[23]

Lanzetta conceived the phrase *via feminina* in relation to the ancient mystical paths of union with God known as the *via positiva* and the *via negativa*. After decades of teaching and research in the spirituality of the mystics and extensive experience in the spiritual direction of women, Lanzetta found herself articulating a third path or road to union with the divine – the way of the feminine:

> Undertaking a feminist reading of women's mystical theology, *via feminina* represents the contemplative paths and processes that break

---

[22] See Lanzetta, *Radical Wisdom*.
[23] Lanzetta, *Radical Wisdom*, p. 8.

through and transform the historical denigration of women encoded in patriarchal cultures. As a new spiritual path with ancient roots in women's experience, it experiments with a particular type of mystical experience – the apophatic or negative – to find the tools women need to pull up the sources of misogyny imbedded in their souls.[24]

In the movement from kataphasis to apophasis, the soul ascends through affirmation to the higher, holier realm of negation, resulting in a language of paradox and a denial of names. As the mystics knew, 'only a language that continually erases itself can capture the unknown divinity'. This transition from affirmation to negation leads into the dark night of the soul, which entails the unsaying of the lower, false self, in order to find the true self. In her feminist mystical theology, Lanzetta articulates this phase of dark night as 'the unsaying of woman'. That is, the *via feminina* begins in the deconstruction of the 'false self' that patriarchy has constructed for women and reinforced with its sacred symbols.[25]

Lanzetta's study explores the subversive power of contemplative feminism and advocates the reclaiming of the divine feminine as a project that is at once personal and political.[26] Contemplative feminism is, in fact, the spiritual praxis of conversion, the transformation whereby women claim their full dignity as subjects of their own lives and agents of justice in the world. As a mystical ethic, it entails a suffering journey of individual transformation that is inseparable from relationships with those who suffer, and with the world itself.

3. Women, Christ, and Salvation

a. Women's Experience of Salvation

a. 1. Women's Spiritual Rights and the Flourishing of the Humanum

The journey of transformation that Lanzetta articulates in her *via feminina* has its origin in the dynamic of *metanoia* that Schillebeeckx identifies as the heart of the experience of negative contrast. More specifically, it has its origin in the fundamental 'yes' that gives rise to the 'no' of resistance to all that threatens the *humanum*.[27] That 'yes' resides in the divine ground of women's being, the place of inchoate knowing that, precisely as women,

---

[24] Lanzetta, *Radical Wisdom*, p. 13.

[25] Lanzetta, *Radical Wisdom*, pp. 14–17.

[26] Lanzetta, *Radical Wisdom*, pp. 20–24.

[27] For Schillebeeckx on mysticism and dark night, see Edward Schillebeeckx, *Church: The Human Story of God* (trans. John Bowden; New York, NY: Crosroads, 1990) pp. 69–71.

they bear the divine image. All that negates or diminishes this feminine divine image threatens women's flourishing. Frequently, women are only aware of their feminine divine ground through the visceral experience of its opposite – in liturgy and symbol, in word and sacrament. The suffering of this 'soul fracture' increases with consciousness; at the same time, deepening consciousness and the resistance to which it gives rise is the only path of healing, salvation, and wholeness for women. Nevertheless, like Jesus' resistance to everything contrary to God's reign, women's mysticism of resistance is typically interpreted by the prevailing authorities as disruptive and disobedient. Wherever the patriarchal status quo is threatened, the place of resistance inevitably becomes the place of the cross. But, as we will reflect later, the place of the cross is also always the place of resurrection.

Jesus enfleshed his own mysticism of resistance and instantiated the reign of God in relationships which privileged the poor and marginalized. Moreover, he accomplished this preeminently through the sharing of meals. Schillebeeckx affirms, '... this fellowship at table is itself, as an eating together with Jesus, an offer here and now of eschatological salvation or "final good"'.[28] This 'here and now' quality of Jesus' eschatological meal-sharing has particular significance for women's experience of both suffering and salvation. The revolutionary power of Jesus' activities is grounded in his intimate communion with God and expressed in his liberating, boundary-dissolving relationships, which restore people to the dignity willed by their Creator. Schillebeeckx stresses: 'Authentic mysticism is never flight from the world but, on the basis of a first disintegrating source-experience, an integrating and reconciling mercy with all things. It is approach, not flight.'[29] So, too, the *via feminina* is a mystical path that unfolds in loving solidarity with all who suffer, especially those who suffer material and social deprivation. Where women's human rights are denied, their primordial spiritual rights are denied and desecrated.[30] Lanzetta advocates for spiritual rights precisely because every abuse perpetrated against women begins in the negation and denial of their right 'to be' *as women*. Every act or symbol of denigration, blatant or subtle, pierces the feminine soul of woman wherein dwells the feminine divinity. From torture and rape in war-torn Sudan to the negation of women's right to publically represent the divine in ecclesial structures – women suffer precisely in and because of their feminine being. It is a crucifixion of the Feminine Body of Christ. The contemplative praxis by which First World women claim their voices is informed by relationship with their sisters who suffer material poverty and overt, tortuous oppression; at the same time, it has implications for their shared salvation.

[28] Schillebeeckx, *Jesus*, p. 218.
[29] Schillebeeckx, *Church*, p. 72.
[30] Lanzetta, *Radical Wisdom*, pp. 182–85.

a. 2. *'Salvations' and Concrete Particularity*

Schillebeeckx's theology is marked by the conviction that it is impossible to define 'salvation' for the same reason that it is impossible to define the *humanum*. The longing for salvation is at one and the same time the longing for human fulfillment, and the origin and destiny of this longing are divine. We dwell in this divine and human Mystery, experiencing fragments of salvation amidst the all too present realities of suffering and evil. Herein we find the necessity for Schillebeeckx's notion of negative contrast: We begin to articulate what salvation could be in counterpoint to the very particular and concrete experience of suffering here and now, and we do so based on fleeting but sure intimations of our own divine ground.

Ecofeminist theologians of diverse cultural backgrounds affirm the centrality of experience in its concrete particularity. They agree that for too long, universal categories of evil and salvation have inappropriately functioned as idolatry, serving patriarchy and bypassing particular instances of suffering and injustice. Each concrete experience of evil involves a search for release and deliverance. Whether we look to women's suffering of personal and spiritual diminishment, or to their suffering of poverty, the salvation they need and long for is indicated over against the particular evil they are experiencing. Ivone Gebara interchanges the terms salvation, deliverance, and resurrection on the one hand, and cross, suffering, and evil on the other. She explains:

> Understanding deliverance within feminist theological reflection begins by noting its signs in daily life, in what befalls us unexpectedly. In actual fact, salvation begins in the experience of what we call the cross or the way of the cross. There lies the sight of multiple resurrections. And this place of cross and resurrection is where one discovers relatedness as necessary for all life, especially all human life.[31]

Gebara embraces an anthropological perspective rooted in life's reality as 'a temporary succession of happy and sad events in our personal and collective existence'.[32] She believes that this anthropological perspective helps us 'to overcome the dualisms characterizing our philosophical and theological tradition', and 'makes a case for proclaiming the unity of the human person in different situations'.[33] This sense of the unity of the human person is complex, and it forms the basis of Gebara's discussion of the meaning of deliverance or salvation amidst the darkness and suffering of daily life. This discussion entails a trenchant critique of the symbol of the cross as it has been used to glorify the redemptive character of male suffering and

---

[31] Gebara, *Out of the Depths*, p. 109.
[32] Gebara, *Out of the Depths*, p. 110.
[33] Gebara, *Out of the Depths*, p. 110.

hide the reality of women's suffering.[34] Ultimately, Gebara concludes that the problem lies not with the cross of Jesus, but rather with its patriarchal interpretations that through the ages have been used to reinforce the suffering and silence of women. She highlights 'the importance of holding the memory of the crucified Jesus together with the memory of others crucified, men and women alike'.[35] Relatedness is not only the condition of being human, it is the matrix out of which we must interpret the cross if it is to have any enduring meaning for real salvation here and now. For the poor, and especially the women, among whom Gebara lives, 'Crosses are always present, but different forms of redemption are present, too. ... Hope is in our bones, walking along with our steps, breathing with our very breath.' She continues: 'We are not dealing with an instrument of torture transformed into victory over death, but with shared bread, wounds healed, gestures of tenderness, the straightened posture of a stooped woman, hunger satisfied for the moment, the birth of a child, a good harvest.'[36] Salvation, then, is what we offer one another and celebrate together in the dailiness of life in the Body of Christ. Moreover, it would seem that this relational immediacy of salvation in the face of human suffering is what Jesus instantiated in his healing, his teaching, and most especially, his 'eschatological meal-sharing'.

b. *Jesus' Constitutive Relation to the Reign of God and the Feminine Body of Christ*

As ecofeminist theologians highlight the personal, relational, and concrete dailiness both of suffering and of salvation, Schillebeeckx emphasizes the importance of connecting Jesus' activities to his person. At the heart of Schillebeeckx's christology is the assertion that Jesus is divine precisely in and through his humanity; his manner of being human is what shows forth his divinity:

> In the light of Jesus Christ, the gospel itself is a hermeneutic of funda-mental human experience. What speaks to us in Jesus is his being human, and thereby opening up to us the deepest possibilities of our own life, and *in this* God is expressed.[37]

This supreme emphasis on the immanent reality of Incarnation is the same emphasis that lies at the heart of Christian ecofeminist theology. In its critique of traditional christological constructs, what ecofeminism seeks to negate is the patriarchal epistemology that has successively overlaid

---

[34] Analyzed in Kathleen McManus, 'Reconciling the Cross in the Theologies of Edward Schillebeeckx and Ivone Gebara', *Theological Studies* 66 (2005), pp. 638–50.

[35] Gebara, *Out of the Depths*, p. 120.

[36] Gebara, *Out of the Depths*, p. 115.

[37] Schillebeeckx, *Christ*, p. 76.

and often distorted the central being and message of Jesus. An honest encounter with this negative critique may enable the official Church to expand its symbolic range in language, ritual, and leadership in a manner more representative of Jesus' inclusive rendering of God's reign. By way of an apologetic for her own stance, Ivone Gebara reflects:

> All the values I regarded as fundamental I found in [Jesus] ... The value of the body, especially the body of the poor ... I came to realize the degree to which suffering and oppressed bodies, silenced bodies, and ostracized bodies had to do with my faith in God's presence, in the *relatedness* of this unfathomable mystery which is so timidly grasped by human flesh.[38]

The relatedness of this unfathomable mystery so timidly grasped by human flesh is, I suggest, precisely what Jesus so consummately grasps in his Abba experience. Schillebeeckx affirms that Jesus' uniquely intimate relation to God as 'Abba' expresses the core of his religious life exactly as the first Christians represented it after his death.[39] This divine relationship that defined Jesus' person and found expression in his community-engendering practices is the paradigm for Christian life. To suggest, as I have in this essay, that Jesus' identification of the Reign of God in and through relationships is uniquely embodied in women's ways of being in the world might appear as a succumbing to the essentialism that ecofeminist epistemology eschews. We walk a fine line here in seeking, nevertheless, to be faithful to the phenomenological method; that is, to be faithful to the witness of what shows itself in reality. Though there is always evidence to the contrary, communities of women who suffer are characteristically marked by a relational solidarity that constitutes a mysticism of resistance harbouring its own seeds of resurrection.

Gebara speaks of God as relatedness wrapped in mystery that, for humans, is personal. She acknowledges that to speak thus of relatedness leads to imprecise discourse, and this is always risky.[40] Christologically, she reflects:

> The Incarnation, the presence of the greatest of mysteries in our flesh, is more than Jesus of Nazareth. In this sense, we could say that Jesus is for us a metaphor of the divine presence, the unfathomable mystery, the unutterable in the human flesh in which we are all included.[41]

In language that evokes Schillebeeckx's assertions of the superior power of God's defenseless vulnerability in Christ, Gebara continues:

---

[38] Gebara, *Longing for Running Water*, pp. 176–77.
[39] Schillebeeckx, *Jesus*, p. 266.
[40] Gebara, *Longing for Running Water*, pp. 108 and 115.
[41] Gebara, *Longing for Running Water*, pp. 184–85.

Jesus is a symbol, a symbol with which we dialogue and in which we include ourselves ... He is the symbol of the vulnerability of love, which in order to remain alive ends up being murdered, killed ... and which then rises again in those who love him, in order to revive the vital cycle of love.[42]

We find ourselves on dangerous ground here in an articulation so phenomenologically faithful to an existential solidarity in the Body of Christ here and now that it seems to deny the cosmically salvific nature of the death and resurrection of one Jesus of Nazareth. There is an agnosticism here about the mysterious and primordial particularity of Jesus' resurrection in favor of the concrete particularity of resurrection life in the community of those who follow Jesus. Yet, it is important that we traverse this ground with Gebara. For too long, over-emphasis on a metaphysical rendering of Christ's cross and resurrection has resulted in a lack of faithfulness to what is revealed in present crosses and resurrections, especially of women. Indeed, such one-sided emphasis has contributed to the suffering of women in the ways indicated in this essay. This is what Gebara rightly decries in her analysis of the oppressive effect of the power we give to traditional truths that are distanced from their origins and from our experience. In her effort to salvage the connection to our experience, however, she neglects the equally important task of connecting such truths to their origin and subsequent development in the tradition.

Gebara's narrative phenomenology, so grounded in the harsh and concrete suffering of women, points to fragmented, salvific human experiences that emerge from or are juxtaposed with such suffering. Particular stories of suffering are related to the particular actions and stories of Jesus in his earthly life, and here hope is identified. What seems lacking, however, is the grounding of concrete stories of suffering in the larger and encompassing total narrative of Jesus' life, death, and resurrection as it has been witnessed to in the unfolding experience of the tradition.

Meaningless suffering, suffering without a cause ... this is what Gebara holds before us, and it is crucial that we contemplate it unflinchingly. She speaks of it in relation to 'the cross as fate', a topic that she feels has not engaged theologians. Yet, Schillebeeckx, too, acknowledges this suffering beyond the suffering of love, beyond the suffering that is a sacrifice for truth or for justice, suffering outside the pale of valor or meaning. Even here, he cites resistance as the only meaningful reaction; 'people must refuse to allow evil the right to exist: They must espouse the cause of good and refuse to treat evil on the same level as good.'[43] Nevertheless, he goes on:

Thus at the deepest level, at the level of our outline of an earthly,

---

[42] Gebara, *Longing for Running Water*, pp. 188–90.
[43] Schillebeeckx, *Christ*, p. 726; *Church*, p. 125.

human future, we are at the same time confronted with the final fiasco of our efforts at resisting evil. Death above all shows us that we are deluded if we think that we can realize on earth a true, perfect, and universal salvation for all and for every individual.[44]

Schillebeeckx shows himself to be no less realistic than Gebara about the concrete and oppressive reality of evil underlying the suffering of the world. The question arises: Does Gebara herself succumb to a certain dualism in granting evil a force equal to that of good, in allowing evil and salvation to operate on the same level? A genuine mysticism of resistance immanently exercised can only have its roots in a transcendent divine reality, the ultimate ground of our being. For Schillebeeckx, 'Christian belief in salvation from God in Jesus as the Christ is the downfall of any doctrine of salvation or soteriology understood in human terms, in the sense of an identity which is within our control and therefore can be manipulated'.[45] While redemption is a task in which humans participate, it is also gratuitous. Over and over, Schillebeeckx insists on the centrality of a love whose power resides in vulnerability:

> Real redemption or salvation always passes over into mysticism: only here can the tension between action and contemplation be sustained. This is existing for others and for the Other, the wholly intimate and near yet 'transcendent God,' with whom Jesus has made us familiar.[46]

4. *Conclusion*

In *Church: The Human Story of God*, Schillebeeckx articulates the concern for the world here-and-now that so preoccupies Mary C. Grey and Ivone Gebara as representative ecofeminist theologians, and Beverly Lanzetta as a proponent of feminist mysticism. He offers four Biblically based metaphors that 'suggest to us the way towards what, according to God's dream for the happiness of men and women and all their fellow creatures, humankind will eventually be'. These are, (a) 'the kingdom of God', which entails 'the definitive salvation or the radical liberation of humankind ... when "God will be all in all"'; (b) the 'resurrection of the body', which 'has everything to do with the personal corporeality in which I lived on earth'; (c) 'the new heaven and the new earth', which is not another world, but the eschatological consummation of an intact ecological environment – 'our earthly world redeemed from being out of joint, though I don't know how to imagine this'. (d) 'Finally,' Schillebeeckx boldly affirms, 'the normative

---

[44] Schillebeeckx, *Christ*, p. 726.
[45] Schilebeeeckx, *Christ*, pp. 836–37.
[46] Schilebeeeckx, *Christ*, p. 838.

role or significance of Jesus ... will become evident to all, being established on the one hand now already from the fragments of the kingdom of God and, on the other hand, also in the final eschatological consummation of this kingdom.' Schillebeeckx articulates each of these hoped-for realities in language that knows its own inadequacy, thus pointing to the necessity of mysticism. He speaks evocatively of 'the uniqueness of Jesus Christ' in terms that are open-ended, testifying to mystery that 'will become transparent to all ... in the midst of so many world religions, in the eyes of God ...'[47] Then he turns to reiterate the concrete ways these four visions of the eschatological future influence and dynamically direct the action of Christians in the world.

For women who suffer precisely as women, the fragmentary concretization of the eschatological reign of God takes a very particular, and in some contexts, revolutionary focus. For women, a mysticism of resistance in the world must begin with the interior mysticism of resistance elaborated by Beverly Lanzetta as the *via feminina*. It is a mysticism rooted in Jesus' intimacy with God which all are called to cultivate, and which women are called to cultivate precisely in their being as women, thus giving rise to feminine and inclusive identifications of God. This mysticism both nourishes and is nourished by solidarity with women suffering poverty both at home and in the Two Thirds world. This solidarity is a participation in the Feminine Body of Christ, the visibility and effectiveness of which is necessary for the fullness of salvation and the coming of the reign of God.

[47] Schillebeeckx, *Church*, pp. 133–34.

THE THREATENED *HUMANUM* AS *IMAGO DEI*: ANTHROPOLOGY AND CHRISTIAN ETHICS

Mary Catherine Hilkert, OP

The poorest and most vulnerable everywhere, but particularly in the developing countries, will be the most affected by the world growth slowdown now being predicted. ... We need most of all to join forces to take immediate action to prevent the financial crisis from becoming a human tragedy ....

– U.N. Secretary-General Ban Ki-moon, *Letter to Leaders of the Group of 20 (G-20) Nations*, 13 November, 2008.

[F]or the first time in human history, [humankind] as such sees itself confronted with the task of taking responsibility as a whole for the consequences of its action. The international solidarity, binding on all [humankind], therefore calls for universally valid *ethical norms or basic principles which apply to all* ... if this situation is not to turn into a farce or a world catastrophe.

– Edward Schillebeeckx, *Christ: The Experience of Jesus as Lord*, p. 661.

Among the 'signs of the times' that Edward Schillebeeckx identified over three decades ago in calling for a new global ethic were: the increasing violence around the globe; the spiraling nuclear race; unrestricted economic growth and the hegemony of multinational corporations; growing ecological devastation; and the development of bio-technologies to control and manipulate human genetic structures, areas all of which are of even greater concern in the third millennium. What contribution, if any, can Christianity make to the present worldwide concern about the future of humankind and the earth?

A number of theologians argue that an authentic Christian contribution to the anthropological and ecological crises of our day should not focus on the question of what constitutes the flourishing of human persons and all forms of life, or on public debates about the most basic requirements for human life in a sustainable ecology. Rather, Christian ethics should be shaped by the Christian community's narrative remembrance of the unique life, death, and resurrection of Jesus Christ, the 'strange new world of the Bible' and counter-cultural Christian discipleship.[1] As Schillebeeckx has argued, however, the question of whether Christian theology should begin with the Bible or with human experience constitutes a false dichotomy. The Christian story itself begins with the human experience of the first Christian disciples, an experience shaped by the interpretive framework of their Jewish heritage and expressed in the language of faith as 'salvation'. Likewise, any narration of the story of Jesus is necessarily selective and shaped by the historical and cultural horizon of the contemporary community and narrator. Schillebeeckx maintains that there is a dimension of human experience which exceeds all interpretive frameworks, but at the same time, all human experience is interpreted experience. His unique contribution to theological anthropology flows from this two-fold conviction. He proposes that a Christian contribution to the meaning of being human should begin with the concrete experiences of suffering that occur in every culture. Yet he remains convinced that the Christian story has a unique contribution to make: 'soteriology, Christology, and anthropology cannot be separated; each clarifies the others'.[2]

This chapter will explore three pivotal and interrelated aspects of Schillebeeckx's claim that the Christian story and the human story are mutually illuminating: his turn to 'the threatened *humanum*' as the starting point for Christian anthropology and ethics; his proposal of anthropological constants as a way forward in the global search for a world-wide ethic which respects cultural and religious pluralism; and his insistence that creation faith and the story of Jesus hold critical and productive power.

---

[1] The phrase 'strange new world of the Bible' is taken from Karl Barth, *The Word of God and the Word of Man* (trans. Douglas Horton; New York, NY: Harper and Brothers, 1957) pp. 97–135. See also: George Lindbeck, *The Nature of Doctrine: Religion and Theology in a Postliberal Age* (Philadelphia, PA: Westminster, 1984); Hans Urs von Balthasar, *The Moment of Christian Witness* [1966] (San Francisco, CA: Ignatius, 1994) pp. 100–13; Robert Barron, *The Priority of Christ: Toward a Postliberal Catholicism* (Grand Rapids, MI: Brazos Press, 2007); and the writings of Stanley Hauerwas.

[2] Edward Schillebeeckx, *Christ: The Experience of Jesus as Lord* (trans. John Bowden; New York, NY: Seabury, 1980) p. 62.

1. *The Turn to the Threatened* Humanum

In a world of violence fueled by religious claims and growing cultural and religious pluralism, Schillebeeckx recognizes that confessional claims cannot provide a common basis for a global ethic. But neither can that ethic be based on some universal understanding of human nature in an era shaped by historical consciousness. The most fundamental reason why historical human nature cannot be articulated in universal terms is that too much historical experience – most specifically, the suffering that results from evil – is utterly irrational. As Schillebeeckx describes these 'historical scraps' which escape any rational analysis:

> There is non-sense in our history: violence, lust for power, coveting at the expense of others, enslavement and oppression – there is Auschwitz, and goodness knows what else in the private sphere and in our own personal life. All of that does indeed fall outside the 'logos' which the historian looks for in history.[3]

The contemporary context requires that the theologian begins not with an abstract ideal of human nature or assumptions about a pre-existing order in human life, but rather, with the reality of those persons and communities whose well-being is at risk or has been violated. Schillebeeckx argues that this is the place where shared ethical commitments and an implicit understanding of the human can emerge in our day. In his words:

> The *humanum*, threatened and in fact, damaged, leads specifically and historically to ethical demand and the ethical imperative, and thus to confrontation with quite definite, negative experiences of contrast. Therefore, ethical invitation or demand is not an abstract norm but, historically, an event *which presents a challenge*: our concrete history itself, [human persons] in need, [humankind] in need.[4]

But each particular experience of suffering or injustice – of 'humankind in need' – is co-determined by elements of interpretation drawn from an irreducible plurality of human cultures, social contexts, and philosophies. Ethicists debate whether it is possible to identify common elements of what constitutes the human given these significant and undeniable differences. Feminist scholars, in particular, resist attempts to universalize human experience which gloss over radical differences such as sex, race, ethnicity, class, and sexual orientation. At the same time, many of these same thinkers are committed to finding some common basis for defending the dignity and rights of those persons who are most vulnerable, especially the women and

---

[3] Edward Schillebeeckx, *Jesus: An Experiment in Christology* (trans. Hubert Hoskins; New York, NY: Seabury, 1979) p. 614.

[4] Schillebeeckx, *Christ*, p. 659 (emphasis in the original).

children who are most often the victims of violence and exploitation around the world. Likewise, the second Parliament of the World's Religions took as the starting point for its 'Initial Document Towards a Global Ethic' the fundamental demand that 'every human being must be treated humanely'.[5]

Rather than proposing a theory of human nature or even a thick description of what constitutes human flourishing in the face of radical cultural and religious pluralism, a growing number of scholars have proposed a more modest goal. They are convinced that it is possible to identify at least enough commonality in human experience to condemn behaviour that is unjust and inhumane. Feminist ethicist Margaret Farley, for example, maintains:

> Whatever the differences in human lives, however minimal the actuality of world community, however unique the social arrangements of diverse peoples, it is nonetheless possible for human persons to weep over commonly felt tragedies, laugh over commonly perceived incongruities, yearn for common hopes. And across time and place, it is possible to condemn recognized injustices and to act for commonly desired goals.[6]

a. Negative Contrast Experience as Universal

For Schillebeeckx, it must be noted that he has been arguing in a similar vein for the past four decades, insisting that the one aspect of human experience which can be described as universal is the experience of resistance to evil and injustice. Borrowing from the writings of critical theorist Theodor Adorno, Schillebeeckx adopts the term 'contrast experience' (later, 'negative contrast experience') to describe those experiences of negativity, both personal and social, that evoke indignation and protest: 'No. It can't go on like this; we won't stand for it any longer!'[7] While human persons in diverse cultures

---

[5] Hans Küng and Karl-Josef Kuschel (eds), *A Global Ethic: The Declaration of the Parliament of the World's Religions* (New York, NY: Continuum, 1998) p. 21.

[6] Margaret A. Farley, 'Feminism and Universal Morality', *Prospects for a Common Morality* (ed. Gene Outka and John P. Reide, Jr.; Princeton, NJ: Princeton University Press, 1993), pp. 170–90 (178); *Just Love* (New York, NY: Continuum, 2006) pp. 57–108; Lisa Sowle Cahill, 'Feminist Ethics, Differences, and Common Ground: A Catholic Perspective', *Feminist Ethics and the Catholic Moral Tradition* (ed. Charles E. Curran, Margaret A. Farley and Richard A. McCormick; New York, NY: Paulist, 1996), pp. 184–204; Jean Porter, 'The Search for a Global Ethic', *Theological Studies* 62 (2001), pp. 105–21; and Cristina L.H. Traina, *Feminist Ethics and the Natural Law* (Washington, DC: Georgetown University Press, 1999).

[7] See: Edward Schillebeeckx, *God the Future of Man* (trans. N.D. Smith; Theological Soundings, 5/1; New York, NY: Sheed and Ward, 1968) p. 136. For another analysis of how indignation gives rise to ethical activity, see: Beverly Wildung Harrison, 'The Power of Anger in the Work of Love', *Union Seminary Quarterly Review* 36 (1981), pp. 41–57.

may disagree about what constitutes human flourishing, Schillebeeckx argues that persons spontaneously recognize that which is dehumanizing: concentration camps, genocide, racial discrimination, homelessness, abuse of children, domestic violence, an economic system in which some face starvation and utter poverty while a small minority controls the wealth and resources of a country.

Underlying the spontaneous ethical response of protest and resistance to evil, Schillebeeckx argues, resides a fundamental trust in reality as trust-worthy and human existence as meaningful.[8] The absence of 'what ought to be' evokes dissatisfaction and action for change which leads in turn to a deeper awareness of what was grasped only inchoately in the initial ethical response – an awareness that human persons are of inestimable value and inviolable. From such experiences of fundamental threat to human survival and dignity emerges not a common philosophical anthropology, but rather a shared concern for 'the *humanum*'. What is universal, according to Schillebeeckx, is not any formulation of what it means to be human, but rather the 'call of and to the *humanum*', which is recognized only *via* its negative and indirect mediation in the critical and practical resistance to threats to humanity.

In the classical language of Christian anthropology and Catholic social teaching, to say that the experience of suffering and marginalized persons is to be given primacy in any account of what it means to be human is akin to saying that the image of God is most fully revealed in human persons when they resist whatever violates the *humanum*. In Schillebeeckx's words:

> If the fundamental symbol of God is the living human being – the image of God – then the place where human beings are humiliated, tortured, and forgotten, as individuals or as a community, by persons or violent structures, is at the same time, the privileged place where religious experience … becomes possible … precisely in and through a human action which seeks to give form to this symbol of God, the human being …[9]

According to Schillebeeckx, however, this fundamental human experience of negativity and the ethical response which it elicits need not be expressed or experienced as a religious impulse. He insists that to name this resistance to evil in religious terms before accounting for the ethical impulse as

[8] That trust has been shaped and confirmed by positive experiences of goodness, meaning, and joy, however fragmentary. See: Edward Schillebeeckx, *Church: The Human Story of God* (trans. John Bowden; New York, NY: Crossroad, 1990) pp. 5–6; Schillebeeckx, *Christ*, pp. 817–19 and p. 897 n. 158; and Edward Schillebeeckx, *The Understanding of Faith: Interpretation and Criticism* (trans. N.D. Smith; London: Sheed and Ward, 1974) pp. 91–101.
[9] Edward Schillebeeckx, *For the Sake of the Gospel* (trans. John Bowden; New York, NY: Crossroad, 1990) p. 164. See also: Schillebeeckx, *Christ*, p. 837.

precisely a human phenomenon is to make a fundamental, categorical mistake. Human ethics has its own integrity, an integrity which remains even when one interprets it within the larger sphere of a theological claim about the presence of God undergirding human existence.

We shall return to the question of the contribution of religious faith to ethics, but first a critical question must be raised about this optimistic evaluation of human persons and basic ethical impulses. Is it, in fact, the case that the spontaneous human response to the violation of the dignity and integrity of others is protest and resistance? Here Schillebeeckx's German colleague Johann Baptist Metz, African American political theologian M. Shawn Copeland, and the Canadian Jesuit Bernard Lonergan have all drawn attention to a more troubling dimension of human existence.

b. *The Question of Bias*

Although Metz shared Schillebeeckx's turn to the concrete suffering of human beings as a necessary starting point for theological anthropology, he did not share Schillebeeckx's optimism about the spontaneous resistance that arises in response to the violation of the human. Writing as a German theologian after Auschwitz, Metz was all too aware of the reality of human apathy and the failure of large numbers of human beings even to see the face of the suffering other, let alone to respond courageously.

Copeland concurs with Schillebeeckx's call for a fundamental shift of paradigms in theological anthropology and has concretized that proposal by claiming that the 'exploited, despised, poor woman of colour' who represents 'the poorest of the poor' needs to become the new anthropological subject of Christian theology.[10] But Copeland demonstrates that the narratives of slaves and of others whose humanity has been systematically violated supports Metz's claim that all too often the human response to the suffering of others is apathy or even some level of participation in the violation, rather than resistance. One incident which Copeland cites serves to underscore this point. An article in the *Times* of London in 1992 detailed the life of a young Somali woman named Fatima Yusef, who went into unassisted labour by the side of a road in Southern Italy while bystanders looked on and taunted her. In that article Ms. Yusef described her humiliation: 'I will remember those faces as long as I live … They would stop and linger as if they were at a cinema careful not to miss any of the show. There was a boy who sniggering, said, "Look what the negress is doing".'[11]

---

[10] M. Shawn Copeland, 'The New Anthropological Subject at the Heart of the Mystical Body of Christ', *Proceedings of the Catholic Theological Society of America* 53 (1998), pp. 25–47 (30).

[11] John Phillips, 'Racists Jeer at Roadside Birth', the *Times* of London, 12 February 1992, p. 8, as quoted by Copeland, 'The New Anthropological Subject', pp. 37–38.

This distressing event is one of many recent examples of human atrocities around the globe that illustrate the failure of persons, communities, or nations to intervene on behalf of the *humanum*. This evidence may corroborate Schillebeeckx's claim that the 'threatened *humanum*' provides the necessary starting point for theological anthropology. But at the same time, it highlights an aspect of his ethical analysis which needs to be more fully developed – the impact of social conditioning and sin on human perception and action, even that of children.[12] Specifically, an analysis of negative contrast experience as revelatory needs to take more account of the power of sin to distort, if not to eradicate, the spontaneous human response of 'no' in the face of evil and injustice.

Here Bernard Lonergan's analysis of the dynamics of bias can help to refine Schillebeeckx's claims about the critical and productive power of negative contrast experiences. According to Lonergan, bias operates on an unconscious level, serving as a filter which inclines the human person to refuse new insights, to resist a shift of values from egoism to the common good, to fail to act even when one realizes that action on behalf of another human being or the common good is needed. What Lonergan describes as 'dramatic bias' or 'scotosis' operates not only at the individual level, but also at the level of social groups (the mob mentality), and at the level of humankind as a whole in the general human resistance to change and conversion and the failure to be self-critical or to consider long-term implications of decisions.[13]

This corrective to Schillebeeckx's claim of a 'spontaneous human response' on behalf of the *humanum* need not undercut the value of Schillebeeckx's insight. But it suggests that the development of authentic human values and responses requires an ongoing process of transformation. Likewise, it emphasizes the power of dramatic bias (in religious terms, social sin) to distort human perception and action and points to the need for the formation of human consciousness and conscience. The religions of the world hold the potential for such formation, but is religious belief necessary to justify the ethical judgement that human persons have an intrinsic value which is inviolable?

---

[12] Schillebeeckx speaks of ethical imperatives arising 'spontaneously' out of experience in *God the Future of Man* (p. 137). In *Church*, he states that indignation seems to be a basic experience of our life in this world. He does add the caveat *'unless we go through it blindly: keen only on consumption, bustle and oblivion … or power'* (p. 5, emphasis added), but the impact of social conditioning and structural sin on the formation of conscience needs further development.

[13] See Bernard Lonergan, *Insight: A Study of Human Understanding* (Toronto: University of Toronto Press, 1992) pp. 191–99, 218–42; 'Healing and Creating in History', *Lonergan: A Third Collection* (ed. Frederick E. Crowe; New York, NY: Paulist, 1985), pp. 100–12.

c. *Is the Ground for Human Hope and Ethical Action Necessarily Religious?*

Schillebeeckx finds support for his conviction that the human ethical demand has priority over religious appeals in referring to Emmanuel Levinas' insight that 'to truly encounter another human being is to realize that she or he is an originally unique transcendent other ... whose existence can make demands on me'.[14] But in terms of an ultimate grounding for human ethics, Schillebeeckx finds the claim that human beings – the 'face of the other' – serves as the ultimate source of value and meaning proves inadequate. Recalling the point stressed above that human beings do not always respond to others with empathy or resist injustice, Schillebeeckx notes that 'the other is not only the origin of an ethical claim on me; he or she is often also potential violence and injustice, just as I am to him or her'.[15] Human beings may indeed act heroically on behalf of the *humanum* in the face of violation towards the other, but as demonstrated above, there is no guarantee that they will, or that when they do, good shall be victorious. Nevertheless, when human persons make heroic choices on behalf of others in the face of the ultimate absurdity of existence, they enact an inexplicable hope in the value of the human which can be viewed as a form of 'ethical martyrdom'.

But what is the ultimate ground for that radical action and implicit hope? Schillebeeckx resists the conclusion that the only possible grounds for the meaningfulness of heroic human action is belief in a transcendent (divine) source of goodness. Rather, he notes that the human judgement that justice is superior to injustice and goodness superior to evil is itself an adequate grounding for an autonomous human ethics. Drawing on the evidence of heroic ethical actions by human persons who were not religious believers, Schillebeeckx argues that belief in God is neither inevitable nor necessary. At the same time, he identifies a crucial limit to a purely human autonomous ethic – it offers no basis for hope for the victims of history, those whose humanity has been violated most radically. In his words, 'the fallen themselves then experience no liberation or redemption'.[16]

d. *Creation Faith*

Offering an alternative ethical analysis from the perspective of 'creation faith', Schillebeeckx argues that it is also credible to interpret the inexplicable commitment to the value of the *humanum* – 'ethical martyrdom'

---

[14] Schillebeeckx, *Church*, pp. 91–99. See also Edward Schillebeeckx, *On Christian Faith: The Spiritual, Ethical, and Political Dimensions* (trans. John Bowden; New York, NY: Crossroad, 1987) pp. 55–64.

[15] Schillebeeckx, *Church*, p. 94.

[16] Schillebeeckx, *Church*, p. 96.

– as grounded in the absolute saving and creative presence of God. This theological perspective claims that the source, sustaining power, and goal of all creation is to be found in the mystery of love, the dynamism of be-ing itself which believers name 'God'. The absolute creative and saving presence of God pervades all of creation, holding it in being and empowering it to achieve its destiny. At the same time, the Creator God has granted a radical autonomy to creation – to nature itself and to human freedom. In terms of human history, it is human beings who create history through the exercise of human freedom, but they do so only as empowered by grace. In Schillebeeckx's concrete language, God has given creation 'a blank cheque'.

Schillebeeckx acknowledges that the validity of faith in a transcendent source of goodness that will have the last word on human history cannot be theoretically demonstrated or proven. He notes, however, that human praxis on behalf of the threatened *humanum* gives testimony to a surplus of hope which goes beyond that which is rationally warranted by the evidence of human history marked as it is by injustice and cruelty as well as by heroism and gratuitous generosity.

On the one hand, Schillebeeckx's theology of creation provides the basis for his conviction that the questions which need to be addressed for human life and a sustainable universe to survive and move toward flourishing are accessible to all reflective human beings. More precisely, the fundamental dimensions of human and ecological well-being can emerge in dialogue among human persons and communities that are willing to engage in dialogue in spite of their differences.[17] Schillebeeckx's delineation of six anthropological constants is an effort to identify those parameters that need to be respected if all human persons are to be able to live with dignity in a sustainable world ecology.

On the other hand, Schillebeeckx remains convinced that creation faith and the story of Jesus hold a distinctively critical and productive power which can foster the flourishing of the *humanum* and the earth. Human impulses and values need to be interpreted and take shape in concrete human history. This is where the human story and the Christian story can intersect in mutually enlightening ways. The Christian conviction that Jesus is both the 'paradigm of humanity' and 'concentrated creation' provides a hermeneutical lens through which Christians interpret (and experience) what constitutes the well-being of humans and the created world. Those who embrace Christian faith acknowledge and experience the power of God at work in their lives, although that does not relieve them from the rational

---

[17] This claim is fundamental, according to Schillebeeckx, if history is not to be ultimately absurd. In the *Jesus* volume he follows Levinas in describing 'the human being-as possibility-of-communication' (p. 614). This is also the wager of David Tracy's volume *Plurality and Ambiguity* (San Francisco, CA: Harper and Row, 1987).

process of ethical discernment or the rigors of ethical dialogue. Others who do not share the same lens and are not committed to or motivated by the Gospel can nevertheless embrace the vision of human life which they see concretized by Jesus and his followers. Before considering that vision, we turn to Schillebeeckx's proposal regarding the central dimensions of human life which are integral to any form of world-wide ethic.

2. Anthropological Constants: Parameters of the Human

The anthropological constants, according to Schillebeeckx, are enduring human impulses or spheres of value, dimensions of which constitute 'personal identity within social culture' in diverse situations, such that constitutive conditions must be presupposed if human persons, cultures and societies are not to be dehumanized and dehumanizing. These are the parameters within which concrete ethical norms need to be worked out in very different cultural and historical contexts. The first parameter for human survival and the promise of ecological flourishing includes embodiment or corporeality as a constitutive dimension of the human person and an ecological commitment to right relationship with all other creatures and with the natural environment (constant #1).[18] Second, survival and the possibility of flourishing are impossible without the twofold awareness that human persons are essentially related to and directed towards others, but at the same time, human persons cannot be reduced to a network of relationships. This commitment to both relationality and autonomy requires the acceptance and affirmation of the other precisely in her or his otherness, freedom, and inviolable dignity (constant #2). But a personalist or interpersonal understanding of the human is not adequate without the further recognition that social and institutional structures are human creations that can either foster or limit personhood and freedom. A commitment to the future of humanity requires active involvement in the political work of changing structures that dehumanize and enslave, as well as developing institutions that encourage human freedom and the well-being of all creation (constant #3).

Tempering the universalist claims of traditional natural law theory, Schillebeeckx joins forces with a host of contemporary Catholic ethicists in recognizing that all human experience is conditioned by multiple variables

[18] Schillebeeckx acknowledges that the ecological and cosmic dimension of his work needs to be developed more fully and has remarked that his theology of creation provides the basis for that. See: Schillebeeckx, *Church*, pp. 234–46, including the reference to 'ecological experiences of contrast' on p. 239; and the text 'I Believe in God, Creator of Heaven and Earth' included in Edward Schillebeeckx, *God Among Us: The Gospel Proclaimed* (trans. John Bowden; London: SCM, 1983) pp. 91–102.

of social location; in his terms, human experience is 'historically, geographically, and culturally conditioned'.[19] This realization carries with it the ethical responsibility of reflecting critically on one's own concrete situation. Thus, Schillebeeckx argues that to be human is a hermeneutical undertaking and that concrete demands arise from one's particular situation and time in history (constant #4). Here Schillebeeckx joins diverse thinkers, from Gustavo Gutiérrez to Pope John Paul II, in stating that the call to solidarity and an option for the poor are human demands in the contemporary globalized world.[20]

But that claim is not only a religious one rooted in the Hebrew and Christian Scriptures. Political philosopher Martha Nussbaum and economist Amartya Sen offer a similar analysis of a minimum threshold of basic human capabilities, all of which are necessary for human survival and therefore are demanded by human justice. In their language, poverty is 'capability deprivation'.[21] This commitment to human justice on a global scale requires reflection, deliberation and the assumption of ethical responsibility for systemic reform, if history and evolution are not to devolve into the survival of the most powerful. For history to be truly human and for life to be sustainable, both reflection and action are required; theory and practice are co-constitutive dimensions of human life (constant # 5).

The sixth constant that Schillebeeckx identifies in philosophical terms is the 'utopian element' in human consciousness that envisions the future in hope. Some form of faith in the ultimate meaning and worthwhileness of life is part of the health and integrity of human life; without it, human persons lose their identity and genuine human action becomes impossible. A wide range of philosophers, psychologists and therapists have made a similar argument about the centrality of hope for the future for human flourishing and its necessity even for survival (constant #6).[22]

Finally, Schillebeeckx recalls that all six factors are integral to the most basic form of meaningful existence, even survival. The six constants are interrelated and need to be held in tension in any attempt to structure human life and shape human history (constant # 7). Thus, for example, the irreducible pluralism in the fourth constant means that societies will

---

[19] In addition to the references in n. 6, see the writings of Charles E. Curran, Richard A. McCormick, Kenneth Himes, Stephen Pope, and James Keenan, among others.

[20] Schillebeeckx notes that 'because of our general prosperity Western [nations] have a duty to international solidarity, above all to poor countries' (*Christ*, p. 739). See: Gustavo Gutiérrez, 'Memory and Prophecy', *The Option for the Poor in Christian Theology* (ed. Daniel G. Groody; Notre Dame, IN: Notre Dame Press, 2007), pp. 17–38; and John Paul II, *Sollicitudo Rei Socialis*.

[21] See: Martha Nussbaum and Amartya Sen, *The Quality of Life* (New York, NY: Oxford University Press, 1993).

[22] See, for example: Viktor Frankl, *Man's Search for Meaning* (Boston, MA: Beacon, 1963); William F. Lynch, *Images of Hope* (Baltimore, MD: Helicon, 1965).

have to learn how to hold together different systems of beliefs and values, while at the same time making common decisions about structures and institutions that will foster human welfare. Likewise, as medical and psychological research has demonstrated, human bodily welfare and the spiritual dimension of hope for the future are interrelated and essential dimensions of human health. But in what sense, if any, are these guidelines for an adequate contemporary anthropology distinctively Christian?

3. *The Christian Story and the Human Story*

Schillebeeckx locates his consideration of the anthropological constants within a larger discussion of what constitutes salvation in Part Four of his *Christ* volume. In Part One of that text he articulates a theology of revelation and argues that human experience is always interpreted from within a framework of tradition. Attention to that twofold context highlights the interrelationship of anthropology, Christology, and soteriology for Schillebeeckx. As he repeatedly observes, for Christians, Jesus is the paradigm of human life. It is true that Christology and the biblical narrative are not the starting points for his discussion of human life and ethics. But as Walter Kasper has wisely observed, Christology need not be the starting point for an anthropology that is genuinely Christomorphic. Rather, Christology provides a corrective and the lens through which Christians read the human situation.[23] For Schillebeeckx, the concrete life of Jesus provides what Christians view as the most adequate hermeneutical key for how the permanent impulses of human life – the anthropological constants – are to be lived out. The path to human flourishing is, for Christians, the life of Christian discipleship.

This does not undercut Schillebeeckx's previous claims that there are shared human experiences (contingency, negative contrast experiences) and ethical convictions which one might arrive at from an alternative reading of human life, whether an alternative religious tradition or humanistic philosophical and ethical analysis. Rather, from the perspective of Christian creation faith, all of creation participates in the absolute creative and saving presence of God and bears witness to it, at least in fragmentary ways. The ethical reflection and praxis of human beings are manifestations – and realizations – of that one saving grace.

What then is the contribution of the life, death, and resurrection of Jesus – and the ongoing Christian telling of that story in word and deed – to human history and the future of all of creation? Christian faith's wager is that the story of Jesus is at once the paradigm and norm of what is possible for humanity and the definitive revelation of the God whose cause is the

---

[23] See: Schillebeeckx, *Christ*, pp. 778–79.

human cause. In his parabolic preaching and his liberating actions and relationships Jesus enfleshed what it means for human persons to be fully alive and to live in the right relationship with others. The concrete contours of human solidarity – and the grounding of that solidarity in God's own solidarity with the *humanum* – are traced and embodied in the narrative accounts of Jesus' words, deeds, and person. From the Christian perspective, Jesus' preaching of the kingdom of God reveals the true *humanum*.[24] In and through his human life lived in solidarity and love, Jesus defines the true meaning of human freedom and the need to challenge religious, political, and social structures that are dehumanizing or destructive of community.

At the core of Jesus' passion for life and his sense of mission, however, was his experience of being sustained by the one he named 'Abba', the Living God whom Jesus proclaimed to be in solidarity with humanity and to be the source of an all-inclusive and forgiving compassion. It is from the life, death, and resurrection of Jesus that Christians have come to the belief of creation faith that there is a transcendent mystery of love at work in the world, opposing evil and injustice and fostering the flourishing of life, especially among those who are vulnerable, exploited, or in need.

Yet Jesus' history, like all human history, took place in the context of finitude and the threat of evil. Hence, Schillebeeckx has interpreted the death of Jesus as a radical experience of negative contrast. When the unconditional love of Abba met definitive resistance and rejection in the cross, Jesus continued to reveal what is possible when human life is lived in the presence of the Spirit by incorporating the failure of his mission into his own surplus of hope. He died in solidarity with all of the innocent victims of history, entrusting the absurdity of his death to God. For Christians, the resurrection becomes the confirmation of Jesus' life and preaching of the kingdom of God, the transformation of the fiasco of his death, and the promise of final salvation offered to all of God's creation.

Schillebeeckx proposes that creation faith, limned concretely in the life, death, and resurrection of Jesus, stands as a radical critique of all other claims to a total vision for human life. Further, Christian faith is not only critical, but also productive. Critical remembrance of the life, death and resurrection of Jesus shapes not only the imagination, but also the action of contemporary Christians. Formation in the Christian story is meant not to remove Christians from the realm of history, but rather to heighten awareness of what constitutes human flourishing and to deepen concern for those who are the concrete faces of the threatened *humanum* and for the new poor of creation itself. In contrast to many narrative approaches to Christology, Schillebeeckx stresses that the Christian story must be enacted by communities of believers if it is to remain a viable way of reframing the

---

[24] See: Schillebeeckx, *Jesus*, pp. 140–42.

human story which has the power to interrupt and challenge competing cultural narratives of human life.[25]

Here we return to the connection between Christology, creation faith, and ethical praxis. Schillebeeckx maintains that the story of the human Jesus makes clear that 'God entrusts to us the struggle against the powers of chaos'.[26] But the other side of God's radical trust of creation is the autonomy and responsibility of human beings for human history and for care of the earth. The resurrection confirms God's immediate saving presence in the most desperate of circumstances, an inexhaustible source of energy and hope, but that presence is always mediated. The story of Jesus – the definitive promise of God for human salvation – continues in history only if his followers mediate that promise in concrete action on behalf of the *humanum*.

However human mediation, while essential, remains fragmentary and finite, and some of the failures of human history are due to the guilty failures of sin.[27] Here, Christian eschatological hope made possible by the Spirit of Jesus stands as a promise for a future for humankind and the earth which remains beyond our grasp or even beyond our imagination. The contours of that promise are available only in the negative categories of what will not be – no more suffering or death or tears (Rev. 21.4) and in the symbolic language derived from the preaching of Jesus and the Christian scriptures in metaphors such as the 'kingdom of God', 'resurrection of the body', and 'new heaven and new earth'.[28] Ultimately, Schillebeeckx suggests that anthropology and soteriology are most adequately considered in the context of Christology. The previous three metaphors are linked to a fourth – the parousia of Jesus Christ – which serves as a critique of all other versions of the definitive meaning of human history and the creation story.[29]

While Christology is not the starting point for the theological anthropology or ethics proposed by Edward Schillebeeckx, his vision of human

---

[25] See: Edward Schillebeeckx, 'Verzet, engagement en viering', *Nieuwsbrief Stichting Edward Schillebeeckx* no. 5 (October 1992), pp. 1–3 (unpublished translation by Robert J. Schreiter: 'Resistance, Engagement and Celebration'). See also: Lieven Boeve, 'The Sacramental Interruption of Rituals of Life', *Heythrop Journal* 44 (2003), pp. 401–17. Boeve argues that more emphasis needs to be placed on the element of discontinuity between the Christian narrative and sacramental praxis and competing cultural narratives, creating a kind of 'Christian contrast experience'.

[26] Edward Schillebeeckx, *Interim Report on the Books* Jesus & Christ (trans. John Bowden; New York, NY: Crossroad, 1982) p. 110.

[27] Schillebeeckx, *Christ*, p. 815 regarding the mystical power of faith persisting despite everything and when one 'weeps over the fiasco of one's life'.

[28] Schillebeeckx, *On Christian Faith*, pp. 29–30. For development, see the text 'I Believe in the Resurrection of the Body', included in Schillebeeckx, *God Among Us*, pp. 128–48.

[29] Schillebeeckx, *Church*, pp. 134–35.

life and our relationship with the cosmos is distinctly Christomorphic. The narrative of Jesus, remembered, proclaimed, celebrated, and lived by his followers around the globe, is not meant to draw his followers into a separate enclave of salvation. Rather the story of Jesus is meant to turn the faces of those who claim his name towards the little ones whose well-being is threatened in our day.

'DARK LIGHT': WRESTLING WITH THE ANGEL AT THE EDGE OF HISTORY[1]

Elizabeth Kennedy Tillar

1. Introduction

An early pioneer in the exploration of religious sensibilities, Harvard psychologist and philosopher William James provides a fitting introduction to this essay, with his mention of the practical application of non-ordinary states of consciousness:

> Our normal waking consciousness, rational consciousness as we call it, is but one special type of consciousness, whilst all about it, parted from it by the flimsiest of screens, there lie potential forms of consciousness entirely different. We may go through life without suspecting their existence; but apply the requisite stimulus, and at a touch they are there in all their completeness, definite types of mentality which probably somewhere have their field of application and adaptation. No account of the universe in its totality can be final which leaves these other forms of consciousness quite disregarded.[2]

More than three decades ago, Stanley R. Dean stated in a letter to the editor of the *American Journal of Psychiatry* his objection to the prevailing

---

[1] In his discussion of mysticism in *Church: The Human Story of God* (trans. John Bowden; New York, NY: Crossroad, 1990), Edward Schillebeeckx refers to Jan Van Ruysbroeck's term 'dark light' to designate the peak of mystical experience, mediated only by negativity in the absence of any positive concepts or images of God (p. 70).

[2] William James, *The Varieties of Religious Experience: A Study in Human Nature* (repr., New York, NY: Longmans, Green, and Co., 1929) p. 388. Originally presented as The Gifford Lectures on Natural Religion at Edinburgh in 1901–02, the groundbreaking classic was first published in the United States by Longmans, Green, and Co. in 1902.

scientific disdain for what he terms the 'ultraconscious' and the need to reexamine 'ancient beliefs that have remained tenaciously ubiquitous despite scientific indifference':

> To deride in the laboratory what one believes in a church is surely one of the supreme ironies of our age. / According to Aldous Huxley mysticism is the only single effective method that has yet been found for the radical and permanent change of personality.[3]

Since that time, research on the human brain has yielded much knowledge that puts religious states of consciousness in a new, more serious scientific light; innovative technologies, daring concepts, and nascent theories have multiplied along with a myriad applications.[4] It seems that we are on the threshold of an age in which science can now help to illuminate states of consciousness classified as mystical without stripping them of their intrinsic value and, in the process, pave the way for their utilization in addressing human dilemmas.

Cultural and religious influences shape the expression, even the experience, of mystical consciousness, of course. Yet there is something essentially similar about mystical encounters that transcends cultural and religious particulars. The mystical experience eclipses ego-attachments and thereby provides an opportunity for greater conscious awareness of what limits conceptualization and often impedes improvement of our flawed human institutions. Because mystical awareness is experiential and characteristically transcends sensory awareness and discursive reason, the intellect does not comprehend in the usual way; it is therefore impossible to communicate such an experience adequately through language, music, or the graphic/plastic arts. Yet through those very channels and others, such as devoted service, something of the mystical experience can be shared and recognized, as any great literature, whether poetry or prose, gives us

---

[3] Stanley R. Dean, 'Metapsychiatry and the Ultraconscious', Letters to the Editor, *American Journal of Psychiatry* 128 (1971), pp. 662–63. In a previous publication, Dean designates the 'ultraconscious' as a 'suprasensory, suprarational level of mentation otherwise known as cosmic consciousness, transcendental illumination, *unio mystica, satori, samadhi, kairos*, etc.' See Stanley R. Dean, 'Beyond the Unconscious: The Ultraconscious', *American Journal of Psychiatry* 122 (1965), p. 471. See also Stanley R. Dean, 'Is There an Ultraconscious Beyond the Unconscious?', *Canadian Psychiatric Association Journal* 15 (1970), pp. 57–62.

[4] Eugene G. d'Aquili and Andrew B. Newberg, 'The Neuropsychology of Aesthetic, Spiritual, and Mystical States', *Zygon* 35/1 (2000), pp. 39–51. See also articles by Carol Rausch Albright, 'Neuroscience in Pursuit of the Holy: Mysticism, the Brain, and Ultimate Reality', *Zygon* 36/3 (2001), pp. 485–92; and by Nina P. Azari of the Heyendaal Institute, University of Nijmegen: 'Georges Bataille: A Theoretical Resource for Scientific Investigation of Religious Experience', *Journal for Cultural and Religious Theory* 4/3 (2003), pp. 27–41.

glimpses of truths that are impossible to apprehend through analysis or convey through explanation.

Jan Van Ruysbroeck's paradoxical 'dark light' and Edward Schillebeeckx's related 'contrast experience' point to a reservoir of practical insight latent in the human condition. A rupture in our customary perception of reality, occasioning *metanoia* or a shift at the seat of consciousness, is the point of departure for an exploration of the salutary potential of mystical knowledge. Such encounters, often elicited by contrast experiences or trauma, open us to dimensions of consciousness that provide insights into the human condition as well as a stimulus to ethical action.[5] Indeed, contends Schillebeeckx, the experiences that have the profoundest impact on our life are those which shatter our former frame of reference:

> The deepest experiences which guide and support our life are, moreover, experiences of conversion, crucifying experiences which evoke *metanoia*, a change of mind, of action and being. Such experiences demolish their own given identity, but do so in order to lead to a new integration, to a better identity.[6]

Additionally, Schillebeeckx identifies the 'principle for the interpretation of reality' as the stubborn resistance of the mundane to human aspirations and projects. Such 'crucifying experiences' evoke a change of being that propels individuals and society toward a new integration and orientation. By bringing us to the very edge of conceptual knowledge, the intransigence of reality confounds our reason and provides a measure of intuitive insight into matters of ultimate concern.[7] The shattering of habitual cognitive structures, eclipsing ordinary consciousness, coupled with the inbreaking of transcendent knowledge, affords a panoramic expansion of awareness and redefinition of human capacities. A mystical experience of God's absence (*apophasis*) seems to occur at the furthest reaches of consciousness and yields the kind of knowledge that Schillebeeckx calls *'pathic' epistemological*

---

[5] Roberta Culbertson, anthropologist and director of the Institute on Violence and Survival, Virginia Foundation for the Humanities, has pioneered the study of trauma and metaphysics on the campus of the University of Virginia in dialogue with interdisciplinary scholars and survivors of trauma. See Roberta A. Culbertson, 'War and the Nature of Ultimate Things: An Essay on Postwar Cultures', *Engaged Observer: Anthropology, Advocacy, and Activism* (ed. Victoria Sanford and Asale Angel-Ajani; New Brunswick, NJ: Rutgers University Press, 2006), pp. 60–75. See also Jess Byron Hollenback, *Mysticism: Experience, Response, and Empowerment* (University Park, PA: The Pennsylvania State University Press, 1996).

[6] Edward Schillebeeckx, *Christ: The Experience of Jesus as Lord* (trans. by John Bowden; New York, NY: Crossroad, 1981) p. 816.

[7] Edward Schillebeeckx, *On Christian Faith: The Spiritual, Ethical, and Political Dimensions* (trans. John Bowden; New York, NY: Crossroad, 1987) p. 48.

intuition.[8] The intellectual insight such an experience imparts; the antidotes it augurs to the plagues of war and structural violence; and its potential to curb other compulsive patterns in human history could help to sustain global renovation over the longer term.

Robert Heilbroner, whom Schillebeeckx cites as one of his sources,[9] says in *An Inquiry into the Human Prospect*, that 'cool reason' alone cannot motivate us to care for posterity, e.g., to forego ozone-depleting conveniences or curb energy-consuming luxuries; nothing short of a 'survivalist ethic' based on a sense of personal responsibility that triumphs over immediate, egoistic interests will impel us to protect the future of humanity.[10] As our species has come to realize, belatedly, we cannot spoil our own eco-niche or perpetuate war without endangering the larger environment and future generations; moreover, not only our physical survival but also our spiritual destiny is at stake.[11]

As a practical approach, social critical theory provides a frame of reference in which experiences of apparently meaningless suffering are construed as potentially valuable insofar as they afford opportunities for insight into reality and for action to improve the human condition. In response to critical theory, Schillebeeckx coined the term 'contrast experience' to refer to any form of negativity, particularly suffering, that reveals a positive value.[12] During the 1970s and 1980s, he integrated into his theology critical theory's 'principle of correlation of critical resistance' to ideologies and inhumane systems so as to interpret suffering for others in a meaningful way – as a critical element in the healing of systems that cause suffering.[13] In keeping with that orientation, the present paper addresses the theoretical-practical value of knowledge acquired primarily in boundary situations, such as violence, illness, poverty, chronic social dysfunction, and infrastructure collapse or crisis ('contrast experiences'), as well as in the positive disclosure experiences of the divine. The necessity of channeling the wellsprings of such knowledge – by way of interpretation, application to the various theoretical and practical disciplines, enculturation, and

[8] Schillebeeckx, *On Christian Faith*, p. 67.
[9] See Schillebeeckx, *Christ*, p. 888 n. 6.
[10] Robert Heilbroner, *An Inquiry into The Human Prospect* (New York, NY: Norton, 1980) pp. 179–86.
[11] Schillebeeckx, *Christ*, pp. 735–36.
[12] Robert J. Schreiter, 'Edward Schillebeeckx: An Orientation to his Thought', *The Schillebeeckx Reader* (ed. Robert J. Schreiter; New York: Crossroad, 1984), pp. 1–24 (18) and Edward Schillebeeckx, 'Living in Human Society', *The Schillebeeckx Reader* (ed. Robert J. Schreiter; New York, NY: Crossroad, 1984), pp. 45-59 (45 [= intr. by Schreiter] and 54–59).
[13] Edward Schillebeeckx, *The Understanding of Faith: Interpretation and Criticism* (trans. N.D. Smith; New York, NY: Seabury, 1974) p. 93.

dissemination of resources – is a perennial catalyst for salvation history. Schillebeeckx writes:

> In forms which will constantly become obsolete and which in fact are obsolete, eschatological salvation must be made visible in fragments on the level of our human history: in human hearts and in structures, because (above all in our contemporary society) the heart or love is also communicated through structures.[14]

2. Mysticism, the 'Contrast Experience', and Critical Negativity

Both suffering for others and the mystical, particularly apophatic, experience of God provide access to knowledge needed to alleviate suffering. In Schillebeeckx's view, ethical consciousness is not simply an acquired value transmitted by tradition and honed through discipline. Human beings are endowed with the capacity for contemplative knowledge and redemptive activity through a personal encounter with transcendent reality, or grace. The intuitive knowledge received through grace motivates people to alleviate suffering and its causes. Moreover, ethical praxis necessarily occurs within social and economic structures as well as diverse theoretical and practical disciplines, all of which constitute the historical medium in which grace is made manifest.

Mystical awareness is linked to the critical element of 'contrast' and dialectically related to the critical negativity of suffering in Schillebeeckx's theology of redemption. As an experience of contrast, suffering contains *in potentia* 'pathic' epistemological insight, which he defines as a critical force 'which leads to new action, which anticipates a better future and seeks to put it into practice'.[15] Schillebeeckx's perception of suffering as a critical tool, with its mystical grounding in the divine Being, is predicated on its singular capacity to plumb the depths of the human condition. Its source is the contrast, or critical negativity, intrinsic to suffering, which holds in

---

[14] Schillebeeckx, *Christ*, p. 745.

[15] Schillebeeckx, *Christ*, p. 818. Schillebeeckx is said to have found the terms *ortho-pathy* and *orthopraxy* in the following passage (Schillebeeckx, *Christ*, p. 888 n. 3):

> Strictly speaking, orthodoxy in religion is concerned only with doctrine or belief, with the intellectual element of spiritual life ... But since religion embraces feeling and activity as well as thought, orthodoxy becomes an inadequate criterion of its worth apart from right experience and right conduct. It ought to have for its correlatives such words as 'orthopathy' and 'orthopraxy', the inward experience and the outward exercise of piety [William A. Curtis, 'Orthodoxy', *Encyclopedia of Religion and Ethics* (vol. 9; Edinburgh, 1917), pp. 570–72 (570)].

counterpoise the contemplative and active possibilities of human nature. The dual character of critical suffering engenders what Schillebeeckx construes as its epistemological potency, which is focused on the future.[16] In short, he perceives the critical element of suffering as a unique means of attaining knowledge of the human condition and of tapping the creative potential inherent in negativity.

Schillebeeckx's insight owes much to Theodor Adorno's negative dialectics, in particular, which has its roots not only in the Frankfurt School of social critical theory but also in Jewish apophatic theology. To encapsulate, for Adorno, the dialectical tension between subject and object is the creative friction of nonidentity, which gives rise to consciousness, reflection, and critical thought.[17] His consistent refusal to define the 'ideal' future of humanity in a positive, concrete way is likened to the Jewish taboo on visible/tangible representations of God: 'Like the Jewish prohibition against graven images of the Holy One, critical theory refused to delineate in an affirmative manner the nature of the "utopia", the "good" and the "truth" towards which it is oriented.'[18]

Similarly, Johann Baptist Metz makes reference to 'the category of the knowledge of absence (which is grounded in anamnestic reason). This kind of knowledge has been nurtured above all in the traditions of negative theology.'[19] Jon Sobrino alludes to the tradition of negative theology contained in scripture: 'It must be remembered that the negative moment of human existence and history has been central to every theology. This can be seen already in the Bible where this negative moment appears in various forms: as ... slavery, meaninglessness, poverty, injustice, etc.'[20] The critical sensibility fostered by apophatic theology and worldly experiences of suffering – Auschwitz, Cambodia, Bosnia, Rwanda and Darfur, etc. – are essential in envisioning and creating a better world; only by way of negative contrast can eschatological reality be discerned:

---

[16] Edward Schillebeeckx, *Jesus: An Experiment in Christology* (trans. Hubert Hoskins; New York, NY: Crossroad, 1981) pp. 621–22.

[17] Joan Alway, *Critical Theory and Political Possibilities: Conceptions of Emancipatory Politics in the Works of Horkheimer, Adorno, Marcuse, and Habermas* (Contributions in Sociology, 111; Westport, CT: Greenwood Press, 1995) p. 64. See Theodor Adorno, *Negative Dialectics* (trans. E.B. Ashton; New York, NY: Continuum, 2nd edn, 1982). See also Elizabeth K. Tillar, 'The Influence of Social Critical Theory on Edward Schillebeeckx's Theology of Suffering for Others', *The Heythrop Journal* 42/2 (2001), pp. 148–72.

[18] J. A. Colombo, *An Essay on Theology and History: Studies in Pannenberg, Metz, and the Frankfurt School* (Atlanta, GA: Scholars Press, 1990) p. 240.

[19] Johann Baptist Metz, *A Passion for God: The Mystical-Political Dimension of Christianity* (trans. J. Matthew Ashley; New York, NY: Paulist, 1998) p. 28.

[20] Jon Sobrino, 'Theology in a Suffering World', *Theology Digest* 41 (1994), pp. 25–30 (26).

> In other words, contrast experiences – the experiences of coming up against reality in its refractory yet revelatory power – reveal fragmentary glimpses of something beyond us. At the same time, because reality is given to us as a gift and because we are part of it, this revelation is also very much our own.[21]

Such contrast experiences are constitutive of human nature: one cannot recognize suffering except in juxtaposition to a foreshadowing of happiness – 'and unjust suffering at least presupposes a vague awareness of the possible positive significance of human integrity'.[22] Therefore, suffering is integral to our apprehension of the kind of world that is possible:

> As a *contrast* experience, the experience of suffering presumes, after all, an implicit impulse toward happiness. And as an experience of injustice, it presumes at least a dim consciousness of the positive prospects of human integrity. As a contrast experience, it implies indirectly a consciousness of an appeal of and to the *humanum*. In this sense, activity which overcomes suffering is only possible on the basis of at least an implicit or inchoate anticipation of a possible, *coming* universal meaning.[23]

Since an eschatological vision assumes points of contrast, the prophetic role of Jesus has its deepest source in the manifest discontinuity between the life God intended for humankind and the history of injustice and suffering: 'In the prophet Jesus, mysticism and the healing of men came from one and the same source: his experience of the contrast between the living God and the history of human suffering.'[24] In his lengthy essay on the structure of Schillebeeckx's Christology, Gabriel Fackre remarks: 'Schillebeeckx believes that his elemental trust in, and intercourse with, God constituted the grounds of Jesus' assurance about the solidarity of God with the human venture – and the resolution of the dilemma of negativity.'[25] The intimate relationship Jesus enjoyed with God – his *Abba* experience – afforded him a rare perspective from which to survey the human condition and proffer the hope of salvation:

> Such a hope, expressed in a proclamation of the coming and already close salvation for men implied in God's rule – now that we have uncovered the unique quality of Jesus' religious life in terms of his (historically exceptional) *Abba* address to God – in Jesus is quite

---

[21] William P. George, 'The Praxis of the Kingdom of God: Ethics in Schillebeeckx' *Jesus* and *Christ*', *Horizons* 12/1 (1985), pp. 44–69 (51).

[22] Schillebeeckx, *Christ*, p. 818.

[23] Schillebeeckx, 'Living in Human Society', p. 55.

[24] Schillebeeckx, *Christ*, p. 821.

[25] Gabriel J. Fackre, 'Bones Strong and Weak in the Skeletal Structure of Schillebeeckx's Christology', *Journal of Ecumenical Studies* 21/2 (1984), pp. 248–77 (257).

plainly rooted in a personal awareness of contrast: on the one hand the incorrigible, irremediable history of man's suffering, a history of calamity, violence and injustice, of grinding, excruciating and oppressive enslavement; on the other hand Jesus' particular awareness of God, his *Abba* experience, his intercourse with God as the benevolent, solicitous 'one who is against evil,' who will not admit the supremacy of evil and refuses to allow it the last word.[26]

Jesus' anticipation of eschatological salvation, like the visions of Micah and Isaiah in which predator and prey are reconciled, is a critical, prophetic dynamism in society: 'Such a prophetic promise is a permanent force, critical of society, which still discovers subtle causes of evil and suffering on the basis of mystical experience of God, where they are not encountered without mystical experience.'[27] Only in mystical experiences of contrast (especially the *via negativa*), to which 'pathic' perception is deeply related, can the subtlest forms and causes of evil and suffering – and their antidote – be detected: 'Mysticism is therefore itself a liberating force.'[28]

Schillebeeckx classifies mysticism as an 'extension of prayer', in which one tries to apprehend God directly but cannot; proximity to God is always mediated. Mysticism is an intense or concentrated form of prayer, which is nevertheless an *indirect* encounter with God. Schillebeeckx uses the term 'mediated immediacy', which contains traces of transcendental Thomism, to express the manner or mode in which creature and creator are related. Janet Callewaert explicates Schillebeeckx's use of the term in her essay on his soteriology:

> 'Mediated immediacy' concerns the unique relationship between finite beings and the infinite God who is absolute origin ... All that is not God derives the totality of its existence and activity from the creator who as absolute freedom transcends all things through interiority. This means that the living God is the depth dimension of all reality. The fundamental medium of the creator is the creation. The relationship between the infinite creator and the finite creature is mediated through an encounter with the world, human history, and human beings.[29]

Moreover, in the furthest reaches of mystical awareness, God is apprehended negatively as a 'dark night' (John of the Cross) or a 'dark light' (Ruysbroeck) in which the experience of communion is not buttressed by

---

[26] Schillebeeckx, *Jesus*, p. 267. See also pp. 621–22.
[27] Schillebeeckx, *Christ*, p. 821.
[28] Schillebeeckx, *Christ*, p. 821.
[29] Janet M. Callewaert, 'Salvation from God in Jesus the Christ: Soteriology', *The Praxis of Christian Experience: An Introduction to the Theology of Edward Schillebeeckx* (ed. Robert J. Schreiter and Mary Catherine Hilkert; San Francisco, CA: Harper and Row, 1989), pp. 68–85 (78). See also Schillebeeckx, *Christ*, pp. 810–17.

positive concepts or images of any kind.[30] Schillebeeckx says of the *via negativa*, or apophatic experience of God:

> This awareness of being grounded in God, of persisting when every empirical foundation and every guarantee have been removed and one weeps over the fiasco of one's life, is the mystical power of faith. When we lose all our supports, even those which can be experienced empirically with some degree of positiveness, the immediacy of the presence of God is in fact experienced as a 'dark night'. All the mystics have experienced this immediacy of the presence of God as a *nada*. One might say that they have experienced it not as a nothingness (*nada*) of emptiness, but as a nothingness of fullness: God's presence as a pure experience of faith, even if this is communicated in a negative way.[31]

There are also positive or joyful experiences that reveal God's hidden presence, of course, both in the workaday world ('the implicit life of prayer') and in '*explicit prayer*'. Schillebeeckx defines the latter as 'man's attempt to see this dimension of immediacy, an attempt to which the believing life of the everyday world as it were drives him, because the believer is aware of the *real* (though mediated) nearness of God'.[32] Mary Catherine Hilkert says that Schillebeeckx perceives both positive 'disclosure experiences' and negative 'contrast experiences' as the basis 'of the religious claim that there is a mystery of graciousness at the depth of human experience and of reality as a whole, the mystery believers identify as "divine" or name "God"!'[33] In short, whether in positive encounters or in negative contrast experiences, one cannot apprehend the divine reality directly; without the veil of mediation, God disappears into invisibility.[34] Furthermore, irrespective of how the mystical encounter is mediated – whether by aesthetic forms, nature, the family or society, the Torah, the *mysterium tremendum*, Christ, etc. – 'it is always an experience of totality: a kind of feeling of the presence of the whole of reality, indeed an experience of the source of everything'.[35]

In either propitious or negative encounters, a contrast with the 'opposite' is implicit, producing intuitions or glimmerings of a better reality. Fackre sees in the single concept of 'contrast' the same two kinds of experiences that Hilkert identifies: 'Negativity and its contrast partner breed a dream of salvation, the righting of every wrong, the mending of every flaw. The

---

[30] Schillebeeckx, *On Christian Faith*, p. 67.

[31] Schillebeeckx, *Christ*, pp. 815–16.

[32] Schillebeeckx, *Christ*, p. 816.

[33] Mary Catherine Hilkert, 'Discovery of the Living God: Revelation and Experience', *The Praxis of Christian Experience: An Introduction to the Theology of Edward Schillebeeckx* (ed. Robert J. Schreiter and Mary Catherine Hilkert; San Francisco, CA: Harper & Row, 1989), pp. 35–51 (41).

[34] Schillebeeckx, *Christ*, p. 816.

[35] Schillebeeckx, *On Christian Faith*, p. 69.

fragmentary shall be made whole, the fleeting permanent, ill-being transformed into well-being.'[36] Whether such intuitions issue from positive disclosures that intensify the 'wrongness' of evil and suffering *or* result from negative experiences that evoke the awareness of a potentially better reality, a vision of change is implicit in them.[37] In a lengthy footnote in *Christ*, Schillebeeckx delineates the nature of the critical force that can emerge from either positive or negative experiences, or more precisely, from their 'dialectical tension':

> As *human*, earthly experiences of meaning are always 'on the way', they are always threatened by the negative and develop a critical and productive force. Thus recollection of positive experiences of meaning and joy refines the concern to track down suffering and strengthens resistance against it. So, too, God is pure happiness and pure goodness; in the light of what is actually evil in the creaturely world, he can therefore only be called the 'anti-evil'. So we have to say that the *critical* practical force does not lie either in the positive or in the negative, but only in their dialectical tension, that is, *in* the experience of contrast in suffering of men who receive and give meaning.[38]

It is essential to bear in mind that in Schillebeeckx's theology, revelation must be wedded to ethical action.[39] Jesus' mystical experience of God was conveyed through his abiding concern for human beings in their situations of suffering: 'As a result, a concept of God is expressed which is both deeply mystical and prophetic; this happens in an indissoluble unity in which ethics combines the mystical element of faith with the political element of the same faith.'[40] For Schillebeeckx, political love or 'praxis of liberation', a contemporary medium of Christian faith, has much in common with the classic mysticism of contemplation:

> This form of love and holiness has its greatest opportunities precisely in our time ... Moreover, this political form of the Christian love of God and neighbour, albeit in another field of experience, knows the same repentance and *metanoia*, the same asceticism and self-emptying, the same suffering and the same dark nights and losing itself in the other as was once the case in contemplative mysticism. This political holiness today already has its own martyrs, for the

---

[36] Fackre, 'Bones Strong and Weak', p. 251.

[37] Fackre, 'Bones Strong and Weak', p. 251.

[38] Schillebeeckx, *Christ*, p. 897 n. 158.

[39] For an interpretation of the transformation of Moses' personality, see the Guest Editorial by Dov Steinmetz, 'Moses' "Revelation" on Mount Horeb as a Near-Death Experience', *Journal of Near-Death Studies* 11/4 (1993), pp. 199–203.

[40] Schillebeeckx, *On Christian Faith*, p. 70.

sake of righteousness among men and women as God's cause; for the mysterious term 'kingdom of God' also denotes that.[41]

The anguish of the disenfranchised transformed into political action receives its Christian impetus from a mysticism of the cross. Even in grave situations of injustice for which there is no human remedy:

> It is possible to speak of a mystical dimension in man's life and this implies that man can oppose repression and violence by giving meaning; in the face of his own impotence to change the objective structures at any given time, he can transcend the situation and affirm the meaning of real humanity.[42]

Jesus suffered the ignominy of a criminal's death, yet through his obedience to God and his willing sacrifice for suffering humanity he defeated the cruelty of human injustice and bestowed on the world the promise of redemption:

> Even in the most apparently hopeless situation, there is always the possibility of mystical opposition through the sacrifice of the cross. This mystical form of criticism is, of course, not immune from possible misuse by the establishment. There are sufficient historical examples of the integration and neutralisation of the 'sacrifice of the cross' so that 'the system' will be perpetuated. In spite of this possibility of misuse, however, I am sure that the dialectical tension between the mystical dimension and the socio-political emancipative dimension is essential to the integrity of our humanity.[43]

The primary role of suffering in the dialectic of mystical contemplation and socio-political action is to add an inner tension (between the 'already now' and the 'not yet') to any understanding of redemption – a tension that galvanizes Christians and others to protest injustice and stand in solidarity with all who suffer.[44] As already stated, mysticism encompasses not only inter-subjective service to individuals but also a critical-cum-practical response to unjust socio-political structures; in other words, salvation must be sought in more than a single dimension of life.[45] 'In the past, mysticism was often identified with contemplation and, given the historical and social situation, love of neighbour had virtually only the form of inter-personal dealings and encounter.'[46] However, in our time, love of neighbour is also

---

[41] Schillebeeckx, On Christian Faith, pp. 73–74.
[42] Schillebeeckx, The Understanding of Faith, p. 146.
[43] Schillebeeckx, The Understanding of Faith, p. 146.
[44] Schillebeeckx, Christ, p. 817.
[45] Schillebeeckx, Christ, p. 812. See also: pp. 716–17.
[46] Schillebeeckx, On Christian Faith, p. 71.

tacitly expressed in human organizational structures and through the application of critical theories and skills:

> So love of God – ultimately mysticism – can enter the concrete social and political commitment of Christians. In that case mysticism and politics are in the same unity in tension for Christians as love of God and love of neighbour, two forms of one and the same theologal attitude.[47]

In addition to the 'unity in tension' of mysticism and politics occasioned by experiences of contrast, the epistemological value peculiar to suffering provides a link between contemplation and various forms of controlling knowledge. It is critical of both contemplative knowledge and science and technology while, at the same time, it can hold in counterpoise the contemplative or aesthetic ('purpose-free') and active or controlling ('purposive') potentialities of the human mind.[48] Only in experiences of contrast, or critical negativity, can suffering form a bridge between contemplation and action, because it alone partakes of both forms of knowledge. The dual nature of critical suffering, derived from a confluence of theoretical and practical knowledge, engenders its 'pathic' epistemological power, which is focused on the future: 'It is a knowledge which looks for the *future* and opens it up.'[49] And its dynamism or 'character of ethical protest' makes it a powerful tool in the removal of injustices.[50]

Precisely by virtue of its critical negativity and its intrinsic connection to contemplation and action, suffering reveals to the discerning conscience the possibility of a more just and compassionate world: 'In other words, qua contrast experience it implies indirectly an awareness of a positive call of and to the *humanum*.'[51] This recognition, derived from the critical mediation of suffering, points toward a new praxis that will usher in human wholeness:

> The long course of human suffering yet possesses a critical cognitive force that calls out for a praxis that will open up 'future'. Passive (suffering) contrast experiences are therefore the negative and dialectical coming to consciousness of a desiderium, a longing, and of a question about meaning 'on its way' and real freedom, wholeness and happiness to come.[52]

Because it is impossible for humanity to eliminate 'every form of alien-

---

[47] Schillebeeckx, *On Christian Faith*, p. 71.
[48] Schillebeeckx, *Christ*, pp. 817–18.
[49] Schillebeeckx, *Christ*, pp. 817–18.
[50] Schillebeeckx, *Christ*, pp. 817–18.
[51] Schillebeeckx, *Jesus*, p. 622.
[52] Schillebeeckx, *Jesus*, p. 622.

ation', Schillebeeckx regards the mystical and liturgical dimensions as indispensable: 'They cannot be dismissed as a phenomenon left over from the past or as a form of compensation, if society still contains elements of repression and violence.'[53] As Winston Persaud expresses it:

> In the face of the appalling suffering in the world, and our witting and unwitting participation in economic and political systems that tear away at the inextricable unity that Christians share in Christ, the Eucharist *re-presents* the suffering of Jesus Christ for the sake of the world and simultaneously *presents* the world of suffering in need of healing.[54]

When understood as a 'living remembrance' of Christ's passion, *anamnesis* – liturgical expression that promotes ethical action to alleviate suffering – has a critical, epistemological force: 'So if it is rightly performed, there is in sacramental symbolic action a powerful historical potential which can integrate mysticism and politics (albeit in secular forms).'[55] Just as socio-political programs can be a 'foretaste of true salvation', so action in the form of technology, or 'manipulative scientific knowledge', can potentially uproot both suffering and its causes.[56]

The 'pathic' epistemological power, intrinsic to contrast experiences, can be operative in scientific technology as well as in political liber-ation movements if the technology or political programme is wedded to ethico-religious consciousness. For that reason the distinction between contemplative and controlling kinds of knowledge is not intellectually palatable to everyone. In his article on Schillebeeckx's ethics, William George acknowledges that Schillebeeckx includes science in his under-standing of God's 'historical communication of grace'.[57] However, George argues that science is not given its proper due in Schillebeeckx's religious ethics, that his work draws too sharp a distinction between intuitive knowledge, with its 'pathic' peculiarity, and scientific knowledge:

> Schillebeeckx affirms that the sciences, along with ethico-political analysis of the problems facing humanity, can be fields of grace... They, too, are part of God's creation. What I wish to emphasize perhaps more strongly than he does is that they can be fields of grace of Jesus Christ, crucified and risen. The *memoria Christi*, it occurs to

---

[53] Schillebeeckx, *The Understanding of Faith*, p. 147.
[54] Winston D. Persaud, 'The Cross of Jesus Christ, the Unity of the Church, and Human Suffering', *The Scandal of a Crucified World: Perspectives on the Cross and Suffering* (ed. Yacob Tesfai; Maryknoll, NY: Orbis, 1994), pp. 111–29 (128).
[55] Schillebeeckx, *Christ*, pp. 820 and 836.
[56] Schillebeeckx, *Christ*, pp. 812–13.
[57] George, 'The Praxis of the Kingdom of God', p. 67; and Schillebeeckx, *Christ*, p. 812.

me, can reside implicitly at the core of a science that truly liberates people from various forms of alienation.[58]

George argues that the contemplative dimension of science is not given sufficient weight in Schillebeeckx's work because of the technological uses and abuses to which science is prone that neglect and obscure the real needs of suffering humanity.[59]

The following egregious example of suffering caused by the misuse of technology sadly illustrates how the compulsion to utilize scientific knowledge, despite known dangers, can dehumanize us and perpetuate suffering. Both the 'deliberate and accidental releases of radioactive materials into the environment' of Mayak (Ural Mountains) and Krasnoyarsk (Siberia), now two of the most toxic areas in the world, have caused sterility, premature births, chronic and terminal diseases, chromosome damage and often-severe birth defects within the affected human populations, tragically manifest in many children and adults.[60] 'For Schillebeeckx, religious consciousness must come to the rescue, reminding science that in its mania for control it cannot run roughshod over human beings and that even the human liberation it brings is only partial.'[61]

Although George concurs with Schillebeeckx's view, he points out that a science given to such excesses is a *counterfeit*, not a true science – a point with which I think Schillebeeckx would agree. In his work, both science and religion are held to the same standard: 'Where religion or science is made absolute, rather than God himself, not only the image of God but mankind itself is disfigured: *ecce homo* – on the cross and on the many crosses which men have set up and keep setting up.'[62] Schillebeeckx's criticism of science is levelled not at science *per se* but at its monopoly on the direction of human progress and its often-flagrant disregard for the dignity of human beings. But when science is properly applied to situations of oppression, illness, or impoverishment in the world, it is an instrument of the earthly component of salvation:

The sciences are children of their time and in their own intrinsic autonomy reflect the hesitations, the blind spots and even the sicknesses of their time ... It is a fact that science and technology cannot bring men their authentic salvation: 'holiness' and wisdom. What they can do is make us considerably more competent, and that

[58] George, 'The Praxis of the Kingdom of God', pp. 67–68.
[59] George, 'The Praxis of the Kingdom of God', p. 67.
[60] 'Mayak/Krasnoyarsk: Contamination and Health Effects', Greenpeace International, October 9, 2000, http://archive.greenpeace.org/~nuclear/waste/mayakkrasnohealth.pdf (last checked on September 21, 2009).
[61] George, 'The Praxis of the Kingdom of God', p. 67.
[62] Schillebeeckx, 'Living in Human Society', p. 50.

in itself is a blessing. Science and technology work miracles when they are used to bring about the freedom of others, solidarity among men and women.[63]

Furthermore, for Schillebeeckx the critical alliance of theology with the social sciences reveals (among other things) vital elements of the history of religious tradition that have been submerged, such as the prominent roles of women in early Christianity or the mystical tradition itself. And secular disciplines are instrumental in the unfolding potentiality of critical remembrance and epistemological intuition to redress social injustice or laxity and alleviate unnecessary suffering. Schillebeeckx contends that embedded in the very structure of the faith tradition is the predisposition of Christians to detect in the workaday world elements in their own tradition that were ignored or quashed by the dominant powers. In the larger environment, then, Christians learn to perceive the lost or dormant possibilities (reminiscences) of their religion and to forge alliances with other emancipatory systems.[64]

> The message of Jesus demands freedom and love for each and everyone, without any exclusiveness. But the latent possibilities of this message are not immediately and automatically revealed 'en bloc', but gradually in the historical progression of the growing human self-awareness. Christian, critical solidarity with the emancipatory history of freedom and a coalition of the theology with critical social theories of humanity can here and now become a necessary dimension of the historically situated *caritas*, of Christian love, and of theology.[65]

Schillebeeckx resolutely maintains that the church must be in dialogue with the secular world in order to discern the truth of its own scriptures. In so doing,

> She will hear the Good News which is always normative for her and which comes to us not only from scripture, but also and equally from every human existential experience which is, in one way or another, always confronted by the grace of the living God.[66]

From the church's perspective, such dialogue is undergirded and guided by the eschatological expectation of the Judeo-Christian tradition, without

---

[63] Schillebeeckx, 'Living in Human Society', p. 49.

[64] Edward Schillebeeckx, 'God, Society and Human Salvation', *Faith and Society/ Foi et société/Geloof en maatschappij: Acta Congressus Internationalis Theologici Lovaniensis 1976* (ed. Marc Caudron; BETL, 47; Leuven: Duculot, 1978), pp. 87–99 (93).

[65] Schillebeeckx, 'God, Society and Human Salvation', pp. 93–94.

[66] Edward Schillebeeckx, *World and Church* (trans. N.D. Smith; Theological Soundings, 3; New York, NY: Sheed and Ward, 1971) p. 105.

which there would be no point in striving for the world's improvement: 'It is precisely because there is an absolute, transcendent, eschatological expectation of salvation for man that commitment to the planning of temporal society and to a world that is more worthy of man is ultimately meaningful.'[67]

In addition, Christianity and theology must recognize their unique 'religio-critical' contribution to the betterment of society and not simply repeat what critical social theories can do more effectively.[68] The interpretations of the world that theology or religion proposes are intrinsically related to the correlative praxis that such interpretations produce. The goals of religious service should spring from the specifically religious experience of the Holy; otherwise, religion is reduced to 'mere magic' or 'pure ethics' (divorced from an experience of *the sacred*).[69] 'Indeed, only in so far as we can recognize the unique critico-hermeneutical force and impulse of religion, can (on account of internal abundance) religion provide a service to the world which is both *specifically religious* and *practically operational* in the world.'[70] That critical-interpretive force – a 'pathic' epistemological power, as identified by one in communion with the divine nature – is an inner consequence of the radical disparity between the life God intended for humanity and the history of injustice and suffering.

3. Practical Applications of Critical Suffering and Epistemological Intuition

Schillebeeckx's system of anthropological coordinates or constants provides the framework for the integration of various elements of his work and the views of other theologians, philosophers, and social scientists as they pertain to the theme of redemptive suffering in the actualization of the *humanum*. His schema of seven coordinates emphasizes the need to integrate the dimensions of human existence *and* presupposes that in our complex world love is very often communicated through structures.[71] For example, global

---

[67] Schillebeeckx, *World and Church*, p. 105.

[68] Schillebeeckx, 'God, Society and Human Salvation', pp. 94–95.

[69] Schillebeeckx, 'God, Society and Human Salvation', p. 95.

[70] Schillebeeckx, 'God, Society and Human Salvation', p. 95.

[71] The proposed anthropological coordinates or constants are as follows: the relation to our corporeality, to nature, and to the ecological environment; the conditioning of human personal identity by relationships with others; our connection with social institutions and structures; the conditioning of people by time and space; the unity of theory and praxis; and the religious or 'para-religious' consciousness of humankind; and the irreducible synthesis of these six dimensions. See Elizabeth K. Tillar, 'Chapter 5: A Synthesis of the Social, Ethical, and Theological Dimensions of Schillebeeckx's Theology of Redemptive Suffering', 'Suffering for Others in the Theology of Edward Schillebeeckx' (unpublished doctoral dissertation, Fordham University, 2000), pp. 59–66.

efforts to curb the spread of AIDS and to provide food and medical care to impoverished or war-torn communities are perhaps the most obvious examples of the reality that *caritas* or healing love is communicated through structures.[72] Often disease is enabled by *preventable* environmental and social factors; in such cases, structures can be reformed or abolished to alleviate suffering and, ideally, eliminate the causes of a given disease.

Political structures and the many agencies of the United Nations as well as the countless non-governmental organizations (NGOs), in order to be most effective, require an ethical infrastructure that is implemented worldwide, a real challenge in a global matrix perceived by many as inevitably pluralistic and even relativistic. On what basis, then, do we decide which values will serve to protect and further the best interest of a diverse *humanum*? Cultural and ethical relativism are useful in generating a healthy respect for diversity; at the same time, consciousness cannot hope to evolve on a global scale if human societies/factions continue to generate or sustain war, genocide, torture, terrorism, and harmful traditional practices. Concerning the last-mentioned phenomenon, the unique value of native and traditional cultures far outweighs any specific dysfunctional aspect of a culture group. It has been a high priority of the U.N. and many private agencies and organizations to assist in preserving cultures, developing their economies, protecting natural resources, facilitating greater self-sufficiency, and immunizing children worldwide. If individual human rights are being violated, however, that will be cause for concern and, often, humanitarian action, since the governments of many countries, including our own, are not always protective and supportive of all members equally.

The humanitarian work of the U.N. agencies and NGOs is facilitated by the body of human rights instruments and other international laws, such as the Convention on the Rights of the Child; the Convention on the Elimination of All Forms of Discrimination Against Women; the Convention Against Torture and Other Cruel, Inhuman, or Degrading Treatment or Punishment, and many others. These instruments serve as the standard by which ratifying nations agree to conduct their domestic and international affairs and provide the legal basis for investigations and implementation of economic sanctions to curb violations of international standards/covenants. Through the prism of embodied ethical criteria, which have their ground in the depth dimension of reality and in lived experiences of contrast, we can and already do collectively establish universal principles and guidelines for the world. Schillebeeckx contends that knowledge to improve society is acquired through the criticism of the history of suffering and that ethical imperatives emerge from such knowledge:

---

[72] See *An Imperfect Offering: Dispatches from the Medical Frontline* (London: Random House, 2008) by James Orbinski, a physician and past president of *Médicins sans frontières*.

In the situation of our existing *condition humaine* and under the conditions of our particular social culture, contemplation and action can only be connected through the criticism of the accumulated history of suffering and the ethical awareness that comes to birth in it. The situation is paradoxical but nevertheless real.[73]

We hear about the failings of the Security Council and bureaucratic issues of the U.N. and criticism is necessary to correct such things, of course. Yet, due to media neglect of the larger reality, there is insufficient awareness of how much is being done by the specialized agencies of the U.N. and many non-governmental organizations to further our survival and development, irrespective of religious and political belief systems, such as the work of Catholic Relief Services in non-Christian countries devastated by natural disasters, war, and drought. During my career, I have engaged in dialogue with the work of NGOs (Amnesty International, Human Rights Watch, the Inter-African Committee, and others) as well as many U.N. agencies (UNICEF, UNESCO, World Health Organization, U.N. Development Programme, U.N. Environment Programme, etc.).[74] Their work is a service of great magnitude and inspired by the desire to make the world a safe, socially just, productive, and healthful place for everyone – in contrast to other forces that shape the world (lust for power, greed, political/ethnic animosities, religious and political ideologies, competition for land and food, and so forth). The desire to create a *humane* and *sustainable* global society is the driving ethical force of the U.N. and allied agencies, with as little encroachment on cultural uniqueness as possible.

People deprived of basic literacy and education; continually subjected to physical cruelty and the resulting trauma; severely limited by food scarcity and malnourishment; divested of basic rights by gender and ethnic discrimination; constantly beset by the anxiety of war; terrorized by personal violence, etc. are often damaged for life – less productive and unable to lead meaningful lives that further their culture's general welfare and the world economy. It is staggering to contemplate the brain power and talent lost to the world at large because the reigning government or the dominant force of a given society does not permit other segments of that same society to flourish and contribute their energies, services, products, and ideas to their own culture (and to the rest of us). Yet, even in the throes of debilitating pain, oppression, and spiritual suffering, there remains the possibility of

---

[73] Schillebeeckx, *Christ*, p. 818.
[74] I conducted research on female genital mutilation (FGM) in 1989–90 while working at the Church Center of the United Nations. My paper on the subject was subsequently published as 'Rights of Passage: Toward the Elimination of Female Circumcision', *International Health and Development* (Journal of the Institute for International Health and Development of the Catholic University of America) 3/1 (1992), pp. 14–22.

divine-human insight and the emergence of new theories and practical skills in the service of the *humanum*. The future is both a divine completion and a divine transcendence of human expectations; it is forever breaking into history in unanticipated ways.[75]

---

[75] Ted Peters, 'Pannenberg's Eschatological Ethics', *The Theology of Wolfhart Pannenberg: Twelve American Critiques, with an Autobiographical Essay and Response* (ed. Carl E. Braaten and Philip Clayton; Minneapolis, MN: Augsburg Publishing House, 1988), pp. 239–65 (248).

PART V
'IT BEGAN WITH AN EXPERIENCE': CHURCH AND TRADITION IN AN AGE OF GLOBALIZATION AND LIQUIDIZATION

PUSHED TO A PRECARIOUS FLEXIBILITY: WHERE TO GO IF TRADITION HAS NO ANSWER AND APOCALYPSE IS NO ALTERNATIVE

Hans-Joachim Sander

1. *Introduction*

Edward Schillebeeckx was a theologian with the size of a century. After his death his theology will continue to surprise. I am especially grateful for two surprises. In 2006, a long interview, given at the occasion of his ninetieth birthday, with the Italian publisher Francesco Strazzari was translated into German.[1] At a certain point, Strazzari referred to Schillebeeckx's famous enterprise of re-discovering virtually all the topics of systematic theology on the basis of Jesus of Nazareth as a person having lived at a particular moment in history (cf. his trilogy *Jesus*, *Christ* and *Church*). Strazzari subsequently asked Schillebeeckx whether he still holds on to his visionary Jesus-matrix. Schillebeeckx replied as follows:

> The German translation of the title *Jesus, die Geschichte eines Lebenden* [lit. 'Jesus, the history of a living one'] no longer satisfies me. Instead of *Geschichte* (history) I would rather prefer *Erzählung* (story), *The story of a living one*, since the way Mark tells this story is different from the way that Matthew tells it, and this differs as

---

[1] Edward Schillebeeckx, *Ich höre nicht auf, an den lebendigen Gott zu glauben* (ed. Francesco Strazzari; trans. Barbara Häussler; Würzburg: Echter, 2006).

well from Luke's version. These three stories are very different from the gospel of John.[2] The second book of the trilogy, *Christ: The Christian Experience in the Modern World* (1980) deals mainly with the Pauline view on Jesus of Nazareth. Proto-Christianity therefore contains different and sometimes contradictory views on Jesus. Nevertheless, they were authentic confessions of faith. The result is surprising and seems to suggest the following: there is no unique and homogenous Christology, instead there are many different forms. In other words: Christology is pluralistic.[3]

For me this answer was a surprise for two reasons. (1) First, it was a surprise since I had misread Schillebeeckx up until this point. I previously thought Schillebeeckx was looking for a Christology related to history, as the New Quest for Jesus had been doing, but with the difference that Schillebeeckx's vision of a historically based Christology depends instead on those people with real historical experiences of Jesus and the narratives people tell about Jesus.[4] Schillebeeckx uses a combination of history and language, of reality in time and signs about this reality, of what is experienced and of what can be told and/or remembered about this experience. I suppose this combination is undivided and unmixed. His Christology is not simply in search of authentic material of the historical Jesus, nor for authentic experiences

---

[2] It should be noted that this problem only concerns the title of the German version of Schillebeeckx's book on Jesus. The title of the Dutch original, *Jezus, het verhaal van een levende* (Jesus, the story of a living one), already used the term 'story' and the English translation changed the title into *Jesus: An Experiment in Christology*.

[3] Schillebeeckx, *Ich höre nicht auf*, pp. 22–23.

[4] Schillebeeckx is replying to his critics that he is definitely not looking for a 'neoliberal' Christology opposed to the Christological dogmas but for a history enlightening the dogma by the disciples' real experience of Jesus. See: Edward Schillebeeckx, *Interim Report on the Books* Jesus & Christ (trans. John Bowden; London: SCM/New York, NY: Crossroad, 1980) pp. 27–35. His critics, among whom Walter Kasper, Leo Scheffczyk and Werner Löser, claim that by reviving a liberal Christology Schillebeeckx is going to relativize Christ's resurrection in favour of Jesus' humanity. But Schillebeeckx's point is the following (Schillebeeckx, *Interim Report*, pp. 31–32):

> I want to pursue the history of dogma with a historical study; in other words, to join with my readers in following along an *itinerarium mentis* the first disciples, who came into contact with a fellow-believer, followed him, and after his death experienced him as Christ and Son of God. Furthermore, when Christians confess that in the life of Jesus of Nazareth God himself has achieved decisive and definitive salvation for the liberation of men, then because of their own confession, the historical life of this man cannot vanish in the mist. ... It is for theological and pastoral reasons, therefore, that I am interested in the historically tangible earthly appearance of Jesus of Nazareth, though this can only be demonstrated in a reflection, the reflection which can be found in the first believing community.

with Jesus, but is searching for authentic narratives about those personal experiences with Jesus as a historical event. I am myself responsible for this aspect of the surprise. My reading of Schillebeeckx had been too narrow. I identified his project, to a too large extent, as a sort of exegetical theology. But his theology, in contrast to what I previously thought, belongs to the field of theologies that use biblical narratives founded upon strict exegesis, so as to open the range of present-day experiences for describing Jesus as an event of a living person.[5]

(2) But there is yet another reason for surprise in Schillebeeckx's remarks. And this part bears his responsibility. Schillebeeckx says that now he would prefer to subtitle his famous book on the living Jesus with 'narrative' instead of 'history'. There is more behind this than simply exchanging synonyms – a change which could be seen as being almost naturally in the line of his thinking of history as implicit theology.[6] In that line, 'history' means story-telling and in this sense 'history' and 'narratives' are indeed synonyms. But the way Schillebeeckx characterizes this story-telling is turning history into something very challenging. It is story-telling which unavoidably creates differences and one cannot explicitly move beyond these differences even if there is an implicit unity between them. One cannot distil a central core from within the various experiences people share with Jesus and the stories they tell about him, not even from the simple fact that they tell these stories in the first place, because distilling such a kernel in the experience of Jesus would necessarily depend upon an abstraction and this would entail leaving the level of experience, which is, as may be remembered, precisely the core of Schillebeeckx's theology. All one can get about Jesus is different stories about his history, stories which are told on the basis of experiences people cannot avoid presenting to others. This is a clue to narratives about

---

[5] Cf. Robert Schreiter, 'Edward Schillebeeckx', *The Modern Theologians: An introduction to Christian Theology in the Twentieth Century* (ed. David F. Ford; Oxford/ Cambridge: Blackwell, 1997), pp. 152–61 (158):

The three insights, then, depend on one another: Experience is grounded in a God who wishes to communicate, the contrast experiences draw us closer to that God, and the experience of God 'mindful of humanity' affirms that act of intuition and faith by making a mediation of the paradoxical experience of the immediate. In doing this, Schillebeeckx achieves a great deal in his hope of making the Christian message of God and the experience of salvation offered in Jesus Christ more available to a secularized society.

[6] Cf. Erik Borgman, *Edward Schillebeeckx: A Theologian in His History* (vol. 1; London: Continuum, 2003) p. 376:

In particular the lecture notes make clear the implications of the revolution which began with Schillebeeckx's adaption of De Petter's philosophical theory of the implicit intuition in the sphere of theology. Finite historical, worldly human existence is the place where God is to be seen in an indirect way, and theological treatment of the tradition is orientated on making visible this existence as such.

Jesus. They are not simply told for the sake of remembering Jesus. They are told for the sake of experiences which are urging to be expressed towards others. It is not purely an object at the heart of this process, i.e. Jesus which is remembered. This object gets a hold on subjects which have to share their experiences in order to have them at all. The most important thing is not that these narratives are different. The most important thing is that they have to be told. Yet, there are differences between these narratives and by holding the different experiences against each other, one cannot get beyond their plurality. Plurality is always part of the picture. In this sense, Schillebeeckx is touching upon the dimension of relativity in all experiences with Jesus. And this relativity belongs to the living person this Jesus still is for people of our times.

Schillebeeckx's remark 'In other words: Christology is pluralistic' sounds all too familiar and it is so easily understood. It sounds as if this plurality is a matter of course. And to some extent it is of course. One can look to the history of Jesus only by way of the narratives of various Gospels. History is simply the praxis of narratives and with each narrative history slightly changes. And of course, one has to accept that there is no such thing as a singular all-embracing Christology, not even in a dogmatic sense. Christology simply implies the dynamics of faith to present Jesus as present here and now. There is not a singular 'one' and a singular 'now' in this experience. The historical event 'Jesus' is open to surprises which may be realized much later than the event. Thus, the singularity shaping Christology has always been put forward in a plurality of ways. And narratives are tools to work with this plurality. But this relativity is not so easy to manage as it sounds. Schillebeeckx's proposal to shift from history to narratives changes the relation between singularity and plurality in his basic argument. And this is a major shift for systematic theology.

2. Singularity in the Mode of Plurality: Relativity and Flexibility at the Centre of Christian Faith

In *Jesus*, Schillebeeckx was looking for a factor uniting Christian faith, one different from the 'historical Jesus' as derived by and analysed from within historical methods and its analysis of the sources about Jesus. It would be absurd simply to focus on that 'historical Jesus' because, as Schillebeeckx put it, 'the first Christians, at any rate, were never confronted with this "historical abstract", which is what a historical-critical picture of Jesus amounts to'.[7] The uniting factor is Jesus as a living person who

---

[7] Schillebeeckx, *Interim Report*, p. 33.

causes an experience of disclosure capable of urging people to a 'metanoia' throughout the centuries in which he has been remembered.

For a person of his historical time, we know a significant amount about Jesus. But at the same time the sources do not provide us with a history of his life continuously developed. One cannot write a biography in the modern sense of that term. We know more about his theology than about his history. On the other hand, kerygma as well as dogma referring to Jesus cannot serve as uniting factors simply because they do not refer to the real history but to different experiences with this history which are not congruent with each other. Instead, these disciplines construct a focus beyond history in order to avoid troubles with the inadequacy of their historical basis as well as to escape potential domination by unanswered critical questions about their concept of Jesus' history. Amid such challenges, Schillebeeckx invented an alternative to the binary code of kerygma or dogma which forces one to decide which one has to be preferred. This alternative insists both on the history of Jesus and at the same time pays tribute to the critical dimension of this history:

> As so far all these sallies have proved to be unsatisfactory, what in the way of a constant unitive factor is left? I would say (and this really is something): the Christian movement itself. In other words a Christian oneness of experience which does indeed take its unity from its pointing to the one figure of Jesus, while none the less being pluriform in its verbal expression or articulation. ... The constant factor here is that particular groups of people find salvation imparted by God in Jesus of Nazareth.[8]

There is a plurality in forms of articulation because there are many disclosures throughout the centuries. But this plurality is based on a singularity, the history of Jesus as a living person for those people who expect their salvation by God in Jesus. This is the 'constant unitive factor' behind all Christology. So, Schillebeeckx's grammar travels from singularity to plurality.

Now, more than 30 years later, Schillebeeckx has changed directions. One has to start with narratives, always being kept apart by differences, in order to get access to a history of experiences with Jesus. At the beginning there is plurality and only on the basis of this plurality a singularity can open up. But this change of direction in the grammar of the argument brings up a precarious factor. Stability which was provided by the initial singular of the history of Jesus is gone even if this does not deny the singularity in this history. In this regard, Schillebeeckx refers to the impact the differences of the various narratives of Mark, Matthew, Luke, John and

---

[8] Edward Schillebeeckx, *Jesus: An Experiment in Christology* (trans. Hubert Hoskins; London: Collins, 1979) p. 56.

Paul have upon each other. One cannot rely simply on one of them and forget about the others. Each one gives new perspectives which the others don't have and each new perspective is a factor in reading one of the others. It is not simply that Mark is different from Matthew, Matthew from Luke, and so forth. It is unavoidable that the differences between the Gospels bring up alternatives for the other narratives of the same Gospel, be it Mark, Matthew, Luke, John or the letters of Paul. So, due to the plurality of narratives, each reference to Jesus is relativized. However, such a relativization doesn't entail complete relativism. As Schillebeeckx has put it in the fragment quoted above: 'Proto-Christianity therefore contains different and sometimes contradictory views on Jesus. Nevertheless, they were authentic confessions of faith.' Relativity and authenticity are here not in contradiction with one another. Each narrative enables the other narratives to bring up their own authentic clues to Jesus. This relativity is not the result of a critical view coming from the outside or the consequence of a misuse of the faithful intentions of the narratives; it is taking place at the very heart of the faith in Jesus. Stability is turned into flexibility.

This suggests that for Schillebeeckx this flexible approach is unavoidable for an honest and intellectual treatment of faith and theological tradition. His change from history to narratives for the (German) title of one of his masterpieces is significant for a major problem within current theological practice. It is an example of liquidity which is a sign for the times we are living in. This liquidity is not yet a sign *of* the times as Vatican II introduced the term as a magisterial category. But it authentically represents the way in which people currently have to organize their lives.

In this sense Schillebeeckx is a major theologian whose theology is living in touch with the human conditions of this time. He accepts for the sake of the truth that relativity is unavoidable in references to Jesus as a living factor in the lives of human beings. The very reference to Jesus as living person is pushing towards a theological praxis capable of dealing with such relativity. It is the livingness of Jesus that causes plurality and differences, because the people experiencing such livingness cannot be summarized by a singular identity. Only a dead Jesus would guarantee such singularity because only then his history could be fixed in principle once and for all. A Jesus no longer alive would lead to a past existence no longer bothered by different experiences. And if one wants to avoid relativity at all costs, one must propose narratives of Jesus as a dead person that excludes his living status throughout the times. This, of course, would be contrary to Christian faith. So, relativity coming out of differences about Jesus is in favour of a faith that believes in him as a living person. Without this relativity the singularity of this living person which was killed at the cross is impossible.

Schillebeeckx has remodelled his own approach to Jesus because of theological reasons. He brings forward what he had realized before in nucleus. At the beginning of his *Church*, he analyses revelation and its relation to history. He claims that there is an ongoing mutuality between tradition and actual situation. Through a mutual relationship between these two factors one can realize what God's revelation means for human beings. Both poles of the binary code, tradition and situation, are important and unavoidable:

> If all this is the case, then it already emerges that for us the identity in the meaning of the gospel cannot primarily lie at the level of the Bible and the past tradition of faith, at least as such, and therefore cannot be found in a material repetition of that past (in any kind of 'funda-mentalism', whether in conservative or progressive forms). Far less, however, can it be found at the level of the situation, then and now, *as such* (whether in a biblicist or a modernist direction). This identity of meaning can only be in the fluctuating 'middle field', in a swinging to and fro between tradition and situation, and thus at the level of the corresponding relationship between the original message (tradition, which also includes the situation of the time) and the situation, then and now, which is different each time.[9]

Next to the basic thesis of a mutual relation between tradition and situation, it is interesting to note that Schillebeeckx speaks of a *fluent oscillating 'middle field'* where both factors meet. In such a 'middle field' there are no sharp contours where tradition ends and situation begins nor *vice versa*. Schillebeeckx's characterization is a theological example of the liquidity which Zygmunt Bauman has analysed as a pressing problem in modern societies. After a long period of a stable and solid modernity closely related to the heavy industries of the nineteenth and twentieth centuries, the powers of globalization are pushing current societies to a precarious liquidity. In almost every work-field, people have to face flexible conditions as they are met with uncertainty over losing their jobs even when their company is posting profits. The order of things has completely changed. The bigger a company has grown and the more it is organized around the globe, the less security it provides for jobs offered. And the financial crisis of 2008 and its aftermath are adding to this problem. Modernity has begun a new phase of its never ending story.

For Bauman, the manufacturing plant of Henry Ford is a symbol for the heavy modernity we have left behind.[10] For the people having worked there,

---

[9] Edward Schillebeeckx, *Church: The Human Story of God* (trans. John Bowden; New York, NY: Crossroad, 1990) p. 41.

[10] Zygmunt Bauman, *Liquid Modernity* (Cambridge: Polity Press, 2000) pp. 115–16: Daniel Bell described one of the most powerful and most envied and emulated of such hotbeds/fortresses/prisons: the General Motors 'Willow Run' plant in Michigan. The site occupied by the plant was two-thirds by a quarter of a mile. All the materials needed to produce cars were gathered under one gigantic roof, in a single monstrous cage. The logic of power and the logic

it was then important to get in. If they managed to be accepted they had a job for their whole working life. Ford's workers had to accept a set of rules and regularities that placed a certain degree of hardship on them. But in return for such hardship, security and stability were provided. At one point Henry Ford even offered a hundred percent increase in pay simply to keep the workers in his plant. He didn't want to lose them to his economic rivals. He was in need of people willing to work in his plant for a long time and he was aware of this. It was a binding relationship that for both partners entailed a clear preference for a lifelong contract. In the car industry, such plants have now been shut down for quite some time, in Detroit and elsewhere throughout the world.

3. *Liquidity as Unavoidable Factor for a Globalized Church*

For a long time the church has functioned in a way similar to Henry Ford's manufacturing plant. It was important to get in and then one was expected not to go out again. The goal was to belong to the true Church and everything else was provided for. Once accepted as a Catholic meant to be Catholic forever. In return, salvation was provided only for people being inside the ecclesial plant, so to speak. Those being outside were considered to be lost. They were not simply lost for the Church but they

> of control were both grounded in the strict separation of the 'inside' from the 'outside' and a vigilant defence of the boundary between the two. Both logics, blended in one, were embodied in the logic of size, organized around one precept: bigger means more efficient. In the heavy version of modernity, progress meant growing size and spatial expansion.
>
> ... Space was truly 'possessed' when controlled – and control meant first and foremost the 'taming of time', neutralizing its inner dynamism: in short, the uniformity and coordination of time. It was wonderful and exciting to reach the sources of the Nile before other explorers managed to find it, but a train running ahead of schedule or automobile parts arriving on the assembly line ahead of other parts were heavy modernity's most gruesome nightmares.
>
> Routinized time joined forces with high brick walls crowned with barbed wire or broken glass and closely guarded gates in protecting the place against intruders; it also prevented all those inside the place from leaving it at will. The 'Fordist factory', that most coveted and avidly pursued model of engineered rationality in times of heavy modernity, was the site of face-to-face meeting, but also a 'till death us do part' type of marriage vow between capital and labour. The wedding was of convenience or necessity, hardly ever a marriage of love – but it was meant to last 'for ever' (whatever that might have meant in terms of individual life), and more often than not it did.

had lost themselves to eternal downfall. Salvation offered by God urged people to stay life-long within the Catholic Church in order to be sure that they were really safe. These people had to accept the strict rules set by the Church for believing and practicing faith. For this they were provided by the Church with everything they needed for a true religious existence and a good personal life. On the other side the Church had to accept that she was to provide these people with what they needed for their salvation. She was responsible for their salvation and she was considered as such by the eternal God. Nothing was to be left out and no one within the Church should have been in need of spiritual values offered outside the Church. Whatever was needed she was able to deliver. So, she had to downplay everything else offered outside of her which she could not have provide people with, e.g. a routine in spiritual reading of the Bible.

Like Henry Ford's manufacturing plants, access to the Church was closely watched by canon law and it was secured by a set of measures excluding people from the outside, while including those people willing to live in accord with such rules. The Church offered salvation only for those willing to accept her terms of trade. She set these rules out of her own means and not by taking over ideas from others. Catholics could be assured that they would receive a salvation that was truly Catholic, which especially meant that it was not Protestant. Such a Church tried to build up a sort of monopoly on religious salvation and for this she guaranteed stable access to the true God. As a kind of iron rule she excluded categorically that one could get access to the deeper truth about God by other religious communities or by other intellectual perspectives.

Benedict XVI's goal of building a solid wall against relativism can be interpreted as a last effort in attempting to restore an ecclesial plant in a Fordist manner. As a major brick in this wall, the historical Jesus has to be secured somewhat along the lines of a living Christ, which entails starting with the Christological creeds in order to find a true access to the historical Jesus. This wall against relativism tries to find security by denying that there can be any flexible liquidity at the centre of the catholic faith. For a Fordist Church, any such liquidity in the relational core between Christ and Jesus is seen as a major threat to the truth-claims of Catholic faith.

For this approach Jesus' history is turned into a sort of supernatural being as it was already pictured in neoscholastics. Then, theology based on this being has to proceed in a Fordist manner. It must not be torn by flexible approaches. It has to be secured at any costs by the truths the Church is providing for. They are stable walls that encourage strict resistance to relativity by the means of faith itself. As soon as this history is proven to be present only in a liquid mode, i.e. if it looses its supernatural character, then faith itself must take over. Then it has to be used as a valid tool to find out what is the very historical truth about Jesus' history. If history cannot guarantee stability then faith has to provide it and has to discipline this history. For this approach it is essential to never leave the universe of faith in order to access to the chosen history. Every history that is unavoidable belongs to the internal affairs of faith and it cannot be placed outside of it. Otherwise the Church may no longer be able to give stability in times of upheaval like ours.

To some extent Schillebeeckx's original search for a stable unitive aspect in Christian relations toward Jesus is a model similar to that of the ecclesial Fordist plant. He has used different means than Joseph Ratzinger but they shared the same goal. In Schillebeeckx's original search the most precarious factor of liquidity at the part of Jesus was not brought up. Jesus is a Jew and so the very centre of Christian faith doesn't belong to the Christian religious community. The very centre of faith cannot be incorporated in the Church as part of her inner life. Jesus will always remain a faith-factor outside of her identity. So, at least the Jewishness of Jesus is tearing down the walls of an ecclesial Fordist plant. One cannot manufacture a Jesus living a Christian faith. This is impossible by history. In this sense the very basis of all ecclesial products, so to speak, is lying outside the walls of a Fordist plant. One has to leave the internal affairs of this plant to come to terms with a true access to Jesus.

By shifting from history to narratives, Schillebeeckx is accepting the need to open the Church to differences coming from outside. In this opening he has run into problems with the Fordist apparatus of the Church, but at the same time he has demonstrated that there is more in the Church than Fordist manufacturing of religious truth-claims. Schillebeeckx's theology has definitely left behind a Fordist grammar for manufacturing theological perspectives. One can no longer hold on to an identity that bestows a singularity, which stands high above the precarious plurality of narratives that show numerous differences. Security by singularity is a fancy ideal but it is neither a reality in the history of faith, i.e. tradition, nor is it a reality one may be able to realize in the increasing plurality of religious affairs, i.e. our globalized situation. The need to concede relativity in terms of Jesus is simply an effect of an increased knowledge about Jesus. Discharging this knowledge would lead to truth-claims that will fail in relation to the historical sources and this would cause a sort of relativism which would be increased just by attacking this relativity. One may even say: the more knowledge one obtains about Jesus, the greater the liquidity one must face for doing theology with this knowledge. Beyond flexible understanding, tradition is turned into fundamentalism.

But this relativity is not the end of a tradition referring to Jesus as a living person. On the basis of not denying this relativity, Jesus has the chance of becoming a globalized figure as a living person. Jesus is simply not the same living person in Brazil or India, in Rome or Istanbul. He may not even be the same in the northern and the southern parts of Belgium. But in each of these places he is a living factor in the lives of people. So, is relativism the fate of faith? Does one has to give up on all security and solidity in theological answers to the problems of today's humankind?

4. Doing Utopian Theology to Escape Relativity: The Luring Power of Apocalypse

There is a short answer to this problem which proceeds by way of power. And there is a difficult one that only has powerlessness to offer. The short answer switches from the beginning to the end of the whole story. If the beginning of Christian faith starts with Jesus the Jew, which cannot be separated from flexibility, then it may be the end of history that can provide for a chance to resist the precarious liquidity of our times. This end is related to the apocalypse. Perhaps a Christian vision of apocalypse offers a way out of liquid uneasiness. The reason is quite simple: There are a lot of reasons for this apocalyptic uneasiness. The Earth is producing a climate change which almost certainly is human-made and this change will cut deep into humankind's way of life. The global ecosystems are losing so many species year by year that one must think of the current loss of species in terms of the five big mass extinctions from the history of the earth put together. NASA's programme to search for potential killers from the asteroid-belt of our solar system gives no reason to stay calm, although they have not yet found a real danger. In the world of politics the first signs of global governance implemented in the hot weeks of the recent financial crisis are not that trustworthy as most people around the globe wished they would be. We have the uncomfortable feeling that our civilization is standing on the edge of collapse. Of course, this is somewhat of an overemphasis. Each generation thinks that the pressing crisis it is compelled to face is an apocalyptic one. But we are definitely living in a time in which the future doesn't look as bright as it did when Schillebeeckx got the idea to write about Jesus as a living person. Some profound changes have occurred and they have brought back apocalyptic scenarios made up of political upheaval, cultural power-claims and religious clashes.[11] And why not fight apocalyptic uneasiness by apocalypse?

Apocalyptic visions have a long tradition in the history of faith. But they are ambivalent. They provide a power of resistance to those which are under pressure and who lack the power to overcome all that is pressuring them. Therefore they are very helpful against violent powers one cannot avoid to be objects of. The book of Revelation exemplifies this. But apocalyptic

[11] For the variety of apocalyptic ideas, see: Fabio Ribeiro de Araujo, *Prophezeiungen über das Ende der Welt: Die Apokalypse und ein neuer Anfang* (Rottenburg: Kopp, 2009). For a recent claim that religious apocalypse is spilling over into politics, see: John Gray, *Black Mass: Apocalyptic Religion and the Death of Utopia* (New York, NY: Farrar, Straus and Giroux, 2007).

visions run the risk of becoming really dangerous if they are brought up from within a position of power or from a position of lust to power. Then they enforce resentment in the Nietzschean sense. This leads to violence against those inside and outside the realm of one's own faith which are not willing to accept the order of things the apocalyptic scenarios are pushing forward.

In this sense apocalyptic scenarios function similar to utopias. In modern times utopias were often used as remedies for ideas which were doomed to failure. By politics of utopia a shattered idea could be believed in beyond the situation which revealed its failure.[12] If one must concede that one does not have the power to change history in one's own religious sense and to resist the powers enforcing powerlessness over oneself, there is still the option to dominate history from the perspective of the end of history. This perspective of the end of history, however, is nothing else than a source of resentment. For the time being, others may have the power not to accept what is good for them despite a collective 'we' telling them otherwise. They may still be powerful enough for not taking seriously our knowledge about the final outcome of history. But these others certainly do not have the power to decide history to the very end. There, at the end, those in power now will be badly surprised and all their power will be gone. This alternative 'we' knows already now what will happen at the end. Those who do not listen now will then be shocked by what will happen to them. This 'we' cannot dominate the progress in our time but the force behind it will ultimately conquer all the others. 'We' know about their fate and this gives us security and stability in the midst of all hardship now.

There is no flexibility in apocalyptic scenarios. The end is already decided and things are already set. There is only stability and security for oneself. In my view, this inflexibility is even applicable to Johann B. Metz's modern political theology, which is eager to secure the fate of the victims of history before God by knowing their final fate. It tries to already fix, both here and now, the justice political theologians think that the victims expect from God and that God is compelled to demonstrate in their favour. Admittedly, the idea of apocalyptic justice for the victims invented by political theology is certainly not brought up to demonstrate power over and against other people. The aim is not oppression of others as it is the case in a fundamentalist approach towards apocalypse. The goals are '*Erinnerung fremden Leids*' (remembering the others' suffering) and '*Erinnerungspathos*' (pathos of remembrance),[13] especially for the victims of the Shoah. This compassion

---

[12] Cf. Barbara Goodwin and Keith Taylor, *The Politics of Utopia: A Study in Theory and Practice* (Oxford: Lang, 2009). For a renaissance of utopias cf. Rolf Steltemeier (ed.), *Neue Utopien: Zum Wandel eines Genres* (Heidelberg: Manutius, 2009).

[13] Johann Baptist Metz, 'Zwischen Erinnerung und Vergessen: Die Shoah im Zeitalter kultureller Anamnesie (1997)', *Zum Begriff der neueren Politischen Theologie 1967–1997* (Mainz: Grünewald, 1997), pp. 149–55 (155).

based upon remembering should be able to build up a contradicting power towards a 'culture of anamnesis'. In this sense, the modern political theology makes a difference between evolutionism, for which time simply goes forward, and apocalypse, wherein time is interrupted by suffering, theodicy, remembering and compassion.

But this difference is not decisive as it only relates to the mode of time. The crucial point is a subject which will finally triumph over the powerlessness of past and present. Modern political theology eagerly seeks to overcome the insecurity of those who suffer by casting itself in solidarity with the victims of history.[14] There has to be a sort of objective final 'happy end' that provides for a just ending to the continuous injustice within history. And God is responsible to guarantee this final outcome of time because he is the partner to this subjective longing for an end to suffering. This finality will prove God's sovereignty over history by a never ending justice. And this sovereignty gives stability against all liquidity and powerlessness resulting from flexibility about this final end. And it will secure the utopias of those who are not able to guarantee justice within history. Without this security their utopias are shaken already in this time. In this sense, apocalyptic claims favoured by political theology are akin to a religious technology that seeks to secure one's own utopias, especially those utopias in relation to victims suffering injustice. It attempts to solve the problem of ambiguity and insecurity of history, since this reveals a modern dilemma. On the one hand history is an open process for modern subjects but its possible negative outcome is not acceptable for those same modern subjects. By reference to the apocalyptic mode as an answer to that problem, political theology reveals that it remains stuck in this modern dilemma. It results from a macrophysics of power in the Foucauldian sense which stabilizes the insecurity of history by a divine apocalyptic power.

Here apocalypse is not simply a faithful approach to God. It is part of a modern identity that avoids liquidity in order to be secured against powerlessness. This identity eagerly seeks grounding in itself – *ego cogito, ego sum*, as the Cartesian mantra goes. This self-related and self-decided identity is longing to dominate history by its own ideas. It needs progress to be sure about itself. And in order to obtain progress, two techniques are employed: exclusion and discipline. In general, one has to be focused on the final goal in order to progress successfully. Thus, one is required to discipline oneself and others so as to maintain the needed level of attention. And furthermore, one has to exclude everything that and everyone who is seen as disturbing this final goal. Utopias are typical representations of this mode of identity.

---

[14] Cf. Johann Baptist Metz, *Glaube in Geschichte und Gesellschaft* (repr., Mainz: Grünewald, 1984) p. 157: 'These fundamental apocalyptical questions – To whom does the world belong? To whom its suffering? To whom its time? – theology appears to be unrivalled in the way it has put them out of action.'

They are places that are not there, 'no-places'. But this doesn't mean that these places do not exist. They are simply not there here and now. They are waiting ahead in the future. Rarely one is capable of tripping up on them, but it is not impossible to get to them; it is only not possible now. But there is a supra-possibility by way of successfully progressing into the future. And this supra-possibility gives discipline already here and now.

Utopias give security for the future and accumulate power in the present. They relativize present powerlessness by pointing to a future power. No liquidity enforced on people here and now can thus contradict utopias. Only one's final success counts. And by this, religious ideas can very easily be combined with utopian expectations. Upon utopian coordinates a final success can be secured through a final word about history issued by a sovereign God. For this purpose it is important for those who are longing for a final judgement about history that God's intentions on history are already known for them. Utopias empowered by such a final divine word can easily overpower any precarious status of a liquid history. People dedicated to such utopias will have a divinely assured place in the future and they can live undisturbed by liquid conditions in the present. No time can demonstrate a utopia as false and misguided if God stands behind this no-place. But the security given by utopias cannot be separated from self-righteousness. For theology this would be disastrous. Every effort to modernize theology would be contradicted because self-righteousness in an attempt to overcome history.

What then should we do with this rather sober result? Is it still possible to hold onto a hopeful outlook towards history, given its critical impor- tance for Christian theology? Is there still a place for the Good News of theology in a highly liquid world which doesn't trust the old utopias any more? If there is, it cannot be found in the future: neither utopias nor apocalypses can re-stabilize theology; theology cannot avoid coming to terms with liquidity in history. And a place for the Good News can neither be found in the past: no tradition can be re-written into stability over a long period of time if Jesus the living person is standing at its heart. There is only one mode of time remaining for a theology that is able to match with the liquidity of history – the present.

5. *The Precarious Liquidity of the Present: A Heterotopia for Doing Theology Today*

Past and future mode of time cannot solve the liquidity problem. The present is not solving it either. It is reinforcing it because the present mode is the most liquid dimension of time. It never really exists in a stable manner. It is already done and turned into past when it appears out of the future. And there is a second factor: the present mode is realized by relativity to what is really there. The present mode is confronted by reality and not with ideal possibilities as the future does. And it consists of confrontations still untold and without narratives as the past requires them. The present mode occurs only relative to what is really there. It is a mode of time which cannot be grounded in itself. It is full of surprises that cannot be deduced from the past nor induced into the future. Alterity takes precedence in places where the present mode unfolds and this alterity remains there. When one is confronted with others one cannot avoid this confrontation. In this sense, the present mode consists of social realities. The past can be turned into a purely personal affair by the narratives one tells or does not tell. In the present a subject is never alone. Here nobody can decide not to be related to others and these others are capable of relativizing one's own stands. In this sense one cannot hold the present on the basis of one's own ideas. On the contrary, one is surrounded by others one cannot avoid to be related to. In a place like this it is not possible to exclude powers, people or facts that one would prefer to exclude from one's own time. Therefore, present times do not encourage the construction of utopias, rather, they confront with surprises that bring up such powerlessness in the first place. For taking seriously present times, neither inductions towards the future nor deductions from the past can do it. Abductions are needed which urge one to rethink one's own truth-telling. This means that one cannot start from that which lies ahead. Abduction starts with what is experienced here and now as surprise.[15] Disciplinary processes of utopias need the future in order to be implemented and by this they avoid surprises, or more precisely: one's own convictions regain power over precarious surprises which can easily be suppressed. Utopias cannot be separated from perspectives of better conditions that still lie ahead. Abductions do not wait for better conditions, they deal with surprises even if they bring forward the worst condition possible, namely to realize how wrong one's own ideas are. The present is such a condition. Therefore, it is a locus which cannot be taken over by utopias. Here a different mode of location with anti-utopian character is needed. That is the reason why in the present heterotopias become visible.

Heterotopias are places alternative to utopias in that they do not provide power over time.[16] They are places that are here, but are easily overlooked or silenced because they are not ruled by the normal order of things. These other-places do not lie ahead in a future and so, discipline and exclusion have no effect. On the contrary, heterotopian places reveal mechanisms of exclusion and practices of discipline and in doing so, relativize utopian

[15] For a fresh perspective to Charles S. Peirce's concept of abduction, see: Atocha Aliseda, *Abductive Reasoning: Logical Investigations into Discovery and Explanation* (Berlin: Springer, 2006).

[16] Michel Foucault, 'Des espaces autres', *Dits et écrits. II: 1976–1988* (Paris: Gallimard, 2001), pp. 1571–81. See also: Michel Foucault, *Die Heterotopien/Der utopische Körper: Zwei Radiovorträge* (Frankfurt a.M.: Suhrkamp, 2005).

power-claims. One of the examples Foucault gives for heterotopias is that of the graveyard. Here the dead are located and everybody can be the next to move to this place. A graveyard challenges what the person may have earlier counted upon. Here, the fragility of utopias is emerging. Another example, not given by Foucault, is Wall Street. In the recent financial crisis, Wall Street has become a heterotopos. Here incredible amounts of money were invested under utopian perspectives which broke down in the crisis. Wall Street has revealed the precarious liquidity of financial products that it itself had previously invented.

So, heterotopias cannot be expected and they cannot be constructed. They simply happen on local terms. At such places, one is compelled to suddenly realize a precarious presence that one can simply not avoid. This precariousness points to an otherness which has an authority to contradict the luring power of utopias. In the presence of heterotopias the narrative mode of tradition previously accepted and the ideal mode of progresses proposed are both relativized by experiences of a plurality of otherness pushing towards alternatives.[17] Facts, people and powers emerge and become significant for one's identity because they attack its preference to be grounded in itself. This may cause a shift in identity.

Since Vatican II, present times have become a unique place for theology. The council took relativity and liquidity of the present as serious challenges for presenting the Gospel. This council followed the programme to deal with *ecclesia ad intra* and *ecclesia ad extra* at the same time and on the same level for authentic teaching. So, it followed a bipolar perspective which cannot be reduced to a singular. This changed the identity of the Church and the mode of doing theology. They were cured from a variety of catholic utopias. The ecclesiology of *societas perfecta*, once taken for granted,[18] was abandoned. Vatican II realized that, as is the case for the modern state, the Church is also living from conditions she cannot guarantee by herself.[19] Her identity is not stable over time, as if she has everything that is needed

---

[17] Cf. Lieven Boeve's idea of recontextualization of tradition through plurality and differences being unavoidable: *Interrupting Tradition: An Essay on Christian Faith in a Postmodern Context* (Louvain Theological and Pastoral Monographs, 30; Leuven: Peeters/Grand Rapids, MI: Eerdmans, 2003).

[18] Cf. Leo XIII's encyclical *Immortale Dei* in 1885 (ASS 18 (1885/6), 162–175) stating that the Church 'is a perfect society of its own kind and its own right (*societas est genere et iure perfecta*), since whatever is necessary for its existence and its effectiveness, in accordance with the will and power of the grace of its Founder, it owns in and of itself (*omnia in se et per se ipsa possideat*)'.

[19] This is the so-called 'paradox of Böckenförde'. See: Ernst-Wolfgang Böckenförde, 'Staat, Gesellschaft, Freiheit', *Recht, Staat, Freiheit: Studien zur Rechtsphilosophie, Staatstheorie und Verfassungsgeschichte* (Frankfurt a.M.: Suhrkamp, 2006), pp. 92–114. This paradox applies to the Church in the same way as it does to the modern secular State.

in herself – a mode I would like to call 'who-identity'. Her identity is, in contrast, structured by the presence of otherness and others, such as other Christian denominations, other religions, human rights not yet realized by the Church, etc. A Church facing those others she cannot avoid because they are simply there in the present, is developing a different mode of identity, an identity for which the locus she is situated in, in the world of today is a major factor. Here, mutuality between 'ad intra' and 'ad extra' is unavoidable which was realized by the Council in the twofold ecclesiology of *Lumen gentium* and *Gaudium et spes*. This means that the Church has to manage a pastorally constituted identity of her own, a mode of identity I would like to call 'where-identity'.

Vatican II invented a binary code for this remodelled where-identity of theology, which counts on the mutuality of both poles. It is the bipolarity of signs of the times and Gospel mentioned in no. 4 – and no. 11 in a slightly different perspective – of *Gaudium et spes*. In presenting the Gospel, the Church is unavoidably linked to social realities being present at her own time at places where people have to struggle so that their human dignity is respected. Vatican II accepts there is no way not to be in solidarity with the people marked by signs of the times. The Church has to give up power-claims in order to live this solidarity. She is in service of the people and of God's presence in the problems of their lives as stated in *Gaudium et spes* no. 3. Not every event in time is a sign of the times. A major factor qualifying an event as a 'sign of the times' is powerlessness inflicted on people by attacks on their dignity, who are therefore in need of solidarity by other people. A sign of the times represents people who have to struggle for their dignity to be respected by others and by society in general. This struggle is a fragile process and this powerlessness is shared by those who decide to be in solidarity with people in this struggle.[20] Such people may be persons living here and now who are endangered by critical living conditions and/or political troubles. But these people may also be persons already

---

[20] Only in this respect do I disagree with Erik Borgman's evaluation of *Gaudium et spes* when he writes the following in his '*Gaudium et spes*: The Forgotten Future of a Revolutionary Document', *Vatican II: A Forgotten Future?* (ed. Alberto Melloni and Christoph Theobald; Concilium, 2005/4; London: SCM, 2005), pp. 48–56 (54):

> If however the Christian message cannot be defined in terms of its substance, but is as it were required to develop afresh again and again in responding to the signs of the times, what then is the foundation of the continuity of this faith? The Pastoral Constitution *Gaudium et spes* avoids this question by giving the impression of merely applying the permanent doctrine of the Church to the present situation.

In contrast to what Borgman claims, there is no adaption of the ecclesial tradition to the present situation in *Gaudium et spes*. The guiding principle is a precarious relativity between both in the mode of a thirdness in the Peircean sense called 'signs of the times'. Then the Christian gospel is not merely an answer to these signs but a discovery based on abductions about this thirdness. Continuity comes out of the need that such discoveries are unavoidable for Christian faith.

deceased like the victims of the Shoah. These victims have a right to be remembered but this right although being a human right is not taken for granted. Remembering the victims of history is not empowering an apocalyptic agenda. People struggling so that their dignity is socially, politically, culturally, religiously respected open the Gospel to a topos which cannot be found otherwise.[21]

Such a confrontation with human beings deeply involved in social crises and political ruptures or deeply linked to mechanisms of exclusion is leading to a special sort of sharing. Those who want to proclaim the Gospel here and now are forced to share the hopes and the sorrows of these people. This sharing means to be confronted with heterotopias for social and political structures accumulating power by dividing human beings of their dignity.[22] For empowering the Gospel in society it would be better to back the normative figures that rule society. But such support would alienate the Gospel from the social, political, cultural and religious meaning of the living person Jesus, which is unavoidably a disturbing factor.

In this sense already, Schillebeeckx and others – by opening theology for modern societies – were eager to link their theologies to a special option for the poor, i.e. liberation theologies. In sharing the fate of the poor the Gospel is closely linked to powerlessness being a political, social, cultural and religious reality in present history. This powerlessness takes away from the Gospel all inclination to secure and stabilize identities grounded in their own selves. It becomes a heterotopic experience by creating loci/topoi of arguments which span a space for alternatives. From then onwards, the Gospel becomes a disturbing factor within societies and policies, as it cannot serve as a yes-factor of identities dominated by self-righteousness. Furthermore, it cannot positively and deliberately stabilize the normal order of things and it cannot even encourage utopias of those who live in solidarity with poor people. Therefore, the Gospel is indeed filled with confrontations of heterotopic dimension and it means to share the powerlessness in them. But this factor of sharing creates a gift in return for which utopias are, by their very nature, unable to give.

---

[21] For *Gaudium et spes* and the *signs of the times* see also Ansgar Kreutzer, *Kritische Zeitgenossenschaft: Die Pastoralkonstitution* Gaudium et spes *modernisierungstheoretisch gedeutet und systematisch-theologisch entfaltet* (Innsbruck: Tyrolia, 2006); Jochen Ostheimer, *Zeichen der Zeit lesen: Erkenntnistheoretische Bedingungen einer praktisch-theologischen Gegenwartsanalyse* (Stuttgart: Kohlhammer, 2008).
[22] Cf. Trygve Wyller (ed.), *Heterotopic Citizen: New Research on Religious Work for the Disadvantaged* (Göttingen: Vandehoeck & Ruprecht, 2009).

6. Sharing the Liquid Conditions of Life: Resisting to Divide God of Present Times

There is a major difference between division, as a source of power that comes out of mechanisms of exclusions, and sharing, as a locus of power-lessness that comes out of liquid social conditions. In division, that what is divided diminishes in favour of the growing power of those who are responsible and capable to implement dividing practices. By contrast, the act of sharing enables growth between those who are involved in the relativity of this social practice. In social practices like knowledge, love, erotic experiences, etc. that which grows does so thanks to its being shared. Shared knowledge leads to greater knowledge, shared love leads to deeper love and shared eroticism means greater erotic intensity. Practices depending on processes of sharing are seriously in danger, or they even fall apart, if they are involved in practices of dividing.

Sharing requires flexibility in social relations and it increases the liquid grammar in them. It is broken if built into strategies of stabilizing. Therefore, it is so hard to institutionalize practices of sharing without losing the personal gift in it. Sharing gives stability only when coming out of precarious flexibility, but it gives no stability against the precariousness of liquid life conditions.

God can be a factor to be shared or to be divided. The Christian tradition to refer to God depends on practices of sharing. Jesus was a Jew and the Christian God – even the dogmatic form of him – deeply depends on the biblical God Jesus himself worshipped. Every time the Christian God-talk was involved into divisions from the Jewish God of Jesus, theology became a factor of hate and violence. This sharing mode of Christian God-talk enables theology to deal with a liquid modernity. If sharing is needed in terms of God then this God cannot be secured by one's own religious identity alone. A God-talk in need of practices of sharing cannot get out of referring and relying on other modes of God-talk. And then God himself becomes a liquid factor for God-talk, especially for theological practices which don't expect surprises with God because he has to secure their utopian expectations. Thus, God is not the starting point of theology. He is a research-programme for theological practice.[23] The sharing-option urges theology to start with present times in order to refer to its tradition and the truths about God which can be found there. Therefore, on the basis of the precariousness of present times, this tradition will be effective into the future. Such God-talk cannot get away with utopias for stabilizing social realities as one would wish them to be.

Yet by this, theology will be given another capacity. By theology's

---

[23] For this perspective, see also: Erik Borgman, ... *want de plaats waarop je staat is heilige grond: God als onderzoeksprogramma* (Amsterdam: Boom, 2008) pp. 81–82.

reconfiguration, it is enabled to refer in an authentic manner to places where heterotopias become visible and, as such, unavoidable. This happens not by chance. It is a result of the biblical grammar of God. The biblical God is deeply connected to places that have a distinct heterotopian quality: the Exodus, the Cross, the forty years journey through the desert, the empty grave, the community of Corinth, the new Jerusalem, etc. At such heterotopian places, the biblical God is connected with people in urgent need of an alternative order of things. He is sharing their sorrows and hopes and they are transformed into a different mode of life. It is not a stable mode of life but a fragile one. But here the liquidity these people cannot avoid to live with has lost its violent nature.

In this sense, the Gospel is a heterotopian power in the living conditions in today's globalized world. It confronts with places one cannot avoid to become aware of because they are significant for the problems people have to go through today. At these places, ruling utopias are today falling apart and people are challenged to share the fate of others in order to overcome the suffering caused by the exclusions and discipline of these utopias. If one is able to make the decision that sharing love becomes true, of which Schillebeeckx refers to when he touched on a God-talk which still is to be developed with the help of that sharing. In answer to the question, 'who is God?', Schillebeeckx responds by a 'where' that is filled by a heterotopic people, devoted to something authentically human:

> In my answer, I will start from the life of Jesus the Christ: from Jesus as a free, human individual who, when he achieves an inner connection to God and calls this Abba-Father, strives for justice and solidary love. This love is mainly focused on the poor and the oppressed. This attitude of Jesus appeals to many people's deepest longings, people who risk their own lives for justice and liberation. There will always be people like that. They are 'like' God. Something of the divine Being becomes visible in these people: the strengthening and spreading of the good and the resistance against evil. All over the world, they are the heart of God. God's essence is passed on in human actions that make life worth living. Indeed, it seems to be the essence of Christianity that, wherever there are people who are willing to devote themselves to something authentically human, an absolute transcendence can be found which has led many to proclaim: 'Surely the Lord is in this place; and I did not know it' (Gen 28,16).[24]

---

[24] Schillebeeckx, *Ich höre nicht auf*, pp. 54–55.

HISTORY AND TRADITION: CATHOLICISM AND THE CHALLENGE OF GLOBALIZED MODERNITY

Oliver Davies

As Catholic theologians who hold to the principle *extra mundum nulla salus*, we find that we live today in times of challenge. Some of the reasons for this are external, having to do with the rise of global political problems such as climate change or world poverty, or the problem of securing the integrity of the world's economic system. Then there are problems posed to the integrity of traditions and to ethical traditions in particular perhaps, from the rapid evolution of a pluralistic multiculturalism, involving the spread of diasporas as global networks (including a form of radical political Islam). The multiplication of ethical traditions within the global arena makes it more difficult to develop consensual and considered political responses to global issues. A central part of the mission and self-understanding of the Church is the pastoral engagement of the Church with such problems, on behalf of the human family, as exemplified in Pope Benedict XVI's recent encyclical *Caritas in Veritate*.

But in seeking to address these concerns of contemporary global modernity, we may find as Church that we are in fact already caught up in these same problematics in ways which lessen our capacity to speak with a properly critical voice. Where we seek to speak to humanity as a whole, for instance, we have to recognize that we do so not only from the ground of a particular revelation (we have always done that) but also from what can be characterized as a particular social and cultural situatedness. This comes into view in the particular cultural memory of narration and also reasoning which developed in the reception of that revelation, and which bears many of the characteristics of distinctively Western schools of thought. Together with the – perhaps unprecedented – globalism of the Catholic Church comes our fundamentally Western orientation of thinking, which is easily identifiable as such within the global frameworks of Church activity. And we suffer visibly from distinctively Western ailments. We are too inclined to think that tradition defines thought, for instance, in the anxiety that any alternative to that will turn out to be some version of the same positivist rationalism which has long since proved untenable. Even the classical philosophical trajectories of Church tradition, whether Aristotelian or Platonic in orientation, while giving a welcome conceptual context to early Christianity, cannot easily be justified as being something other than embedded tradition, with their own particular, historically determined points of departure. Perhaps we have not always found the right tools to protect ourselves from becoming ourselves too post-modern. As disciples in Christ, we may share in the apostolic critical distance to the world, but as living and thinking human beings who have been highly educated in the ways of today, and in particular at universities, we may inevitably find it difficult to extricate ourselves from the same relativist landscape that we may wish to critique.

And so the question arises: how can we be non-relativistically present in a pluralistic and globalized world? How can we be more than a tradition among other traditions? And how can we lay legitimate and reasonable claim to being that without simply increasing the volume of our presence as tradition? In matters of relativism, size does not count, and so even such a global and yet substantially unified presence as the Catholic Church, must be confronted by the persistent anxiety that we have no greater claim to being more than a 'tradition' than does any other community, Christian, religious or secular. If we make such a claim, then it can immediately be countered by the view that it is precisely a claim which forms part of our tradition, which is to say our cultural and social memory. What is there then to which we can point which might reasonably make the case to others (as well as ourselves) that this tradition is more than a tradition? For an answer to this question we shall have to look to the concept of history.

In this recognition of the contribution of Edward Schillebeeckx, we will need to make a distinction then between 'tradition' and 'history'. These words extensively overlap in much current usage, and it is not in fact always clear in much contemporary theology where the boundary between tradition and history lies. But though related, tradition and history must remain distinct concepts if Catholic tradition is to be able to claim that as tradition it is *historical* and distinctively so. After all, Christian tradition holds that it is founded uniquely upon historical revelation as incarnation in space and time. In the unity of present and past which defines human communities, including the Catholic Church, the term 'tradition' tends in fact to emphasize memory (always a present event) and the synchronic character of community who are bound together by common narratives and practices which express, perpetuate or are otherwise associated with that recalling. 'History' on the other hand invites us to think – potentially at least – of our existence as embodied agents in the causal flow of material reality. In straightforward terms, the language of history urges us to go beyond memory and the present and to consider, on the one hand, human action as that which has real effects upon other people, and, on the other, events from the past, including actions in the past, which have real effects even when they are not captured by or reproduced in human memory and traditions. History is about acts and the effects of acts. It is as much about *discovery* in the present as it is about insight into the past.

From a Christian perspective, history is always bound up with the unrepeatable act whereby God entered history and died for us on the Cross. It is an act whose effects are received in tradition but are received there also as discovery: as history that is constantly to be discovered within the vitality of present memory. As the living Word made flesh, he is the presence in whom and from whom we receive history as a living reality to be thought and lived. In the confession that Christ still lives, and does so in the integrity of his risen embodied life as fully human and fully divine, there is the claim that it is his risen body, wounded and glorified, that grounds the continuity of history which is the foundation of the Church's transformed life in space and time. As living, Jesus Christ is fully historical; and Christians who participate in his life, through baptism, come to share in the universal particularity of his historicality. Nowhere do we see that more clearly represented in human life than in the Eucharist, where the Church directly shares in the continuing life of Christ, mediated in his sacramental presence as sacrifice, in the midst of the Church.

But if we are to be clear about the distinction between 'tradition' and 'history' in such a way that we can begin to establish a claim for Christianity as a tradition that is uniquely *historical*, then we have to be clear also about how Christ is present to us in the Eucharist and how he is not. He is not present to us, for instance, in the fullness of his embodied life. Traditional sacramental theology states that he is (only) substantially present in the Eucharistic species, whereas he is fully or 'locally' present in heaven.[1] This means to say that it is in heaven that the risen Christ occupies space and time in accordance with his continuing, transformed or glorified humanity, and not in the Eucharist.[2] Eucharistic presence requires that the Eucharistic species of bread and wine remain constant in space and time. We do not claim to see the body and blood of Christ directly, as being in this place at this time (what tradition means by 'local' existence). Rather we 'see' him by discerning that he is really present as hidden within the Eucharistic species. We receive him, in his substance, clothed in the bread and wine.

---

[1] See Thomas Aquinas, ST III, q. 76, art. 5.

[2] For sources and themes in the traditional understanding of the Ascension more generally, see my comments in Oliver Davies, Paul Janz and Clemens Sedmak, *Transformation Theology: Church in the World* (London/New York, NY: T&T Clark, 2007) pp. 15–21.

This traditional way of speaking of the Eucharist uses the language of mediation therefore rather than the more modern trend to the language of substitution. There is an important difference between the two. The former implies that the Eucharistic presence is not self-sustaining but is rather the mediatory making present of Jesus Christ in the fullness of his divinity and continuing transformed humanity. We have to make a fundamental distinction between the mode of Christ's 'substantial' embodiment for us in the Eucharist and how he appeared to St Paul on the road to Damascus, for instance.[3] Traditionally, sacramental theology looks to the ascended Christ as the one whose presence is mediated to us and among us in the Eucharist. It is the ascended Christ himself however, in the primordial integrity of his full bodily life, or heavenly 'locality', who St Paul encountered on the road to Damascus. Unlike Eucharistic presence, this was historical revelation, in the sense that it was an active calling and commissioning of St Paul in Lordship into the service of the Church as the 'servant' (or 'slave') of God. Although we cannot share the revelatory character of this event (unlike St Paul, we encounter the living Christ not directly but through the Church and in the Spirit), we can recognize the quality of this encounter as being a personal encounter with present Christ in the fullness of his Lordship, and as the foundation of Christian vocation as transformative summons or 'hearing the call'. This is to encounter Christ in space and time according to his dominical authority, as the one who as Lord over space and time calls us into his service within the particularity of our individual spatio-temporal existence. In other words, if it is the case that it is the ascended Christ who comes into presence in the Eucharist, then St Paul's experience of the living Christ in his ascended embodiment, shows us that he becomes present for us also through calling, commissioning and vocation. This is an experience which comes to us in the Spirit, through the Church, and it is not revelation. But it remains a properly historical presence for us, as it was for St Paul, in that it is active and requires our own responsive reception in active obedience to the command of God made present to us in Christ, through the Spirit and the Church, within the particularity of our daily living.

But despite the denser historicality of the commissioning mode of Christ's presence, it is likely to be the case that we will think of the Eucharist as the *primary* presence of Christ in the world. The pre-modern Christian would have pointed to Christ in heaven (well represented on medieval maps as located on the farthest crystalline ring of the pre-Copernican finite universe[4]) as his continuing or present embodiment in the scriptural world

---

[3] Acts 9.3–19; 22.6–16; 26.12–18. Davies, Janz and Sedmak, *Transformation Theology*, pp. 44–55.

[4] For the place of heaven within traditional cosmology, see W.G.L. Randles, *The Unmaking of the Medieval Christian Cosmos 1500–1760: From Solid Heavens to Boundless æther* (Aldershot: Ashgate, 1999) and Edward Grant, *Planets, Stars*

of 'heaven' and 'earth', and to heaven as the place to where the Christian hoped to go at death, following Christ, in order to live with the blessed in the presence of God. The modern Christian cannot point to Christ in this way at all however, since heaven cannot be located in our universe in such a way that anyone could point to it. Rather the modern Catholic Christian would be likely to point to the Eucharist as the site of the Real Presence for the present immediacy of God to us in the world of space and time. But this in turn implies that Christ ascended is in fact a mode of Christ's *absence*, rather than the fullness that Pentecost and traditional sacramental theology suggests it is.[5] And it also sets up a profound tension between Eucharist and rite as the site of Christ's primary presence in the world and the world itself with all its complex and detailed social and political problematics. Eucharist begins to seem an alternative to world in this view, rather than the disclosure of the truth of the world, as the place of incarnation and Christ's continuing historicality, which it must most fundamentally be.

We cannot make the claim to be a properly historical religion then unless we first retrieve the full and integral historicality of Jesus Christ, which means his continuing historicality as active presence in space and time, however unique that presence or embodied life may be. And it certainly is a unique form of personal and embodied presence since St Paul himself does not tell us that he actually sees the body of Christ at all, even though he does clearly identify the light he sees and the voice he hears, as being the Galilean.[6] This remains a presence in hiddenness therefore, though it is precisely presence none the less and not absence.

There is no doubt that a retrieval of the doctrine of the ascension is long overdue. We do not need its ancient cosmology of height, exaltation and ascending, but we do need its faith conviction that Jesus Christ remains

---

 and Orbs: The Medieval Cosmos (Cambridge: Cambridge University Press, 1996). For further references and a brief summary of current scholarship on pre-modern heaven, see Oliver Davies, *The Creativity of God: World, Eucharist, Reason* (Cambridge: Cambridge University Press, 2004) pp. 16–21.

[5] In his substantial study of the Ascension and Church, Douglas Farrow deploys the paradigm of a dialectical presence and absence. See Douglas Farrow, *Ascension and Ecclesia* (Edinburgh: T&T Clark, 1999), in which he may implicitly be following a Barthian account of revelation. This dialectic will always tend towards a substitutive rather than mediatory account however. The Ascension needs to be grasped as a fundamentally different mode of Christ's presence in the world. See, for instance, the young Joseph Ratzinger's comment that the Ascension marks not the 'withdrawal of Christ to an Empyrean which is beyond the world, but is a visible expression for our participation in the mode of his being in the world: through the Spirit, Christ is not absent from the world but present in a new way, as the kingdom of God is realized on earth' (Joseph Ratzinger, 'Himmelfahrt Christi. II: Systematisch', *Lexikon für Theologie und Kirche* [ed. Michael Buchberger *et al.*; vol. 5; Freiburg/Basel/Vienna: Herder, 2nd rev. edn, 1960] col. 361).

[6] See also Gal. 1.11–24 and 1 Cor. 15.8.

within space and time, or in continuity with what we generally understand as space and time, in the final fullness of his – transformed – humanity and divinity. Ancient cosmology allowed the Christian Church to affirm that Jesus Christ had not gone away but only withdrawn from sight: that he was, in fact, hidden from us by the great distance of 'heaven above' from 'earth below'. We do not calculate that divide in terms of distance as the pre-moderns naturally did, according to their cosmology, but the principle remains the same. Now that his human body no longer conceals him, following his full glorification, the body is withdrawn from our senses until he 'comes again', and he is hidden within the material, historical world. And if Jesus is still present in space and time, then he can still disrupt us, as living bodies do, and as St Paul was 'disrupted' on the road to Damascus. To speak of disruption in this way is already to begin to speak of history rather than tradition or, more precisely, it is to speak of a tradition which is irreducibly historical in its capacity to receive and respond to the disruption-discovery which is the presence to us of the living body of Christ. It is this very distinctive disruption which is the particular form of Christian discipleship, as the reception or living out of doctrine in a life which is repeatedly trans-formed by the disruptive life of the 'ascended' Christ.[7] Disruption is the mode in which the disciple discovers the historical Christ.

Disruption always happens in the here and now. We recognize the 'disruptive' qualities of the parable of the good Samaritan or of the passages in Matthew 25, where Christ accuses his listeners of not having cared for him in the poor, the vulnerable and disadvantaged. But the loss of the theological meaning of the 'ascended' Christ, which is the embodiment in which Christ disrupts us, means that contemporary Christians cannot share the intellectual, or theological, confidence of the pre-modern Christian that it is truly Jesus himself who is disruptively present to us in our encounter with the needs or vulnerability of the other. In other words we struggle to make sense of how Christ can be truly present to us on such occasions of eschatological disruption when we do not really know what it is *for Christ still to be alive in the fullness of his humanity and divinity*. We cannot make sense of the scriptural and classical affirmation that Christ's continuing life in our universe is as hidden by distance. That heaven as 'above' we can read only as metaphor, what scripture and tradition otherwise took to be as a literal reference. For us, the theological failure of the ascended Christ which

---

[7] Lieven Boeve has argued that the Christian narrative itself signals its own 'inter-ruption' and allows us to identify this interruption – by life, by the nodal events of human existence – as a *theological* interruption: 'Interruptions cause the narrative to collide with its own borders.' We can thus begin to read the narrative as being, uniquely, 'a narrative of interruption', and the Christian life as a life of witness to the active, disruptive and ultimately transformative power of God at work in history (Lieven Boeve, *God Interrupts History: Theology in a Time of Upheaval* [New York, NY/London: Continuum, 2007] pp. 42 and 45).

seems to be a condition of modernity inevitably obstructs the possibility of a fuller reflective integration of caritative love into the foundational economy of faith. This is a failure not of history but of tradition which struggles to understand itself as *historical* tradition precisely at this point of disruptive encounter with the living, historical Christ.

But what can we do about this? We are separated from pre-modern Christians by the unbridgeable gulf of cosmology, which gives a different imaginative experience of the world as well as a different intellectual one. This is also a revolution in cosmology which was closely associated with the rise of a technological understanding of matter, leading over time to a shift in human embodiment as technology colonized the place of the here and now. We live in a public and global world in which disembodied modes of thinking associated with the performance of complex social, technological and communicative systems predominate, with their need for transferability, accountability and transparency. In their link with science, technology, professional life and universities, all of these are deemed as prestigious modes of thinking. But this kind of transparency is bought at the cost of an ever increasing complexity that increasingly fails to be adequate to the complex particularity of real life. The need to regulate human action, for whatever appropriate reason, is leading to a society which undervalues those forms of reasoning in the face of the immediacy of life – as in family life, for instance, in our close relationships, or in our pastoral work – which are most attuned and appropriate to complex reality in the unrepeatable here and now. Embodied forms of reasoning that are learned over time from repeated experience, within a culture of learning, have relatively low prestige, for these are not system-based forms of reasoning and are not tractable to transparency and transferability. How can we return to an embodiment of Christ in which he is known precisely in his intentionality for us, as the new born infant knows her mother, when so much in our culture wants to control the disruptive-historical on account of its unrepeatability? Is there not even in our own Catholic theology sometimes the wish to use the intellect to control the unpredictability of the disruptive discovery that is at the centre of our faith?

It is here again that we need to consider the Eucharist. A substitutive understanding of the Eucharist can only deepen the divide between the meaning of worship and the meaning of caritative acts in the Christian life, which is to say between 'tradition' as narrative, rite and memory and 'history' as the actuality of events, in which we are disrupted. A retrieval of the doctrine of the ascension as the continuing presence in hiddenness of Christ, which is the traditional ground of Eucharistic theology, allows for a proper *mediatory* understanding of the Eucharist and therefore unlocks a profound continuity between the two. Most importantly, the Eucharist offers us a hermeneutics of this incarnational presence in hiddenness, which is precisely the discernment through the Spirit of the actuality of Christ's presence in hiddenness to us in materiality. We 'see' him in the Eucharistic elements, as truly present, in the bread and wine. If the Eucharist is no longer asked to *substitute* for the living embodied Christ who has 'departed' from the world, then it can begin to instruct us on where and how he is to be found in the world and in the actuality of human historical life.

After all, Christ is present in the Eucharist as *sacrifice*. And sacrifice, in the Christian sense, is the language of history. Sacrifice is the purity of act, and it is a profoundly embodied phenomenon since, in the willing self-sacrifice which is Christ's self-offering for us on the Cross, the body itself becomes the free and loving instrument of our historical agency. When we act self-sacrificially, for the sake of the other or others, we ourselves become free material cause. We become properly *historical*. Christ's presence in hiddenness then in the Eucharist is fundamentally a *historical* mode of presence, since his sacrifice for us, by which he made himself one with the will of the Father, is paramountly *act*. And it is by our free acts that we can as human beings realize our belonging as embodied agents in the causal flow of history.

Here again then a distinction needs to be drawn if the Eucharist is to be properly secured in history and if Christian tradition as such is properly to become visible as *historical* tradition or as tradition which has a fundamental and unique orientation to history as the domain of an event that is antecedent to or 'outside' memory. It is not a different Christ who we meet in particular situations of moral calling and challenge from the Christ of Eucharistic presence, but such situations rather constitute two different historical ways in which we can know him, by virtue of our own complex historical nature. In the Eucharist we celebrate as Church our being in a world which is undergoing and which shall undergo so radical a transformation in the power of the risen Christ. The world is and shall be drawn into conformity with the irreversible triumph of God in Jesus Christ, for the sake of the world. In the Eucharist we celebrate the superabundant meaning of a world entering the freedom of the New Creation. This is to be within history as the unfolding of events and as the cosmic realization in space and time of the free design of God for the world as God's world.

But the self-sacrificial act of caritative action is equally historical though in a different way. Here it is not history as cosmic process in the unfolding of space and time, ultimately held in the transforming power of God, which comes into view, but rather history as the moment in which we make the world *this* world rather than another. This is history as a dynamic becoming of which we ourselves are part. It is history as that to which we can, under circumstances of the act, become internal. Being internal to it, we precisely do not understand its directionality. Here we feel only what it is we must do (or perhaps what we should *not* do in the sense of walk away from our responsibilities). Coming to our best judgement, beyond the comfort of secure knowledge, we make a difference as this person, freely and lovingly acting in this place and time. Yet still, in this area of human freedom, responsibility and risk, we are in the power of God. But we are now in that power in a different kind of way. We are in it by being in the powerless stranger and the poor man through whose self-sacrificial death God entered history as one who takes space and time to himself. We share that poverty, which is precisely the poverty of being historical as we enter, with responsibility, into the irreversibility of the historical act in the face of, or in the midst of, life's irreducibly complex particularity. This is to enter the power of the poor one who was raised and in whose rising, became – according to his humanity – an instrument for the inexpressible power of God in history, precisely at the points where the world becomes this world and not another.

A retrieval of the doctrine of the Ascension can eschew the archaic cosmology but retain the primary Christological affirmations which came to expression in that cosmological form, concerning the continuing fullness of the – now fully transformed – humanity and divinity in Jesus Christ whose risen life we proclaim at Easter. Such a retrieval must lead to a new relation between Eucharist and the caritative act, which is at the same time a new and newly interdependent relation between tradition and history. It must bring Eucharist and practical love back to their original complementarity and so establish Christianity, even in its most modern and deconstructive environments, as *historical* tradition, whose truth is witnessed to and lived out in the meaningfulness of a distinctively historical life as disciple.[8]

That meaning is constituted in the act, or sequences of acts and their sustaining practices, in which we allow ourselves to become free and loving material cause for others. In the moment of our own free act for the sake of the other, in loving obedience to the divine command made present to us in Christ through such a moment of historical determinacy, the disciple embraces her own materiality and contingency. In that moment of freely becoming material cause, or sacrifice, for the sake of the other, we become like the Eucharistic elements. For the very moment of our act, or embodiment of love, becomes the manner of Christ's hiddenness within materiality, and thus a mode of his presence in the world, as Lord of space and time. And again in parallel with the Eucharist, with its hermeneutics of revelation, in such a moment there opens up for us the possibility of an ecclesial 'seeing' through the Spirit, when we can discern him in us and ourselves in him. Then we can discover, in the mind of the Church, that the same Jesus Christ lives for us as real presence in hiddenness in both Eucharist and caritative acts, both of which are mediations of his living

---

[8] The central role played by Matthew 25 and by the eschatological requirement of the Christian to address the needs of the poor during the high patristic period of the fourth century is often poorly understood. Susan R. Holman's book *The Hungry Are Dying* (Oxford: Oxford University Press, 2001) goes a long way to redress this imbalance.

or 'ascended' embodiment as sacrifice. And so, while the act itself remains individual in its responsibility, the meaning of the act is the Lordship of Christ as sacrifice which we receive and celebrate in the Eucharist.

We have to ask then, in the final part of this contribution, how this new theological turn to history, from within a Eucharistic theology, stands within Catholic theological tradition? It has much in common with a range of Catholic thinkers, from Pierre Rousselot to Maurice Blondel and the *nouvelle théologie* and, more remotely, to liberation theology and the option for the poor. But it is also strongly non-cognitivist in orientation and so at odds in a certain respect with either the Transcendental Thomism of Karl Rahner or the aesthetic cognitivism of Hans Urs von Balthasar. Beyond those thinkers who have thought most deeply about the act, the natural point of alignment is with Edward Schillebeeckx, in whose work the slightly off-beat theological impulses of North West Europe come to their fullest expression.[9] There are two aspects that come to our attention.

The first is an orientation towards praxis as a way of addressing the problem of world. Speaking of world is always perilous in that it suggests a totalization which can be resolved only conceptually. World, which must be fundamentally about sensible reality, becomes an *idea*, and a totalizing one, when spoken about. World as it exists in actuality is always something of which we ourselves are a part, and thus something which itself contains the very act of reflecting about it. Even as observer, we are in the world. This means that if we wish to speak of world, we shall have to do so indirectly, by addressing such themes, as Schillebeeckx does, as Church, sacrament and ministry. If we are to speak of 'world' in ways that are adequate, then we must do so stealthily.

The second factor is the 'non-cognitivism' which Schillebeeckx learned from his Dominican teacher. De Petter developed the notion of 'implicit intuition', which was significantly at odds with the movement which became Transcendental Thomism, in its implicit appeal to the fundamental role of more imaginative and embodied dimensions in the reception of revelation. This non-cognitivism was strengthened in important ways by Schillebeeckx's turn to apophaticism in the negativity of his 'negative contrast experience' and the political orientation of his later work (the 'no' to the world as it is, in its social fallenness).[10] Here protest and apophatic

---

[9] M.M. Bakhtin, *Towards a Philosophy of the Act* (trans. and notes Vadim Lapiunov; ed. Michael Holquist and Vadim Liapunov; Austin, TX: Texas University Press, 1993); Maurice Blondel, *Action* [1893] (trans. Oliva Blanchette; Notre Dame, IN: Notre Dame University Press, 1984); Hannah Arendt, *The Human Condition* (Chicago, IL: Chicago University Press, 2nd edn, 1998). Act as practice is also a major theme more directly in the Frankfurt School, where it is worked out in terms of class interests rather than the self-sacrificial pursuit of the universal good.

[10] See in particular Edward Schillebeeckx, *Jesus in our Western Culture: Mysticism, Ethics and Politics* (trans. John Bowden; London: SCM Press, 1987).

negativity mix in what is fundamentally a unitive experience of the divine. The inability to capture God in concepts, to which the apophatic tradition attests, is itself an expression of the proximity of God, mediated to us in the compassionate politics of solidarist social action.

What I take from Schillebeeckx's work most fundamentally however is his passionate and compassionate commitment to the principle that action in the world is not an adjunct to faith but the very foundation of faith. *Caritas in Veritate* seems to come close to echoing this insight. A contemporary retrieval of the doctrine of the 'ascension' can build upon this 'apophatic practical theology' (reminiscent in some respects of the medieval Franciscans) within a more intensified environment of pluralistic and globalized exchange. We can only know the 'ascended' Christ in continuity with St Paul's knowledge of him, as encounter and challenge in the midst of life. The body is known in and through the Holy Spirit and the Church as the disruptive intentionality of its life. Christ lives as sacrifice. But it is the *real body* that is known through the mediation of the act in its intentionality for us just as it is the real body that is known through the mediation of the Eucharist, in its world-meaning for us. Here too then we find an echo of Schillebeeckx's 'negative contrast experience', for the 'not-knowing' of the body of Christ conceptually and representationally is a pre-condition for the 'knowing' of the body of Christ in terms of its intentionality for us and its transformative power of act. It is by the power of that act that we as Christians meaningfully live.

THE CHURCH WITH
A HUMAN FACE

Marc Dumas

1. Introduction

In 1985, Edward Schillebeeckx published *The Church with a Human Face*,[1] a new and extended version of a book he had published some years before and in which Schillebeeckx took account of the critical reception his earlier work had received. The original Dutch title of the 1985 book, *Pleidooi voor mensen in de Kerk: Christelijke identiteit en ambten in de Kerk* (Plea in Favour of Humans in the Church: Christian Identity and Ministry in the Church), more explicitly states the author's commitment to changing humanity's place and praxis in the Church. The book is Schillebeeckx's exhortation to the Church to exit from the impasse in which it finds itself. Noting that social and historical developments have always affected the way the community of believers is organized, Schillebeeckx invites us on a historical journey to clearly show us how the different forms of ecclesial life have unfolded. The various conceptions and forms of ministerial organization did not suddenly fall from heaven: throughout the ages they developed and sometimes were fundamentally transformed in order to give room for a greater diversity of other possibilities, but without breaking the fundamental unity and the apostolicity of the New Testament. In this regard, Schillebeeckx searches for acceptable models of ministerial organization in the history of the Church in order to unlock forgotten truths which can contribute pastorally to overcoming the contemporary aporia and shattering the ideological deviances which stifle the creativity of the community of God. In the light of the contemporary situation Schillebeeckx proposes a hermeneutics of tradition in order to discover and evaluate, in a critical manner, the way in which community life can express itself in our contemporary context both in terms of local communities of faith as well as in regard to official authorities.

---

[1] Edward Schillebeeckx, *The Church with a Human Face: A New and Expanded Theology of Ministry* (trans. John Bowden; New York, NY: Crossroad, 1985).

Five years later, *Church*[2] (Dutch original: *Mensen als verhaal van God*) was published. In the final section of this book, Schillebeeckx reflects upon a new model for the Church, a model that can benefit from the accomplishments of democracy, reserving an important place for everyone's freedom, and that can finally position itself differently within today's *pluri-religious* world. Almost everywhere in the West, Christian communities are becoming increasingly weaker in number and in influence. There are insufficient numbers of skilled and engaged ministers and volunteers are wearing themselves out. Yet, one is still reluctant to change existing structures and to recognize the charisma of women, married men, defrocked priests and lay people. Without disavowing its role in mediating faith in Jesus Christ, the Church must be able to actualize itself, in a new context, in a way that affirms Christianity's identity and particular situation amidst a concert of other religions. For Schillebeeckx, the question of a democratic gesture of God's community becomes necessary. The community's present structure does not take the new context sufficiently into account, and this handicaps its service to the world. Can the Church avoid the dual traps of absolutism and relativism? Can the Church witness to its mission without arrogance and feelings of superiority while explicating the unique nature of Christianity in a plural context? Furthermore, can the Church acknowledge, through the other and through plurality, the intangible and fertile richness of God? Believers discover, in the story of Jesus of Nazareth, the life and the true being of God, but how can they account for this faith and live it today?

Whereas the twentieth century was largely spent assessing the results of twentieth century theology, interest has lately been shifted to theology's possible future. The symposium in which this paper was originally presented is but another example of this endeavour, and the challenges awaiting us are numerous. Arguably, while theology was always able – at least this is what one could be led to believe – to pursue a stable course even through stormy weather it is now considerably weakened. Could theology be on the way to extinction? Could it be in danger of disappearing, as the dinosaurs once did in olden times, or as may be the looming fate for today's polar bears? In this regard, Michel de Certeau speaks of the 'misery of theology' pointing to the temptation theology faces of mutating into religious studies or humanities.[3] He says that theology's task is twofold:[4] first, theology should revisit those places in the tradition where the fundamental relation was elaborated between the always particular option for Christian faith and the forms,

---

[2] Edward Schillebeeckx, *Church: The Human Story of God* (trans. John Bowden; New York, NY: Crossroad, 1990).

[3] See Michel de Certeau, 'La misère de la théologie', *La faiblesse de croire* (ed. Luce Giard; Esprit; Paris: Seuil, 1987), pp. 253–63.

[4] See de Certeau, 'La misère de la théologie', pp. 261–62.

religious or not, in which the praxis and consciousness of a society have taken shape in the past; second, theology must be an active participant in society, as society's accomplice both in its ambitions and its risks, engaging with societal conflicts in a critical way, which entails distancing itself from the tendency to exclude the excess of and the opening to the Other. This demand for a connection between faith and society, on the one hand, and the commitment to the life of the city, on the other, in order to attain to '*le théologal*'⁵ appear to me as two intuitions already present in Schillebeeckx's work. We will come back to them below.

Several theological training programmes are disappearing today. Theology departments are seeing a decrease in the number of teachers, and in many countries these programmes are confronted with a steady decrease in the number of students. After all, why would anyone want to study theology? Indeed, who is asked to deal with religion in the public realm? Most of the time this task is being carried out by historians, psychologists, sociologists or anthropologists. When theologians do interact with the media or speak in public spaces they do so more often than not under another title (bishop, professor, or ethicist). Even the theologian's natural habitat, namely, his or her own community, is often inhospitable to the exercising of his or her work in a critical manner ... In short, a brief glance at the current situation shows that the issue of 'identity' is the theologian's major challenge: what does it mean to do theology *hic et nunc*? What are the conditions that make the theological task possible? And lastly, why do we do theology at all, and for whom?

There can be many, even contradictory, answers to these questions. For a number of theologians, on the one hand, there is no identity problem at this point in time. They continue to believe, in a more or less naïve way, that everything will continue to go on as it has for the better. For others, however, the crisis is so serious that one cannot even know whether a 'native' theological service can continue to be offered to the dioceses due to a lack of well-trained and interested staff. Certain theologians may be reproached for having so opened themselves up to culture, to become specialists in the study of religion, that they lose sight of the essential and organic ecclesiastic service they should be giving to the institution. These theologians invariably answer that they couldn't do otherwise, since

---

⁵ There is a slight difference in French between the terms '*théologal*' and '*théologique*'. The emphasis with the '*théologal*' rests on the Presence of the Trinity (Father, Son and Holy Spirit). Through metaphors, the Bible brings to the fore the Presence of God in different ways: the burning bush with Moses, the bliss of the wind with Elija, and so forth. This Presence ('*théologal*') is precisely what the theologians have to find in, through, and within the world. Thus to reflect on that Presence of God is a theological task. In the following text, I shall either use the word '*théologal*' between inverted commas or the expression 'theological experience' in order to render the Presence of God.

they have a responsibility to speak about God not only in ways that are adequate for contemporary needs but, also, in upholding this responsibility, to speak with and to today's men and women in order to be able to inscribe faith in Jesus Christ into this world.[6]

In what follows, I will consider first certain ancestral reflexes that should be taken up again today. Second, I will add some precision to these reflexes in order to understand them with a view toward my Western, North American, Quebecers context. Recontextualized in this way, they can become new tools for performing the contemporary act of theology. This reflection should lead to some considerations regarding the faithful and ecclesial community which will help to explain the title of this paper.

2. Ancestral Reflexes of the Theological Act

The first two reflexes of the theological act that we find in Schillebeeckx are qualified by de Certeau as urgent. (1) To have the capacity to revisit the different moments in the tradition in which different figures of the relation between faith in Jesus and the context are unfolded is an encounter, not simply with knowledge and intellectual tours de force, but rather a discovery of the motivations, experiences, circumstances and concretizations in a particular time and place of the interpretation of the encounter with the crucified and risen Jesus. The proposed course in *The Church with a Human Face* illustrates well the patient work of this historian, exegete, hermeneutist, and theologian who works with the material in order to show clearly the various possible valences in accordance with the contexts and the reflex to be taken up again to respect the dynamics of faith, which unfolds itself when new circumstances have arisen. (2) The second reflex is a committed participation in the life of contemporary people, in their projects, in their defeats, in their anxieties, and in their successes. The theologian cannot comfortably hold a view from above, remaining out of the game when everything is at stake; rather, it is through this dedication and commitment to participation in contemporary life that the theologian will be touched by his or her contemporary's realities, desires, sufferings and hopes. What happens if the theologian only moves between the horizons of Antiquity and Middle Ages or if his or her language is inaccessible or unable to be understood by the majority? What happens if he or she is insensitive to the religious, philosophical, political, economic, cultural, and media pursuits of his contemporaries? The theologian may then be a

---

[6] See Michel Beaudin and Anne Fortin, 'Lectures et relectures inconclusives', *Des théologies en mutation: Parcours et trajectoires* (ed. Michel Beaudin, Anne Fortin and Ramon Martinez de Pison; Héritage et projet, 65; Montréal: Fides, 2002), pp. 391–411 (394).

great scholar, but he or she will not be able to collaborate in the religious and spiritual quests of his or her time. In my opinion, this second reflex is as pressing as it is unavoidable: without a committed theological interpretation of the context (the latter not only being a decor or a pretext to do theology), how would one shed light on the underlying logics, where would one find a hermeneutical fulcrum, how would one distance oneself from this context and find a terrain from which to criticize it and to open up a space for a possible experience of the '*théologal*', a space for excess and for an overflow of the Other within the heart of human lives?

The theologian develops the capacity to interpret Tradition for today so that he or she may accompany those who search for meaning and interrogate the faith, since disappointment and despair often shake our hopes. *The Church with a Human Face*, with its identification of the Church's dead-ends and its analysis of post-Vatican II events, pointedly shows Schillebeeckx's devotion to diagnosing the current situation and to searching for viable solutions which could be proposed as a ministerial theology which would be significant for the communities.

However, theologians are also in need of developing one last reflex, namely to use epistemological and methodological tools which are comprehensible to their contemporaries. Conceptual abstractions and arguments relying on an authority which is pulled out of the Tradition have lost their weight. Where and how, in our era, is it still possible to account for the Christian faith? For instance, certain more inductive and narrative linguistic approaches, or the integration of more recent cultural and philosophical analyses, might be helpful. Schillebeeckx gives, for an example, a predominant place to experience.[7] His analyses take into account specific approaches in order to better delineate what 'experience' might imply. Furthermore, this gives him the opportunity to offer a balance between politics (commitment) and mysticism and to leave a space for spiritual life in his theological activity. By doing so, he makes use of the believer's experience who encounters God.

So new contexts await us – one must take into account not only religion's growing complexity but also its mutations outside of institutions into more individualistic forms when speaking of secularization, pluralism, interreligious dialogue and ecological crisis – and new difficulties must be addressed (e.g. identity crisis, outdated ecclesial models, insignificance of words) to speak of God in an adequate manner in this day and age. But when used adroitly the dialogue with contemporaries is indispensable for rejoining them, to perceive their wounds and failings, their hopes and desires, to speak to them of God, and to interpret God's presence in the midst of their world.

---

[7] See for instance the synthesis of Schillebeeckx's analysis on experience: *Church*, pp. 15–21.

As a hermeneutical and critical theologian, Schillebeeckx first analyses the new context and the problems posed by this context, naming the resulting theological challenges. He then uses the new historical and exegetical research to revisit the places where faith in Jesus Christ emerges as well as the multiple theological, ecclesial, and ministerial crystallizations throughout time and space. Finally, with audacity and sagacity, he recaptures the work of our ancestors in faith by offering new ways appropriate for the present time due to the change in contexts. For this method, it is not sufficient to simply transpose knowledge from the past or from somewhere else. Rather, we have to appropriate the dynamic of faith anew by recalling that the theological act is forever moving, perpetually challenged, and in constant transformation. In this regard, I understand the theological act as a sort of passage-way or transition, one which offers an understanding of faith for those around us who interrogate us wanting to understand what is happening to their life when verticality either strikes them or seems absent.

3. Achieving Transitions (Passages)

Like Schillebeeckx, we all go through a number of transitions in the course of our research and theological work. For him, such a transition occurred in passing from Neo-Scholasticism to hermeneutics, from a traditional Christology to one which incorporates exegetical works, and, lastly, from the Catholic Church's relatively secure universe to the contemporary world. Through this last move, Schillebeeckx went on to new tasks of thinking, articulating, and organizing his frame of mind in a totally different way with the help of sociology, critical theory and hermeneutics. Has Schillebeeckx accomplished these transitions in a radical way? Only his later, more penetrating, works can help us adequately answer this question.

As for ourselves, analogous transitions await us, albeit with other elements, problems, contexts, and methods. The term 'passage' reminds us of those passing by on the street, the ones who cross borders but also of Easter, where the messenger draws us to the Crucified and Resurrected. The term 'passage' likewise calls us to action, to transformation, for a transfiguration of the subjects practising theology. These transitions necessarily modify the practitioner as much as it modifies the practice of theology itself. And, to my mind, these transitions are necessary if we want to take up the challenge presented by the present age. Doesn't theology have to continuously take up its task in the face of new situations? Aren't we operating in unprecedented situations, situations which call us to do theology in a context in which individualism and pluralism have made humans more vulnerable, in a context in which our society's values, symbols and imagination are mutating? I see theologians as passers-by, both welcoming the spiritual quest and the quest for sense of their contemporaries and reviewing them in a critical fashion. Now, I would like to identify some transitions which must be undergone in order to place ourselves on the path toward a meaningful practice of theology today. My statement is that of a pilgrim and a searcher. It is not the declaration of one who has reached the pinnacle.

a. *Passage toward a Contextual Theology for the Here and Now*

It is remarkable to see how theology travels through the ages and through space. Having experienced the theology of these other times and other places, it is nonetheless important to make a theology for the here and now. This demands both an awareness of the strengths and the limits, and the wounds and stories of the people surrounding us. Although it is important to speak theoretically to consider the main tendencies in our Western societies, it is just as important to take theologically into account what is being experienced concretely and to note the concrete consequences of some problematic on cultural challenges within our own societies, to incorporate the humanist, religious and spiritual quests of our days no matter if the people are related or not to any ecclesial institution. Isn't it important to develop an indigenous and original theology if we want to discern the seeds of hope, which come to life in our societies, and if we want to avoid the excesses of idolatry, of indifference, and even of religious illiteracy in the face of its own legacy? All this entails the opening of a passage by listening to the echoes of reality and by sticking to life as it is lived; it is a transition that comes from the bottom-up, from the outskirts or the margins, and which aims at taking up once again and anew the movement of the ancestors in faith, who also had to think about and to speak of the intelligibility of their faith with the instruments then available in their situation.

It is surprising, for example, that in Quebec we have rapidly transitioned from a Catholic country to a secular one and that we now speak of a *pluri-religious* land. Is this due only to the advent of immigrants, or is it because people from Quebec craft a spirituality for themselves *à la carte*? If the Church of Quebec wants to heal its people's memory – a memory focusing only on abuse of people's conscience, clericalism, sexual abuses in Indian boarding schools, etc., it has to re-read its recent history in a more positive way. Before the sixties, this past was not all negative, but was also a prolific seed of the Gospel (cooperative associations, support of social justice, draft impediment, etc.), something of which the Quebec people could be proud of. It is also amazing to see that Quebec gives the impression of being a society marked by an anthropology of (material) plenitude, whereas previously we upheld an anthropology of material lack, which provided an opportunity for social and communal organizations. If plenitude marks our anthropology, why are there so many young people dropping out of school? Why are there suicides among the elderly? Why do so many people live in distress, as if hope had run out? If we are in an existential dead-end, if our plenitude is not marked by transcendence, if the exit of the clergy from our public institutions has only given us the opportunity to be harsh towards ecclesial heteronomy, and if, nonetheless, this country has not advanced towards a collective mobilizing project and a way of living together, then we must denounce this situation and meet some of its challenges, among which lies the redefinition of Christian identity in the face of a seemingly evanescence of all things sacred along with the articulation of how the individual can cope with the encounter of plurality. This is but an example of where the questions are situated, and it illustrates how these same questions call the theologian to criticize dead-ends and to find within them possibilities for veritable life.

b. *Methodological and Epistemological Passage*

However, drawing special attention to the contemporary situation is not enough to create a theology. Marked by divisions and crises, by projects and dreams, the contemporary situation must be integrated into the theological act. This passage touches upon theological method and epistemology. The questioning of the secular authority of theology in modernity has driven it to transform its practice in a modern, scientific and specialized practice. This has permitted theology to gain some credibility, approaching that of the other sciences. However, while this kind of discourse was plausible in the past, it is now being put in question, since it cannot take into account our fragmented, even pulverized, reality. These scientific theologies were simply too good to be true, and some of their frameworks and horizons didn't have any link to reality at all. What can we do once our patch job hasn't worked and when our repeated attempts to do so fail over and over again when faced with defeat, loss and suffering?

Let us start from scratch! Let us try another way. Let us revisit texts from the Tradition with new questions and new approaches, new methods and attitudes in order to develop another relationship with the scriptural, dogmatic, and ministerial Tradition – a more mystical relation, if I may say so. If for those ancestors it was a question of life and death of the faith, shouldn't we put these elements at stake in our reflections as well? This passage demands another relationship with the foundational texts and a reprise of the efforts undertaken in the Tradition to appropriate the Christ event. It likewise demands the exploration of theological elements capable of reading the sensibilities of today, elements which could favour vitality, hope and inspiration. Narrative theologies, eco-feminist theologies, or theologies having recourse to experience, seem promising for the construction of such a new theology, because they answer to the new conditions of the human frame of mind and its consequences for theological work in a better and more appropriate way.

c. *Passing to theology (and to the* 'théologal'*)*

And Easter! The passing of the Resurrected Crucified. Is this not the passage to faith, namely through that place where all our secure feelings flee, where we take the risk to empty ourselves to listen, where well put words sound empty, if they aren't really filled with this gift? And let us pay attention in this passage to what is forbidden, to the margins, to gaps and to interruptions, because isn't this precisely where God reveals his presence within the heart of our humanity? Doesn't this transition lead theology to discover a new space to position itself in the world – a space oriented not so much toward what has already been established, but rather that seeks for traces of the absent one, of an absentee, in the heart of suffering humanity, in the heart of desperate lives, but present at the same time in the heart of liberations, healings, and in the growth towards more humanity.

This transition calls for an enhanced integration of the '*théologal*' – Presence of God – in theology. Scientific requirements have properly situated theology within a theoretical space, useful and profitable at the time. However, does this not incur the risk of reducing theological experience to the parameters of science, which have little interest in this experience – if any at all. If theology must open itself to other discourse, it is equally necessary for us not to loose our own spirit, not to loose what is constantly slipping out of our hands, what is, and continues to be, unspeakable. This transition to theological experience, therefore, does not exclude the opening to others, but it presupposes a mutual enrichment and a reciprocity which highlights the differences between dialogue partners as well. And theology's specific task is to support theological experience by trying to find the words with which this experience can be expressed or expresses itself, to find the theological experience within our very lives.

If the function of theology is mainly to incite reflection upon faith – a reflex emerging from people's encounters with God, from those who have been deeply moved by the Crucified and Resurrected Jesus, and from those who gather as a Church – does it mean that theologians should open up their horizons of faith to the diverse horizons of cultures and confessions, which clearly mediate the '*théologal*' – Presence of God – since the beginning throughout different situations, epochs and ages? Can we imagine a passage out into open waters to see how and where theological experience is present in the midst of our lives, in the here and now? Can we imagine that God's followers could be somewhere else than where we expect to find them?

These three passages or transitions (contextual, methodo/epistemological and '*théologal*') ultimately point towards a place for research into the heart of people's lives at this place and time. Contexts are more complex; both pluralism and individualism seem to be difficult to accommodate reasonably. Theological experience should not only open a passage to contexts, but it should also, and above all, open up a passage towards people and communities, towards real people, in flesh and bone, people who call and challenge us, who are looking for actual ways to answer to their questions, distress, and desires. New sensibilities are expressed. Having demolished totalitarian thought, we set our focus now on the periphery, the gap, the excess, the overflow. Furthermore, our thought has become fragmentary, which allows for greater imagination. All this allows us to attend to our contemporary's speech and to respond to their situation in better ways. However, these new peripheries could lead us to further loosen our ties with ecclesial tradition, which, all in all, does not seem to be very significant for today's youth. This leads us to the crucial question facing the Church today.

4. *The Church with a Human Face*

In contrast to the earlier ecclesial and dogmatic universe, Quebec's theologians, in the past few decades, are becoming more and more concerned with subjects in search of meaning and they are willing to accompany them in the expression of faith in Jesus Christ. Following the contemporary process of individualization (such individualization seems to be the last entrenchment when everything is falling apart), Quebec's theologians have paid attention to those subjects' spiritual experiences – sometimes even to the detriment of communal and ecclesial dimensions – to the point that one must even ask how it could be possible to balance individualism and community, solitude and solidarity.

What kind of Church do we have? Locally, fatigue is manifest. From a management perspective, we are in a downsizing mode, looking for ways to avoid disasters. We are always trying to do more with fewer resources; not to mention the fact that these resources are aging. Can we do it any other way? Can we start from scratch and have the audacity to do things differently? Could we benefit from the emergence of a new paradigm of interdependency, which is beginning to emerge on the horizon, and use this as a lever to build Church upon? We speak a lot about networking in research and of interdependency in sustainable development. Interdependency is directed towards establishing a new relational model based on something other than dependency or autonomy, two old patterns which ought to be overcome. Interdependency highlights the fact that we are all dependent upon one another, so our relationship to others must radically change if we want to live through the present environmental crisis.

How to affirm and live faith in Christ in this new emerging paradigm? How to reconstruct God's congregation? My proposal is simple: build from the bottom-up, along common affinities, and see to what extent these small local groups can become ecclesial cells, which open up to others in order to make Church happen. A friend of mine, who is a priest, works with the homeless. He sees Church everywhere, especially where others don't see it. He thinks that Church is both one who thirsts and one who quenches one's thirst. Everything begins with this essential icon of sharing and of profound communion, of relation to another, which testifies to a third party and opens a path to life, freedom, and happiness.

A Church with human faces. Could it not be possible to imagine Church from those everyday small deeds which take on an unsurpassable meaning, especially for those deprived of any such meaning? Could it not also be there that you will find men and women committed to live in and change the world, where solidarities are created and fraternity shapes itself, where Churches can originate? I am imagining gatherings made by affinities, social, artistic and cultural activities, temporary or long term charitable activities, local, national or international support for prisoners, etc. The list of places/ecclesial cells goes on and on. It is where we try to change the miserable human faces around us into serener faces, where small, modest, less spectacular histories are shared, but histories which lead to hope for a more *humane* humanity, and with it, increasingly *human* humans.

A Church with human faces brings with it the possibility of a new beginning, with young men and women creating new basic communities, and with these communities organizing themselves into models of a humble and meaningful presence around them. In turn, individuals and groups invest discretely and fairly to offer microcredit to the poorest of the poor, to give them the opportunity of recovering their dignity; original parishes are reorganized, aimed at key periods of community life; student groups meeting with those who are left out; others journeying, accompanying, sharing and dialoguing with people who think and live God otherwise. In short, ecclesial cells are being formed around people's interests, and oftentimes exist in the margins of the great ecclesial trends; these communal renewal groups sometimes form small closed groups, but there are also ecclesial cells which are like the seeds of the Gospel in the world.

The Church has promoted a freed humanity, a humanity standing tall in the face of God; it has campaigned for the symbol of the Crucified God, which should allow, to a certain extent, a new frame of mind in favour of liberating the individual and of inscribing him/her into community affairs, which in turn, opens up to interdependence.

In his proposal of a theology of ministry, Schillebeeckx outlines perfectly the way in which social context acts upon the Church's organization. It becomes possible and probably desirable to unfold various faith community models side by side. Those various ministries, which are at the service of leadership and which take the interests of the Gospel to heart, will undergo, in the near future, the effects of the impact of this emergent paradigm of interdependency within society.

If Church is God's congregation, that it is a particular group reunited to celebrate, pray, share the Word, and committed to changing the world, rather than functioning as a hierarchical structure with the pretentions of being universal, then why would it not have ecclesial cells in all sorts of different associations?

If Church is precisely the home of Trinitarian life, because of its relation to the Son, the Father, and the Holy Spirit, as well as a relation to another and the others, then how could the Church remain self-enclosed? Isn't it, on the contrary, always drawn to open itself up to the world; to tell the theological experience; to share the bread; to move along with the poor and the indigent, and to work for more justice?

What we wish for, is that the fall of Church, which was lived abruptly in our country, can be the occasion for the Church to reinvent itself. Isn't it, in fact, when we hit rock bottom that unexpected developments and creativity occur? Indeed, instances of hope are sometimes neglected, and a flood of ecclesial cells is urgently needed in our times, so that the right words and appropriate action may drive us into a new world, to a profound interdependency, to a freedom, and to a more fraternal way of living together (in caring and healing), toward a more respectful attitude towards the planet.

5. Overture to a closing

Let us summarize before we conclude. We have tried to shed light on a certain number of elements in Schillebeeckx's theological act, in order to see whether or not, and how, they are still relevant today. I have paid special attention to three of these acts: the analysis of the present faith context, the analysis of the unfolding of the faith experience throughout the centuries, and the criticism of deviations and ideologies in order to bring back the 'théologal' in the current context. The Schillebeeckxian theological work is both an exploration of the beginning and the historical unfolding of the theological tradition as well as an analysis of our present time which allows us to propose an adequate correspondence between that tradition and the experience of faith for our contemporaries.

The theological act is situated and inscribed at the place where the feet, the heart, and the head of the theologian are located. No theologian is an island; his work is linked to men and women in a quest and a request for meaningfulness: meaningfulness to live and to understand, to have faith, to hope, and to love. It is for them that he or she strives to grasp the problematic, to explore Scripture and the Tradition in order to dig up positions which take down the barriers of today's people. He or she criticizes impasses, wrong tracks and ideologies. The theologian hunts down the theological experience in his or her encounter with a culture. God's community starts where a human who is thirsty receives something to drink

from another one; where, in the most natural way, a relationship acknowledges its interdependency, a welcoming of the difference, the gap, and a
meeting that is fruitful. It is not a reduction to the same, nor a flattening to
the identical, but a fecundity that shares in the gratuitous presence of the
Other. It is through faces both brightened by satisfaction and darkened by
struggle that the Church can unfold itself again, because a presence of the
theological experience paves the way to satisfaction and, in turn, sends out
an invitation to satisfy the struggling.

PART VI
PHILOSOPHY AND THEOLOGY

IMPLICIT FAITH:
PHILOSOPHICAL THEOLOGY
AFTER SCHILLEBEECKX

Stephan van Erp

1. *Divisions in theology: Notes towards a Philosophical Theology*

a. *The Anti-Modern Slant*

'Only theology overcomes metaphysics.' This is John Milbank's conclusion in a chapter bearing that very same title in his book *The Word Made Strange*. Theology, he there writes,

> If it wishes to think again God's love, and think creation as the manifestation of that love, ... must entirely evacuate philosophy, which is metaphysics, leaving it nothing (outside imaginary worlds, logical implications or the isolation of *aporias*) to either do or see, which is not – manifestly, I judge – malicious.[1]

Based on the content of the rest of the chapter, it is important to note that Milbank does not suggest disconnecting theology entirely from all philosophy. Philosophy, he argues, serves a purpose as long as it is oriented towards 'an always in any case implicit abstract reflection on the "context" of our ascent'. By this, he means a philosophy that is able to 'convert the given into a gift, to receive love' and to 'admit the mediation of appearing and revelation via the judgement and right desire of "the inspired man", even if it be equally the case that judgement and right desire are themselves entirely given'.[2] And he adds that he is referring to a concept of revelation

---

[1] John Milbank, *The Word Made Strange: Theology, Language, Culture* (Oxford: Blackwell, 1997) pp. 36–52 (50).
[2] Milbank, *The Word Made Strange*, p. 49.

which dates prior to early modernity, after which it became 'distorted' into a positive, actual content.[3]

Coming to a different conclusion but also referring to a premodern conception of faith, John Caputo has argued that theology and philosophy are closely connected insofar as they are inwardly structured by the sort of faith that is at work in each. He claims that:

> [Faith] turns out to have a stronger hand to play, which is why ... the premoderns were onto something important. For faith is an elemental form of human life, a basic ingredient in our existence, as necessary as the air we breathe, and it proves to be an indispensable requirement for philosophy as well as for theology, which it turns out differ from each other in virtue of the difference between the faith that is in them, that is in each of them.[4]

Caputo concludes that the distinction between philosophy and theology is between two kinds of interpretative angles on faith, which is a given that both the philosopher and the theologian have in common.

Milbank's analysis of a rigid separation of modern philosophy and theology has radical consequences for his critique of theological reason and for the recognition of theological sources in particular. The givenness of judgement contradicts, according to him, the possibility of an independent phenomenology that could inform theology or even evoke new theological content. Theology therefore, he concludes, should resist metaphysics and avoid resulting in representational knowledge, but instead continue to be susceptible to the infinite source that has shaped the history of human ascent. Caputo claims that this infinite source is already and always present in metaphysical and representational knowledge, which are therefore not opposed to receiving the gift of the divine, but instead are the interpretative results of it.

Milbank however argues that only theological judgement participates in that which is given from this infinite source, and in order to maintain that participation, it should remain non-metaphysical through the active response to the givenness of the ongoing history it is part of. He considers modern philosophy however as being 'metaphysical' and positivist. He defines it as rooted in the secular immanentism of ancient philosophy, which forces it to seek a graspable, immanent security. Hence, it is unsuitable for theology. Theological judgement in turn is described by Milbank as

---

[3] In the chapter 'Theology overcomes metaphysics', Milbank expresses an adamant opposition to the philosophy of Jean-Luc Marion, claiming that Marion's position leads to asserting the truth of Christianity merely on the level of appearance, without giving any account of revelation as a historical continuity.

[4] John D. Caputo, *Philosophy and Theology* (Nashville, TN: Abingdon, 2006) pp. 57–58.

revealed judgement, and he disqualifies modernity for its misrepresentation of revelation as being co-constructible through knowledge and language, which according to him results in viewing the world, at its best, as 'a series of givens to be known, rather than gifts to be received and returned'. In short, according to Milbank, theological judgement is and should remain non-phenomenological, non-metaphysical and should be considered as revealed. Consequently, he argues, it cannot take its sources from modern philosophy or any cultural or social practice whatsoever, but instead it originates from and seeks its way to, what he describes as a pure form of *theologia*.

And yet, why is it that this theological origin should not be reflected upon with the help of modern philosophy? I would here like to argue against anti-modern and 'neo-orthodox' positions such as Milbank's. Resisting or resigning to the use of modern philosophy in contemporary theology unnecessarily leads to the division of theologians into so-called orthodox or revisionist and liberal camps. Dividing philosophical and theological schools into 'premodern', 'modern' and 'postmodern' groups is the result of modern philosophy itself and it does not do justice to a chronological description of the history of philosophy. Moreover, confirming these divisions involves a diversion from theology's core business, which is to reflect on God's salvific act in history.[5] School divisions in contemporary philosophy and theology are not very helpful to the furtherance of theological reflection and frequently result in methodological debates about the relationship between disciplines or cultural periods.[6]

b. *The Modern Angle*

Through a rereading of Edward Schillebeeckx's theological metaphysics, I would like to show that contemporary theology can be the fruitful outcome of an ongoing conversation and connection of faith with modern philosophy. In my opinion, Schillebeeckx's application of a Kantian interpretation of an Aristotelian-Thomist metaphysics to modern theology is a clear example of this. Theologians should continue that conversation instead of presenting themselves as opponents of the modern. This is not only needed for reasons of analytics and academic or secular communication, as David Tracy suggested by distinguishing theology's audiences, in which philosophy

---

[5] Cf. John Webster, 'Theology after Liberalism', *Theology after Liberalism: Classical and Contemporary Readings* (ed. John Webster and George P. Schner; Blackwell Readings in Modern Theology; Oxford: Blackwell, 1998), pp. 52–64; John Webster, 'Theologies of Retrieval', *The Oxford Handbook of Systematic Theology* (ed. John B. Webster, Kathryn E. Tanner and Iain R. Torrance; Oxford: Oxford University Press, 2007), pp. 583–99.

[6] Cf. Ingolf Ulrich Dalferth, *Theology and Philosophy* (repr.; Eugene, OR: Wipf & Stock, 2001).

served as a rhetorical tool to reinforce theology's accountability within the academy.[7] Apart from the formal support that philosophy adds to the study of faith, I would like to claim that it is perfectly capable of reflecting on the material content of theology without 'maliciously distorting' it, as Milbank suggests. Instead, philosophy adds to or complements theology, precisely because, as Caputo claimed, it is motivated by the faith that has shaped both philosophy and theology.

A counterproposal to current neo-orthodox tendencies in philosophy and theology is the further development of a *philosophical theology*, which distinguishes but neither identifies nor separates practices of the given faith from its traditional and tradition-bound resources, discourses and worldviews. One of the distinctions theologians should particularly reflect upon nowadays is that between secular worldviews and the world of faith. Philosophy, like other academic disciplines applied to theology, is needed to make these distinctions. Instead of evacuating philosophy from theology in order to uncover a 'pure' theological centre of judgement, I would like to propose that philosophy is actively involved in discovering *and* forming constructive judgements of faith, and in understanding what constitutes theology *as* theology. The latter does not entail understanding revelation as an added, authoritative or decisive theological argument against an otherwise nihilist modernism. Here, Milbank's criticism of theology as a type of representational knowledge could equally be applied to a certain brand of authoritative traditionalism or positivism of revelation. Instead, philosophy adds to the (re)discovery and understanding of revelation as the actual, here and now dynamics of the divine Word in the world, also, and perhaps even especially there and then, where it is not or not fully confirmed as such, if only for acknowledging the experience that when it is confirmed or represented, it points at the particular contingency of its representation, rather than at the universality of its infinite source.[8] What we need to explore therefore, is implicit faith, at least in order to understand why more or less explicit forms of faith are inadequate or valuable. But also, from a Christian perspective, to understand why the contingency of life and the real is not an absolute limit, but ever anew susceptible to the revelatory event of the incarnation in Christ.[9]

---

[7] David Tracy, *The Analogical Imagination: Christian Theology and the Culture of Pluralism* (Ann Arbor, MI: Crossroad, 1981).

[8] Cf. Edward Schillebeeckx, *Church: The Human Story of God* (trans. John Bowden; New York, NY: Crossroad, 1990) pp. 72–77.

[9] Cf. Schillebeeckx, *Church*, pp. 27–28.

2. *Understanding Being: De Petter's Theory of the Implicit Intuition*

Which phenomenology and which metaphysics could provide the material for the exploration of an 'implicit faith'?[10] According to Schillebeeckx himself, in twentieth-century Catholic theology, the choice was between the metaphysics of either Joseph Maréchal or Dominique De Petter, who was Schillebeeckx's philosophy teacher.[11] Both developed post-neothomist ontologies closely connected with modern epistemology. Maréchal argued that the validity of abstract concepts is founded on a non-intellectual dynamic of the mind. Knowledge then, is considered a projective act in which the concept transcends itself towards the infinite.[12] Maréchal's metaphysics is based on Kantian epistemology, which denies the possibility of knowing the *Ding an sich*. The *Ding an sich* functions merely as the transcendental limit of knowledge. De Petter criticized Maréchal for finding a solution for the antinomy of concept and reality outside the intellectual act itself, and ultimately denying true knowledge of reality itself. Although Maréchal tries to bridge the gap between reason and reality through a transcendental dynamic of the mind, he needs a non-intellectual patch to do so. De Petter, in turn, proposed to found his realist metaphysics on an intellectual act: 'implicit

---

[10] See also: Jeffrey D. Bloechl, *Religious Experience and the End of Metaphysics* (The Indiana Series in the Philosophy of Religion; Bloomington IN: Indiana University Press, 2003); Hermann Deuser (ed.), *Metaphysik und Religion: Die Wiederentdeckung eines Zusammenhanges* (Veröffentlichungen der Wissenschaftlichen Gesellschaft für Theologie; Gütersloh: Gütersloher Verlagshaus, 2007).

[11] The Swiss theologian Hans Urs von Balthasar presented the choice for a theological metaphysics as one between Kant or Goethe. According to him, Rahner, following Maréchal, chose Kant and Balthasar himself chose Goethe. Cf. Michael Albus, 'Geist und Feuer: Ein Gespräch mit Hans Urs Von Balthasar', *Herder Korrespondenz* 30 (1976), pp. 72–82 (76).

[12] Cf. Karl Rahner, *Hearers of the Word* (rev. Johann Baptist Metz; trans. Ronald Walls; London/Sydney: Sheed and Ward, 1969) p. 59:

Consciousness grasps its particular object in a pre-concept of being (as we wish to designate this process of reaching out to grasp the 'more') and hence of the absolute breadth of its possible objects. In each particular cognition it always reaches out beyond the particular object, and thus grasps it, not just as its unrelated, dead 'thisness,' but in its limitation and reference to the totality of all possible objects. This is because consciousness, by being close to the particular in order to know it, also always reached out beyond the particular as such. The pre-concept is the condition for the possibility of the universal concept, of the abstraction which in turn is what makes possible the objectification of the datum of sense perception and so of conscious subsisting-in-oneself.

intuition'.[13] My proposal for the exploration of implicit faith resonates with the title of De Petter's article, 'Implicit Intuition'.[14] In it, De Petter tries to conquer the critical problem, that is, the antinomy of concept and reality. In this section I will offer a reconstruction of De Petter's metaphysics and clarify the philosophical background of Schillebeeckx's theology and my own thoughts towards a theology of implicit faith.[15]

a. *Being Constitutes the Intellect, but the Intuition of Being is Intellectual*

'Implicit intuition', as De Petter defines it, is the direct intellectual grasping of the concrete. 'Intuition', therefore, should not be understood as a sudden, accidental insight, which at best can be trained as if it is a certain type of sensibility or something to which one can 'open one's mind'. Nor should it be understood as a preparatory phase, from which all knowledge develops. Implicit intuition is not a pre-reflexive given either, which precedes active and conscious knowledge. It is however performed by the intellect, De Petter claims, while, on the other hand, implicit intuition enables the intellectual act to be a true grasping of reality. Therefore, implicit intuition is not an epistemic characteristic that is present in the intellect. It is a condition for knowledge that needs to be realized by the act of knowledge itself. This is why implicit intuition is not a warranty, serving thus as a coping-stone for a naive realist philosophy. The intellect and the abstract concepts it forms, play an essential part in the act called implicit intuition. Implicit intuition is 'a moment of intuition which is essentially included in the intellectual act, from which it has received its most essential meaning and in which it could be discovered through reflective effort'.[16]

De Petter's set-up for a Kantian influenced, but nevertheless realist metaphysics is an attempt to conquer every dualism between the knowing subject and the known object, despite the difference between reality's concrete particularities and the intellect's abstract and necessarily unifying constructions. According to him, both concrete particularity and abstract

---

[13] Cf. Edward Schillebeeckx, *The Concept of Truth and Theological Renewal* (trans. N.D. Smith; Theological Soundings, 1/2; London/Sydney: Sheed and Ward, 1968) pp. 18–22.

[14] Dominicus Maria De Petter, 'Impliciete intuïtie', *Tijdschrift voor Philosophie 1* (1939), pp. 84–105.

[15] For an English interpretation of De Petter's metaphysics, see Philip Kennedy, *Deus Humanissimus: The Knowability of God in the Theology of Edward Schillebeeckx* (Ökumenische Beihefte zur Freiburger Zeitschrift für Philosophie und Theologie, 22; Fribourg: Universitäts-Verlag, 1993); cf. also: Robert J. Schreiter, 'Edward Schillebeeckx', *The Modern Theologians: An Introduction to Christian Theology in the Twentieth Century* (ed. David F. Ford; Oxford/Cambridge: Blackwell, 2nd edn, 1997), pp. 152–61.

[16] De Petter, 'Impliciete intuïtie', pp. 101–02.

construction are an expression of the unity of being, which in turn is also the most fundamental and constitutive unity of the intellect, albeit implicitly and inadequately expressed in abstract concepts. This inadequacy however, he argues, is a characteristic of the concept and the intellect, not of the unity of being itself.

In short, De Petter argues that implicit intuition is an indispensable aspect of the intellectual act. This aspect only becomes explicit in the formation of knowledge through abstract concepts, which are expressions of truth, a truth that always presupposes the unity of being. Being is implied in the abstract expression, whereas the abstraction in itself cannot express this being. A concept is called abstract, because it does not encompass concreteness. In relation to the concrete, abstraction is forever imperfect. It is imperfect compared to complete unity, that is, the unity through which the abstract and the concrete can be understood together in their singularity of being. De Petter claims that this singularity of being or unity of being is the constitutive foundation of the unity of knowledge (truth), which is forever implicitly and non-conceptually implied in the intellect which makes itself explicit. This can only become clear through the activity of the intellect itself, when it expresses itself through the act of judgement and the formation of abstract concepts.

The being that is expressed with the abstract concept, guarantees the objectivity of the concept, De Petter stipulates. The abstraction has to be integrated into an ontological consciousness, because the unity of concept and reality is performed by the intellect, not by the abstract concept itself. The human mind can only form these concepts because of this ontological consciousness that is implied in the intellect. The realization of the inadequacy of the abstract concept diffusely explains how the abstract concept is the expression of an intellectual identity. Through this realization of the difference between the ontological consciousness and the abstracting intellect, the intellect finds the explanation for this difference in itself. This is the full meaning of the term 'implicitness'.[17]

b. *The Judgement is Real, Intuitive and Intellectual*

Abstract expression is part of an explicit judgement which lays claim to the epistemic truth because of its movement from the abstract to the concrete. Yet De Petter questions how this movement is possible. The abstraction itself cannot complete the movement into the concrete. This, he claims, is only possible because of an implicit moment in the expression. In principle, this implicitness is identical in the judgement and the concept, but in the judgement (e.g. A is B), only that which is implied by the abstraction is to some extent made explicit by means of the copula 'is'. However, the copula

---

[17] De Petter, 'Impliciete intuïtie', pp. 86–87.

'is' can only function as the bridge between the abstract and the concrete if, apart from the standard copulative value, it is also given a judicative value. After all, if the term 'being' denotes the implicit consciousness of being, this term has a judicative value, because, according to De Petter, only the consciousness of being has the objective value of judgement.

A judgement therefore is not merely conceptual, but it also consists of a retracing of the abstract content to a concrete reality. The act of abstraction does not include the concreteness of the actual being, however. Therefore, to be meaningful, a judgement consists of a supplementary act by which the abstract content of a judgement is traced back to concrete reality. The structure of a judgement corresponds to that particular function: It consists of a predicate, as that which has to be traced back to the concrete; and a copula, as that which brings about the tracing. Now that the meaning and the function of a judgement have been defined as a supplement to the abstraction, it needs to be explained how a judgement connects the abstract content with the concrete. This is the question regarding the foundation of a judgement, to which the answer can be found in the moment of intuition of a judgement.

The solution of traditional Thomist philosophy for the problem of reaching the concrete from the abstract by means of a judgement is untenable, according to De Petter. This solution is the *conversio ad phantasmata*, i.e. reaching the concrete through a judgement by means of a reflection on the contents of sensory perception on which the abstractions are dependent. De Petter questions whether it can be taken for granted that, because of the dependence of the abstractions upon sensory contents, a judgement could retrace those sensory contents in the abstract concept, and in doing so, reach the concrete again. For De Petter's rigid realism, the act of the imagination is no option for connecting a judgement with the particular. The intellect cannot grasp concreteness in any other quality than that which is characteristic to it, that is, its intelligibility. The antinomy of the peculiar function of a judgement, of connecting the abstract and the concrete, is replaced by an antinomy of the sensory and the intellectual. Sensory perception does not grasp the concrete as concreteness. Although it experiences it as concreteness, the objectivity of an object can only be grasped by the intellect. Sensory perception however has to be regarded as a link between the concrete and the intellect, for how else would the intellect be able to define the function of sensory perception as a full experience of concreteness if it was not able to fully grasp concreteness itself, through the sensory perception?

216

c. *The Intuition is not Transcendental but Manifests Being as the Act of God*

Because of the conceptual unity, which the transcendental contents (being, one, thingness, etc.) of a judgement maintain in relation to the concrete, it has become clear that these transcendental contents are not interchangeable with implicit intuition itself. After all, implicit intuition itself has no conceptual unity and is therefore never expressed in the abstract concept. Intuition is the implicit expression of transcendental concepts in judgements and abstract concepts. With regard to the transcendental content, implicit intuition is the possibility of its functioning. This is how De Petter distinguishes intuition in the abstraction from the intuition in the transcendental contents of judgement. With regard to the abstraction, it functions as a way of reaching the concrete, whereas with regard to the transcendental contents it functions as the way in which the abstraction is able to reach the concrete.

According to De Petter, being is a pure act. By 'being', he means the fundamental constitutive act of the consciousness of being by which the intellect intrinsically and totally performs itself and forms the basic principle of its activity and self-realization. Being is not a static condition, but an ever-changing current of events and relations. Yet, metaphysical unity expressed by the term 'being' is a unity that is present in the fluid reality of the multiple, individual beings; even if it is a unity which can only be established in metaphysical reflection, as a principle for structuring, used by the human intellect in reality. Although the unity present in multiplicity can only be found by means of philosophical reflection and is not part of a spontaneous and explicit knowledge, this does not mean that it is only a metaphysical concept – that is, only used logically and formally – and not something which is present in reality. According to De Petter, metaphysical unity is being as act. The act of knowledge implicitly confirms its own foundation, as being itself. Being as such is not the *quod* of the act of knowledge, but the *quo*, the internal principle from which every conceptual expression derives its intellectual meaning and value.

In the last section of his article, De Petter identifies the unity of being with God, and the implicit intuition with the divine act that is pure intellect in itself. Without any sufficient explanation, De Petter concludes his article by saying that his theory of the implicit intuition shows the necessary complementary value of the Augustinian doctrine of illumination to the Aristotelian-Thomist doctrine of knowledge.[18] What else, he wonders, could manifest itself so completely in inadequate beings that create equally inadequate abstract concepts? And it is this supplementary statement that is unaccounted for, which would probably raise Milbank's attention, since

[18] De Petter, 'Impliciete intuïtie', pp. 103–04.

it comes so close to his own correction of Thomist metaphysics with an Augustinian Neo-Platonism.

3. Understanding Faith: Schillebeeckx's Speculative Theology

a. Anticipation against Participation

In the first volume of the trilogy on Christology, Schillebeeckx explicitly dissociated himself from De Petter's theory of implicit intuition. According to him, this type of metaphysics leaves no space for history and time, and for that matter, no space for context. The answer, he writes, to the Christological question of whether God's salvific acts are present in Jesus of Nazareth, should be demonstrable in historical experiences. He himself regards this as a clear break with De Petter and even with Thomas Aquinas. He argues that Aquinas was able to confirm the implicit participation of the totality of being in each and every particular experience and each and every separate abstract expression as self-evident, because it was also a socio-cultural reality, and therefore part of people's experiences there and then. Schillebeeckx believes however that in a secularized society that offers different religious options, the idea of *participation* that lies behind the metaphysics of the implicit intuition needs to be replaced by the idea of *anticipation*, so as to recognize that being is becoming in history. Consequently, Schillebeeckx adds, every universal truth claim will have to justify itself to critical reason, to which it can only present itself as a hypothesis: 'Being able to demonstrate the personal, socio-political, secular, historical relevance of the Christian faith (within a critical stance towards society and culture) thus becomes an indirect test of religious, faith-motivated utterances.'[19]

Schillebeeckx's Christology would therefore involve a clear break with the metaphysics of unity of his fellow Dominican and philosophical teacher De Petter, but also with that of Thomas Aquinas, and this for philosophical and social-cultural reasons. At this point, one could wonder whether Schillebeeckx has allowed contextuality and culture to fully determine and change the metaphysical foundations of (his) theology, or at least, the way in which he justifies the relation between the context and the content of faith. In the first part of his last monograph *Church: The Human Story of God*, where he meditates on the word 'God' and the experiences it expresses and produces, Schillebeeckx describes philosophical reflection on God as a 'distant context' in which people use the word 'God'. According

---

[19] Edward Schillebeeckx, *Jesus: An Experiment in Christology* (trans. Hubert Hoskins; New York, NY: Seabury, 1979) p. 619.

to him, philosophical traditions used to be rational and theoretical explorations of a presupposed belief in God. In this sense, he argues, it must be acknowledged that religions are the primary contexts of the use of the word 'God'. So, Schillebeeckx's pluralist concerns in his last book not only apply to religious traditions' internal differences or differences between religious traditions, but also to the difference of contexts in which philosophy and theology emerge.[20]

Should it be acknowledged, after De Petter's attack on a Thomist epistemology, and after Schillebeeckx's criticism of unifying metaphysical systems of participation and his recognition of philosophy emerging from a context different from theology, that we are far removed from Thomist philosophy as a foundation or natural conversation partner for theology?[21] Is this the consequence of Schillebeeckx's anticipation for the challenges for contemporary theology: religious pluralism, nonfoundationalism and postmodern thought, and the attention given to otherness, difference, absence, and historicity?[22] Like nonfoundationalists and postmodern thinkers, Schillebeeckx seems to reject metaphysics or first philosophies in favour of historical experience. Is therefore Milbank's criticism valid here, that these challenges have led to the confirmation of the world as a series of givens to be known, rather than gifts to be received and returned? Is there no independent phenomenology or type of metaphysics that could incorporate history and particular experiences into a theology that reflectively returns these gifts?

I would like to propose that for answering these questions, both the philosophy of De Petter and the theology of Schillebeeckx will prove to be most helpful, and indeed, in doing so, I am implying that I disagree with Schillebeeckx on his radical break with his philosophy teacher, although I do acknowledge their differences in language and focus as significant. But more importantly, rereading De Petter and Schillebeeckx from the perspective of contemporary theology could offer some tools for my explorations into implicit faith.

First, let us return to De Petter's metaphysics. His stress on the performance of the intellect as a necessity for being to appear as the implication of every judgement, is thoroughly historical. He does not claim that the intellect constructs being as such, nor does he support the type of phenomenology which claims that without the performing transcendental

---

[20] Cf. Schillebeeckx, *Church*, Chapter 1.

[21] Despite the strong analytical Thomist tradition in contemporary theology, see, for instance, John Haldane, *Faithful Reason: Essays Catholic and Philosophical* (London/New York, NY: Routledge, 2004) pp. 3-15; and Fergus Kerr, *After Aquinas: Versions of Thomism* (Malden, MA/Oxford: Blackwell, 2002) pp. 74–76.

[22] Cf. Thomas G. Guarino, *Foundations of Systematic Theology* (Theology for the Twenty-First Century; New York: T&T Clark, 2005) pp. 1–39.

subject, there is no being, because being by definition would be being-for-me. On the contrary, De Petter advocates a strong realism, without claiming that being *as* being is fully available in concepts or judgements, although it needs the intellect's performance to understand that the totality of being lies at the origin of every intellectual act. Intellectual judgement reveals its origin by being inadequate and diffuse, in other words, by implying that which it cannot reveal through its performance of grasping the real.[23] In De Petter's later works, he expresses a strong aversion to the concept of the *esse commune*, precisely because it ignores the historicity of the performing intellect. The contingency of beings, he claims, defies a confirmation of their unity, and the experience of their contingency can only negatively point at a unity that is absolute and fully transcendent.

It is this last statement that led to Schillebeeckx's conclusion that De Petter's metaphysics is a metaphysics of participation, which offers a worldview founded on a concept of absolute Being, and is undesirable for a contemporary culture in which the pluralism and historicity of events and ideas should be confirmed rather than transcendentally grounded. But Schillebeeckx himself, in contrast with his own criticism of De Petter's metaphysics, has been perfectly capable of combining a metaphysics of participation and a theology of historical experience.

b. *Speculative Theology*

To demonstrate this, I would like to point toward two moments in Schillebeeckx's historical development, one in his early years and one in his later years. Both moments signify his own struggle with a metaphysical ambivalence that is integral to every experience of practiced faith, and which has led to reflexive forms of both positive and speculative theology. In the collection of articles in *Revelation and Theology*, Schillebeeckx defines positive theology as seeking insight into the development of revelation in the scriptures and the mystery of Christ into dogmatic theology.[24] According to him, a necessary condition for understanding this development is the reconstruction of historical experiences of salvation and the communal, ecclesial life that it shaped. This reconstruction however makes use of a reason that is illuminated by faith and allied with the history of faith. Neither the illumination of reason nor the historical continuity can be part of magisterial teaching alone, he argues, but should be performed

---

[23] Cf. David Tracy, 'On Longing: The Void, the Open, God', *Longing in a Culture of Cynicism* (ed. Stephan van Erp and Lea Verstricht; Zürich/Berlin: LIT, 2008), pp. 15–32.

[24] On 'positive theology', see: Edward Schillebeeckx, *Revelation and Theology* (trans. N.D. Smith; Theological Soundings, 1/1; London/Melbourne: Sheed and Ward, 1967) pp. 118–23.

by speculative theology. Speculative thought continues to intellectually regenerate the connection of present day experiences with scripture and tradition. Apart from furthering the knowledge of faith through a reflection on the cohesion of the mysteries of faith and through the reconstruction of historical theological developments, speculative theology could also discursively rethink positive statements. But it should at the same time not overstate its demand of intelligibility. And he concludes:

> Theology is always a 'stammering' in the face of the transcendent mystery of faith ... this humility [ought to be] not merely a question of words, but also something that must be apparent in the manner in which theology is practised. The attention of theology must always be directed to the mystery of salvation that is announced and not to the human means which help us to approach it. ... In the content of faith there is both a tendency towards incarnation in human thought and a funda-mental resistance to rationalisation. On the one hand, theology should not sink into so-called 'evangelism', which is only aware of the mystery and the 'folly of faith', nor should it tend towards an uncontrolled incarnation, which is only conscious of the meaningful intelligibility of faith. ... Sound theology can only develop if it progresses diffidently between this Scylla and that Charybdis. It must actively maintain a constant tension between incarnation and disincarnation, between transcendence and humanising. ... the harmonious relationship between the impulse towards incarnation and disincarnation, at the level of theological thought, only come[s] about dramatically in conflicts and polemics, between stern excommunications and splendid syntheses. Throughout history, therefore theology is always passing through a crisis or growth, as a result of which its true face is always appearing in a purer form 'until we all attain to the unity of the faith' (Eph 4:13).[25]

c. Mystical Theology

In *Church*, Schillebeeckx develops a mystical theology based on the notion of an 'absolute limit', of a radical finitude and contingency, which resonates with his balancing of speculative and positive theology, but also with his theory of the anthropological constants as theological foundations.[26] Both believers and non-believers, he acknowledges, share the experience of a radical finitude and contingency. By this, he hastens to add, he is not referring to situations in which people find themselves when they are most vulnerable, for example, when they are seriously ill or dying. (Schillebeeckx's concept of the 'contrast experience' is sometimes wrongly interpreted as

---

[25] Schillebeeckx, *Revelation and Theology*, pp. 176–77.
[26] Schillebeeckx, *Church*, pp. 77–80.

such, as if it only occurs during or after certain dramatic events.) Neither is the experience of the absolute limit the same as Schleiermacher's *schlechthinniges Abhängigkeitsgefühl*, as it is not an immediate revelatory experience, a deep insight of some sorts. On the contrary, the experience of the absolute limit is given within every human experience as real. As the real in human experience, it refers to something that is not a by-product of experience, but to the implied confirmation of reality in every experience. Here, we find clear traces of De Petter's implicit intuition in the work of the later Schillebeeckx. The latter however moves from the epistemological to the theological. It is at the absolute limit that all religious and secular world-views emerge, he continues. The modern view of religion as the choice to create another world, a supernature beyond limits of the secular, is misrepresenting religious interpretations of this experience, as if religion, contrary to secular worldviews, does not do justice to contingency, but instead contradicts it with the escape to a transcendent reality outside the limit of finitude. Yet, there is, according to Schillebeeckx, a difference between religious and secular worldviews, in as far as the believer interprets the limit as a salvific divine presence in history, while the non-believer is 'locked up within the absolute limit, lonely with fellow human beings'.

Twenty years after Schillebeeckx wrote this, it may not be that easy to distinguish between believers and non-believers. In Western Europe and America, secularization has been followed by a cultural trend that some describe as the resurgence of religion. This does not mean that secular worldviews are diminishing. Instead, secular views mediate religious views, and not seldom implicitly or in language and forms that are yet to be recognized as religious. I am not just referring to the grey area of those ideas and rituals of people who are exploring forms of spirituality both old and new. Nor am I pointing at the so-called religious market in pluralist or multicultural societies. Instead, I think this is a time and an age to acknowledge new ways in which people with secular worldviews are associated with the history of an incarnate God, and are therefore connected with the people in the church. Theologians should explore the implicit associations and connections of contemporary secular culture with its religious past and present. This would not only serve the purpose of understanding the ongoing reform of churches and theologies or the appeal of conversions to Christianity, as Charles Taylor has done in his *A Secular Age*.[27] It would also make explicit what otherwise could be easily overlooked: the implicit faith in a divine and salvific presence in history.

With the support of philosophy, theology should be the study of the experiences at the absolute limit, asking why some believe or decide that the limit confronts them with a divine presence in the world and why some

---

[27] Charles Taylor, *A Secular Age* (Cambridge, MA: Belknap Press/Harvard University Press, 2007) pp. 728–72.

do not. Moreover, theology's new task is one of description and under-standing at the limits of contingency, seeking to comprehend both where and how the hopes and fears that people share assist in constructing their worldviews. At first sight, these constructions appear as the reassembly of the remnants of communities in history of which future generations may or may not be part. To be able to discover newness in that reassembly, however, it might prove necessary to disconnect positive from speculative theology, temporarily, for the sake of a specific type of descriptive explo-ration, a phenomenology of practiced faith in places where it is as yet not expected to appear. Schillebeeckx's mystical theology of the absolute limit thus points toward new tasks for contemporary theology: understanding the beliefs of non-believers as a different outcome of shared experiences at the absolute limit of contingency and exploring implicit faith in a world full of meaning, shared by believers and non-believers alike.

Conclusion

One of theology's philosophical tasks – and philosophy's tasks for theology – is to speculatively search for and articulate an actual and ongoing incar-nation of the divine in the world, in order to retrace and confirm *theologia* before it has become theology, which in its turn can only reflectively confess it, but certainly not speak it. Thus, it opens the possibility of an unexpected *locus theologicus*: implicit faith moves between the Scylla of revelation and tradition as imposed or exclusive theological foundations, and the Charybdis of culture and context as providers of ever-new theological embodiments. Modern philosophy, as the expression of, and reflection on worldviews, could well prove to be a carrier of implicit faith and one of the mediators of the *passivum theologicum*, as Schillebeeckx has discussed it.[28] Although the *passivum theologicum* signifies expressions of the remnants of a religious past, it may also provide the material for composing a future of hope. I have argued that phenomenology, metaphysics, or any form of speculative philosophy should not be ignored or excluded from constructive theology. Against Milbank, who has suggested that the present needs a theology proper, a positivist theological metaphysics of the gift, I have argued that the speculative and the mystical are needed to explore implicit faith, in order to be receptive to what is given in that, which manifests itself as fully secular. Therefore, modern philosophy should turn out to be the indispensable conversation partner for theology, because it perceptively and descriptively gathers experiences and expressions that might not immediately manifest themselves as responses or confessions of a giving and self-revealing God, but will in the end.

[28] Schillebeeckx, *Church*, pp. 65–66.

CONVERSATION, IDENTITY AND TRUTH

Benoît Bourgine

For theology, the relationship with philosophy remains fundamental. Of course, social and human sciences are also crucial, but theology *vis-à-vis* philosophy is a far more essential condition of validity and relevance. Edward Schillebeeckx's theological achievements illustrate this point. In his works, the application of historical and (literary) critical studies on biblical texts is significant. Nevertheless, they could not by themselves prevent his theology to fall into the narrowness of the *Leben-Jesu-Forschung* approach. On the contrary, philosophical hermeneutics and phenomenology inspired Schillebeeckx's works in their relation to the biblical narratives in a valid way such that the gap between exegesis and dogmatics could be filled, while recovering the unity of the theological interpretation. Similarly, Edward Schillebeeckx has been able to argue for the historicity and rationality of theology against Neo-Scholastic positivism or biblical fundamentalism on the ground of philosophical reflections.

In following Schillebeeckx's lead, we argue that contemporary challenges lead theology in two directions: the dialogical imperative with modernity and the challenge of identity in a postmodern context. In both of these directions, the crucial question relates to the concept of *truth* and appropriate relationship to it – this is the reason why philosophy takes such a decisive part in the job.

Modernity has determined different levels of truth in such a way that scientific knowledge, ethical or political legitimacy and ultimate beliefs belong to distinctive orders, even if they can't be adequately separated. On each of these levels, theology has to engage in a critical dialogue in order to maintain contact with the activities of these other human spheres, as well as with the changing way of being human in such complex societies. Theology has to recover an assumption of the unity of truth as eschatological in order to avoid fundamentalism as well as relativism (part 1).

Postmodernity has placed on the agenda the question of identity. The incredulity towards meta-narratives has left people without marks, second or third generations of immigrants are looking for their identity, and globalization has situated various religions and cultures into close contacts. In the end, a cultural and religious radicalization is visible, as multicultural and multireligious societies are still having to find a *modus vivendi*. How can theology help Christians and Church in that context? What resources can theology offer to communities and to societies so that they'll be able to relate to themselves and to others, while avoiding radicalization and violence? (part 2)

1. *Theology in Conversation with Modern Rationality*

The first vital challenge pertains to the question of *dialogue*. The apologetical question, understood as the dialogue between theology and other rationalities, can't be solved unless the contemporary crisis of truth is faced on three levels: truth that is worthy of our *knowledge;* truth that we can propose to our individual and collective *action*; and truth in which we may rightfully *believe*. No author has described this better than Jean Ladrière, who has given in his works a useful analysis of the project of modern rationality.[1] How can philosophy help to relate theological truth with the truth of the objective world, the truth of the social world, the truth pertaining to the ultimate concern? Let us analyse this three-level challenge in a more detailed way.

a. *Kantian issues and Jefferson's pride*

'What can I know? What ought I to do? What may I hope?'. In accordance with these issues that summarize Kant's philosophical agenda, modern rationality has distinguished between these three primary ways as capable of meeting truth and thus, has pursued three main projects: the project of science, the project of democracy and the project of individual autonomy in choosing the meaning, value and norm of existence. Thomas Jefferson, an important actor within this revolution, epitomizes these distinctive traits in a remarkable way. Despite serving eight years as President of the United States and his many other glorious accomplishments, Jefferson, who is buried at his home in Monticello, Virginia wrote a very precise epitaph for his tombstone: 'Author of the Declaration of American Independence, of the Statute of Virginia for Religious Freedom and Father of the University of Virginia.' A three dimensional achievement is emphasized: his contribution to science, to democracy and to religious pluralism.

On the level of knowledge, theology of the 21st century must continue

---

[1] Jean Ladrière, *Bibliographie de Jean Ladrière* (Bibliothèque philosophique de Louvain, 66; Leuven: Peeters, 2005).

to face the ever evolving vision of man and cosmos coming from scientific rationality. Ecology, astrophysics and Darwinian theory of evolution (applied to biology, genetics and neurosciences) are continuously determining anew the scales of time and space in which the human person is situated and must understand himself accordingly. In this respect, the cosmos and the human life in the history of nature have to be inserted within a meaningful narrative. Otherwise how could the biblical story still be proclaimed? And furthermore, how should the biblical story be told in a critical manner, in line with the scientific *status quaestionis*? Theology has to object to creationism and Intelligent Design Theory, as well as to concordism and scientific materialisms with a serious *epistemology*. The current Roman Catholic responses to these challenges are not appropriate. Recently, Cardinal Schönborn has expressed his affinity with Intelligent Design Theory, which led Benedict XVI to pronounce ambiguous declarations on the issue.[2] If we speak about Darwinian evolutionary theory, the issue is very serious since 'nothing in biology makes sense except in the light of evolution', as Theodosius Dobzhansky puts it.[3] The problem here is in developing an up-to-date philosophy of science which is able to receive the new state of knowledge. And in turn, philosophical categories have to be renewed. On this issue the philosophical background is undoubtedly decisive.[4] For a critical conversation with science, theology needs the help of a philosophy of science in line with the new scientific paradigms. Theology has to learn the logic of science as if this logic was a new language. Otherwise theology will become a stranger to the common language of this world.

On the ethical and political level, theology of the 21st century must face new challenges arising from the complexity of multiethnic and multireligious western societies. Politics is in a profound crisis. Is the hypothesis of intercultural societies valid? Must the values of modern European humanism arising from a Jewish-Christian background be imposed upon migrant Islamic populations? Is a negotiation on values such as civil equality between men and women possible or desirable? Can the 'human rights', as understood in the West, become a political programme for the

---

[2] Christoph Schönborn, *Hasard ou plan de Dieu? La création et l'évolution vues à la lumière de la foi et de la raison* (trad. Monique Guisse; Paris: Cerf, 2007); Stephan Otto Horn and Siegried Widenhofer (eds), *Creazione ed evoluzione: Un convegno con Papa Benedetto XVI a castel Gandolfo* (intr. Card. Christoph Schönborn; Bologna: Edizioni dehoniane, 2007). See my review in *Revue théologique de Louvain* 39 (2008), pp. 549–51.

[3] Title of a famous article he wrote in *The American Biology Teacher* 35 (1973), pp. 125–29.

[4] The works of John Haught offer a good example of a valid response to this challenge, especially for his accurate philosophical conversation with Whitehead, Teilhard, Polanyi and Jonas.

whole world? What is the proper place of the Christian believer and of the Christian Church in Western society? And what response will emerge from increasing Islamic demands for greater social visibility? Here too, theological reason has to learn the language of current political reason in order to enter in critical dialogue with its logic. The French model of separation between State and Church excludes religious arguments in political deliberation and ignores communities' membership in shaping social life. But are secular reasons really all that neutral, especially when secular reason is performed as a 'reasoning in terms of comprehensive nonreligious doctrines'?[5] But can such ideas of autonomy avoid individualism on a large scale? The conversation with political philosophers[6] or classical authors such as Tocqueville are crucial to inspiring a balanced theological position in these issues. But this can't be a one-way conversation. Theology has to receive the creative input of political and social ideas for its own area. The public relevance of Church and theology depends on the fact that their practices are in accordance with their discourse. The Church can't proclaim the equality of men and women in societies in which inequalities tend to be reduced, while at the same time allow for the gap between men and women to persist in ecclesial decision making. The Church can not both praise democratic political systems and keep them out of its proper walls. How could responsible citizens of a democratic society take seriously their participation in the Church in which they have nothing to say and nothing to decide? Is responsible citizenship contrary to the law of love, or is it incompatible with order and authority in the Christian community as Schillebeeckx rightly puts it?[7]

On the level of ultimate concern, theology of the 21st century must face the encounter with pluralism. Theology has to reflect on the various tendencies and pathologies of the contemporary act of believing; on moral autonomy; on the ethics of dialogue between religions; and above all, on the tension between particularity and universality of Christianity. Does pluralism necessarily lead to relativism? Is the pretention of universality out of time in the radical plurality of postmodern context? The relationship with other cultures and religions is here on the agenda.

We argue that from a philosophical and theological perspective, the most consistent attitude in the dialogue with other religions is by maintaining the uniqueness and universality of the salvation in Jesus Christ.[8] This dialogue remains fruitful, but under no circumstances can it lead to the idea that

---

[5] John Rawls, 'The Idea of Public Reason Revisited', *The Laws of Peoples* (Cambridge, MA: Harvard University Press, 1999), pp. 129–81 (152).
[6] Let's nominate in the French area Pierre Manent, Paul Valadier, Marcel Gauchet, Agnès Antoine or Jean-Marc Ferry.
[7] See Chapter 4 of Edward Schillebeeckx, *Church: The Human Story of God* (trans. John Bowden; New York, NY: Crossroad, 1990).
[8] See Joseph Moingt as an inspiring reference, *Dieu qui vient à l'homme* (3 vols; Paris: Cerf, 2002/2005/2007).

the Gospel could be only one way among others. Jesus Christ is a human person, with a temporal and particular story. But in that limited space of time and existence, God the Father has revealed Himself in Jesus in a faithful and complete way. He has spoken *Himself*. This particular story is designed as salvation for all men and women. Can God give a finite as well as a true, faithful and complete communication of Himself? The answer of the Christian theology of revelation is clear: 'Yes, He can.' Reflection over universal salvation must take into account both the uniqueness and the universality of this salvation. And in doing so, metaphysics is here unavoidable: metaphysics is unavoidable in building a model of truth in which transcendence can inhabit immanence. Thus, I disagree with the position adopted by Schillebeeckx on this subject.[9]

We argue that from a philosophical and theological perspective, the most consistent attitude in the conversation between the Gospel and other cultures is that no universal point of view can fully express the understanding of the Gospel. Consistent with the previous thesis, we argue that the Gospel, designed for all men and women, must then be fully received inside each and every culture. Such a process is both long and delicate. And it is a challenge for the unity of faith and of the Church. But we can't be afraid of such a necessary process. The distinction between Gospel and its cultural vehicle has to be made: no culture can pretend to any superiority, not excluding Greek antiquity. I disagree here with Benedict XVI who sees the translation of the Gospel in the cultures as a stage of dehellenization, the impact of which must be limited.[10] Local Churches are to be set free in their attempt to fully receive the Gospel in their language and traditional cultures. The normative character of the Scriptures as well as the patristic moment and the great councils can't be used as an excuse to stand in the way of processes of enculturation. The Gospel has the capability to be received seriously and plainly in all the cultures. That reception is compatible with the communion of faith and is aptly expressed in a truth model whereby transcendence and immanence can inhabit each other. No universal expression can pretend to be the unique way of saying Jesus Christ, but mutual recognition of the faithfulness of the different cultural translations of the Gospel can pave the way to unity between local churches.

---

[9] See chapter 3 of Schillebeeckx, *Church*.

[10] See his 'Faith, Reason and the University: Memories and Reflections', Lecture during a meeting with the representatives of science at the University of Regensburg, 12 September 2006, http://www.vatican.va/holy_father/benedict_xvi/speeches/2006/september/documents/hf_ben-xvi_spe_20060912_university-regensburg_en.html (last checked on 23 January 2010).

b. *Theological Challenges*

Theology must learn these new languages as specific aspects of truth that modernity has definitely distinguished. Theological language has to relate to the language of science in a critical way. In turn, theological language is compelled to relate to the ever changing logic of the political and social order. In this regard, theology has to distinguish between religious content and cultural vehicle and vector. The challenge is to have a dialogue that respects distinction without separation or confusion between these different languages. It is a translation that allows theology to relate to these human spheres of activity and to take responsibility for a critical task and a propositional task in these different areas. While inventing itself anew, theology receives its own identity as a specific rationality in conversation with other logics. It is the only way to inhabit this present century and not a past one.

In this reconfiguration of Christian theology within contemporary modernity, theology's conception of truth is decisive.[11] We should not underestimate the contribution of Christianity's understanding of truth as inevitably eschatological, with regard to the present mode of rationality: in present rationality, the dynamics of democracy supposes the ideal of life according to reason as its horizon, while the dynamics of science supposes an ideal of complete knowledge of the reality as its goal. But these ideals are not only remote targets, they are indeed at work while reason tries hard to reach these goals. These ideals are at work as well in the *eschaton* as a working of Christian life, which we can liken to an attractor. Ladrière has taken the Christian theological concept of *eschaton* to name the ideal of reason and has spoken about the eschatological nature of this rationality. Truth has not yet come but truth is already at work. Fundamentalism takes for granted the given unity of truth – which in reality is a matter of hope. On the contrary, we argue, as an example, that there is always a tension between theological truth and scientific truth. The effort to relate theological truth to scientific truth is to be done anew and again at each period of time. However, no synthesis can ever be a definitive one.

Philosophy appears thus as an essential medium in this task. It is too much for theology, in both its language and means, to succeed in crossing bridges through these different worlds. Philosophy gives theology an external point of view that enables theology to make conversation with other rationalities and logics.

---

[11] Paul Ricœur, 'L'histoire de la philosophie et l'unité du vrai', *Histoire et vérité* (Paris: Seuil, 1967), pp. 51–68 as well as 'Vérité et mensonge' in the same book (pp. 187–218); Jean Ladrière, *Sens et vérité en théologie: L'articulation du sens III* (Cogitatio Fidei, 237; Paris: Cerf, 2004) p. 156; Louis Perron, *L'eschatologie de la raison selon Jean Ladrière pour une interprétation du devenir de la raison* (Sainte-Foy: Les presses de l'Université Laval, 2005).

2. *Theology and the postmodern Quest for Identity*

The second challenge theology faces pertains to the problem of *identity* in the context of globalization. Here, we outline a sketch of the issue. To do so, there are two connected issues. First is the identity of the Christian believer described by Paul the Apostle. The second issue is the identity of the Self in the postmodern context. The answer to the first issue will size up the theological input to the second issue.

In his life and writings, Paul has given us a model of Christian identity that can be described as a transgression of identities. There is Paul, the Jew, both ethnically and religiously. Then there is Paul, the cultural Greek. And finally, there is also Paul, the Roman, on a civic level. All of which, we name 'Paul', the man of several borders. First, we must notice that Paul shows loyalty towards all of these belongings. At the same time, he fights against a model of identity understood in terms of closure or exclusion. For him, identities are not fixed species and so he breaks the traditional borders with freedom. Paul the Pharisee pleads on behalf of the Gentiles to be admitted in the Community without the imposition of the Jewish Law. With Paul, the Christian model of the acceptance of new believers has become ethnically indifferent: the door is as widely open as possible. In the epistle to the Romans (Chapter 8), Paul, the Greek, includes the Cosmos in the dynamic process of the history of Salvation: 'The creation waits with eager longing for the revealing of the children of God' (Rom. 8.19). Paul, the Roman citizen, organizes the Christian communities taking into account the principles of hierarchy, authority and order, however these principles are submitted to the law of love: 'God has so arranged the body, giving the greater honour to the inferior member, that there may be no dissension within the body, but the members may have the same care for one another' (1 Cor. 12.24–25). While Paul, in his ultimate dimension, relates to the life given by Christ, the life Christ is sharing with him, so that his life is Christ and nothing else. This life is widely open to communion without limitation in such a way that Paul breaks the borders of his different identities. 'There is no longer Jew or Greek, there is no longer slave or free, there is no longer male and female; for all of you are one in Christ Jesus' (Gal. 3.28). Being a Christian is not an identity in the same way as that of being Belgian or French, man or woman. Being a Christian doesn't belong to the present form of the world that is passing away (1 Cor. 7.31). Neither does being a Christian take oneself out of the world. For Paul, being a Christian trans-forms all the identities that define himself to submit them to the imperative of love and universal communion. Faith leads one in overstepping the limits of fixed identities. Here then is a model of absolute existential truth that doesn't lead to violence but to freedom towards belongings, a model of absolute existential truth where one may find himself and transform his relationship to the world in the cause of communion.

What can such a model of identity tell to us in a time of emphasis on cultural difference?[12] In short, it can say a lot. I refer to five contemporary philosophical attempts to read Paul in such a perspective.[13] For Badiou, Paul is building a very useful model of universal truth, emerging from an event, the Resurrection, and he builds a theory of the Self without a fixed identity. For Žižek, Paul breaks out of the traditional and cosmic order of the world to open it to universality by means of Agapè. For Agamben, Paul has transformed the conception of time in the Western countries into a messianic one. For Sichère, Paul's model can inspire a revolution against present nihilism. According to Sichère, the human person seen as a separate and an autonomous subjectivity can't take that measure as the universal measure. For the human person, the decision to be himself needs a larger horizon, the horizon of the Being which calls for an ultimate responsibility.

These researches can't be underestimated in a time in which the trends towards ethnic oriented policies and fixed identities place in danger the neutrality of law. Such philosophically creative inputs may help us to argue over the possibility of universal values and the possibility of community belonging which could be open identities and not exclusive ones.[14]

The conversation between philosophy and theology is indeed finding new ways. To conclude, mention must be made of the promising attempts within French phenomenology to think anew theological concepts in its own philosophical perspective.[15] Theology could receive from these essays a fresh look at its concepts and language and can learn how to bring out new treasures from old ones.

---

[12] Jean-Claude Guillebaud, *Le commencement d'un monde* (Paris: Seuil, 2008).

[13] Giorgio Agamben, *The Time That Remains: A Commentary on the Letter to the Romans* (trans. Patricia Dailey; Meridian: Crossing Aesthetics; Standford, CA: Stanford University Press, 2005); Alain Badiou, *Saint Paul: The Foundation of Universalism* (trans. Ray Brassier; Cultural Memory in the Present; Standford, CA: Standford University Press, 2003); Stanislas Breton, *Saint Paul* (Coll. Philosophies; Paris: PUF, 1988); Bernard Sichère, *Le jour est proche: La révolution selon Paul* (Paris: Desclée de Brouwer, 2003); Slavoj Žižek, *The Fragile Absolute: Or, Why Is the Christian Legacy Worth Fighting For?* (Wo es war; London/New York, NY: Verso, 2000). See Benoît Bourgine, 'Saint Paul et la philosophie: Crise du multiculturalisme et universel chrétien', *Revue théologique de Louvain* 40 (2009), pp. 78–94.

[14] François Jullien, *De l'universel, de l'uniforme, du commun et du dialogue entre les cultures* (Paris: Fayard, 2008).

[15] Emmanuel Housset, *L'intériorité d'exil: Le soi au risque de l'altérité* (Paris: Cerf, 2008); Jean-Luc Marion, *Au lieu de soi: L'approche de Saint Augustin* (Épiméthée: Essais philosophiques; Paris: PUF, 2008); Emmanuel Falque, *Dieu, la chair et l'autre: D'Irénée à Duns Scot* (Paris: PUF, 2008).

PART VII
LOOKING BACKWARD, LOOKING FORWARD: THE PAST AND FUTURE OF SCHILLEBEECKX'S THEOLOGICAL PROJECT

RETRIEVING GOD'S CONTEMPORARY PRESENCE: THE FUTURE OF EDWARD SCHILLEBEECKX'S THEOLOGY OF CULTURE

Erik Borgman

1. *Theology of Retrieval*

Maybe the most innovative contribution of John Webster's to *The Oxford Handbook of Systematic Theology* is the introduction to the category of 'theologies of retrieval'.[1] Theologies of retrieval are theologies that consider modernity to be an ambivalent episode of human history to which theologians cannot simply submit themselves. Modernity as we know it, and as it understands itself, cannot be the hidden *norma normans non normata* that decides what can and cannot be said and done in contemporary theology. On the contrary, it is the task of theologians to critique modernity by retrieving aspects of the Christian tradition that tend to be forgotten and ignored as theology becomes 'modern'. Strangely enough the most obvious candidate for the title 'theologian of retrieval' (and the theologian John Webster probably knows best), Karl Barth, is not presented as such by Webster. Though his disciple Eberhard Jüngel is, as are the proponents of the Radical Orthodoxy movement.[2] Joseph Ratzinger would also have been

---

[1] John Webster, 'Theologies of Retrieval', *The Oxford Handbook of Systematic Theology* (ed. John B. Webster, Kathryn E. Tanner and Iain R. Torrance; Oxford: Oxford University Press, 2007), pp. 583–99.

[2] One may suspect that the whole idea of 'theologies of retrieval' would not have been thought up had John Milbank not published his *Theology and Social Theory: Beyond Secular Reason* (Oxford: Blackwell, 1990).

an obvious candidate, but he is mentioned only once and very casually in *The Oxford Handbook*.

Speaking of 'theologies of retrieval' makes clear that what they are up to is not some direct form of theological conservatism or 'neo-orthodoxy'. The retrieval of what is forgotten is considered as a precondition to a fuller – that is: a more fully *theological* – understanding of modernity, one which is supposed to contribute to a better life in the given context of modernity. Theologians of retrieval do not advocate a simple return from modern theology to what they consider to be a more authentic Christian teaching from the past. Some of them may rhetorically suggest that, but ultimately their point is that to respond adequately to our situation, we have to search for what would be a true orthodoxy here and now. This implies that orthodoxy, as authentic Christian teaching, cannot be seen as an unchanging substance, but has to be reinvented in relation to contemporary issues. In order to do that, theologians of retrieval bring the almost forgotten themes and focuses or points of view that are marginalized in contemporary thought, back into intellectual circulation. This is indeed not a straightforward traditionalism and the argument given is not simply that because something is part of the tradition, it should now be received as authoritative.

However, there is of course a claim for authority made in any theology of retrieval. Pointing at what is wrong in the contemporary situation, the suggestion put forth is that this might be a consequence of losing something essential from the Christian tradition along our way to late modernity. The task of retrieving these elements is thus presented as necessary in order to rescue our civilization.

a. *Nouvelle théologie*

Along with Jüngel and Milbank, Webster also introduces theologians like Henri De Lubac and Yves Congar, representing the Roman Catholic movement of the so called *nouvelle théologie*, into the ranks of his 'theologians of retrieval'. It is not clear whether Webster understands how daring this gesture is. The fact of the matter is that *nouvelle théologie* has usually been and is still interpreted as a variety of theological modernism. In a centralized Roman Catholic Church that considered anti-modernism to be the core of its identity, *nouvelle théologie* seems first and foremost a cautious and clever attempt to open up to the contemporary world in the only way possible after the so-called Modernist crisis: by radically re-interpreting the texts on which the anti-modernist stance of the Church was said to be based, i.e. the work of Saint Thomas Aquinas.[3] Presenting *nouvelle*

---

[3] For this image of *nouvelle théologie*, see the still very influential book by Ted Mark Schoof, *Breakthrough: Beginnings of the New Catholic Theology* (Logos Books; Dublin: Gill and Macmillan, 1970).

théologie as a 'theology of retrieval', Webster draws attention to the fact that its representatives – and, as we shall see, the documents of Vatican II in line with them – did not want to open up to the contemporary world because they craved for intellectual prestige among their contemporaries. Neither did they think that this was the best strategy for the Church to again become a factor of influence in contemporary society and culture. All talk by theologians after the Second Vatican Council about a correlation between the theological tradition and the contemporary world notwithstanding, *nouvelle théologie* defended its opening up to the contemporary world ultimately by *theological* arguments.

For the proponents of *nouvelle théologie*, the very confession of the incarnation breaks down the typically modern – nominalist – presupposition that the finite and the infinite, the natural and the supernatural are separated by an unbridgeable gap. This means that it can no longer be argued that there is no intrinsic connection between the immanent and the transcendent, between the world and the divine. They read the oeuvre of Thomas Aquinas, which was presented by the hierarchy of their Church as normative in the way it connected philosophy and theology, nature and grace, as contradicting the dominant Catholic approach, although this approach also claimed to be founded on Aquinas' system of thought. In neo-scholasticism, theological doctrines supposedly based on the authority of the Church given to her by Jesus Christ himself, were extrinsically added to an analysis of the phenomena of the world. If left to itself, the world was bound to show its insufficiency and, without supernatural assistance, it could only come to a crisis. This was evident from the catastrophes of poverty and violence so prominently present in Modernity with its wars and its 'social question', as the hierarchy of the Roman Catholic Church had argued since the middle of the nineteenth century. This allegedly demonstrated why the natural world, in order to be saved, needed the revealed truth entrusted to the Catholic Church.[4]

According to *nouvelle théologie*, this was not a genuinely Catholic, but very much a typically modern way of thinking. Based on their reading of Aquinas and what they saw as the consequences of the doctrine of incarnation, the proponents of *nouvelle théologie* felt that theology had to analyse the way in which the natural and the supernatural, nature and grace, and the world and God were connected already, as a consequence of God's gracious initiative. To cultivate a connection with modernity does not imply for them a surrender to what is foreign to the Christian faith. Modernity itself was founded in the tradition of that faith, but had during

---

[4] Cf. Pierre Thibaul, *Savoir et pouvoir: Philosophie thomiste et politique cléricale au XIXe siècle* (intr. Émile Poulat; Histoire et sociologie de la culture, 2; Quebec: Presses de l'Université Laval, 1972); Émile Poulat, *L'église, c'est un monde: L'ecclésiosphère* (Sciences humaines et religions; Paris: Cerf, 1986).

its course lost sight of this fact. The Christian tradition, *nouvelle théologie* claims, has its own view on authority. This view is distinctly different from the early modern view on the hierarchy and delegated sovereignty that the Catholic Church used until the sixties of the last century in order to present its authority. It lives from the idea that grace does not have to be authoritatively added to the world as it is. In their reading of the Christian tradition, to understand the world adequately, one needs to see its connection with God and its dependence on the divine gift of grace.

Thus *nouvelle théologie* brings to light the imperative that to do theology is ultimately not to intervene in the world as it is from the outside, but to think about the situation in which the theologian, in his or her theologizing, participates. There are not a series of first substantial theological views, themes or topics that are then, in a second step, connected to the contemporary context. In particular, Marie-Dominique Chenu has shown how thinking about the incarnation of the Divine in Jesus Christ is itself a manner of thinking about and critiquing the contemporary situation in world and Church. Theological thinking is thinking about the contemporary situation in which it participates. It is not judging the situation from a position supposedly outside that situation, as neo-scholasticism would have it.[5]

This means that the world and the situation it is in, and the debate on what is the case and what is the matter, what our situation is and how we should act in it – is open in principle to contributions from a religious background. The world *is* God's world because it is created, whether people acknowledge it or not. History is God's history because it is redeemed, and this redemption has left its traces in human lives, whether this is confessed to or not. Public opinion or dominant voices in the public domain may not always be hospitable to religious and theological contributions, but the debate on who and where we are, and where we are heading, should seduce theologians to make their contribution anyway. By doing so they not only make their theological views public, but bring to light the truth that what is at stake in the public sphere is ultimately, and profoundly, religious.

b. *Retrieval of the Religious*

This background enables a theological understanding of what is commonly called the 'return' or the 'resurgence' of religion in the contemporary world, and the debates on what this 'return' could mean. Peter Berger's 1999 book on *The Desecularization of the World* notwithstanding, the 'resurgence of

---

[5] Cf. Christophe F. Potworowski, *Contemplation and Incarnation: The Theology of Marie Dominique Chenu* (McGill-Queen's Studies in the History of Ideas, 33; Montreal: McGill-Queen's University Press, 2001).

religion' does not mark the end of secularization.[6] Our habitat does not cease to be, in the words of Charles Taylor, 'a secular age'.[7] At the same time, however, and in the heart of this secular world, religious visions, religious involvement, religious symbols and religious theories re-emerge and are re-invented. The struggle of religious worldviews and philosophies of life, and the contest between secular and religious interpretations of situations and developments, are in fact part and parcel of modern history. In this sense religion *is* an integral part of modernity: as a contested ground, a polemical field, an issue of combat over who and what has authority and why. With the return of religion in our contemporary debates, we have a chance to theologically rediscover and/or redefine the essence of modernity by reconsidering and redefining the place of religion in it.

Taylor's important book *A Secular Age* seems about as ambivalent as the age it describes. Modernity is irreversibly secular, Taylor claims, in that modern people no longer seek to participate in a divine order and do not argue their cases from divine norms that are invested with an unchallengeable authority. In this light, Joseph Ratzinger's argument, that modernity needs to be founded in absolute norms it cannot develop and maintain itself, and that it is the mission of the Catholic Church to provide these norms, seems to be fighting an already lost battle.[8] As an epoch, modernity is in an ongoing process of leaving traditional norms and authorities, and finding and developing new ones within the same process. The true novelty of modernity, only fully uncovered in our late modern era, is that it has no foundation and does not rely on any prior belief people need to hold in regard to certain truths or moral maxims. In late modernity people become modern not by believing in modern values or by considering a modern worldview as the most adequate or as the true one, but by having enough trust – in the sense that modern democracy *does* require faith – to participate in the modern culture of doing things in a certain way, and discussing and solving issues in accordance with certain procedures but with no absolute limits or prior consensus.

In 2005, in a debate with the future pope of the Roman Catholic Church, German philosopher Jürgen Habermas demonstrated precisely this point.[9] According to Habermas religion is relevant in a new and unpredicted way in late modernity. But this relevance is not to be found in its ability

[6] Peter L. Berger (ed.), *The Desecularization of the World: Resurgent Religion and World Politics* (Grand Rapids, MI: Eerdmans, 1999).

[7] See: Charles Taylor, *A Secular Age* (Cambridge, MA: Belknap Press/Harvard University Press, 2007).

[8] Cf. Joseph Ratzinger, *Values in a Time of Upheaval* (San Francisco, CA: Ignatius, 2006), esp. pp. 31–44.

[9] Cf. Jürgen Habermas, 'Pre-political Foundations of the Democratic Constitutional State?', *The Dialectics of Secularization: On Reason and Religion* (ed. Florian Schuller; San Francisco, CA: Ignatius 2006), pp. 19–52.

to provide a solid foundation for our culture or our national community. In moments of crisis, when we discuss the foundations of our culture and our community, a resurgence of religious viewpoints and arguments can be observed. In the late modern era these arguments can contribute to the discussion on what is true or good, according to Habermas, but to modern people they do not and should not provide authoritative answers. Ratzinger was – and from his new position as universal pontiff still is – suggesting a return to the lost authority of the Catholic Church as the solution to the problems modernity itself is unable to solve. This has been the Catholic hierarchy's message to the world since Leo XIII published *Rerum novarum* in 1891. In 1891, however, one could still think that modernity was based on a faith in human freedom, and that debating this faith by stressing the need of authority made sense. Today, behaving as a free and autonomous subject is the only way people can function in contemporary society. To rely unconditionally on authority has become impossible, because appealing to authority as a foundation has – to state it paradoxically – lost all authority. In this situation the question becomes: how are we to have faith in community, the common good and a graciously given future, without an authoritatively founded belief?

In the last part of *A Secular Age*, Charles Taylor suggests, rather than argues, that in a secular age religion can and does return in a wide variety of forms and shapes. In his view there are two privileged ways in which religion, the religious and religious engagement can, and indeed does, resurface in late modernity.

First, the religious is looked for and found in attempts to escape the experience of the world as being whatever we make of it. Here post-romantic, modernist art is paradigmatic for Taylor. Modernist writers do not want to tell the story they freely think up, using form and language as tools to tell their tale as efficiently and adequately as possible. Since the early twentieth century, Modernist literary forms have attempted to subvert storytelling itself, to loosen its control and to abandon the writer's sense of autonomy that enables him or her to write an unambiguous text and the reader's autonomy that enables him or her to produce an unambiguous reading, one, thus actively making space for whatever may want to reveal itself in the process of writing and reading. Analogously, experimentalist painters since the middle of the twentieth century no longer used the most sophisticated techniques possible in attempting to express their unique view of the world. They were instead searching for the moment in which they lost control over the painting process wherein something can be recognized as revealing itself in and through this moment. In other words, it has been typical of modernity that the rational subject it created not only struggles to stay in power, but also searches for ways to get rid of its central place and the power that comes with it. The hope is for something that is not produced, but, in one way or another, received – if not as an authority, then at least as something to rely on or something to be disturbed by.

Secondly, Taylor points at the possibility of the Christian tradition, as one of the supposed sources of Western civilization, being grasped by the subject and grasping the subject in return, inspiring and challenging people time and again. According to Taylor's analysis, the typical twentieth-century convert to Christianity returns to what he or she has come to see as the source of meaning and an ordered life in a culture of increasing commoditization and instrumentalization. As a result of the process of rationalization, as analyzed by Max Weber, places of inspiration, community and meaning become few and small. They are only able to survive at the margins of the dominant, rationalized culture. This marginalization of what once was at the core of culture may, on the one hand, seem a tragic loss of influence, but it also, on the other hand, makes art and religion possible spaces of criticism. This marginalized criticism is by definition, according to Weber, powerless. It enables people to psychologically compensate for what is painfully lacking in their daily lives, again according to Weber, and this is an important compensation, but only on an existential level.[10]

I would suggest, however, that this is an analysis of a sociologist who thinks he can point out a priori what really matters in a society *qua* society. Inspired artists and genuine believers, however, did, do and will consider the particular *niche* they found as a new center of the world from which it is possible to start to change the whole of culture. There is no way of knowing in advance whether they are right or not. Or maybe one should even say that they *are* right. They and their contributions to the world did, do and will change the culture they live in, although usually not in the way they had hoped or expected to. Without their marginal attempts to retrieve meaning that are threatened with becoming lost, and the representations of what they founded within the debates that built what we call the public sphere, culture would be different. The fact that in late modernity art has become a privatized matter, both in its production and its consumption, does *not* necessarily imply that it is socially irrelevant. The fact that religion becomes more and more privatized and de-institutionalized, also does *not* make it necessarily socially irrelevant. The social relevance of the private sphere and of private practices has to be researched thoroughly. Provisional results do suggest, however, that privately experienced religious meaning can have a strong social impact. It even enables people to live the events in the secularized social and public sphere not just as possibilities to express

---

[10] Max Weber, 'Wissenschaft als Beruf', *Gesammelte Aufsätze zur Wissenschaftslehre* (ed. Johannes Winkelmann; Uni-Taschenbücher, 1492; 7th repr., Tübingen: Mohr Siebeck, 1988), pp. 582–613 (612).

their religious convictions, but also as sources of religious meaning in their own right.[11]

2. *Edward Schillebeeckx, Vatican II and the Theological Retrieval of Modernity*

It is within this context that Edward Schillebeeckx's theology is still relevant. Of course the content of the theology Schillebeeckx developed since 1945 is not necessary meaningful in all of its aspects today. But the way in which he developed it is still pertinent. This is in line with what Schillebeeckx himself wrote about the continuing relevance of Jesus' words and deeds. In his farewell lecture as professor at the University of Nijmegen in 1983, Schillebeeckx explicitly endorsed the theory of Brazilian liberation theologian Clodovis Boff that not what Jesus said and did had to be imitated by contemporary Christians, but the way Jesus, by his acts and words, *related* to his own context: this is what has to be reproduced in our contexts. Schillebeeckx was looking for a relational or, as he himself called it, a 'proportional' continuity: what is and should be constant in the Christian tradition is the proportional relation of Christians to the ever-changing situations in which they find themselves.[12] Here, Schillebeeckx reveals himself as a true representative of *nouvelle théologie*: the religious and Christian relevance of the contemporary is to be retrieved. There is much we can learn from Schillebeeckx here, especially in the way he redis-covered the relation between the Christian and Catholic traditions and the dynamics of human history.

a. *The Dynamics of History*

Historical dynamics revealed itself especially and clearly in Modernity. Modernity is in many ways the era of dynamism and change, not just in fact – all human history has in fact been dynamic, even though people have considered their lives as repetitions of an eternal, unchanging scheme – but also in terms of self-consciousness. Modernity is the era in which

---

[11] I am currently involved in a large research project on the questions of whether, where and how people in the thoroughly secularized Dutch society experience 'higher value' or 'spiritual meaning' in their lives. Provisional results suggest that to a surprisingly large degree the experiences are private in nature, but the value or meaning is social in content.

[12] Edward Schillebeeckx, *Theologisch geloofsverstaan anno 1983* (Baarn: Nelissen, 1983); later the passage was revised in Edward Schillebeeckx, *Church: The Human Story of God* (trans. John Bowden; New York, NY: Crossroad, 1990/London: SCM, 1990).

fundamental historical changes became part of the awareness of humanity as not only something unavoidable, but also as not necessarily threatening and dangerous. Change can be positive and the world has to change.

French philosopher and historian of ideas Marcel Gauchet rightly suggested that Modernity thus realized a core idea of the Christian tradition, namely that God is not a static, but a dynamic presence, related not to a stable order and a given state of affairs, but to the dynamics of a world opening itself up to a new future it can only receive as a gift.[13] The Catholic church, however, resisted the idea of historical change and the possibility of progress through this change for quite some time. Since the second half of the nineteenth century especially, she militantly presented herself as a rock of security and stability in the midst of chaotic, threatening and arbitrary change. It was only in the 1960s at the Second Vatican Council that the Roman Catholic Church broke away from its fixation on constancy and unchanging order. It opened itself up to the dynamics of history and located God's presence in its connection to the world and its changes, especially in the Pastoral Constitution on the Church in the Modern World, *Gaudium et spes*. In the fourth paragraph of its introduction, *Gaudium et spes* says:

> Today, the human race is involved in a new stage of history. Profound and rapid changes are spreading by degrees around the whole world. Triggered by the intelligence and creative energies of man, these changes recoil upon him, upon his decisions and desires, both individual and collective, and upon his manner of thinking and acting with respect to things and to people. Hence we can already speak of a true cultural and social transformation, one which has repercussions on man's religious life as well.

Here the argument is no longer that the Catholic heritage has to be defended against the sinful modern will to change everything that should remain stable as the unshaken foundation of the truly, Divinely-willed good life. The message is that in this situation of profound change and transformation, we have to find out anew what the Gospel message is. It makes sense to try and find out, according to *Gaudium et Spes*, because God remains faithfully present to the changing world. Here we see the influence

---

[13] Marcel Gauchet, *Le désenchantement du monde: Une histoire politique de la religion* (Paris: Gallimard, 1985); English translation: Marcel Gauchet, *The Disenchantment of the World: A Political History of Religion* (trans. Oscar Burge; intr. Charles Taylor; New French Thought; 1st pb. print, Princeton, NJ: Princeton University Press, 1999). See also: Jean-Luc Nancy, 'Le déconstruction du Christianisme', *Les études philosophiques* 4 (1998), pp. 503–19; English translation: the chapter 'The Deconstruction of Christianity', in: Jean-Luc Nancy, *Dis-Enclosure: The Deconstruction of Christianity* (trans. Bettina Bergo, Gabriel Malenfant and Michael B. Smith; Perspectives in Continental Philosophy; New York, NY: Fordham University Press, 2008), pp. 139–57.

of *nouvelle théologie* as a theology of retrieval in the document. The faithfully present God reveals him/herself in ever new ways for a Church that lives up to its 'duty of scrutinizing the signs of the times and of interpreting them in the light of the Gospel' (no. 4).

From the very beginning of his career as a theologian immediately after the Second World War, Edward Schillebeeckx participated in the movement of those trying to develop a theology of creation, of the world, of what was then called the 'earthly realities'. *Gaudium et spes* can be seen as a result of these attempts. The Constitution states that the world, 'which is the theater of human history and the heir of human energies, human tragedies and human triumphs', is the same world

> the Christian sees as created and sustained by its Maker's love, fallen indeed into the bondage of sin, yet emancipated now by Christ, Who was crucified and rose again to break the strangle hold of personified evil, so that the world might be fashioned anew according to God's design and reach its fulfillment (no. 2).

The question is of course what it means to see the world in this way, and to live in it and to be a part of the divine dynamics. This question is at the core of the later Schillebeeckx and it is in this respect that we can still learn from him.

b. *The Struggle for the Interpretation of the Documents of Vatican II*

There is a massive debate, however, concerning the proper way to see the inheritance of the Second Vatican Council. Pope Benedict XVI has made the hermeneutics of the documents of Vatican II into a major issue almost from the very start of his pontificate – if not long before that. In an address to the Roman Curia dated December 22, 2005 – roughly eight months after his election as pope and roughly forty years after the closing of the Council – Joseph Ratzinger drew a sharp contrast between the two ways of interpreting the Council and its documents:

> On the one hand, there is an interpretation that I would call 'a hermeneutic of discontinuity and rupture'; it has frequently availed itself of the sympathies of the mass media, and also one trend of modern theology. On the other, there is the 'hermeneutic of reform', of renewal in the continuity of the one subject-Church which the Lord has given to us. She is a subject which increases in time and develops, yet always remaining the same, the one subject of the journeying People of God.[14]

---

[14] Cf. http://www.vatican.va/holy_father/benedict_xvi/speeches/2005/december/documents/hf_ben_xvi_spe_20051222_roman-curia_en.html. As far as it is concerned with the interpretation of Vatican II, the document is quoted at length in Matthew L. Lamb and Matthew Webb Levering (eds), *Vatican II: Renewal within Tradition*

This statement is much more than an instruction on the way Church documents should be read: always related to other documents, always related to and in continuity with the history in which they participate. Ultimately, what is at stake is the proper understanding of the Church and its relation to Modernity and the modern world.

Already ten years after the Council, in 1975, then not even Bishop or Cardinal, but Professor Joseph Ratzinger of Regensburg University protested in an article to the way in which the Pastoral Constitution on the Church in the Modern World *Gaudium et spes* had in his view been used in Europe, especially in the Netherlands, to justify a close identification of the Church with the concerns of world. It was mistakenly because of this, in his view, that the Church tended to give up its critical distance to Modernity. Ratzinger thereby accused the introduction of *Gaudium et spes* of being too optimistic, although he feels the rest of the document redeems this flaw. The main point Ratzinger wants to make, however, both in the 1975 article and in the address thirty years later, is that only by being truly independent of its worldly context is the Church justifiably to be called the dwelling place of God's truth. Only then can the faithful consider themselves truly *cooperatores veritatis*, 'co-workers of the Truth', as it is said in the third letter of John (3 John 8) – Ratzinger chose *cooperatores veritatis* as his motto when he became the archbishop of Munich and Freising in 1977.

Ultimately, a 'hermeneutics of discontinuity' of the documents of the Second Vatican Council is wrong according to Ratzinger for the very same reason that to him a 'hermeneutics of discontinuity' of Scripture is wrong, as he explains in his 2007 book on Jesus.[15] It endangers the credibility of the Church as a truthful witness to the Truth entrusted to her by God through Jesus Christ. As I previously quoted from the December 2005 address: The Church is in Ratzinger's view a 'subject which increases in time and develops, yet always remaining the same'. Later on, it is said in the same address: 'The Church, both before and after the Council, was and is the same Church, one, holy, Catholic and apostolic, journeying on through time.' This means a return to the supposed contradiction between a chaotic and threatening fragmentation of Modernity and the salvific ordered unity of the Church of the nineteenth century.[16]

(Oxford/New York, NY: Oxford University Press, 2008) pp. ix–xv. The quoted fragment is printed on p. x.

[15] Cf. Joseph Ratzinger/Benedict XVI, *Jesus of Nazareth* (New York, NY: Doubleday, 2007).

[16] See already Joseph Ratzinger, *Principles of Catholic Theology: Building Stones for a Fundamental Theology* (San Francisco, CA: Ignatius, 1987).

c. *Continuity and Discontinuity*

Now there is no denial, of course, that it is part of the Catholic tradition to believe that the Church is one, holy, Catholic and apostolic. But the question still remains as to whether this makes it necessary to think of it as 'one subject-Church', journeying sovereignly through history, in the process of developing and reforming itself but never discovering in this process something that was not already part of it?

Historically it is hard to see how one could deny that the Church has always learned from the world in which she participates. Of course, the truth it often encountered was in a deep sense the same truth that it has the mission to witness to from within Scripture and its tradition, but in ways that were impossible to anticipate before this encounter. And it is also hard to deny that the Second Vatican Council was in some aspects a break with the immediate and older past. The Church for a long time contradicted the legitimacy of religious freedom, but at the Council endorsed it, to name but one example. This is not a minor change. At the same time, it is also true that in *Dignitatis humanae* the Second Vatican Council presents a view on religious freedom that differs considerably from the dominant one, thus making an important contribution from the Christian and Catholic traditions to the discussion on what religious liberty is and why it is important. In other words, leaving behind the idea of a Church having everything essential within itself does not necessarily imply that the Church should or does lose its distinctive role and relevance.

One of the important things we can learn from Edward Schillebeeckx, I think, is that we do not need to think of the Church as one subject in possession of the truth in order to hold on to the confession of her continuity in response to God's continuous faithfulness. Vatican II declared a revolution in terms of understanding the Church, not by breaking away from continuity, and thus speaking only of 'discontinuity and rupture', but by thinking differently about the continuity of the Church. 'The Church', says the Dogmatic Constitution on the Church *Lumen gentium*, 'is in Christ like a sacrament', that is a 'sign and instrument both of a very closely knit union with God and of the unity of the whole human race' (no. 1). In the introductory paragraphs of *Lumen gentium*, God is presented as the Creator and Redeemer of the world, who can be, and is, known in the world through the Church (LG 2–4). The suggestion here is that the continuity of the Church is the continuity established in her mission to and her role within the world, receiving God's presence at least partly through her openness for and her solidarity with the world, hence existing in a role that is ever changing. Schillebeeckx was among those who, following the work of the French theologian and historian Marie-Dominique Chenu (1895–1990), developed between 1945 and

1960 a new and positive understanding of theological development and historical change in the Church.[17]

Since the second half of the nineteenth century, dominant neo-scholasticism considered doctrinal development as a result of pure logical deduction. Combining two statements that were considered to be divinely revealed and therefore absolutely certain, one could in principle draw a conclusion that was equally certain. Thus the fullness of truth present in the inheritance of the Church from the beginning was enfolded and developed. After the Second World War there was, on the one hand, the movement striving for what was called *resourcement*, a return to the sources. Typically, it was not the Bible but the Church Fathers that were considered to embody the true and living source of theology, and, what was more, the true way of understanding the position of the theologian. Neo-scholasticism was strongly influenced by an enlightenment epistemology of pure reason and a logically consistent system of related truths. The movement of *resourcement* saw the Church Fathers presenting the Christian faith as an organic whole that, from its own, internal and divine source, captured the whole of life, including intellectual life. It is in line with this *resourcement*-movement, of which the French Jesuit Jean Danielou (1905–1974) was the leading intellectual, that one has to see the work of Joseph Ratzinger situated.[18]

On the other hand, the French Dominican Marie-Dominique Chenu became convinced in the 1930s that theology exists as a reflection on the current situation of mankind and on God's involvement in it. As an historian, Chenu saw the great theological synthesis of Thomas Aquinas in particular not as a self-contained and self-sufficient system, as neo-scholasticism did, nor as a moment in the self-enfolding consciousness of the Church in line with the *resourcement*-movement. Chenu regarded Aquinas' oeuvre, considered as their main inspiration by neo-scholastic theologians and good theology in general, as a reflection on the contemporary situation from the point of view of a specific, historically situated spirituality embedded in a specific, historically situated culture. Contemporary theologians, according to Chenu, had to express their culture and its spirituality in thought, just as Aquinas had expressed his culture and its spirituality in thought. The *resourcement*-movement changed the neo-scholastic view on how continuity within 'the one subject-Church' is maintained: not by way of correct reasoning, but by organic and intrinsic development. In Chenu's

---

[17] Cf. my *Edward Schillebeeckx: A Theologian in His History. Volume I: A Catholic Theology of Culture (1914–1965)* (trans. John Bowden; London/New York, NY: Continuum, 2004).

[18] This also means that in my view Ratzinger is not, as often is suggested, a progressive turned conservative. All the major themes of his later work, and its tendency, are already present in his *Introduction to Christianity* (London: Burns & Oates, 1969) (German original in 1968).

view the whole idea of 'the one subject-Church' disappears. The continuity of the Church is not maintained by a separate process of internal development, but by remaining in relation to history, because history is the place of God's ongoing presence and revelation. This at least was the core of the idea of incarnation according to Chenu's interpretation of the Christian tradition.

3. Edward Schillebeeckx: Discontinuity as Continuity

It is from this starting point that Edward Schillebeeckx goes forward. In what follows, I will concentrate on the concepts of continuity and the identity of the Church as present in his trilogy on Jesus as Christ. The first volume is supposedly about Jesus in his historicity, the second volume is allegedly about the faith of the early Church in Jesus as Christ, and the third is said to speak of the Church as the community of the followers of Jesus. These characteristics can be highly misleading, however. For my part, I consider all three volumes to be attempts to show what it means that Christianity, in its very core and from its beginning, is a way of reading the world, leading one thus to interpret one's own involvement in it in light of the presence of God revealed in the history of Jesus' words and deeds, his passion, death and resurrection.

a. Continuously Open to the New

That Christianity is a way of reading history is especially clear in the second volume of Schillebeeckx's trilogy, published in the Netherlands in 1977 as *Gerechtigheid en liefde, genade en bevrijding*. For the Americans, its title was translated as *Christ: The Experience of Jesus as Lord*, and for the English, the book was called *Christ: The Christian Experience in the Modern World*.[19] The subtitle of the English edition suggests that there is a connection with the Pastoral Constitution on the Church in the Modern World *Gaudium et Spes*, and rightly so. The American edition suggests that the book is on the Christian view of Jesus, which is also correct. The point is that both issues are closely connected according to Schillebeeckx. Understanding Jesus as Lord means seeing him as the one able to disclose God's presence to the ambivalent, awful and scary, but also beautiful and hopeful world of which we are part.

In the first half of his second volume, Schillebeeckx shows how new questions and new ways of understanding salvation and redemption,

---

[19] Edward Schillebeeckx, *Christ: The Experience of Jesus as Lord* (trans. John Bowden; New York, NY: Seabury, 1980); *Christ: The Christian Experience in the Modern World* (trans. John Bowden; London: SCM, 1980).

new ways of longing and hoping for it and of living in its anticipatory presence brought to light by Jesus' life, death and resurrection, made the first generations of Christians interpret the history of Jesus in previously unanticipated manners. In other words, what we see here is continuity by way of discontinuity, by being open to what is unexpectedly new. In the second half of the second volume, Schillebeeckx presents modern ways of longing for redemption and salvation in the way people try to live their personal, but especially – and this was still innovative in the 1970s, with political and liberation theologies still in the process of developing – their collective lives. In the struggles for a new and better society in their various shapes, Schillebeeckx located secularized forms of Christian hope. As a consequence, he analysed various forms and expressions of these struggles, and the theories behind them, extensively. This accounts for the fact that the second volume of his trilogy is such a thick monster of a book. This seems to be the consequence of really taking seriously the statement in the first paragraph of *Gaudium et spes* that 'nothing genuinely human fails to raise an echo in [the] hearts' of the followers of Christ, and then trying to show in earnest what this implies.

Schillebeeckx's, message here is that the discontinuity that characterizes Modernity, especially in its relation to its religious inheritance, is in fact – or can and should be analysed as – a form of continuity. The history of Christianity has always been characterized by a history of new experiences leading to the necessity to re-interpret traditions coming from the past. Thus they see these experiences in light of what the traditions represent on the basis of past experiences, as well as the other way around.[20] I have focused on the second volume of Schillebeeckx's Christological trilogy, because it makes undeniably clear the fact that Schillebeeckx's project is not simply to return to the origins of the Christian traditions, i.e., to Jesus Christ Himself and therefore to argue that everything that was not part of Jesus' original message should not be considered an integral part of the Christian faith, as Hans Küng does in *On Being a Christian*. Schillebeeckx, in a way, argues the other way around: what does ultimately not contribute to the fullness of our vision of God as the one giving us his kingdom as our future, should not be considered part of the Christian faith. In his first volume, both in England and America called *Jesus: An Experiment in Christology*, Schillebeeckx shows how, in the New Testament, the plurality of confessions to Jesus and his religious significance are expressions of experiences with God's unexpected presence to the world through and because of him.[21]

---

[20] Cf. Schillebeeckx's reflections on hermeneutics, especially in his *The Understanding of Faith: Interpretation and Criticism* (trans. N.D. Smith; London: Sheed and Ward, 1974).

[21] Edward Schillebeeckx, *Jesus: An Experiment in Christology* (trans. Hubert Hoskins; New York, NY: Seabury, 1979/London: Collins, 1979).

The history of Jesus within the community of his disciples shows how God is revealed as a concerned, passionate, present and liberating God to the poor, the marginalized and the excluded. This means that continuity cannot mean holding on to what is said before, not even to what is said by Jesus himself. It means reading the world as it is and as it develops, using Jesus Christ as a lens. This, Schillebeeckx argues, is what Christians have always done, and it is this approach to history that should be retrieved from the Christian tradition to enable theology to become truly modern, and truly Christian – and in this sense: orthodox – at the same time.

Continuity, in the context of the Christian faith and of the Church, according to the view Schillebeeckx presents, should mean being open to the new ways in which this ever unexpected and 'new' God that is revealed in the past, is now revealed in new and unprecedented ways (*God Is New Each Moment* is the title of a book length interview with Edward Schillebeeckx from the nineteen eighties[22]).

Continuity is not something the Church owns or could define as a characteristic belonging to its identity. This is rather what Ratzinger suggests by talking about a 'subject-Church' which 'increases in time and develops, yet always remaining the same'. Continuity is given to the Church through God's faithfulness to human history. In this regard, the Church should open herself to the unexpected changes of history and the discoveries made in the human responses to it. This view on being-Church is what Schillebeeckx tries to present in the third volume of his Christological trilogy: *Church: The Human Story of God*, published in Dutch in 1989.[23] The English title is perhaps misleading as Schillebeeckx clarifies in this volume that all people in their lives and histories are God's story; the original Dutch title, *Mensen als verhaal van God*, would read in English something like 'Human Beings as God's Story'. It is, again, *Gaudium et spes*: the Church is not religiously significant in spite of the fact that it participates in human history, but because it participates in it and by participating in it.[24] Because it is in and through history that the Church meets its God.

b. *Theologically Retrieving Contemporary Experience*

Of course the Church should participate in contemporary human history in a specific Christian way. This is what Schillebeeckx is trying to express

---

[22] Edward Schillebeeckx, *God Is New Each Moment* (in conversation with Huub Oosterhuis and Piet Hoogeveen; trans. David Smith; Edinburgh: T&T Clark, 1983/ New York, NY: Seabury, 1983).

[23] For reference, see note 12 above.

[24] The questions this implies concerning the unity and the Catholicity of the Church are explored and discussed in Gerard Mannion, *Ecclesiology and Postmodernity: Questions for the Church in Our Time* (Louisville, KY: Liturgical Press, 2007).

when he speaks about – I referred to it already – a *proportional* continuity of the tradition. Christians should be part of their world in a manner analogous to Jesus' participation in his world. This is concretized in Schillebeeckx's reflections on 'experiences of contrast' as analogous to the Christian way of speaking about the relation between redemption and judgement. In concrete situations of suffering or oppression, God's salvific presence is experienced as absent, but this experience itself is a redemptive experience of unexpected presence; salvation is anticipated in the struggle to change the situation. Thus Schillebeeckx makes clear how the God Jesus preached and embodied is often contradictory to contemporary culture, but this contradiction is itself closely connected to and incarnated within this culture. God is again ever new and unexpected in the way s/he reveals him/herself in concrete situations as the same God of whom Jesus is the icon.

It is impossible to predict what we ultimately may discover in this regard. Even the most careful reading of Schillebeeckx's oeuvre is unable to tell us that. But reading helps us to discover how to learn theologically from the world and to retrieve the place where we are established as 'holy ground' (Exod. 3.5).[25]

---

[25] Cf. my programmatic essay ... *want de plaats waarop je staat is heilige grond: God als onderzoeksprogramma* [... for the place where you stand is holy ground: God as research programme] (Amsterdam: Boom, 2008).

SCHILLEBEECKX AND THEOLOGY IN THE TWENTY-FIRST CENTURY

Robert J. Schreiter

Introduction

The purpose of this chapter is to bring together some reflections on the conference that gave rise to the chapters in this book, about the significance of Edward Schillebeeckx's thought for theology in the twenty-first century. These remarks are not intended as a summary of what occurred at the conference or appears here (although the authors will be referred to); the wealth of insight is simply too rich to condense into a few words. Rather, it is meant to pick up on insights and place them in a larger context, and to look at them, at times, from a slightly different angle. Nor are these remarks intended to provide a platform for promoting Schillebeeckx's published work as a basis in and of itself for doing theology in the twenty-first century. Throughout his career, Schillebeeckx has made clear again and again that he was not interested in founding a 'school' of theological thought. He has always deemed it more important that theologians engage their own experience and contexts with the resources of the Tradition through the lenses of appropriate and critical methodologies.

This chapter also tries to do this by noting some of the distinctive features of the twenty-first century that have been raised in this book that intersect and thus interact with Schillebeeckx's own concerns and interpretations. One of the signal achievements of his work has been to help Catholic theology make the transition from the pre-modern to the modern situation. In his later years, he has touched also on issues of postmodernity, but has not engaged them to the same extent as those of modernity. Nonetheless, the methodologies he has proposed and utilized in his own work do open doors to engaging postmodernity. Corrections he has made on his own methods (as, for example, his understanding of correlation as a method in theology) naturally create a heuristic for engaging new methods as well. In what follows, I want to point to four areas where Schillebeeckx's work connects with such postmodern concerns: (1) how the concerns of the present time engage enduring questions in theology; (2) how some salient questions are engaged – questions that seem to us to be urgent; (3) indicate some of the prospective questions for the present time that are now just emerging; and (4) propose some matters that I would deem important, but have not been raised here explicitly.

I will try to do this in three steps. First of all, I will propose and then work from a frame for the discussion that can be derived from Schillebeeckx's own work and has had some influence upon the work of the authors brought together in this volume. Second, I will offer some remarks on five areas or themes that have been salient in Schillebeeckx's thought and have been addressed in this book, looking particularly at what they might offer to theology in the current situation. And third, I will note two important and much discussed areas in contemporary theology that have not been addressed here, and suggest how Schillebeeckx's work might be used to engage them.

1. *A Frame for Schillebeeckx's Thought:* Extra mundum nulla salus

In the letter he addressed to the 2008 conference and which was at the beginning of this book, Schillebeeckx proposed a theme to serve as a kind of *leitmotif* for the investigation that was being undertaken: *extra mundum nulla salus* ('outside the world there is no salvation'). He noted that many commentators and critics of his theology had placed too great an emphasis on the *mundus* or 'world' in his thought, thereby depicting his theology as a reductive humanism. In responding to that, he noted that such a reading overlooks the *salus* or 'salvation' that is completely the work of God. In his own words: 'The expression *extra mundum nulla salus* has to do with the reality that the creative, saving presence of God is mediated in and through human beings.' It is these two dimensions: a thorough commitment to the reality of God, and to the reality of the world, that are brought together in his theology. *Salus* suffuses the *mundum*. To separate this dynamic inter-action, or to reduce in any way the one to the other does not represent this fundamental insight of Schillebeeckx. Consequently, the categories in the one have counterparts in the other: one cannot speak of nature, for example, without speaking also of creation; one cannot speak of human society without speaking also of a political theology; one cannot recount history without speaking too of the narratives of God's action within it; and one cannot speak of humanity itself without seeing it as a window into the very Godhead in whose image and likeness humanity has been created. The *mundus* is a *sacramentum* – a sacrament – of the divine.

It thus becomes important to keep these two foci in his thought always in interaction with each other. Not to maintain this tension distorts Schillebeeckx's thought. It was perhaps the innovations he brought in method, and how he used these to analyze the world, that has led some to develop a one-sided reading of his work. By taking a more inductive approach – starting with the world, and then seeing how it receives God's grace – Schillebeeckx reversed the perspective that has prevailed in so much of Western theology where one begins with God and then somehow tries to fit the world and human experience within the transcendent.

The Catholic University at Leuven and the Radboud University, Nijmegen have served in recent years as the 'axis' of reflection on Schillebeeckx's overall project. Lieven Boeve has suggested here that the two universities have taken slightly different tacks in their reading of Schillebeeckx. In this most recent period Leuven has concentrated especially on a hermeneutical reading of Schillebeeckx's work, especially as it engages modernity and postmodernity. This is certainly a legitimate way to approach his work. Schillebeeckx introduced hermeneutical thinking into Catholic theology in 1967, and brought about a fundamental shift in how Catholic theology was to engage twentieth-century developments in method.[1] Nijmegen, on the other hand, has focused on Schillebeeckx's project as a theology of culture (that is, on the culture and society of the West, and Northwestern Europe in particular, since 1945). This approach too finds ample foundation in his work, starting with his very first publications on the situation in post-war France in 1945[2] through to his 1986 Abraham Kuyper-Lectures at the Free University of Amsterdam.[3]

But even with this necessary emphasis on the 'world' dimension of his project, the 'salvation' dimension cannot be forgotten. By focusing on salvation rather than simply on God, Schillebeeckx underlines the economy of God's presence and work in the world, thus engaging that world as it is, rather than according to some abstract design. It is this theological vision

---

[1] Cf. Edward Schillebeeckx, 'Naar een katholiek gebruik van de hermeneutiek: Geloofsidentiteit in het interpreteren van het geloof', *Geloof bij kenterend getij: Peilingen in een seculariserend christendom* (FS Willem Hendrik van de Pol; ed. Hendrik van der Linde and A.M. Fiolet; Roermond: Romen, 1967), pp. 78–116. The English version, 'Toward a Catholic Use of Hermeneutics', may be found in Edward Schillebeeckx, *God the Future of Man* (trans. N.D. Smith; Theological Soundings 5/1; New York, NY: Sheed and Ward, 1968/London/Sydney: Sheed and Ward, 1969), pp. 1–49.

[2] See his three essays under the common title 'Christelijke situatie' in *Kultuurleven* 12 (1945), pp. 82–95, 229–42 and 585–611.

[3] These are available in English as Edward Schillebeeckx, *On Christian Faith: The Spiritual, Ethical, and Political Dimensions* (trans. John Bowden; New York, NY: Crossroad, 1987). In the original Dutch edition, the subtitle read: *Jezus in onze Westerse cultuur* ('Jesus in Our Western Culture'). On the occasion of his eightieth birthday in 1994, *Tijdschrift voor theologie* devoted a special issue to his work as a theologian of culture.

that has made his theological project so exciting to so many people, seeking to make sense of their experience of God in a modern, secular setting. And it is through this bifocal lens of world and salvation, if you will, that I will explore themes that have been central to his work.

2. *Schillebeeckx in the Twentieth and Twenty-First Century*

Schillebeeckx's theological work falls mainly in the second half of the twentieth century, and it is the challenges and issues of that period that were his preoccupation. For Catholic theology, this meant both a renewal of theology by returning to patristic and medieval sources (the subject of Schillebeeckx's dissertation[4]) and the encounter with modernity. As has already been noted, Schillebeeckx offers a theology of modernity inasmuch as he tried to meet this phenomenon on its own ground, sympathetically but critically. By the latter stages of his publishing, postmodernity (however defined) seemed to have displaced modernity in many ways. Postmodernity's focus on fragmentation over coherence, disruption over continuity, and the margins over the center are not without echo and even direct treatment in Schillebeeckx's writings in the 1980s and 1990s, but postmodernity's issues and methods for addressing them were not at the center of his work.

By the twenty-first century, many have argued that we are in yet another phase, called the post-postmodern, the second modern, or the post-secular. In different ways and from different perspectives, the nomenclature draws attention to various dimensions of the current era: that the postmodern has exhausted itself in its celebration of instability and people are now looking for a new coherence (post-postmodern);[5] that modernity is reasserting itself as a reformed and chastened version of itself in light of postmodern critique (a second modernity);[6] that the resurgence of religion now has displaced the hegemony of the secular in the West and now must share the stage with religion (post-secular).[7]

---

[4] Edward Schillebeeckx, *De sacramentele heilseconomie: Theologische bezinning op St. Thomas' sacramentenleer in het licht van de traditie en van de hedendaagse sacramentsproblematiek* (Antwerpen: 't Groeit, 1952).

[5] See Robert J. Schreiter, 'A New Modernity: Living and Believing in an Unstable World', *New Theology Review* 20/1 (2007), pp. 51–60.

[6] Sociologist Ulrich Beck calls this the *'zweite Moderne'*. See the series he edits for Suhrkamp Verlag by the same name.

[7] The post-secular is exemplified in the work of Jürgen Habermas since 2001; see the essays collected around this theme in his *Zwischen Naturalismus und Religion* (Frankfurt a.M.: Suhrkamp, 2005). The post-secular is explored even more emphatically in Charles Taylor's *A Secular Age* (Cambridge, MA: Belknap Press/Harvard University Press, 2007).

In what follows I want to look at Schillebeeckx's project under five headings, and indicate the continuing fecundity of his thought within the questions posed to him by twentieth-century thought, and how his work is being extended into the twenty-first century. The five headings are: method, God, the human, the social, and suffering.

a. *Method*

As has already been indicated, questions of method have been a central feature of Schillebeeckx's work. Beginning within the fields of Thomism and phenomenology, he began from the middle 1960s a trajectory through the major developments in method in European thought: hermeneutics, analytic philosophy, critical social theory, and semiotics. These have all left marks in his published writing. In addition, his lectures on hermeneutics from the 1970s until his retirement in 1983 show him engaging structuralism, post-structuralism, and linguistic philosophy as well. Chapters in this book show authors engaging his work in Thomism and phenomenology (Anthony Godzieba, Erik Borgmann, and Stephan van Erp) and hermeneutics (Lieven Boeve, Benoît Bourgine, and Marc Dumas). All of these show the continuing relevance of these methods and approaches, rooted as they are in the first half of the twentieth century, for the early twenty-first century as well.

Two methodological approaches with special relevance to the current situation also surfaced in the discussions. (1) The first is the use of communicative studies in theology, something that Vincent Miller brought forward. He focused here especially on the role of narrative and media studies. In North America, communicative theology has been influenced especially by theory deriving from media studies (especially aural and visual media) and studies of cultural practices. In Europe, theologians have extended the work of Habermas on communicative theory into theology.[8] Schillebeeckx has not engaged media studies directly, and his use of Habermas has focused primarily on Habermas' earlier work, on critical social theory, dating from the 1960s and early 1970s. Yet Schillebeeckx's interest in narrative, dating from the mid-1970s, is a natural platform for extending that interest into both media studies and a communicative theology.[9]

(2) A second methodological approach that has taken on greater salience in the twenty-first century is intercultural hermeneutics. The impact of globalization has been such that it is now necessary to find ways to bridge

---

[8] Notable here is the work of Edmund Arens. See his *Gottesverständigung: Eine kommunikative Religionstheologie* (Freiburg: Herder, 2007).

[9] A study in Schillebeeckx and cinema is that of Antonio Sison, *Screening Schillebeeckx: Theology and Third Cinema in Dialogue* (New York, NY: Palgrave Macmillan, 2006).

interpretation and understanding across a variety of boundaries, social and cultural. Schillebeeckx in his own writing gives evidence of this in his appreciation of feminist theologies and in his appropriation of themes from theologies of liberation, especially in his soteriology. Formal work in intercultural hermeneutics, while begun in both feminist and liberation theologies, came mainly—as a concern for culture as such—only in the 1990s and the early twenty-first century.[10] Three authors in this book took up the challenges of an intercultural hermeneutics in a more specific way: Gemma Cruz, in addressing issues of global migration; and Kathleen McManus and Elizabeth Tillar, looking at the intersection of feminism and human suffering. Feminist theory continues to undergo development and growth, as is evidenced in all three of the papers here. McManus' and Tillar's previous work on suffering has taken Schillebeeckx as a central author, and are two of the most important scholars on Schillebeeckx's work on suffering, a theme that will be returned to below.

Schillebeeckx, like most theologians of his era, has focused his own work primarily on Western thought and its contexts, especially around the questions of dealing with modernity. At the same time, however, he was one of the first theologians in Europe to call attention to the Latin American theologies of liberation and to incorporate insights from this movement into his own work. It is not surprising, then, that students writing disser-tations since the mid-1990s have rather easily been able to extend his hermeneutical work into the new field of intercultural hermeneutics.

Advances in method figured strongly in discussions among the authors, the results of which can be found in various chapters of this book. Attempts were made to overcome binary thinking, something Schillebeeckx himself has long espoused. Triadic possibilities were explored, and Hans-Joachim Sander argued especially for nuanced forms of dialectic (dialectic being perhaps more at home in the Hegelian and idealist traditions of the German-speaking world than in the Low Countries) as ways of overcoming the polarities implicit in binary thinking. Of special interest was how to construe universality in non-hegemonic ways, with proposals about iterative procedures (Manemann) and finding common ground (Cruz). Tied especially to this was how thinking about particu-larities and singularities in turn inform understandings of universality. In a globalized world, where issues of power and its distribution are being rethought, how universality is construed and claimed has taken on new dimensions that still need to be explored. Along with that come under-standings of 'pluralism' that need to be sharpened (a point made strongly by Sander). The methods that take on the questions of how to bring

[10] See Robert J. Schreiter, *The New Catholicity: Theology between the Global and the Local* (Maryknoll, NY: Orbis, 1997); D.N. Premnath (ed.), *Border Crossings: Cross-Cultural Hermeneutics* (Maryknoll, NY: Orbis, 2007).

disparate concepts together (in binaries, triads, or dialectically and of how to relate universality and particularity) will each shape those discourses in particular ways. Overall issues about how to proceed therefore are of special importance, as both Boeve and Borgman indicated, and Marc Dumas illuminated in a special way by his use of the work of Michel de Certeau.

b. *God*

God is of course a central theme in any theology, indicated in the term 'theology' itself. It was an explicit topic of discussion in the conference as is evidenced in the chapters of this book. The twin themes of God as limit and God as immanent came out in many ways, especially in the work of Frederiek Depoortere (on themes of God and science, and God and the 'new atheism'), as well as that of Bourgine and van Erp. Grappling with how to talk about God in the twenty-first century world, beset as it is with both the new atheism of Dawkins and Hitchens,[11] but also with religious resurgence in so many parts of the world, remains a daunting challenge. Looking both at limit (in senses of horizon, transcendence, and the ineffable, of the *Deus absconditus*), and immanent (issues of theodicy, of grace, of providence) as categories for talking about God's presence to and in the world remain major tasks for the twenty-first century.

Schillebeeckx's encounters with British analytic philosophy in the 1960s, building upon his Thomism, have provided in some ways the most important frame of reference for his speaking about God as limit. His interest in human experience and how it comes to encounter divine revelation, as well as his extended reflections on the nature of human suffering, have informed his speaking about God as 'a God of human beings' ('*een God van mensen*').

Here too the theme of salvation comes forward, one of the two great themes in Schillebeeckx's thought. Much has been written about Schillebeeckx's understanding of suffering – that which calls forth the cry for and the need for salvation. More will be said about suffering below. I would like to focus attention here on the soteriological questions we are facing in the twenty-first century. The biggest question is how to imagine salvation at the present time. Utopian thinking and the related aspects of theologies of hope and of liberation dominated theological thinking from the late 1960s to the early 1980s. But by the mid-1980s the optimism that drove utopian thinking began to crumble (as exemplified in the two Vatican declarations on liberation theology at that time). Some of this may

---

[11] Richard Dawkins, *The God Delusion* (New York, NY: Houghton Mifflin Harcourt, 2006); Christopher Hitchens, *God is Not Great: How Religion Poisons Everything* (New York, NY: Twelve, 2007).

have been connected to postmodern assertions about the collapse of master narratives. The fall of the Berlin wall in 1989 ushered in a brief resurgence of optimism (talk of an Hegelian 'end of history'), but that optimism was soon dampened by the upsurge of conflicts around the world, and talk of the 'clash of civilizations'. In the midst of that brief period of optimism there was also a deflation of socialist utopian thinking after the collapse of the Communist states in Eastern Europe ended at least one kind of utopian design for many. To speak of God's salvation for the world requires, it seems to me, some kind of master narrative. But a master narrative that can capture the cry for salvation and the response to that cry – beyond simply a call to solidarity with those who are suffering and more towards imagining a world beyond suffering – is something that still eludes our grasp.[12] Whether a new master narrative about God's bringing salvation to the world can be found that can generate and direct enthusiasm is a major task for the twenty-first century.

Another emerging field for thinking about God is that of interreligious dialogue. This field has of course been prominent for nearly half a century, but has taken on new urgency with globalization, the migration of peoples, and the resurgence of religion. Schillebeeckx addressed interreligious dialogue most directly in the third volume of his trilogy and other writings at the end of the 1980s. The issues at that point had not yet been sharpened by the movement of peoples (such as Islam into Western Europe) or the variety of conflicts that involved religious difference in one form or another.[13] Jean-Louis Souletie focused special attention here by delving into some of the substantive issues within the dialogue.

This emerging field becomes increasingly urgent on a number of fronts – from a global ethic through multicultural and multireligious living to peacebuilding. Work on it requires at some stage a relatively strong grasp of the respective religious traditions and the cultures surrounding them, something that the youngest generation of scholars is now trying to undertake.[14]

---

[12] Some have suggested that the heightened interest in reconciliation is a result of the collapse of utopian thinking: because we cannot see ahead, we have turned more toward healing the past. Still others have suggested that the rapid growth of Pentecostal and Charismatic Christianity is filling this void.

[13] See Hans G. Kippenberg, *Gewalt als Gottesdienst: Religionskriege im Zeitalter der Globalisierung* (Munich: C.H. Beck, 2008).

[14] Notable here is the 'comparative theology' movement, led by Francis X. Clooney, SJ of Harvard University. At this point comparative theology is primarily concerned with comparing religious texts, but it may come to move further afield into the practical areas of interreligious dialogue.

c. *The Human*

The *humanum* played a central role in Schillebeeckx's own imagining of the utopian in his work in the 1970s and 1980s. This concept, drawn from the thinking of the Frankfurt School, and indirectly from the work of the philosopher Ernst Bloch, represented an attempt to anticipate the future of a liberated humanity. The vision of the *humanum* continues to animate thinking as both Mary Catherine Hilkert and Elizabeth Tillar indicate here. Although we may be living through a time of eclipse for utopian thinking (as a result of the collapse of the utopian ideologies that were so present in the twentieth century, especially those of Marxism and socialism), the *humanum* continues for some to provide a point of departure (one thinks of the slogan of the World Social Forum: 'Another world is possible'). Feminist theologians especially find it a useful point of departure for their work.

With this comes the larger question of theological anthropology, an area of theology that holds a central place in the twenty-first century much as Christology did in the last quarter of the twentieth century. The meaning of culture amid the migration of peoples, questions about the boundaries of human life raised in the biomedical sciences, questions of sex and gender, the continuing evolution of thinking about human rights – all of these are deeply anthropological questions. A striking feature of the conversations at the conference was the continued salience of Schillebeeckx's proposal of 'anthropological constants', found in the second volume of his trilogy, *Christ*, as a way of ordering the principal axioms that need to be kept in mind in any discussion of the human.

d. *The Social*

Schillebeeckx's work is replete with social themes. Along with Johann Baptist Metz, he was the pre-eminent expositor of the role of the social dimension of humanity in Catholic theology. Here the 'world' dimension of his thought comes into its own. Questions of how to periodize the social dimension (modern, postmodern, etc.) have already been discussed above. Sander went to some length to speak of the liquidity of the current age (following Zygmunt Bauman's use of the term) and its apocalyptic dimensions. Both he and Oliver Davies proposed models of looking at the current state of the social dimension in our time.

Perhaps the most extensive discussions of the social dimension were about the political forum, proposed in different ways by Miller, Manemann, and Sander. Differences among them were at least partially about their different contexts in North America and Europe, as well as the authors to whom they appealed. Schillebeeckx himself was much in conversation with Metz at the time he was writing about the political (the 1970s and 1980s), and this is reflected in his writing. The political figures prominently in his work in those years, not so much in a political-partisan way or in reference to the *polis*, but rather to the soteriological ramifications of the encounter between God and the world.

Within the current situation, the discussion here intersects with that about pluralism, and how to negotiate differences in multicultural societies. This is an area that is essential to current discourse, and one that is still inadequately theorized. Discourse in Europe and elsewhere has shifted away from a postmodern celebration of multiculturalism as diversity and fragmentation, to exploring the limits of multicultural accommodation and interaction, and finding models of multicultural engagement for the sake of a healthy public sphere or, in the language of Catholic Social Teaching, the common good. This shift began on the political right[15] but now is engaged by the political left as well.[16] It is another example of the transit out of the postmodern into something different, however this is yet to be named.

e. *Suffering*

Schillebeeckx's work on suffering has been one of the most fertile areas of his thought for a younger generation of scholars. At least five dissertations have been devoted to his views on suffering since the late 1990s.[17] The heuristic values of his concept of negative contrast experiences, both as an epistemological device to shift people out of being overwhelmed by suffering to resistance to it, and as a theological anticipation of salvation from God, have been noted by many, and have been taken up here by Cruz, Hilkert, McManus, and Tillar. It is striking – and by no means accidental – that all four of these authors are women, taking women's experience as a point of departure for their work. Women's oppression is well responded to within the framework of negative contrast experiences. Schillebeeckx's preoccupation with suffering has been especially attractive to scholars in the so-called Third World, where the degree of human suffering in

---

[15] See for example Paul Scheffer, *Het land van aankomst* (Amsterdam: De Bezige Bij, 2007).

[16] Robert D. Putnam, '*E pluribus unum*: Diversity and Community in the Twenty-First Century. The 2006 John Skytte Prize Lecture', *Scandinavian Political Studies* 30/2 (2007), pp. 137–74.

[17] Kathleen McManus, 'The Place and Meaning of Suffering in the Theology of Edward Schillebeeckx' (Toronto, 1999); Elizabeth Tillar, 'Suffering for Others in the Theology of Edward Schillebeeckx' (Fordham, 2000); Derek Simon, 'Provisional Liberations, Fragments of Salvation: The Practical Critical Soteriology of Edward Schillebeeckx' (Ottawa, 2001); Aloysius Rego, 'Suffering and Salvation: The Salvific Meaning of Suffering in the Later Theology of Edward Schillebeeckx' (Melbourne, 2001); Antonio Sison, 'Political Holiness in Third Cinema: The Crystallization of Edward Schillebeeckx's Eschatological Perspective in Kidlat Tahimik's "The Perfumed Nightmare"' (Nijmegen, 2004).

poverty and oppression is especially strong. For these reasons, it is one of Schillebeeckx's most enduring contributions to theology for the twenty-first century. Dealing with suffering today can no longer lean upon the optimism that marked the utopian ideologies in which the experience was sometimes framed in the past. At the same time, suffering cannot be confronted without some measure of hope that it can be overcome. Peace studies and reconciliation have become a major venue for exploring how salvation from suffering might be found, especially in looking at the reconstruction of societies after conflict. The local theologies of the World Church in most of the world have no credibility if they do not address suffering. Schillebeeckx's formulation of suffering and human experience remains one of the most effective ways of approaching the reality and seeming intractability of human suffering.

3. Issues Left Unaddressed

This review of themes appearing in Schillebeeckx's thinking in the twentieth century has tried to show how they continue to have salience for the twenty-first century. But if one is thinking about theology in the twenty-first century, then it is important to note also areas that are much discussed in theology today that have not figured in the discussions here. I would like to mention just two that stand out in a special way.

(1) The first much-discussed area is that of aesthetics. The discussion has two sides. One, following especially upon the work of Hans Urs von Balthasar, seeks to establish a theology of the beautiful alongside the more commonly known theologies developed around the transcendentals of the good and the true.[18] While trying to explore a transcendental theme that has not been adequately examined, this effort runs the risk of separating off the beautiful from the other two transcendentals, leaving an inward-looking concentration on individual perception and holiness. On the other side, there is another movement, most notably present among U.S. Latino theologians, that emphasizes more the political dimensions of beauty and holiness.[19] Schillebeeckx's own work on political holiness from the latter 1980s (see footnote 3, above) would make an appropriate point of

---

[18] Balthasar's trilogy begins with *Herrlichkeit* (the beautiful), and is followed by *Theodramatik* (the good), and *Theologik* (the true). Originally published by Johannes Verlag in Einsiedeln, an English translation is available from Ignatius Press in San Francisco.

[19] See for example, Alejandro García-Rivera, *The Community of the Beautiful* (Collegeville, MN: Liturgical Press, 1999); Roberto Goizueta, *Christ Our Companion: Toward an Theological Aesthetics of Liberation* (Maryknoll, NY: Orbis, 2009).

departure for such a work, which would serve as a corrective on the more inward-looking aesthetics found among some of the followers of Balthasar.

(2) The other unaddressed area is a movement within contemporary North Atlantic theology that is highly critical of modernity and seeks to mount an alternative theology drawing especially on a reading of Augustine against Aquinas. This movement has no agreed-upon name; it is associated with the journal *Communio*, and with the Anglo-American movement known as Radical Orthodoxy. In Leuven, it has been studied under the name of 'Neo-Augustinian postmodernism'.[20] Because of the association of the current pope with this movement, this movement is finding a great deal of favor in English-language theological circles today.

Schillebeeckx could not in any way be reckoned as part of this movement; on the contrary, it is his kind of theology that they are trying to counter. A re-reading of the current state of Western society – as post-postmodern, post-secular, or what have you – is a theological task that could be undertaken profitably. But it should be careful not to rearrange recent history to suit some of its more polemical purposes. This is especially true of a recasting of the significance of the Second Vatican Council for the Church. This new historiography plays down the reforms and new insights of the Council in favour of seeing primarily continuity with the Church before the Council. An edition and translation of Schillebeeckx's writings from the Council, which is now under way, would be an occasion to address this rereading of history that is being put forward.

4. *Conclusion*

What will Schillebeeckx's theology mean for the twenty-first century? In 1989, I was asked to address the enduring significance of his theology, and suggested four topics that would likely be seen as part of his legacy to the theological enterprise.[21] These were: (1) working inductively as a theological method, (2) the narrative character of experience, (3) the mystery of suffering and contrast, and (4) the primacy of the soteriological. Certainly all four of these have found resonance here as part of Schillebeeckx's ongoing contribution to theology in the twenty-first century, as evidenced in the chapters in this book. At the same time, one of his caveats should be noted here

---

[20] See the results of a 2006 conference held there: Lieven Boeve, Mathijs Lamberigts and Maarten Wisse (eds), *Augustine and Postmodern Thought: A New Alliance Against Modernity?* (BETL, 219; Leuven: Peeters, 2009).

[21] Robert J. Schreiter, 'Edward Schillebeeckx: His Enduring Significance', *The Praxis of Christian Experience: An Introduction to the Theology of Edward Schillebeeckx* (ed. Robert J. Schreiter and Mary Catherine Hilkert; San Francisco, CA: Harper and Row, 1989), pp. 147–55.

again: Important is not so much that the results of his own investigations be constantly replicated and repeated by a younger generation of theologians, as that they carry on their own theological work in the spirit of his own. As he put it in his letter to the Conference that was the origin of this book: 'I thank you all for your willingness to take my thought as the starting point for doing theology for the 21st century – but only as a starting point.' That the impulses he brought to theology in modernity – both in method and in themes to be treated – could still prove so resilient in a new time and a new situation is testimony to why his thought and legacy will live well into the twenty-first century.

THEOLOGY FOR THE 21ST CENTURY: A COMMENTARY ON THE SYMPOSIUM

Kathleen Dolphin, PBVM

At the end of the first decade of the twenty-first century, arguably one of the most tumultuous in recent history for both church and world, theologians are wise to pause and take stock of the contemporary challenges facing theology itself. Identifying real challenges in the real world – and placing them in mutually critical dialogue with the richness of the Christian tradition – is the first step in a praxis-oriented theological methodology, the type exemplified in the work of Edward Schillebeeckx for over fifty years. Inspired by Schillebeeckx's approach, participants in the symposium *Theology for the 21st Century: The Enduring Relevance of Edward Schillebeeckx for Contemporary Theology* likewise explored ways to meet the new challenges theology faces in our own day.

As a theologian whose work has focused on Schillebeeckx's sermons as enactments of practical theology, my own interest has been in the mutually enriching relationship between theology and spirituality. In this capacity I was invited to present, at the conclusion of the symposium and here, a response to the symposium as a whole; that is to say, to offer a general commentary on the presentations at the symposium. I do so from a particular stance; i.e., a pastoral stance at the juncture of theology and spirituality. My lens is that of a North American Catholic theologian.

1. *The Current Situation*

In this commentary I analyse how each of the symposium speakers addressed specific challenges to theology. Before doing that, however, I offer an overview of the current situation with regard to the relationship between theology and spirituality, particularly in the United States. Before proceeding further, a definition of spirituality seems in order. I have been

265

influenced by Sandra Schneiders' definition: 'Spirituality is the experience of consciously striving to integrate one's life in terms not of isolation and self-absorption, but of self-transcendence toward the ultimate value one perceives.'[1] Schneiders notes that for Christians, the 'ultimate value' is the Triune God. It is that Christian, mainly Catholic, perspective that I adopt in this commentary.

The flourishing of spirituality depends in great measure on the adequacy of the theology that grounds it, and vice versa. Any challenge to theology impacts the spirituality praxis that not only expresses that theology but in turn influences it. Take, for example, the effect of new cosmological discoveries on traditional images of God. Scientists tell us that the universe has no edge and no centre, or to put it another way, every point is the centre. For many seekers, that piece of information has profound implications for theology and spirituality. Reflecting on the infinity of the universe (or the 'multiverse', as we are encouraged to call it, now that there are at least hints that ours is not the only universe in existence), we are prompted to adjust our spirituality practices to include reflection not only on the living presence of God in our own familiar venue of planet Earth, but also on the living presence of God in an ever expanding universe. This requires shifts in both theology and in spirituality praxis. For example, Schillebeeckx asserts, 'Something of a sigh of mercy, of compassion, is hidden in the deepest depths of reality ... and in it believers hear the name of God.'[2] At the 'centre' of the universe is this infinite sigh of compassion. His helpful theological insight here aids spiritual praxis; in this case it offers new ways of addressing God in prayer.

The striking claim that creation reveals God as infinite compassion emerges from Schillebeeckx's notion of 'creation faith', wherein he insists on the possibility of God's transcendence being revealed through God's immanence in creation. Attention to the power of the Catholic sacramental imagination to hold binaries like transcendence and immanence in creative tension is a particularly effective feature of Schillebeeckx's thought. It holds great promise for addressing issues related to the many dimensions of the question of God in modernity/post-modernity, and to the important dynamic between theology and spirituality.

Theology informs spirituality. On the other hand, spirituality can influence theology. Moving from cosmological heights to a more 'down to earth' level, a case in point is how the use of gender inclusive language, in public and private prayer, can have a gradual, positive impact on theological consciousness of theologians and worshippers alike.

---

[1] Sandra Schneiders, 'Spirituality in the Academy', *Theological Studies* 50 (1989), pp. 676–97 (684).

[2] Edward Schillebeeckx, *Church: The Human Story of God* (trans. John Bowden; New York, NY: Crossroad, 1990) p. 6.

In addition, while theologians are doing their scholarly work, the social and cultural world remains extremely fluid. On the one side, interest in spirituality has increased remarkably during the past several decades in public discourse, in the realm of personal search for meaning – and even in academia. Even a casual stroll through a bookstore or a brief Internet search will reveal the intensity and extensiveness of this interest in the theories and practices of spirituality. Further, the revival is manifested both within and beyond institutionalized religious settings. Certainly the interest within traditional Christianity is far-reaching in both Catholic and Protestant circles, but becoming more and more evident is the emergence of what James R. Lewis and others have described as a large-scale, decentralized religious subculture that draws its inspiration from sources outside the Judeo-Christian tradition.[3] These alternative spiritualities, typically quite individualistic in tone, are attractive to some who have become disenchanted with the institutional structures of organized religion. 'I'm not religious but I am spiritual' is a commonly heard statement. A recent poll in the U.S. indicated that 15% of those surveyed claim no religious affiliation.[4] These seekers have become unmoored, so to speak, from stable faith communities, which in the past were the loci where the faith was passed on to the next generation. Needless to say, issues of belonging and disengagement constitute important challenges facing practical theologians as they attempt to address the laity in an engaging way at a time when the level of theological literacy in the U.S. culture(s) seems to be quite low.

At the other end of the spectrum, within Catholicism, there is a flurry of interest in styles of spirituality popular in the mid-19th to mid-20th centuries. This resurgence of pre-Vatican II spirituality is characterized by a fascination with religious garb, Mass in Latin, practices to gain indulgences, devotions to Mary that assign to her divine attributes, adoration of the Blessed Sacrament (disengaged from the Eucharistic liturgy), and so forth. While these practices may be a source of comfort and nostalgia for some older adult Catholics who suffered through the sometimes vapid and ultra-casual liturgies of the 1970s, some young people look upon these practices as novel, even 'cool' – high praise indeed! But a question arises: what to do when the 'coolness' cools, so to speak? Fads come and go. Can the revival of an isolated practice, such as trying to gain indulgences, sustain faith over the long haul in the way that regular participation in a Eucharistic

[3] James R. Lewis (ed.), *Oxford Handbook of New Religious Movements* (New York, NY: Oxford University Press, 2004).

[4] *The American Religious Identification Survey* (2008), conducted by Barry Kosmin and Ariela Keysar at Trinity College, Hartford, Connecticut, surveyed 54,461 adults (http://www.americanreligionsurvey-aris.org). A similar survey, the *U.S. Religious Landscape Survey* (2008), conducted by the Pew Forum on Religion and Public Life, found similar results (http://religions.pewforum.org).

community can, especially a community liturgy based on excellent sacramental theology? Nothing replaces sound theology and sound spirituality.

2. Schillebeeckx as Resource for 21ˢᵗ Century Theology and Spirituality

The challenges to theology that were discussed in the *Theology for the 21ˢᵗ
Century* symposium are challenges to spirituality as well. Eight challenges
were identified and addressed: (1) the question of God in modernity, (2)
the social role of theology, (3) theologies of inter-religious dialogue, (4)
Christology and suffering, (5) the role of experience as a theological starting
point, including an attentiveness to feminist concerns, (6) issues related to
community, Eucharist, ministry, and the full flourishing of the *humanum*,
(7) the philosophy/theology interface, and (8) an evolving understanding of
the history of salvation and eschatology. These eight challenges are crucial
issues that theology must address effectively.

To do so requires a fruitful method. Schillebeeckx's method, and
the application thereof, produced a valuable legacy. For purposes of
brevity here, I summarize Schillebeeckx's approach in terms of the four
basic movements outlined by practical theologian Don S. Browning. These
four movements or 'moments' are: (1) A descriptive moment: a thick
description of a particular situation/human experience, including articulation of a precise question; (2) a historical moment: placing that situation
and question in conversation with the history of the Christian tradition; (3)
a systematic moment: taking the result of that 'conversation' and organizing new insights not only from theology, but from other disciplines as well
and (4) a strategic moment: the call to effective action.[5] These movements
are traceable in Schillebeeckx's sermons.[6] Besides the possibility of viewing
his sermons as enactments of practical theology, another reason I am
interested in his sermons is that the audience of this genre is a believing
community, gathered specifically for prayer and reflection either in a
formal worship service or in some other prayerful setting. Schillebeeckx's
integration of practical theology and spirituality is brought out in greater
relief in his sermons than elsewhere in his work. Further, a close reading of
these texts reveals criteria for judging whether the theology produced by
this method is sound. The criteria I have discerned to be operative in his
work are these three, formulated here in questions: (1) Grounded in this

---

[5] Don S. Browning, *A Fundamental Practical Theology: Descriptive and Strategic
Proposals* (Minneapolis, MN: Fortress, 1991) pp. 223–26.

[6] Schillebeeckx, *God Among Us: The Gospel Proclaimed* (trans. John Bowden; New
York, NY: Crossroad, 1983) and *For the Sake of the Gospel* (trans. John Bowden;
London: SCM, 1989).

particular theology, does the praxis have an incarnational dimension? (2) Is it some way relational? (3) And does it have the potential to transform favourably both the individual and community? In other words, the norms are incarnationality, relationality, and transformationality.

My reflections focus on the eight challenges posed at the symposium. My comments will incorporate Schillebeeckx's method and particularly his norms as outlined above. In this way I highlight how the participants address 21st century challenges to their work as theologians *with the assistance of Schillebeeckx as a resource*. In each participant's paper, I pinpoint at least one major insight (among many) that seems to illustrate one of the three norms with particular clarity as the writer deals with one of the challenges. Moreover, an overall view of the papers reveals that the norms implicit in Schillebeeckx's work appear in the participants' work as well, even though the particular challenges to these 21st century theologians were framed somewhat differently than would have been the case in the mid-to-late 20th century when Schillebeeckx was doing his work. The pattern that emerges bodes well for the future of theology.

a. *Incarnationality*

(1) Addressing the challenge posed by philosophy and theology: The indisputable significance of life experience, as a starting point for theology and spirituality, must not be allowed to eliminate the role of speculative reason and even rational grounding for both theology and spirituality. After all, the human being, considered as both embodied spirit and inspirited body (to use the notion of perspectival seeing discussed by Frederiek Depoortere), does have a mind – and *intellectual* experience! And Schillebeeckx insists that all experience is interpreted experience. Appreciation for this intellectual dimension of humanness is expressed by Stephan van Erp. Indeed, van Erp suggests a way that Schillebeeckx might have continued to use, rather than abandon, philosophical theology as rooted in Dominique De Petter. Benoît Bourgine agrees with van Erp on this critique of the later Schillebeeckx. Bourgine argues for the use of philosophy and reason in an even wider role than van Erp does. Bourgine underlines the importance of reason and philosophy for theology's dialogue with science, with the political and social order, and with a thoroughly pluralized culture.

(2) Addressing the challenge 'It began with an experience': the experience of faith, tradition, and hermeneutics: Like van Erp and Bourgine, Hans-Joachim Sander also discusses the value and limits of rational grounding. Whether Sander is correct in asserting that belief in an ultimate destiny for the world eliminates incentive to study and improve the world, is subject to dispute. Indeed, Elizabeth Tillar does dispute this point in her symposium contribution. Oliver Davies' hermeneutical retrieval of the tradition of the Ascension promotes renewed faith in this central doctrine

and its implications for regarding Jesus as universal saviour. On this point he not only agrees with Bourgine's insistence on Jesus as universal saviour, but he also brings more specificity to Bourgine's more general assertion. His interpretation of the Ascension calls for grace-filled human action as participation in the salvific work of Jesus Christ.

(3) Addressing the challenge 'The Church with a human face': community, Eucharist, ministry: In her reflection on the full flourishing of the *humanum*, Mary Catherine Hilkert starts with Schillebeeckx's notion of negative contrast experience, and moves to a consideration of his anthropological constants. As she notes, a valuable feature of these anthropological constants is that they provide a possible basis for a reconstituted natural law ethic. Her helpful delineation of components of Creation faith is complemented by her insistence that Christology, soteriology, and anthropology are inseparable. Just as Vincent Miller provides a frank analysis of the U.S. ecclesial situation, Marc Dumas provides a description of the Quebec-Canadian ecclesial situation, which, sadly, amounts to a negative contrast experience at this time. The hope that Hilkert offers for human possibilities in general is found in more specific terms in Dumas' hope for the Church, including hope for a renewed Eucharistic community and a re-energized ministry.

(4) Addressing the challenge 'Extra mundum, nulla salus': History of salvation and eschatology: Elizabeth Tillar calls for a correction to the relative lack of attention to mystical experience, including both positive and negative contrast experiences. Further, Tillar, like Schillebeeckx, insists that the mystical cannot be separated from the political. Hence she affirms that salvation cannot be separated from the experience of the world. Erik Borgman notes that there are two opposing interpretations of the history of salvation and theology. One demands an idealized, seamless continuity in that history. The other, held by Borgman and Schillebeeckx, affirms the inevitability of ruptures and discontinuities in that history, which make responses to cultural shifts necessary, even amidst the *proportional* continuity of the tradition. Which of the two approaches the Church chooses will dramatically impact on the direction the Church takes at this critical time. The second approach will have the Church engage the world as a key component of the salvific process.

b. *Relationality*

(5) Addressing the challenge to theology presented by 21st century understanding of the social role of theology: Vincent Miller provides a coherent defense of Schillebeeckx against charges that he radically separates religion and politics. Miller bases this claim on Schillebeeckx's 'creation faith' and on his sacramental theology. Humans discover God by engaging in public efforts to establish a just social order both within and outside the church.

Miller rehabilitates the centrality of the virtue of prudence in political discernment as a means of avoiding what he helpfully describes as the current U.S. overemphasis on ideological identity and the resulting exclusionisms that are so antithetic to authentic relationality. Jürgen Manemann specifies democracy as an ideal form of this authentic relationality, for which humans should strive. Indeed he regards democracy as a theological value since radical respect for the other needs religion in order to be well grounded. Further, religion can keep democracy from ultimately crushing dissent or destroying the political importance of the individual.

(6) *Addressing the challenge of theologies of, and dialogue among, religions:* Gemma Cruz discusses the features and deficiencies of the once commonly used categories of exclusivism, inclusivism, and pluralism. She has valuable suggestions about what the dialogue between Christianity and Asian religions would look like. Her proposal to incorporate concerns of women and the poor could alleviate possible skepticism about being able to discern cross-cultural themes.

c. Transformationality

(7) *Addressing the challenge to theology presented by modernity and post-modernity:* Frederiek Depoortere presents a portrait of a world so totally dominated by the Enlightenment and science that even faith itself becomes an illusion. Anthony Godzieba portrays humans as entrapped ultimately by the illusion of Enlightenment progress. Thus they are both open to the sheer transforming luxury of God's freeing grace.

(8) *Addressing the challenge of Christology and suffering:* Kathleen McManus and Jean-Louis Souletie highlight the potential of 'negative contrast experiences' to produce salvific transformation through the mediation of Christology. The key concept of the 'negative contrast experience' is focused upon by both McManus and Cruz, who highlight the experience of women and the poor in particular. Souletie emphasizes that the salvific process of transformation includes action undertaken, empowered by Christ.

3. Conclusion

In my concluding remarks at the closing session, I called attention to a cartoon that depicted two fellows down on their luck and sitting on a street corner, each holding a tin cup and wearing a sign. One sign said 'Please help me. I'm an unpaid theologian.' The other fellow's sign said, 'Please help me. I am a *paid* theologian.' Needless to say, we are not in this line of work for the money, fame, and glory. Why then do we go through the rigours of doctoral studies? Why do we plan conferences and journey across oceans to meet with colleagues for a sustained dialogue? Why do we engage in the asceticism of writing, of preparing for public speaking engagements, of teaching – all the while juggling professional commitments with a myriad of personal commitments? We do it because this is our vocation; because this is where our deep passion for learning meets the deep hunger of a troubled world.[7] Indeed, 'the love of learning and the desire for God' have met in a beautiful way at the symposium.[8] When good results are produced, one's vocation is affirmed. Edward Schillebeeckx's extraordinary body of work – and its ongoing relevance – is a tribute to how well he fulfilled his vocation. His legacy has been apparent throughout the work of this symposium. Fulfilling their own vocations, these theologians are confronting challenges to theology in the new millennium, using Schillebeeckx effectively as a resource. As Robert Schreiter pointed out in his particularly insightful response at the closing session, the legacy of Schillebeeckx has been apparent thoughout the work of this symposium. Fulfilling our own vocations as theologians, we are confronting challenges to theology in the new millennium, using Schillebeeckx effectively as a resource.

---

[7] Here I paraphrase Frederick Buechner's definition of vocation: 'The place God calls you to is the place where your deep gladness and the world's deep hunger meet' in his *Wishful Thinking: A Seeker's ABC* (New York, NY: Harper One, 1993) p. 95, first published as *Wishful Thinking: A Theological ABC* (New York, NY: Harper & Row, 1973).

[8] Jean Leclercq, *The Love of Learning and the Desire for God: A Study of Monastic Culture* (New York, NY: Fordham University Press, 1961).

BIBLIOGRAPHY

1. Works by Edward Schillebeeckx

To keep things surveyable, two separate lists are provided here: a list with works of Schillebeeckx in Dutch and a list with works in English. The lists only contain those works which have been cited in the present volume, though, for matters of completeness, the original Dutch version of the works listed in the list with English works has been added to the list with the Dutch works, even when that original version has not been mentioned in the main text. The one book from Schillebeeckx in German that has been cited is added to the list with Dutch works. For a complete bibliography of Schillebeeckx, readers are asked to refer to Ted Mark Schoof and Jan van de Westelaken, *Bibliography 1936–1996 of Edward Schillebeeckx O.P.* (Baarn: Nelissen, 1997). This bibliography was renewed and completed in 2008 and can be downloaded from http://schillebeeckx.nl/documenten/bibliography.pdf.

a. *Works in Dutch*

'Christelijke situatie', *Kultuurleven* 12 (1945), pp. 82–95, 229–42, 585–611.

De sacramentele heilseconomie: Theologische bezinning op St. Thomas' sacramentenleer in het licht van de traditie en van de hedendaagse sacramentsproblematiek (Antwerpen: 't Groeit, 1952).

'Theologie', *Theologisch woordenboek* (vol. 3; Roermond/Maaseik: Romen, 1958), col. 4485–542 (included in: *Openbaring en theologie*, 1964, pp. 71–121; English translation in: *Revelation and Theology*, 1967, pp. 95–183).

Op zoek naar de levende God (Redes uitgesproken aan de Katholieke Universiteit Nijmegen; Utrecht: Dekker en van de Vegt, 1959) (included in: *God en mens*, 1965, pp. 20–35; English translation in: *God and Man*, 1969, pp. 18–40).

Openbaring en theologie (Theologische peilingen, 1; Bilthoven: Nelissen, 1964) (English translation in: *Revelation and Theology*, 1967 and in: *Revelation and Theology II* (US)/*The Concept of Truth and Theological Renewal* (UK/Australia), 1968.

God en mens (Theologische peilingen, 2; Bilthoven: Nelissen, 1965) (English translation: *God and Man*, 1969).

Wereld en kerk (Theologische peilingen, 3; Bilthoven: Nelissen, 1966) (English translation: *World and Church*, 1971).

'Naar een katholiek gebruik van de hermeneutiek: Geloofsidentiteit in het interpreteren van het geloof', *Geloof bij kenterend getij: Peilingen in een seculariserend christendom* (FS Willem Hendrik van de Pol; ed. Hendrik van der Linde and A.M. Fiolet; Roermond: Romen, 1967), pp. 78–116 (included in: *Geloofsverstaan*, 1972, pp. 11–41; English translation in: *God the Future of Man*, 1968, pp. 1–49).

'Zwijgen en spreken over God in een geseculariseerde wereld', *Tijdschrift voor theologie* 7 (1967), pp. 337–59 (English translation in: *God the Future of Man*, 1968, pp. 51–90).

'Het nieuwe Godsbeeld, secularisatie en politiek', *Tijdschrift voor theologie* 8 (1968), pp. 44–66 (English translation in: *God the Future of Man*, 1968, pp. 167–207).

Geloofsverstaan: Interpretatie en kritiek (Theologische Peilingen, 5; Bloemendaal:

Nelissen, 1972) (English translation [without 'Naar een katholiek gebruik van de hermeneutiek', 1967]: *The Understanding of Faith*, 1974).

Jezus, het verhaal van een levende (Bloemendaal: Nelissen, 1974) (English translation: *Jesus*, 1979).

Gerechtigheid en liefde, genade en bevrijding (Bloemendaal: Nelissen, 1977) (English translation: *Christ*, 1980).

Tussentijds verhaal over twee Jezusboeken (Bloemendaal: Nelissen, 1978) (English translation: *Interim Report*, 1980).

'Een nieuwe aarde: Een scheppingsgeloof dat niets wil verklaren', *Evolutie en scheppingsgeloof* (ed. Sjoerd L. Bonting; Baarn: Nelissen, 1978), pp. 167–76.

Kerkelijk ambt: Voorgangers in de gemeente van Jezus Christus (Bloemendaal: Nelissen, 1980/2nd edn: 1981 [marginally adapted]) (English translation of the 1980 edn: *Ministry*, 1981).

Evangelie verhalen (Baarn: Nelissen, 1982) (English translation: *God Among Us*, 1983).

God is ieder ogenblik nieuw: Gesprekken met Edward Schillebeeckx (ed. Huub Oosterhuis and Piet Hoogeveen; Baarn: Ambo, 1982) (English translation: *God is New Each Moment*, 1983).

Theologisch geloofsverstaan anno 1983 (Baarn: Nelissen, 1983) (included as first chapter in: *Mensen als verhaal van God*, 1989; English translation in: *Church: The Human Story of God*, 1990).

'Theologie als bevrijdingskunde', *Tijdschrift voor theologie* 24 (1984), pp. 388–402.

Pleidooi voor mensen in de kerk: Christelijke identiteit en ambten in de kerk (Baarn: Nelissen, 1985) (English translation: *The Church with a Human Face*, 1985).

Als politiek niet alles is... Jezus in onze westerse cultuur: Abraham Kuyper-lezingen 1986 (Baarn: Ten Have, 1986) (English translation: *Jesus in our Western Culture: Mysticism, Ethics and Politics* [in the UK]/*On Christian Faith: The Spiritual, Ethical, and Political Dimensions* [in the US], 1987).

Om het behoud van het evangelie: Evangelie verhalen II (Baarn: Nelissen, 1988) (English translation: *For the Sake of the Gospel*, 1990).

Mensen als verhaal van God (Baarn: Nelissen, 1989) (English translation: *Church*, 1990).

'Terugblik vanuit de tijd na Vaticanum II: De gebroken ideologieën van de moderniteit', *Tussen openheid en isolement: Het voorbeeld van de katholieke theologie in de negentiende eeuw* (ed. Erik Borgman and Anton van Harskamp; Kampen: Kok, 1992), pp. 153–72.

'Verzet, engagement en viering', *Nieuwsbrief Stichting Edward Schillebeeckx* no. 5 (October 1992), pp. 1–3 (unpublished translation by Robert J. Schreiter: 'Resistance, Engagement, and Celebration').

Theologisch testament: Notarieel nog niet verleden (Baarn: Nelissen, 1994).

'Het gezag van de traditie in de theologie', *Jezus, een eigentijds verhaal* (ed. Maurice Bouwens, Jacobine Geel and Frans Maas; Zoetermeer: Meinema, 2001), pp. 76–87.

Ich höre nicht auf, an den lebendigen Gott zu glauben (ed. Francesco Strazzari; trans. Barbara Häussler; Würzburg: Echter, 2006).

b. *Works in English*

Revelation and Theology (trans. N.D. Smith; Theological Soundings 1/1; London/Melbourne: Sheed and Ward, 1967/New York, NY: Sheed and Ward, 1967) (partial translation of *Openbaring en theologie*, 1964).

BIBLIOGRAPHY

God the Future of Man (trans. N.D. Smith; Theological Soundings, 5/1; New York, NY: Sheed and Ward, 1968/London/Sydney: Sheed and Ward, 1969).

Revelation and Theology II (trans. N.D. Smith; Theological Soundings 1/2; New York, NY: Sheed and Ward, 1968).

= *The Concept of Truth and Theological Renewal* (trans. N.D. Smith; Theological Soundings 1/2; London/Sydney: Sheed and Ward, 1968) (partial translation of *Openbaring en theologie*, 1964).

God and Man (trans. Edward Fitzgerald and Peter Tomlinson; Theological Soundings, 2; London/Sydney: Sheed and Ward, 1969/New York, NY: Sheed and Ward, 1969) (Dutch original: *God en mens*, 1965).

World and Church (trans. N.D. Smith; Theological Soundings, 3; London/Sydney: Sheed and Ward, 1971/New York, NY: Sheed and Ward, 1971) (Dutch original: *Wereld en kerk*, 1966).

The Understanding of Faith: Interpretation and Criticism (trans. N.D. Smith; London: Sheed and Ward, 1974/New York, NY: Seabury, 1974) (Dutch original: *Geloofsverstaan*, 1972).

'God, Society and Human Salvation', *Faith and Society/Foi et société/Geloof en maatschappij: Acta Congressus Internationalis Theologici Lovaniensis 1976* (ed. Marc Caudron; BETL, 47; Leuven: Duculot, 1978), pp. 87–99.

Jesus: An Experiment in Christology (trans. Hubert Hoskins; New York, NY: Seabury, 1979/London: Collins, 1979/New York, NY: Crossroad, 1981/New York, NY: Vintage, 1981) (Dutch original: *Jezus, het verhaal van een levende*, 1974).

Christ: The Christian Experience in the Modern World (trans. John Bowden; London: SCM, 1980).

= *Christ: The Experience of Jesus as Lord* (trans. John Bowden; New York, NY: Seabury, 1980/Crossroad, 1981) (Dutch original: *Gerechtigheid en liefde, genade en bevrijding*, 1977).

Interim Report on the Books Jesus & Christ (trans. John Bowden; London: SCM, 1980/New York, NY: Crossroad, 1980) (Dutch original: *Tussentijds verhaal over twee Jezusboeken*, 1978).

Ministry: A Case for Change (trans. John Bowden; London: SCM Press, 1981).

= *Ministry: Leadership in the Community of Jesus Christ* (trans. John Bowden; New York, NY: Crossroad, 1981) (Dutch original: *Kerkelijk ambt*, 1980).

God Among Us: The Gospel Proclaimed (trans. John Bowden; London: SCM, 1983/New York, NY: Crossroad, 1983) (Dutch original: *Evangelie verhalen*, 1982).

God Is New Each Moment (in conversation with Huub Oosterhuis and Piet Hoogeveen; trans. David Smith; Edinburgh: T&T Clark, 1983/New York, NY: Seabury, 1983) (Dutch original: *God is ieder ogenblik nieuw*, 1982).

'Living in Human Society', *The Schillebeeckx Reader* (ed. Robert J. Schreiter; Edinburgh: T&T Clark, 1984/New York, NY: Crossroad, 1984), pp. 45–59.

The Church with a Human Face: A New and Expanded Theology of Ministry (trans. John Bowden; New York, NY: Crossroad, 1985/London: SCM, 1985) (Dutch original: *Pleidooi voor mensen in de kerk*, 1985).

Jesus in our Western Culture: Mysticism, Ethics and Politics (trans. John Bowden; London: SCM, 1987).

= *On Christian Faith: The Spiritual, Ethical, and Political Dimensions* (trans. John Bowden; New York, NY: Crossroad, 1987) (Dutch original: *Als politiek niet alles is...*, 1986).

For the Sake of the Gospel (trans. John Bowden; London: SCM, 1989/New York, NY: Crossroad, 1990) (Dutch original: *Om het behoud van het evangelie*, 1989).

Church: The Human Story of God (trans. John Bowden; New York, NY: Crossroad, 1990/London: SCM, 1990) (Dutch original: *Mensen als verhaal van God*, 1989).

'The Religious and the Human Ecumene', *The Future of Liberation Theology: Essays in Honor of Gustavo Gutiérrez* (Maryknoll, NY: Orbis, 1989) (included in: *The Language of Faith*, 1995, pp. 249–64).

The Language of Faith: Essays on Jesus, Theology and the Church (intr. Robert J. Schreiter; Concilium Series; Maryknoll, NY: Orbis/London: SCM, 1995).

'Documentation: Religion and Violence', *Religion as a Source of Violence* (ed. Wim Beuken and Karl-Josef Kuschel; Concilium, 1997/4; Maryknoll, NY: Orbis/London: SCM, 1997), pp. 129–42.

'The Uniqueness of Christ and the Interreligious Dialogue', A lecture delivered on April 22, 1997 at the Catholic Academy in Munich, Bavaria, unpublished manuscript.

'Prologue: Human God-Talk and God's Silence', *The Praxis of the Reign of God: An Introduction to the Theology of Edward Schillebeeckx* (ed. Mary Catherine Hilkert and Robert J. Schreiter; New York, NY: Fordham University Press, 2nd edn, 2002), pp. ix–xviii.

2. Works on Edward Schillebeeckx

The following list of works on Edward Schillebeeckx contains those works on Schillebeeckx which have been cited in the present volume. Next to these, a number of publications on Schillebeeckx by contributors to the present volume has been added here, even when they are not cited in the main text. Finally, also a number of publications by other Schillebeeckx-scholars which were considered, either by participants to the symposium or by Ted Mark Schoof, to be key-texts for Schillebeeckx-scholarship have been added. For a much more complete bibliography of secondary works on Schillebeeckx readers are asked to refer to http://schillebeeckx.nl/documenten/bibliography_secundair.pdf.

Auwerda, Richard, *Dossier Schillebeeckx: Theoloog in de kerk der conflicten* (Bilthoven: Nelissen, 1969).

—— *Dossier Schillebeeckx* (trans. Paul Bourgy; Études religieuses, 787; Bruxelles: CEP/Print: Soledi (Liège), 1970).

van Bavel, Tarsicius Jan, 'Hermeneutische knelpunten in een theologisch dispuut', *Tijdschrift voor theologie* 20 (1980), pp. 340–60.

Boeve, Lieven, 'L'interruption sacramentelle des rites d'existence', *Questions liturgiques: Studies in Liturgy* 83 (2002), pp. 30–51.

—— 'The Sacramental Interruption of Rituals of Life', *Heythrop Journal* 44 (2003), pp. 401–17.

—— 'Experience according to Edward Schillebeeckx: The Driving Force of Faith and Theology', *Divinising Experience: Essays in the History of Religious Experience from Origen to Ricoeur* (ed. Lieven Boeve and Laurence Paul Hemming; Studies in Philosophical Theology, 23; Leuven: Peeters, 2004), pp. 199–225.

Borgman, Erik, 'Theologie tussen universiteit en emancipatie: De weg van Edward Schillebeeckx', *Tijdschrift voor theologie* 26 (1986), pp. 240–58.

—— 'Op zoek naar Maria... en verder! Schillebeeckx' mariologie en haar actuele betekenis', *Tijdschrift voor theologie* 33 (1993), pp. 241–66.

—— 'Van cultuurtheologie naar theologie als onderdeel van de cultuur: De toekomst van het theologisch project van Edward Schillebeeckx', *Tijdschrift voor theologie* 34 (1994), pp. 335–60.

—— *Edward Schillebeeckx: Een theoloog in zijn geschiedenis. Deel 1: Een katholieke cultuurtheologie (1914–1965)* (Baarn: Nelissen, 1999).

—— 'La teolofa de Edward Schillebeeckx como un arte liberador', *Aternativas: Revista de análisis y reflexión teolólogica* 7/15 (2000), pp. 149–58.

—— 'Theology as the Art of Liberation: Edward Schillebeeckx's Response to the Third World Theologians', *Exchange* 32/2 (2003), pp. 98–108.

—— *Edward Schillebeeckx: A Theologian in His History. Volume 1: A Catholic Theology of Culture (1914–1965)* (trans. John Bowden; London/New York, NY: Continuum, 2004).

—— 'Deus humanissimus? Christelijk geloof bij Edward Schillebeeckx als excessief humanisme', *Humanisme en religie: Controverses, bruggen, perspectieven* (ed. J. Duyndam, M. Poorthuis and Th. de Wit, Delft: Eburon 2005), pp. 229–46.

—— 'Openheid voor de sporen van de God van heil: Edward Schillebeeckx over dominicaanse identiteit', *Ons rakelings nabij: Gedaantevaranderingen van God en geloof, ter ere van Edward Schillebeeckx* (ed. M. Kalsky *et al.*; Zoetermeer: Meinema, 2005), pp. 58–72.

—— 'The Ambivalent Role of the "People of God" in Twentieth Century Catholic Theology: The Examples of Yves Congar and Edward Schillebeeckx', *A Holy People: Jewish and Christian Perspectives on Religious Communal Identity* (ed. M. Poorthuis and J. Schwarz; Leiden/Boston: Brill, 2006), pp. 263–77.

—— 'Edward Schillebeeckx: een kritische cultuurtheoloog', *Toptheologen: Hoofdfiguren uit de theologie van vandaag* (ed. Josephus B.M. Wissink; Tielt: Lannoo, 2006), pp. 66–87.

Bowden, John, *Edward Schillebeeckx: Portrait of a Theologian* (London: SCM, 1983).

Callewaert, Janet M., 'Salvation from God in Jesus the Christ: Soteriology', *The Praxis of Christian Experience: An Introduction to the Theology of Edward Schillebeeckx* (ed. Robert J. Schreiter and Mary Catherine Hilkert; San Francisco, CA: Harper and Row, 1989), pp. 68–85.

Chia, Edmund, 'Towards a Theology of Dialogue: Schillebeeckx's Method as Bridge between Vatican's Dominus Iesus and Asia's FABC Theology' (unpublished doctoral dissertation, University of Nijmegen, 2003).

D'hert, Ignace, *Een spoor voor ons getrokken: De Jezustrilogie van Edward Schillebeeckx* (Baarn: Nelissen, 1997).

Dumas, Marc, 'Expériences et discours théologiques', *Laval théologique et philosophique* 56/1 (2000), pp. 3–15.

—— 'Corrélation: Tillich et Schillebeeckx', *Précis de théologie pratique* (ed. Gilles Routhier and Marcel Viau; Bruxelles: Lumen Vitae/Ottawa: Novalis, 2004), pp. 71–83.

—— 'Corrélations d'expériences?', *Laval théologique et philosophique* 60/2 (2004), pp. 317–34.

Dupré, Louis, 'Experience and Interpretation: A Philosophical Reflection on Schillebeeckx' *Jesus* and *Christ*', *Theological Studies* 43 (1982), pp. 30–51.

Fackre, Gabriel J., 'Bones Strong and Weak in the Skeletal Structure of Schillebeeckx's Christology', *Journal of Ecumenical Studies* 21/2 (1984), pp. 248–77.

George, William P., 'The Praxis of the Kingdom of God: Ethics in Schillebeeck' *Jesus* and *Christ*', *Horizons* 12/1 (1985), pp. 44–69.

Häring, Hermann, 'Verlossing – ondanks Jezus' lijden en dood?', *Meedenken met Edward Schillebeeckx: Bij zijn afscheid als hoogleraar te Nijmegen* (ed. Hermann Häring, Ted M. Schoof and Boniface Ad Willems; Bloemendaal: Nelissen, 1983), pp. 171–87.

—— 'Met mensen op weg, voor mensen op weg: Over het theologisch denken van Edward Schillebeeckx', *Mensen maken de kerk: Verslag van het symposium gehouden op 11 november 1989 bij gelegenheid van de 75^e verjaardag van Edward Schillebeeckx* (ed. Huub ter Haar; Baarn: Nelissen, 1989), pp. 27–46.

—— 'God – "puur verrassing": Edward Schillebeeckx' doorbraak naar een nieuwe theologie', *Tijdschrift voor theologie* 45 (2005), pp. 13–32.

Hilkert, Mary Catherine, 'Towards a Theology of Proclamation: Edward Schillebeeckx's Hermeneutics of Tradition as a Foundation for a Theology of Proclamation' (unpublished doctoral dissertation, Catholic University of America, 1984).

—— 'Hermeneutics of History in the Theology of Edward Schillebeeckx', *The Thomist* 51 (1987), pp. 97–145.

—— '"Grace-Optimism": The Spirituality at the Heart of Edward Schillebeeckx's Theology', *Spirituality Today* 43 (1991), pp. 220–39.

—— 'Edward Schillebeeckx', *A New Handbook of Christian Theologians* (ed. Donald W. Musser and Joseph L. Price; Nashville, TN: Abingdon Press, 1996), pp. 411–18.

—— 'Edward Schillebeeckx, O.P. (1914–): Encountering God in a Secular and Suffering World', *Theology Today* 62 (2005), pp. 1–12.

—— 'Discovery of the Living God: Revelation and Experience', *The Praxis of Christian Experience: An Introduction to the Theology of Edward Schillebeeckx* (ed. Robert J. Schreiter and Mary Catherine Hilkert; San Francisco, CA: Harper & Row, 1989), pp. 35–51.

—— 'Experience and Revelation', *The Praxis of the Reign of God: An Introduction to the Theology of Edward Schillebeeckx* (ed. Robert J. Schreiter and Mary Catherine Hilkert; New York, NY: Fordham University Press, 2nd edn, 2002).

Hilkert, Mary Catherine, and Robert J. Schreiter (eds), *The Praxis of Christian Experience: An Introduction to the Theology of Edward Schillebeeckx* (San Francisco, CA: Harper & Row, 1989).

—— *The Praxis of the Reign of God: An Introduction to the Theology of Edward Schillebeeckx* (New York, NY: Fordham University Press, 2nd edn, 2002).

van Iersel, Bas, 'Van bijbelse theologie naar bijbelse theologen: Is het einde van een klein schisma in zicht?', *Meedenken met Edward Schillebeeckx: Bij zijn afscheid als hoogleraar te Nijmegen* (ed. Hermann Häring, Ted M. Schoof and Boniface Ad Willems; Bloemendaal: Nelissen, 1983), pp. 54–68.

Iwashima, Tadahiko, *Menschheitsgeschichte und Heilserfahrung: Die Theologie von Edward Schillebeeckx als methodisch reflektierte Soteriologie* (Themen und Thesen der Theologie; Düsseldorf: Patmos, 1982).

Kennedy, Philip, *Schillebeeckx* (Outstanding Christian Thinkers; Collegeville, MN: Liturgical Press, 1993).

—— *Edward Schillebeeckx: Die Geschichte von der Menschlichkeit Gottes* (Mainz: Grünewald, 1994).

—— *Deus Humanissimus: The Knowability of God in the Theology of Edward Schillebeeckx* (Ökumenische Beihefte zur Freiburger Zeitschrift für Philosophie und Theologie, 22; Fribourg: Universitäts-Verlag, 1993).

—— 'God and Creation', *The Praxis of the Reign of God: An Introduction to the Theology of Edward Schillebeeckx* (ed. Mary Catherine Hilkert and Robert J. Schreiter; New York, NY: Fordham University Press, 2nd edn, 2002), pp. 37–58.

McManus, Kathleen, 'The Place and Meaning of Suffering in the Theology of Edward Schillebeeckx' (unpublished doctoral dissertation, Toronto, 1999).

—— 'Suffering in the Theology of Edward Schillebeeckx', *Theological Studies* 60 (1999), pp. 476–91.

—— *Unbroken Communion: The Place and Meaning of Suffering in the Theology of Edward Schillebeeckx* (Lanham, MD: Rowman & Littlefield, 2003).

—— 'Embracing Life, Embracing the Cross: Edward Schillebeeckx and Suffering', *The Way* 44/1 (2005), pp. 61–73.

—— 'Edward Schillebeecckx: The Making of a Theological Vocation', *Doctrine & Life* 55/3 (2005), pp. 23–31.

—— 'Reconciling the Cross in the Theologies of Edward Schillebeeckx and Ivone Gebara', *Theological Studies* 66 (2005), pp. 638–50.

Portier, William, 'Interpretation and Method', *The Praxis of Christian Experience: An Introduction to the Theology of Edward Schillebeeckx* (ed. Robert J. Schreiter and Mary Catherine Hilkert; San Francisco, CA: Harper & Row, 1989), pp. 18–34.

Rego, Aloysius, 'Suffering and Salvation: The Salvific Meaning of Suffering in the Later Theology of Edward Schillebeeckx' (unpublished doctoral dissertation, Melbourne, 2001).

—— *Suffering and Salvation: The Salvific Meaning of Suffering in the Later Theology of Edward Schillebeeckx* (Louvain Theological and Pastoral Monographs, 33; Leuven: Peeters, 2006).

Schoof, Ted Mark (ed. and intr.), *De zaak Schillebeeckx: Officiële stukken* (Bloemendaal: Nelissen, 1980).

—— *The Schillebeeckx Case: Official Exchange of Letters and Documents in the Investigation of Fr. Edward Schillebeeckx, O.P. by the Sacred Congregation for the Doctrine of the Faith, 1976–1980* (trans. Matthew J. O'Connell; New York, NY: Paulist, 1984).

Schoof, Ted Mark, '"... een bijna koortsachtige aandrang...": Schillebeeckx 25 jaar theoloog in Nijmegen', *Meedenken met Edward Schillebeeckx: Bij zijn afscheid als hoogleraar te Nijmegen* (ed. Hermann Häring, Ted M. Schoof and Boniface Ad Willems; Bloemendaal: Nelissen, 1983), pp. 11–39.

—— 'E. Schillebeeckx: 25 Years in Nijmegen', *Theology Digest* 37 (1990), pp. 313–331; 38 (1991), pp. 31–44.

—— 'In de verdediging voor mensen in de kerk', *Tijdschrift voor geestelijk leven* 65/1 (2009), pp. 127–37.

Schreiter, Robert J., 'Edward Schillebeeckx: An Orientation to His Thought', *The Schillebeeckx Reader* (Edinburgh: T&T Clark, 1984/New York, NY: Crossroad, 1984), pp. 1–24.

—— 'Edward Schillebeeckx', *A Handbook of Christian Theologians* (ed. D.G. Peerman and M.E. Marty; Nashville, TN: Abingdon 1985), pp. 625–38.

—— 'Edward Schillebeeckx', *The Modern Theologians: An Introduction to Christian Theology in the Twentieth Century* (ed. David F. Ford; Oxford/Cambridge: Blackwell, 2nd edn, 1997), pp. 152–61.

—— 'Edward Schillebeeckx: His Enduring Relevance', *The Praxis of Christian Experience: An Introduction to the Theology of Edward Schillebeeckx* (ed. Robert J. Schreiter and Mary Catherine Hilkert; San Francisco, CA: Harper & Row, 1989), pp. 147–55.

—— 'Edward Schillebeeckx: His Continuing Significance', *The Praxis of the Reign of God: An Introduction to the Theology of Edward Schillebeeckx* (ed. Mary Catherine Hilkert and Robert J. Schreiter; New York, NY: Fordham University Press, 2nd edn, 2002), pp. 185–94.

Schreiter, Robert J. (ed.), *The Schillebeeckx Reader* (Edinburgh: T&T Clark, 1984/ New York, NY: Crossroad, 1984).

Schreiter, Robert J. and Mary Catherine Hilkert (eds.), *The Praxis of Christian Experience: An Introduction to the Theology of Edward Schillebeeckx* (San Francisco, CA: Harper & Row, 1989).

—— *The Praxis of the Reign of God: An Introduction to the Theology of Edward Schillebeeckx* (New York, NY: Fordham University Press, 2nd edn, 2002).

Simon, Derek J., 'Provisional Liberations, Fragments of Salvation: The Practical Critical Soteriology of Edward Schillebeeckx' (unpublished doctoral dissertation, Ottawa, 2001).

—— 'Salvation and Liberation in the Practical-Critical Soteriology of Schillebeeckx', *Theological Studies* 63 (2002), pp. 494–520.

Sison, Antonio, 'Political Holiness in Third Cinema: The Crystallization of Edward Schillebeeckx's Eschatological Perspective in Kidlat Tahimik's "The Perfumed Nightmare"' (unpublished doctoral dissertation, Nijmegen, 2004).

—— *Screening Schillebeeckx: Theology and Third Cinema in Dialogue* (New York, NY: Palgrave Macmillan, 2006).

Swidler, Leonard, and Piet F. Fransen, *Authority in the Church and the Schillebeeckx Case* (New York, NY: Crossroad, 1982).

Thompson, Daniel Speed, *The Language of Dissent: Edward Schillebeeckx on the Crisis of Authority in the Catholic Church* (Notre Dame, IN: University of Notre Dame Press, 1993).

Tillar, Elizabeth K., 'Suffering for Others in the Theology of Edward Schillebeeckx' (unpublished doctoral dissertation, Fordham University, 2000).

—— 'The Influence of Social Critical Theory on Edward Schillebeeckx's Theology of Suffering for Others', *The Heythrop Journal* 42/2 (2001), pp. 148–72.

—— 'Eschatological Images of Prophet and Priest in Edward Schillebeeckx's Theology of Suffering for Others', *The Heythrop Journal* 43/1 (2002), pp. 34–59.

—— 'Critical Remembrance and Eschatological Hope in Edward Schillebeeckx's Theology of Suffering for Others', *The Heythrop Journal* 44/1 (2003), pp. 15–42.

Van de Walle, Ambroos R., 'Theologie over de werkelijkheid: Een betekenis van het werk van Edward Schillebeeckx', *Tijdschrift voor theologie* 14 (1974), pp. 463–90.

Willems, Boniface Ad, 'Die endlose Geschichte des Edward Schillebeeckx', *Katholische Kirche, Wohin? Wider den Verrat am Konzil* (ed. Norbert Greinacher and Hans Küng; Serie Piper, 488; München/Zürich 1986), pp. 411–23.

—— 'The Endless Case of Edward Schillebeeckx', *The Church in Anguish: Has the Vatican Betrayed Vatican II?* (ed. Hans Küng and Leonard Swidler; San Francisco, CA: Harper & Row, 1987), pp. 212–22.

3. *Other Works Cited*

Adorno, Theodor, *Negative Dialectics* (trans. E.B. Ashton; New York, NY: Continuum, 2nd edn, 1982).

Agamben, Giorgio, *The Time That Remains: A Commentary on the Letter to the Romans* (trans. Patricia Dailey; Meridian: Crossing Aesthetics; Standford, CA: Stanford University Press, 2005).

Albright, Carol Rausch, 'Neuroscience in Pursuit of the Holy: Mysticism, the Brain, and Ultimate Reality', *Zygon* 36/3 (2001), pp. 485–92.

Albus, Michael, 'Geist und Feuer: Ein Gesprach mit Hans Urs Von Balthasar', *Herder Korrespondenz* 30 (1976), pp. 72–82.

Aliseda, Atocha, *Abductive Reasoning: Logical Investigations into Discovery and Explanation* (Berlin: Springer, 2006).

Alway, Joan, *Critical Theory and Political Possibilities: Conceptions of Emancipatory Politics in the Works of Horkheimer, Adorno, Marcuse, and Habermas* (Contributions in Sociology, 111; Westport, CT: Greenwood Press, 1995).

Amaladoss, Michael, 'The Church and Pluralism in the Asia of the 1990s', *FABC Papers No. 57e* (Hong Kong: FABC, 1990).

Appadurai, Arjun, *Modernity at Large: Cultural Dimensions of Globalization* (Minneapolis, MN: University of Minnesota Press, 1996).

d'Aquili, Eugene G., and Andrew B. Newberg, 'The Neuropsychology of Aesthetic, Spiritual, and Mystical States', *Zygon* 35/1 (2000), pp. 39–51.

de Araujo, Fabio Ribeiro, *Prophezeiungen über das Ende der Welt: Die Apokalypse und ein neuer Anfang* (Rottenburg: Kopp, 2009).

d'Arcais, P. Flores, 'Ist Amerika noch eine Demokratie?', *Die Zeit*, 20 January 2005.

Arendt, Hannah, *Was ist Politik? Fragmente aus dem Nachlaß* (ed. Ursula Ludz; intr. Kurt Sontheimer; München/Zürich: Piper, 1993).

—— *The Human Condition* (Chicago, IL: Chicago University Press, 2nd edn, 1998).

Arens, Edmund, *Gottesverständigung: Eine kommunikative Religionstheologie* (Freiburg: Herder, 2007).

Azari, Nina P., 'Georges Bataille: A Theoretical Resource for Scientific Investigation of Religious Experience', *Journal for Cultural and Religious Theory* 4/3 (2003), pp. 27–41.

Badiou, Alain, *Saint Paul: The Foundation of Universalism* (trans. Ray Brassier; Cultural Memory in the Present; Standford, CA: Standford University Press, 2003).

Bakhtin, M.M., *Towards a Philosophy of the Act* (trans. and notes Vadim Lapiunov; ed. Michael Holquist and Vadim Liapunov; Austin, TX: Texas University Press, 1993).

von Balthasar, Hans Urs, *The Moment of Christian Witness* [1966] (San Francisco, CA: Ignatius, 1994).

Barron, Robert, *The Priority of Christ: Toward a Postliberal Catholicism* (Grand Rapids, MI: Brazos Press, 2007).

Barth, Karl, *The Word of God and the Word of Man* (trans. Douglas Horton; New York, NY: Harper and Brothers, 1957).

Bauerschmidt, Frederick C., 'The Politics of Disenchantment', *New Blackfriars* 82 (2001), pp. 313–34.

Bauman, Zygmunt, *Liquid Modernity* (Cambridge: Polity Press, 2000).

Beaudin, Michel, and Anne Fortin, 'Lectures et relectures inconclusives', *Des théologies en mutation: Parcours et trajectoires* (ed. Michel Beaudin, Anne Fortin and Ramon Martinez de Pison; Héritage et projet, 65; Montréal: Fides, 2002), pp. 391–411.

Beck, Ulrich, *Die Erfindung des Politischen: Zu einer Theorie reflexiver Modernisierung* (Frankfurt a.M.: Suhrkamp, 1993).

Beinert, Wolfgang, 'Faith', *Handbook of Catholic Theology* (ed. Wolfgang Beinert and Francis Schüssler Fiorenza; New York, NY: Crossroad, 1995), pp. 249–53.

Berger, Peter L., *The Desecularization of the World: Resurgent Religion and World Politics* (Grand Rapids, MI: Eerdmans, 1999).

Bloechl, Jeffrey D., *Religious Experience and the End of Metaphysics* (The Indiana Series in the Philosophy of Religion; Bloomington IN: Indiana University Press, 2003).

Blondel, Maurice, *Action* [1893] (trans. Oliva Blanchette; Notre Dame, IN: Notre Dame University Press, 1984).

—— *The Letter on Apologetics and History and Dogma* (ed. and trans. Alexander Dru and Illtyd Trethowan; Grand Rapids, MI: Eerdmans, 1994).

Böckenförde, Ernst-Wolfgang, 'Was heißt heute eigentlich "politisch"?', *Demokratiefähigkeit* (ed. Jürgen Manemann; Jahrbuch Politische Theologie, 1; Münster: LIT, 1995), pp. 2–5.

—— 'Staat, Gesellschaft, Freiheit', *Recht, Staat, Freiheit: Studien zur Rechtsphilosophie, Staatstheorie und Verfassungsgeschichte* (Frankfurt a.M.: Suhrkamp, 2006), pp. 92–114.

Boeve, Lieven, 'Schatbewaarder en spoorzoeker: het één niet zonder het ander', *Jezus, een eigentijds verhaal* (ed. Maurice Bouwens, Jacobine Geel and Frans Maas; Zoetermeer: Meinema, 2001), pp. 87–91.

—— *Interrupting Tradition: An Essay on Christian Faith in a Postmodern Context* (Louvain Theological and Pastoral Monographs, 30; Leuven: Peeters/Grand Rapids, MI: Eerdmans, 2003).

—— *God Interrupts History: Theology in a Time of Upheaval* (New York, NY: Continuum, 2007).

—— 'Theological Truth, Particularity and Incarnation: Engaging Religious Plurality and Radical Hermeneutics', *Orthodoxy: Process and Product* (ed. Mathijs Lamberigts, Lieven Boeve and Terrence Merrigan; BETL, 227; Leuven: Peeters, 2009), pp. 323–48.

Boeve, Lieven, Mathijs Lamberigts and Maarten Wisse (eds), *Augustine and Postmodern Thought: A New Alliance Against Modernity?* (BETL, 219; Leuven: Peeters, 2009).

Borgman, Erik, *Sporen van een bevrijdende God: Universitaire theologie in aansluiting op Latijnsamerikaanse bevrijdingstheologie, zwarte theologie en feministische theologie* (Kerk en theologie in context, 7; Kampen: Kok, 1990).

—— *Alexamenos aanbidt zijn God: Theologische essays voor sceptische lezers* (Zoetermeer: De Horstink, 1994).

—— 'Gods gedaanteverandering: De metamorfosen van de religie en hun theologische betekenis', *Tijdschrift voor theologie* 44 (2004), pp. 45–66.

—— '*Gaudium et spes*: The Forgotten Future of a Revolutionary Document', *Vatican II: A Forgotten Future?* (ed. Alberto Melloni and Christoph Theobald; Concilium, 2005/4; London: SCM, 2005), pp. 48–56.

—— *Metamorfosen: Over religie en moderne cultuur* (Kampen: Klement, 2006).

—— *... want de plaats waarop je staat is heilige grond: God als onderzoeksprogramma* (Amsterdam: Boom, 2008).

Bourdieu, Pierre, *Distinction: A Social Critique of the Judgement of Taste* (trans. Richard Nice; Cambridge, MA: Harvard University Press, 1984).

—— et al., *The Weight of the World: Social Suffering in Contemporary Society* (trans. Priscilla Parkhurst Ferguson; Cambridge: Polity Press, 1999).

Bourgine, Benoît, review of *Creazione ed evoluzione*, by Stephan Otto Horn and Siegried Widenhofer (eds), *Revue théologique de Louvain* 39 (2008), pp. 549–51.

—— 'Saint Paul et la philosophie: Crise du multiculturalisme et universel chrétien', *Revue théologique de Louvain* 40 (2009), pp. 78–94.

Bradshaw, Brendan, 'Transalpine Humanism', *The Cambridge History of Political Thought 1450–1700* (ed. James Henderson Burns and Mark Goldie; repr., Cambridge: Cambridge University Press, 2004), pp. 95–131.

Breton, Stanislas, *Saint Paul* (Coll. Philosophies; Paris: PUF, 1988).

Browning, Don S., *A Fundamental Practical Theology: Descriptive and Strategic Proposals* (Minneapolis, MN: Fortress, 1991).

Buechner, Frederick, *Wishful Thinking: A Theological ABC* (New York, NY: Harper & Row, 1973).

—— *Wishful Thinking: A Seeker's ABC* (New York, NY: Harper One, 1993).

Cahill, Lisa Sowle, 'Feminist Ethics, Differences, and Common Ground: A Catholic Perspective', *Feminist Ethics and the Catholic Moral Tradition* (ed. Charles E. Curran, Margaret A. Farley and Richard A. McCormick; New York, NY: Paulist, 1996), pp. 184–204.

Caputo, John D., *Philosophy and Theology* (Nashville, TN: Abingdon, 2006).

Casanova, José, *Public Religions in the Modern World* (Chicago, IL: University of Chicago Press, 1994).

de Certeau, Michel, 'La misère de la théologie', *La faiblesse de croire* (ed. Luce Giard; Esprit; Paris: Seuil, 1987), pp. 253–63.

Chaput, Charles J., *Render Unto Caesar: Catholic Witness and American Public Life* (New York, NY: Doubleday, 2008).

Chia, Edmund, 'Dialogue with Religions of Asia: Challenges from Within (1) (Part II)', http://www.sedos.org/english/within_chia.html (accessed on 24 November 2008).

Chowers, Eyal, *The Modern Self in the Labyrinth: Politics and the Entrapment Imagination* (Cambridge, MA: Harvard University Press, 2004).

Coleman, John A., *The Evolution of Dutch Catholicism, 1958–1974* (Berkeley, CA: University of California Press, 1978).

Colombo, J.A., *An Essay on Theology and History: Studies in Pannenberg, Metz, and the Frankfurt School* (Atlanta, GA: Scholars Press, 1990).

Copeland, M. Shawn, 'The New Anthropological Subject at the Heart of the Mystical Body of Christ', *Proceedings of the Catholic Theological Society of America* 53 (1998), pp. 25–47.

Culbertson, Roberta A., 'War and the Nature of Ultimate Things: An Essay on Postwar Cultures', *Engaged Observer: Anthropology, Advocacy, and Activism* (ed. Victoria Sanford and Asale Angel-Ajani; New Brunswick, NJ: Rutgers University Press, 2006), pp. 60–75.

Curtis, William A., 'Orthodoxy', *Encyclopedia of Religion and Ethics* (vol. 9; Edinburgh, 1917), pp. 570–72.

Dalferth, Ingolf Ulrich, *Theology and Philosophy* (repr., Eugene, OR: Wipf & Stock, 2001).

Davie, Grace, *Religion in Modern Europe: A Memory Mutates* (Oxford: Oxford University Press, 2000).

Davies, Oliver, *The Creativity of God: World, Eucharist, Reason* (Cambridge: Cambridge University Press, 2004).

Davies, Oliver, Paul Janz and Clemens Sedmak, *Transformation Theology: Church in the World* (London/New York, NY: T&T Clark, 2007).

Davison, Anne, 'Learning to Live in a Europe of Many Religions: A Curriculum for Interfaith Learning for Women', World Council of Churches (2000), http://www.wcc-coe.org/wcc/what/interreligious/cd35–18html (accessed on 3 September, 2005).

Dawkins, Richard, *The God Delusion* (London: Bantam Press, 2006/New York, NY: Houghton Mifflin Harcourt, 2006).

Dean, Stanley R., 'Beyond the Unconscious: The Ultraconscious', *American Journal of Psychiatry* 122 (1965), p. 471.

—— 'Is There an Ultraconscious Beyond the Unconscious?', *Canadian Psychiatric Association Journal* 15 (1970), pp. 57–62.

—— 'Metapsychiatry and the Ultraconscious', Letters to the Editor, *American Journal of Psychiatry* 128 (1971), pp. 662–63.

Dennett, Daniel C., *Breaking the Spell: Religion as a Natural Phenomenon* (New York, NY: Penguin, 2005).

De Petter, Dominicus Maria, 'Impliciete intuïtie', *Tijdschrift voor Philosophie* 1 (1939), pp. 84–105.

Derrida, Jacques, *Adieu to Emmanuel Levinas* (trans. Pascale-Anne Brault and Michael Naas; Meridian: Crossing Aesthetics; Palo Alto, CA: Standford University Press, 1999).

Deuser, Hermann (ed.), *Metaphysik und Religion: Die Wiederentdeckung eines Zusammenhanges* (Veröffentlichungen der Wissenschaftlichen Gesellschaft für Theologie; Gütersloh: Gütersloher Verlagshaus, 2007).

Dobzhansky, Theodosius, 'Nothing in Biology Makes Sense Except in the Light of Evolution', *The American Biology Teacher* 35 (1973), pp. 125–29.

Donneaud, Henry, 'Chalcédoine contre l'unicité absolue du Médiateur Jésus-Christ? Autour d'un article récent', *Revue thomiste* 102/1 (2002), pp. 43–62.

Doré, Joseph, 'La présence du Christ dans les religions non-chrétiennes', *In Chemins de dialogue* no. 9 (1997), pp. 13–50.

D' Souza, Diane, 'Inter-faith Dialogue: New Insights from Women's Perspectives', *Ecclesia of Women in Asia: Gathering the Voices of the Silenced* (ed. Evelyn Monteiro and Antoinette Gutzler; Delhi: ISPCK, 2005).

Dubiel, Helmut, *Ungewißheit und Politik* (Frankfurt a.M.: Suhrkamp, 1994).

Dumeige, Gervais (ed. and trans.), *Textes doctrinaux du Magistère de l'Eglise sur la foi catholique* (Paris: Editions de l'Orante, 1975).

Dupont, Jacques, *Essais sur la christologie de Saint Jean: Le Christ, Parole, Lumière et Vie, la Gloire du Christ* (Bruges: Editions de l'Abbaye de Saint-André, 1951).

Dupuis, Jacques, *Who Do You Say I Am? Introduction to Christology* (Maryknoll, NY: Orbis, 1994).

—— *Toward a Christian Theology of Religious Pluralism* (Maryknoll, NY: Orbis, 1997).

—— *Christianity and the Religions: From Confrontation to Dialogue* (New York, NY: Orbis, 2001).

—— 'Le Verbe de Dieu, Jésus Christ et les religions du monde', *Nouvelle revue théologique* 123/4 (2001), pp. 529–46.

Eck, Diana, *A New Religious America: How a 'Christian Country' Has Become the World's Most Religiously Diverse Nation* (San Francisco, CA: Harper One, 2002).

Eckhart, Meister, *Traités et sermons* (trans. F.A. and J.M.; intr. M. de Gandillac; Philosophie de l'esprit; Paris: Aubier, 1942).

Falque, Emmanuel, *Dieu, la chair et l'autre: D'Irénée à Duns Scot* (Paris: PUF, 2008).

Farley, Margaret A., 'Feminism and Universal Morality', *Prospects for a Common Morality* (ed. Gene Outka and John P. Reide, Jr.; Princeton, NJ: Princeton University Press, 1993), pp. 170–90.

—— *Just Love* (New York, NY: Continuum, 2006).

Farrow, Douglas, *Ascension and Ecclesia* (Edinburgh: T&T Clark, 1999).

Featherstone, Mike, *Consumer Culture and Postmodernism* (London: Sage, 1991).

Federation of Asian Bishop's Conferences, *For All the Peoples of Asia* (4 vols., Quezon City: Claretian, 1997/1997/2002/2007).

Finkielkraut, Alain, *The Wisdom of Love* (trans. Kevin O'Neil and David Suchoff; intr. David Suchoff; Texts and Contexts, 20; Lincoln, NE: University of Nebraska Press, 1997).

Flew, Antony, R.M. Hare and Basil Mitchell, 'Theology and Falsification', *New Essays in Philosophical Theology* (ed. Antony Flew and Alasdair MacIntyre; 7th impression, London: SCM, 1969), pp. 96–130.

—— 'Theology and Falsification: A Symposium', *The Philosophy of Religion* (ed. Basil Mitchell; Oxford Readings in Philosophy; Oxford: Oxford University Press, 1971), pp. 13–22.

Foucault, Michel, 'Des espaces autres', *Dits et écrits. II: 1976–1988* (Paris: Gallimard, 2001), pp. 1571–81.

—— *Die Heterotopien/Der utopische Körper: Zwei Radiovorträge* (Frankfurt a.M.: Suhrkamp, 2005).

Fox, Thomas C., *Pentecost in Asia: A New Way of Being Church* (New York, NY: Orbis, 2002).

Frankl, Viktor, *Man's Search for Meaning* (Boston, MA: Beacon, 1963).

Gabriel, Karl, 'Religion und Kirche im Spiegel- und Diskursmodell von Öffentlichkeit', *Glaube und Öffentlichkeit* (ed. Ingo Baldermann *et al.*; Jahrbuch für Biblische Theologie, 11; Neukirchen-Vluyn: Neukirchen, 1996), pp. 31–51.

García-Rivera, Alejandro, *The Community of the Beautiful* (Collegeville, MN: Liturgical Press, 1999).

Gauchet, Marcel, *Le désenchantement du monde: Une histoire politique de la religion* (Paris: Gallimard, 1985).

—— *The Disenchantment of the World: A Political History of Religion* (trans. Oscar Burge; intr. Charles Taylor; New French Thought; 1st pb. print, Princeton, NJ: Princeton University Press, 1999).

Gebara, Ivone, *Longing for Running Water: Ecofeminism and Liberation* (Minneapolis, MN: Fortress, 1999).

—— *Out of the Depths: Women's Experience of Evil and Salvation* (Minneapolis, MN: Fortress, 2002).

Geffré, Claude, *Croire et interpréter: Le tournant herméneutique de la théologie* (Paris: Cerf, 2001).

Godzieba, Anthony J., 'As Much Contingency, As Much Incarnation', *Religious Experience and Contemporary Theological Epistemology* (ed. Lieven Boeve, Yves De Maeseneer and Stijn Van den Bossche; BETL, 188; Leuven: Peeters, 2005), pp. 83–90.

—— 'Knowing Differently: Incarnation, Imagination, and the Body', *Louvain Studies* 32 (2007), pp. 361–82.

—— '"Refuge of Sinners, Pray for Us": Augustine, Aquinas, and the Salvation of Modernity', *Augustine and Postmodern Thought: A New Alliance against Modernity?* (ed. Lieven Boeve, Mathijs Lamberigts and Maarten Wisse; BETL, 219; Leuven: Peeters, 2009), pp. 147–65.

Goizueta, Roberto, *Christ Our Companion: Toward an Theological Aesthetics of Liberation* (Maryknoll, NY: Orbis, 2009).

Goodwin, Barbara, and Keith Taylor, *The Politics of Utopia: A Study in Theory and Practice* (Oxford: Lang, 2009).

Grant, Edward, *Planets, Stars and Orbs: The Medieval Cosmos* (Cambridge: Cambridge University Press, 1996).

Gray, John, *Black Mass: Apocalyptic Religion and the Death of Utopia* (New York, NY: Farrar, Straus and Giroux, 2007).

Greenpeace International, 'Mayak/Krasnoyarsk: Contamination and Health Effects', 9 October, 2000, http://archive.greenpeace.org/~nuclear/waste/mayakkrasno health.pdf (last checked on 21 September 2009).

Grey, Mary C., *Sacred Longings: The Ecological Spirit and Global Culture* (Minneapolis, MN: Fortress, 2004).

Guarino, Thomas G., *Foundations of Systematic Theology* (Theology for the Twenty-First Century; New York, NY: T&T Clark, 2005).

Guillebaud, Jean-Claude, *Le commencement d'un monde* (Paris: Seuil, 2008).

Gutiérrez, Gustavo, 'Memory and Prophecy', *The Option for the Poor in Christian Theology* (ed. Daniel G. Groody; Notre Dame, IN: Notre Dame Press, 2007), pp. 17–38.

Habermas, Jürgen, *Zwischen Naturalismus und Religion* (Frankfurt a.M.: Suhrkamp, 2005).

—— 'Pre-political Foundations of the Democratic Constitutional State?', *The Dialectics of Secularization: On Reason and Religion* (ed. Florian Schuller; San Francisco, CA: Ignatius 2006), pp. 19–52.

Haldane, John, *Faithful Reason: Essays Catholic and Philosophical* (London/New York, NY: Routledge, 2004).

Harris, Sam, *The End of Faith: Religion, Terror, and the Future of Reason* (New York, NY: Norton, 2005).

Harrison, Beverly Wildung, 'The Power of Anger in the Work of Love', *Union Seminary Quarterly Review* 36 (1981), pp. 41–57.

Heckel, Martin, 'Das Säkularisierungsproblem in der Entwicklung des deutschen Staatsrechts', *Christentum und modernes Recht: Beiträge zum Problem der Säkularisierung* (ed. Gerhard Dilcher and Ilse Staff; Frankfurt a.M.: Suhrkamp, 1984), pp. 35–95.

Heelas, Paul, 'Introduction: Detraditionalization and Its Rivals', *Detraditionalization: Critical Reflections On Authority and Identity* (ed. Paul Heelas, Scott Lash and Paul Morris; Malden, MA/Oxford: Blackwell, 1995), pp. 1–30.

Heilbroner, Robert, *An Inquiry into The Human Prospect* (New York, NY: Norton, 1980).

Hendrikse, Klaas, *Geloven in een God die niet bestaat: Manifest van een atheïstische dominee* (Amsterdam: Nieuw Amsterdam, 2007).

Hervieu-Léger, Danielle, *Religion as a Chain of Memory* (trans. Simon Lee; New Brunswick, NJ: Rutgers University Press, 2000).

Hill Fletcher, Jeanine, *Monopoly on Salvation? A Feminist Approach to Religious Pluralism* (New York, NY: Continuum, 2005).

—— 'Religious Pluralism in an Era of Globalization: The Making of Modern Religious Identity', *Theological Studies* 69 (2008), pp. 394–411.

Hitchens, Christopher, *God Is Not Great: The Case Against Religion* (London: Atlantic Books, 2007).

—— *God Is Not Great: How Religion Poisons Everything* (New York, NY: Twelve, 2007).

Hollenback, Jess Byron, *Mysticism: Experience, Response, and Empowerment* (University Park, PA: The Pennsylvania State University Press, 1996).

Holman, Susan R., *The Hungry Are Dying* (Oxford: Oxford University Press, 2001).

Honneth, Axel, 'Das Andere der Gerechtigkeit', *Freiheit oder Gerechtigkeit: Perspektiven Politischer Philosophie* (ed. Peter Fischer; Leipzig: Reclam, 1995), pp. 194–240.

Horn, Stephan Otto, and Siegried Widenhofer, *Creazione ed evoluzione: Un convegno con Papa Benedetto XVI a castel Gandolfo* (intr. Christoph Schönborn; Bologna: Edizioni dehoniane, 2007).

Housset, Emmanuel, *L'intériorité d'exil: Le soi au risque de l'altérité* (Paris: Cerf, 2008).

Hunter, James Davison, *Culture Wars: The Struggle to Define America* (New York, NY: Basic Books, 1991).

James, William, *The Varieties of Religious Experience: A Study in Human Nature* (repr., New York, NY: Longmans, Green, and Co., 1929).

Johnson, Elizabeth A., *Women, Earth, Creator Spirit* (Mahwah, NJ: Paulist, 1993).

—— *Quest for the Living God: Mapping Frontiers in the Theology of God* (New York, NY: Continuum, 2008).

Jullien, François, *De l'universel, de l'uniforme, du commun et du dialogue entre les cultures* (Paris: Fayard, 2008).

Kasper, Walter, *An Introduction to Christian Faith* (trans. V. Green; New York, NY/Ramsey, NJ: Paulist, 1980).

—— *The God of Jesus Christ* (trans. M.J. O'Connell; repr., New York, NY: Crossroad, 2005).

Kerr, Fergus, *Immortal Longings: Versions of Transcending Humanity* (Notre Dame, IN: University of Notre Dame Press, 1997).

BIBLIOGRAPHY

—— *After Aquinas: Versions of Thomism* (Malden, MA/Oxford: Blackwell, 2002).
Kippenberg, Hans G., *Gewalt als Gottesdienst: Religionskriege im Zeitalter der Globalisierung* (Munich: C.H. Beck, 2008).
Knitter, Paul, *No Other Name: A Critical Survey of Christian Attitudes toward the World Religions* (Quezon City: Claretian, 1985).
—— 'The Place of the Church and Missionary Activity in Theocentric and Soteriocentric Approaches to Dialogue', *Mission & Dialogue: Theory and Practice* (ed. Leonardo N. Mercado and James J. Knight; Manila: Divine Word Publications, 1989), pp. 186–221.
—— 'Toward a Liberation Theology of Religions', *The Myth of Christian Uniqueness: Toward a Pluralistic Theology of Religions* (ed. John Hick and Paul Knitter; New York, NY: Orbis, 1987), pp. 178–200.
—— *Introducing Theologies of Religions* (Maryknoll, NY: Orbis, 2002).
Kreutzer, Ansgar, *Kritische Zeitgenossenschaft: Die Pastoralkonstitution* Gaudium et spes *modernisierungstheoretisch gedeutet und systematisch-theologisch entfaltet* (Innsbruck: Tyrolia, 2006).
Küng, Hans, and Karl-Josef Kuschel (eds), *A Global Ethic: The Declaration of the Parliament of the World's Religions* (New York, NY: Continuum, 1998).
Ladrière, Jean, *Sens et vérité en théologie: L'articulation du sens III* (Cogitatio Fidei, 237; Paris: Cerf, 2004).
—— *Bibliographie de Jean Ladrière* (Bibliothèque philosophique de Louvain, 66; Leuven: Peeters, 2005).
Laing, Ronald D., *The Politics of Experience* and *The Bird of Paradise* (repr., Harmondsworth: Penguin, 1977).
Lamb, Matthew L., and Matthew Webb Levering (eds), *Vatican II: Renewal within Tradition* (Oxford/New York, NY: Oxford University Press, 2008).
Lanzetta, Beverly J., *Radical Wisdom: A Feminist Mystical Theology* (Minneapolis, MN: Fortress, 2005).
Leclercq, Jean, *The Love of Learning and the Desire for God: A Study of Monastic Culture* (New York, NY: Fordham University Press, 1961).
Lefort, Claude, *Fortdauer des Theologisch-Politischen* (Vienna: Passagen, 1999).
Léon-Dufour, Xavier, *Lecture de l'Evangile selon Saint Jean* (vol. 1; Paris: Seuil, 1988).
Levinas, Emmanuel, *Otherwise than Being: Or, Beyond Essence* (trans. Alphonso Lingis; Martinus Nijhoff Philosophy Texts, 3; The Hague: Nijhoff, 1981).
—— 'The Trace of the Other', *Deconstruction in Context* (ed. Mark C. Taylor; Chicago, IL: University of Chicago Press, 1986), pp. 345–59.
Lewis, James R. (ed.), *Oxford Handbook of New Religious Movements* (New York, NY: Oxford University Press, 2004).
Liebsch, Burkhard, *Gastlichkeit und Freiheit: Polemische Konturen europäischer Kultur* (Weilerswist: Velbruck, 2005).
Lindbeck, George, *The Nature of Doctrine: Religion and Theology in a Postliberal Age* (Philadelphia, PA: Westminster, 1984).
Lonergan, Bernard, 'Healing and Creating in History', *Lonergan: A Third Collection* (ed. Frederick E. Crowe; New York, NY: Paulist, 1985), pp. 100–12.
—— *Insight: A Study of Human Understanding* (Toronto: University of Toronto Press, 1992).
Lynch, William F., *Images of Hope* (Baltimore, MD: Helicon, 1965).
Lyon, David, *The Steeple's Shadow: On the Myths and Realities of Secularization* (Grand Rapids, MI: Eerdmanns, 1987).
—— *Jesus in Disneyland: Religion in Postmodern Times* (Cambridge: Polity Press, 2000).

Manemann, Jürgen, *Carl Schmitt und die Politische Theologie: Politischer Anti-Monotheismus* (Münster: Aschendorf, 2002).
—— *Rettende Erinnerung an die Zukunft: Essay über die christliche Verschärfung* (Mainz: Grünewald, 2005).
—— *Über Freunde und Feinde: Brüderlichkeit Gottes* (Kevelaer: Topos, 2008).
Mannion, Gerard, *Ecclesiology and Postmodernity: Questions for the Church in Our Time* (Louisville, KY: Liturgical Press, 2007).
Marchart, Oliver, 'Demonstrationen des Unvollendbaren: Politische Theorie und radikaldemokratischer Aktivismus', *Demokratie als unvollendeter Prozess: Documenta11_Platform1* (ed. Okwui Enwezor et al.; Ostfildern: Hatje Cantz, 2002), pp. 291–306.
Marion, Jean-Luc, *Au lieu de soi: L'approche de Saint Augustin* (Épiméthée: Essais philosophiques; Paris: PUF, 2008).
Massa, Mark, *Catholics and American Culture: Fulton Sheen, Dorothy Day and the Notre Dame Football Team* (New York, NY: Crossroad, 1999).
McGrath, Alister E., *The Twilight of Atheism: The Rise and Fall of Disbelief in the Modern World* (Garden City, NY: Doubleday, 2004).
Menke, Christoph, *Spiegelungen der Gleichheit* (Berlin: Akademie Verlag, 2000).
—— 'Grenzen der Gleichheit: Neutralität und Politik im Politischen Liberalismus', *Deutsche Zeitschrift für Philosophie* 50/6 (2002), pp. 897–906.
Metz, Johann Baptist, *Theology of the World* (London: Burns and Oates/New York, NY: Herder and Herder, 1969).
—— '"Politische Theologie" in der Diskussion', *Diskussion zur politischen Theologie* (ed. Helmut Peukert; Mainz: Grünewald, 1969), pp. 267–301.
—— *Glaube in Geschichte und Gesellschaft: Studien zu einer praktischen Fundamentaltheologie* (Mainz: Grünewald, 1977/repr., Mainz: Grünewald, 1984).
—— *Zur Theologie der Welt* (repr., Mainz: Grünewald, 1984).
—— 'Zwischen Erinnerung und Vergessen: Die Shoah im Zeitalter kultureller Anamnesie (1997)', *Zum Begriff der neueren Politischen Theologie 1967–1997* (Mainz: Grünewald, 1997), pp. 149–55.
—— *A Passion for God: The Mystical-Political Dimension of Christianity* (trans. J. Matthew Ashley; New York, NY: Paulist, 1998).
—— 'Under the Spell of Cultural Amnesia? An Example from Europe and Its Consequences', *Missing God? Cultural Amnesia and Political Theology* (ed. John K. Downey, Jürgen Manemann and Steven T. Ostovich; Münster: LIT, 2006), pp. 5–10.
—— *Memoria passionis: Ein provozierendes Gedächtnis in pluralistischer Gesellschaft* (Freiburg/Basel/Vienna: Herder, 2006).
Milbank, John, *Theology and Social Theory: Beyond Secular Reason* (Oxford: Blackwell, 1990).
—— *The Word Made Strange: Theology, Language, Culture* (Oxford: Blackwell, 1997).
Miller, Vincent J., *Consuming Religion* (New York, NY: Continuum, 2004).
—— 'Where Is The Church? Globalization And Catholicity', *Theological Studies* 69 (2008), pp. 412–32.
Moingt, Joseph, *Dieu qui vient à l'homme* (3 vols.; Paris: Cerf, 2002/2005/2007).
Moltmann, Jürgen, *Politische Theologie – Politische Ethik* (Fundamentaltheologische Studien, 9; München: Kaiser, 1984).
Mouffe, Chantal, 'Für eine antagonistische Öffentlichkeit', *Demokratie als unvollendeter Prozess: Documenta11_Platform1* (ed. Okwui Enwezor et al.; Ostfildern: Hatje Cantz, 2002), pp. 101–12.
—— *On the Political* (Thinking in Action; Abingdon/New York, NY: Routledge, 2005).

288

Nancy, Jean-Luc, 'Le déconstruction du Christianisme', *Les études philosophiques* 4 (1998), pp. 503–19.

—— 'The Deconstruction of Christianity', *Dis-Enclosure: The Deconstruction of Christianity* (trans. Bettina Bergo, Gabriel Malenfant and Michael B. Smith; Perspectives in Continental Philosophy; New York, NY: Fordham University Press, 2008), pp. 139–57.

Nietzsche, Friedrich, *Werke in drei Bänden* (ed. Karl Schlechta; vol. 3; repr., Munich: Hanser, 1966).

Nussbaum, Martha, and Amartya Sen, *The Quality of Life* (New York, NY: Oxford University Press, 1993).

O'Neill, Maura, *Mending a Torn World: Women and Interreligious Dialogue* (New York, NY: Orbis, 2007).

Orbinski, James, *An Imperfect Offering: Dispatches from the Medical Frontline* (London: Random House, 2008).

Ostheimer, Jochen, *Zeichen der Zeit lesen: Erkenntnistheoretische Bedingungen einer praktisch-theologischen Gegenwartsanalyse* (Stuttgart: Kohlhammer, 2008).

Painadath, Sebastian, 'Federation of Asian Bishops' Conferences' Theology of Dialogue', *Dialogue? A Resource Manual for Catholics in Asia* (ed. Edmund Chia; Bangkok: Federation of Asian Bishops' Conferences, 2001), pp. 102–05.

Perron, Louis, *L'eschatologie de la raison selon Jean Ladrière pour une interprétation du devenir de la raison* (Sainte-Foy: Les presses de l'Université Laval, 2005).

Persaud, Winston D., 'The Cross of Jesus Christ, the Unity of the Church, and Human Suffering', *The Scandal of a Crucified World: Perspectives on the Cross and Suffering* (ed. Yacob Tesfai; Maryknoll, NY: Orbis, 1994), pp. 111–29.

Peters, Ted, 'Pannenberg's Eschatological Ethics', *The Theology of Wolfhart Pannenberg: Twelve American Critiques, with an Autobiographical Essay and Response* (ed. Carl E. Braaten and Philip Clayton; Minneapolis, MN: Augsburg Publishing House, 1988), pp. 239–65.

Peters, Tiemo Rainer, *Johann Baptist Metz: Theologie des vermissten Gottes* (Mainz: Grünewald, 1998).

Philipse, Herman, *Atheïstisch manifest: Drie wijsgerige opstellen over godsdienst en moraal* en *De onredelijkheid van de relgie: Vier wijsgerige opstellen over godsdienst en wetenschap* (Amsterdam: Bert Bakker, 2004).

Phillips, John, 'Racists Jeer at Roadside Birth', the *Times* of London, 12 February 1992, pp. 8.

Pieris, Aloysius, *God's Reign for God's Poor: A Return to the Jesus Formula* (Kelaniya: Tulana Research Centre, 1999).

Polednitschek, Thomas, *Diagnose Politikmüdigkeit: Die Psychologie des nicht-vermissten Gottes* (Berlin: Wichern, 2003).

Porter, Jean, 'The Search for a Global Ethic', *Theological Studies* 62 (2001), pp. 105–21.

Potworowski, Christophe F., *Contemplation and Incarnation: The Theology of Marie Dominique Chenu* (McGill-Queen's Studies in the History of Ideas, 33; Montreal: McGill-Queen's University Press, 2001).

Poulat, Émile, *L'église, c'est un monde: L'ecclésiosphère* (Sciences humaines et religions; Paris: Cerf, 1986).

Premnath, D.N. (ed.), *Border Crossings: Cross-Cultural Hermeneutics* (Maryknoll, NY: Orbis, 2007).

Putnam, Robert D., '*E pluribus unum*: Diversity and Community in the Twenty-First Century. The 2006 John Skytte Prize Lecture', *Scandinavian Political Studies* 30/2 (2007), pp. 137–74.

Race, Alan, *Christians and Religious Pluralism: Patterns in the Christian Theology of Religions* (London: SCM, 1983).

Radford Ruether, Rosemary, 'Feminism and Jewish-Christian Dialogue: Particularism and Universalism in the Search for Religious Truth', *The Myth of Christian Uniqueness: Toward a Pluralistic Theology of Religions* (ed. John Hick and Paul Knitter; New York, NY: Orbis, 1987), pp. 137–48.

Raguin, Yves, *Un message de salut pour tous* (Vie chrétienne: Supplément, 406; Paris: Vie chrétienne, 1996).

Rahner, Karl, *Hearers of the Word* (rev. Johann Baptist Metz; trans. Ronald Walls; London/Sydney: Sheed and Ward, 1969).

—— *Foundations of Christian Faith: An Introduction to the Idea of Christianity* (trans. W.V. Dych; New York, NY: Crossroad, 1978).

Rahner, Karl, and Herbert Vorgrimler, 'Revelation', *Theological Dictionary* (ed. Cornelius Ernst; trans. Richard Strachan; New York, NY: Herder and Herder, 3rd edn, 1968), pp. 409–13.

Randles, W.G.L., *The Unmaking of the Medieval Christian Cosmos 1500–1760: From Solid Heavens to Boundless æther* (Aldershot: Ashgate, 1999).

Ratzinger, Joseph, 'Himmelfahrt Christi. II: Systematisch', *Lexikon für Theologie und Kirche* (ed. Michael Buchberger *et al.*; vol. 5; Freiburg/Basel/Vienna: Herder, 2nd rev. edn, 1960), col. 361.

—— *Introduction to Christianity* (London: Burns & Oates, 1969).

—— *Principles of Catholic Theology: Building Stones for a Fundamental Theology* (San Francisco, CA: Ignatius, 1987).

Ratzinger, Joseph/Benedict XVI, 'Address of His Holiness Benedict XVI to the Roman Curia Offering Them His Christmas Greetings', 22 December 2005, http://www.vatican.va/holy_father/benedict_xvi/speeches/2005/december/documents/hf_ben_xvi_spe_20051222_roman-curia_en.html (last checked on 23 January 2010).

—— *Values in a Time of Upheaval* (San Francisco, CA: Ignatius, 2006).

—— 'Faith, Reason and the University: Memories and Reflections', Lecture during a meeting with the representatives of science at the University of Regensburg, 12 September 2006, http://www.vatican.va/holy_father/benedict_xvi/speeches/2006/september/documents/hf_ben-xvi_spe_20060912_university-regensburg_en.html (last checked on 23 January 2010).

—— *Jesus of Nazareth* (New York, NY: Doubleday, 2007).

Rawls, John, 'The Idea of Public Reason Revisited', *The Laws of Peoples* (Cambridge, MA: Harvard University Press, 1999), pp. 129–81.

Ricœur, Paul, 'L'histoire de la philosophie et l'unité du vrai', *Histoire et vérité* (Paris: Seuil, 1967), pp. 51–68.

—— 'Vérité et mensonge', *Histoire et vérité* (Paris: Seuil, 1967), pp. 187–218.

Rottländer, Peter, 'Alterität versus anamnetische Ethik?', *Demokratiefähigkeit* (ed. Jürgen Manemann; Jahrbuch Politische Theologie, 1; Münster: LIT, 1995), pp. 238–249.

Samartha, Stanley, *One Christ, Many Religions: Toward a Revised Christology* (Maryknoll, NY: Orbis, 1991).

Scheffer, Paul, *Het land van aankomst* (Amsterdam: De Bezige Bij, 2007).

Schmitt, Carl, *Politische Theologie: Vier Kapitel zur Lehre von der Souveränität* (repr., Berlin: Duncker & Humblot, 1993).

—— *Political Theology: Four Chapters on the Concept of Sovereignty* (ed. and intr. George Shwab; foreword by Tracy B. Strong; Studies in Contemporary German Thought; Cambridge, MA: MIT Press, 1985).

Schneiders, Sandra, 'Spirituality in the Academy', *Theological Studies* 50 (1989), pp. 676–97.

Schönborn, Christoph, *Hasard ou plan de Dieu? La création et l'évolution vues à la lumière de la foi et de la raison* (trans. Monique Guisse; Paris: Cerf, 2007).

Schoof, Ted Mark, *Breakthrough: Beginnings of the New Catholic Theology* (Logos Books; Dublin: Gill and Macmillan, 1970).

Schreiter, Robert J., *The New Catholicity: Theology between the Global and the Local* (Maryknoll, NY: Orbis, 1997).

—— 'A New Modernity: Living and Believing in an Unstable World', *New Theology Review* 20/1 (2007), pp. 51–60.

Sichère, Bernard, *Le jour est proche: La révolution selon Paul* (Paris: Desclée de Brouwer, 2003).

Smedes, Taede A., *God en de menselijke maat: Gods handelen en het natuurwetenschappelijk wereldbeeld* (Zoetermeer: Meinema, 2006).

Sobrino, Jon, 'Theology in a Suffering World', *Theology Digest* 41 (1994), pp. 25–30.

Steinmetz, Dov, 'Moses' "Revelation" on Mount Horeb as a Near-Death Experience', *Journal of Near-Death Studies* 11/4 (1993), pp. 199–203.

Steltemeier, Rolf (ed.), *Neue Utopien: Zum Wandel eines Genres* (Heidelberg: Manutius, 2009).

Sternberger, Dolf, *Die Politik und der Friede* (Frankfurt a.M.: Suhrkamp, 1986).

Suchocki, Marjorie Hewitt, 'In Search of Justice: Religious Pluralism from a Feminist Perspective', *The Myth of Christian Uniqueness: Toward a Pluralistic Theology of Religions* (ed. John Hick and Paul Knitter; Maryknoll, NY: Orbis, 1987), pp. 149–61.

Swidler, Leonard, *After the Abslolute: The Dialogical Future of Religious Reflection* (Minneapolis, MN: Fortress, 1990).

Taylor, Charles, *A Secular Age* (Cambridge, MA: Belknap Press/Harvard University Press, 2007).

Thibaul, Pierre, *Savoir et pouvoir: Philosophie thomiste et politique cléricale au XIXe siècle* (intr. Émile Poulat; Histoire et sociologie de la culture, 2; Quebec: Presses de l'Université Laval, 1972).

Tillar, Elizabeth K., 'Rights of Passage: Toward the Elimination of Female Circumcision', *International Health and Development* 3/1 (1992), pp. 14–22.

Tracy, David, *The Analogical Imagination: Christian Theology and the Culture of Pluralism* (Ann Arbor, MI: Crossroad, 1981).

—— *Plurality and Ambiguity* (San Francisco, CA: Harper and Row, 1987).

—— 'The Uneasy Alliance Reconceived: Catholic Theological Method, Modernity and Postmodernity', *Theological Studies* 50 (1989), pp. 548–70.

—— 'On Longing: The Void, the Open, God', *Longing in a Culture of Cynicism* (ed. Stephan van Erp and Lea Verstricht; Zürich/Berlin: LIT, 2008), pp. 15–32.

Traina, Cristina L.H., *Feminist Ethics and the Natural Law* (Washington, DC: Georgetown University Press, 1999).

Trinkaus, Charles, *In Our Image and Likeness: Humanity and Divinity in Italian Humanist Thought* (Chicago, IL: University of Chicago Press, 1970).

Van Herck, Walter, *Religie en metafoor: Over het relativisme van het figuurlijke* (Tertium Datur; Leuven: Peeters, 1999).

Vroom, Hendrik, *No Other Gods: Christian Belief in Dialogue with Buddhism, Hinduism, and Islam* (Grand Rapids, MI/Cambridge: Eerdmans, 1996).

Wacker, Bernd, and Jürgen Manemann, ' "Politische Theologie": Eine Skizze zur Geschichte und aktuellen Diskussion des Begriffs', *Politische Theologie – gegengelesen* (ed. Jürgen Manemann and Bernd Wacker; Jahrbuch Politische Theologie, 5; Münster: LIT, 2008), pp. 28–65.

Weber, Max, 'Wissenschaft als Beruf', *Gesammelte Aufsätze zur Wissenschaftslehre* (ed. Johannes Winkelmann; Uni-Taschenbücher, 1492; 7th repr., Tübingen: Mohr Siebeck, 1988), pp. 582–613.

Webster, John, 'Theology after Liberalism', *Theology after Liberalism: Classical and Contemporary Readings* (ed. John Webster and George P. Schner; Blackwell Readings in Modern Theology; Oxford: Blackwell, 1998), pp. 52–64.

—— 'Theologies of Retrieval', *The Oxford Handbook of Systematic Theology* (ed. John B. Webster, Kathryn E. Tanner and Iain R. Torrance; Oxford: Oxford University Press, 2007), pp. 583–99.

Wilfred, Felix, *Sunset in the East?* (Madras: SIGA, 1991).

—— 'Towards a Better Understanding of Asian Theology', *Vidyajyoti Journal of Theological Reflection* 62/12 (1998), pp. 890–915.

Wisdom, John, 'Gods', *Proceedings of the Aristotelian Society: New Series* 45 (1944–45), pp. 185–206.

Wuthnow, Robert, *The Restructuring of American Religion* (Princeton, NJ: Princeton University Press, 1990).

—— *After Heaven: Spirituality in America since the 1950's* (Berkeley, CA: University of California Press, 2006).

Wyller, Trygve (ed.), *Heterotopic Citizen: New Research on Religious Work for the Disadvantaged* (Göttingen: Vandehoeck & Ruprecht, 2009).

Yong, Amos, *Hospitality and The Other: Pentecost, Christian Practices, and the Neighbor* (Maryknoll, NY: Orbis, 2008).

Žižek, Slavoj, *The Ticklish Subject: The Absent Centre of Political Ontology* (Wo es war; London/New York, NY: Verso, pb edn, 2000).

—— *The Fragile Absolute: Or, Why Is the Christian Legacy Worth Fighting For?* (Wo es war; London/New York, NY: Verso, 2000).

INDEX OF NAMES

293

INDEX OF NAMES

INDEX OF SELECTED TOPICS
FROM THE WORK OF
EDWARD SCHILLEBEECKX

9 780567 181602